The Language, Ethnicity and Race Reader

'An excellent overview of an important and complex interdisciplinary area, provided through a varied set of texts which are engaging and challenging, but still accessible.'

Mark Sebba, *Lancaster University, UK*

The Language, Ethnicity and Race Reader is an invaluable guide for students navigating the current debates surrounding language and diversity, colonialism, migration and identity.

Packed with editorial material, the book draws together key articles in the field and puts them in their thematic and social contexts. Including extracts written between 1920 and the present, and spanning a number of disciplines and countries, the book explores changing ideas of ethnicity and race, and considers the ways in which these ideas shape human communication.

Features include:

- a general introduction exploring and connecting the debates
- organisation into three thematic sections, each with an editors' introduction
- suggestions for further reading

Extracts by: Mervyn Alleyne, Bill Ashcroft, Les Back, Michael Billig, Wendy Bokhorst-Heng, John Taggart Clark, Cecilia Cutler, Joshua Fishman, Kenneth Gospodinoff, John Gumperz, Monica Heller, Eduardo Hernández-Chavez, Roger Hewitt, Jane H. Hill, Ray Honeyford, Otto Jespersen, Alamin Mazrui, R. P. McDermott, Ngũgĩ wa Thiong'o, Susan U. Philips, Randolph Quirk, Ben Rampton, John Rickford, Edward Sapir, Jacqueline Urla, Benjamin Lee Whorf.

Roxy Harris is Lecturer in the School of Social Science and Public Policy, King's College, London, UK. His publications include *Language and Power* (with I. Schwab and L. Whitman, 1990).

Ben Rampton is Professor in the School of Social Science and Public Policy, King's College, London, UK. His publications include *Crossing: Language and Ethnicity among Adolescents* (1995).

The Language, Ethnicity and Race Reader

Edited by

Roxy Harris and
Ben Rampton

Routledge
Taylor & Francis Group

LONDON AND NEW YORK

First published 2003
by Routledge
11 New Fetter Lane, London EC4P 4EE

Simultaneously published in the USA and Canada
by Routledge
29 West 35th Street, New York, NY 10001

Routledge is an imprint of the Taylor & Francis Group

Typeset in Perpetua and Bell Gothic by
Florence Production Ltd, Stoodleigh, Devon
Printed and bound in Great Britain by
TJ International Ltd, Padstow, Cornwall

British Library Cataloguing in Publication Data
A catalogue record for this book is available from the British
Library

Library of Congress Cataloging in Publication Data
A catalog record for this book has been requested

ISBN 0–415–27601–2 (hbk)
ISBN 0–415–27602–0 (pbk)

Contents

SECTION THREE:
Language, Discourse and Ethnic Style

Acknowledgements

We are particularly indebted to the many students we have worked with over the last decade, and to our close colleagues Constant Leung and Celia Roberts.

The editors and publishers wish to thank the following for permission to use copyright material.

Alleyne, Mervyn (1989) 'Language'. From *The Roots of Jamican Culture*. London: Pluto Press.

Ashcroft, Bill (2001) 'Language and race'. *Social Identities* 7(3). Website: http://www.tandf.co.uk

Back, Les (1995) 'X amount of Sat Siri Akal! Apache Indian, reggae music and intermezzo culture'. From A. Ålund and R. Granqvist (eds) *Negotiating Identities: Essays on Immigration and Culture in Present Day Europe*. Amsterdam: Rodopi.

Billig, Michael (1995) 'Remember banal nationalism' and 'Flagging the homeland daily'. From *Banal Nationalism*. London: Sage Publications.

Bokhorst-Heng, Wendy (1999) 'Singapore's *Speak Mandarin Campaign*: language ideological debates in the imaging of the nation'. From J. Blommaert (ed.) *Language Ideological Debates*. Berlin: Mouton de Gruyter.

Clark, John Taggart (2003) 'Patrolling class and ethnic borders through lingusitic stylization'. In Gon, Nisha Merchant, Amanda R. Doran and Anastasia Cole (eds) *Proceedings of the Seventh Annual Symposium about Language and Society*. Austin, Texas: University of Texas Department of Linguistics, vol. 43, Texan Linguistics Forum.

Cutler, Cecilia (1999) 'Yorkville crossing: white teens, hip hop and African American English'. *Journal of Sociolinguistics*, vol. 3, reprinted by permission of Blackwell Publishing, Oxford.

Fishman, Joshua (1972) 'The impact of nationalism on language planning', from *Language in Sociocultural Change*. Stanford: Stanford University Press.

Gumperz, John (1979) 'Interview with John Gumperz'. Originally published in J. Gumperz, T. Jupp and C. Roberts (1979) *Crosstalk*, London: BBC. Republished in J. Twitchin (1990) *Crosstalk: An introduction to cross-cultural communication*. London: BBC, pp. 46–55.

Gumperz, John and Hernández-Chavez, Eduardo (1972) 'Bilingualism, bidialectualism, and classroom interaction' reprinted by permission of the publisher from C. Cazden, V. John and D. Hymes, *Functions of Language in the Classroom*. Teachers College Press: New York, © 1972 by Teachers College, Columbia University. All rights reserved, pp. 84–108, 370–394.

Heller, Monica (1999) 'Alternative ideologies of *la francophonie*'. *Journal of Sociolinguistics*, vol 3, reprinted by permission of Blackwell Publishing, Oxford.

Hewitt, Roger (1992) 'Language, youth and the destabilisation of ethnicity' from *Ethnicity in Youth Culture*. C. Palmgren, K. Lovgren and G. Bolin (eds). Stockholm: Youth Culture at Stockholm University.

Hill, Jane H. (1995) 'Junk Spanish, covert racism and the (leaky) boundary between public and private spheres'. *Pragmatics* 5(2), reprinted by permission of the authors.

Honeyford, Ray (1995) 'The language issue'. From *Integration or Disintegration: Towards a Non-racist Society*. London: The Claridge Press.

Jespersen, Otto (1922/64) 'The origin of speech'. From *Language: Its Nature, Development and Origin*. London: George Allen & Unwin.

Mazrui, Alamin (1997) 'The world bank, the language question and the future of African education'. *Race and Class* 38(3).

McDermott, R. P. and Kenneth Gospodinoff (1981) 'Social contexts for ethnic borders and school failure' from *Culture and the Bilingual Classroom*. H. Trueba, G. Guthrie, J. Au (eds). Rowley: Newbury House.

Ngũgĩ wa Thiong'o (1986) 'The language of African literature'. From *Decolonizing the Mind: The Politics of Language in African Literature*. London: James Currey.

Philips, Susan U. (1972) 'Participant structures and communicative competence: Warm Springs children in community and classroom'. Reprinted by permission of the publisher from C. Cazden, V. John, D. Hymes.

Quirk, Randolph (1990) 'Language varieties and standard language'. *English Today* 21, Cambridge: Cambridge University Press.

Rampton, Ben (1990) 'Displacing the "native speaker": Expertise, affiliation and inheritance'. *ETL Journal* 44(2) reprinted by permission of Oxford University Press.

Rickford, John (1997) 'Suite for ebony and phonics' *Discover Magazine* 18(12).

Sapir, Edward (1963) 'Language, race and culture'. From *Language: An Introduction to the Study of Speech*. London: Rupert Hart-Davis.

Urla, Jacqueline (1995) 'Outlaw language: creating alternative public spheres in Basque radio'. *Pragmatics* 5(2) (reprinted by permission of the authors).

Whorf, Benjamin Lee (1956–73), 'An American Indian model of the universe.' In J. N. Carroll (ed.) *Language Thought and Reality: Selected Writings of Benjamin Lee Whorf*. Cambridge, MA: The MIT Press.

While the publishers and editors have made every effort to contact authors and copyright holders of works reprinted in *The Language, Ethnicity and Race Reader*, this has not been possible in every case. They would welcome correspondence from individuals or companies they have been unable to trace.

INTRODUCTION

Our aims and organisational rationale

S OME COLLECTIONS OF READINGS represent a discipline, and in doing
so, they can aim to be authoritative, selecting a series of influential articles
that have helped to define a particular field. Many of the articles in this collection
have also been written by very influential scholars, but our volume centres on a
topic rather than a discipline, and the topic is itself rather contentious. So instead
of being a series of papers showing the development of a more or less consensual
disciplinary perspective, this Reader tries to:

- show a range of the different ways in which language has been involved in
  arguments about race and ethnicity;
- capture some of the major lines of disagreement; and
- indicate some of the broad shifts in the terms of debate over time.

We can't of course avoid the constraints of our own London-based academic backgrounds in education, sociolinguistics and cultural studies, but overall, we would
like to see this collection as a set of argumentative dialogues, more about contrast
and difference than the consolidation of a particular way of looking at language,
ethnicity and race.[1] In line with this, we hope that these readings will help to
provide people in a wide range of academic and professional fields with some illumination and clarification of the many ways in which language and ethnicity
intersect.

We are not assuming that our readers have any specialist knowledge about
language. In addition, we wouldn't want to foreclose on the diverse articles that
follow by trying to offer our own over-arching theory of what language is and does.
But two broad points can be made right at the outset.

First, the social processes and arenas where language and ethnicity are seen to interact vary very considerably in their scale. Language, ethnicity and race have been taken together in discussions that focus on long-term historical processes and on wide-ranging global ones, they have featured together in accounts of state policy and institutional practice, they have figured in analyses of the fine-grain of how individuals interact with one another face-to-face, and they have been key issues in attempts to describe how individuals think. This range is loosely reflected in the way we have divided the collection into three parts, moving from phenomena and processes that are longer and larger down into ones that are smaller and briefer. Although the fit is by no means always very tidy, we've divided the extracts in this collection into three sections:

- Colonialism, imperialism and global process.
- Nation states and minorities.
- Language, discourse and ethnic style.

Second, people mean a great many different things when they refer to 'language'. In view of the fact that it's so pervasively and intimately bound into the ways that humans do things together, this is hardly surprising, and in the articles that follow, among other things, language and languages are viewed:

- as sets of conventions for making sense that are shaped in distinctive ways within particular social groups – conventions operating at the level of sounds, words, grammar and/or ways of organising spoken and written texts (discourse);[2]
- as emblems of allegiance, as objects of disdain, as emotive symbols that create intimacy, solidarity or distance;[3]
- as forms of representation that shape, facilitate but also sometimes challenge group stereotypes and a sense of 'us' and 'them';[4]
- as valued and unevenly distributed modes of communication that include, develop and privilege some people, while excluding and disadvantaging others.[5]

In fact, far from providing a neutral vantage point above the fray, the academic study of language is itself well-established as an ideological enterprise, influencing our perceptions of ethnicity and race.[6] Indeed, if we look across the collection as a whole, we can see that when the Anglo and European world encounters populations it commonly deems to be 'Other', scholars appear to wrestle with one of two dualistic frameworks of interpretation. With the first and older of these frameworks, scholars work with, for, and against, a governing assumption that the 'West' is civilised, advanced, 'modern', and that the Others are primitive, traditional, 'pre-modern'. When the second framework becomes salient, the assumptions of Anglo and European modernity are thrown open to question, hitherto dominant categories and evaluations of language and ethnicity are destabilised, and a 'post-' or 'late modern' view of the world starts to assert itself. We can elaborate on these two highly influential interpretive tensions as follows.

In the first, pre-modern Others are described from the viewpoint of 'western' modernity, in an encounter that has been enormously important for social science. According to Anthony Giddens, sociology had its origins in the shift from the traditional to the modern, in 'the arrival of industrialism, the transfer of millions of people from rural communities to cities, the progressive development of mass democracy',[7] and between them, sociology, anthropology and linguistics built images of traditional society as an agrarian world of 'tribes' and 'natives', of kinship and folk customs, of ritual oratory and oral narrative. In fact, through processes of contrast, these representations constructed a vision of the 'Other' that helped to define what Anglo and European modernity itself should be. Instead of tribes and kinship, modernity was characterised by an orientation to citizenship and nation-states, to reason rather than custom, to literacy above oracy, argument above narrative, and education over traditional socialisation. And this scheme of oppositions continued to operate when the focus on distant places moved back home to the Anglo and European world. Exotic 'tribes' became 'ethnic minorities', and the preoccupation with difference was translated into debates about whether and how modern institutions like schools might become more hospitable to the diversity of putatively 'non-modern' others in their midst.

In recent years, however, this vision of a binary contrast between tradition and modernity has started to lose its power, giving way to the second 'problematic'. Here, the claim is that contemporary versions of free market capitalism have undermined the authority of the modern nation-state, and that globalisation has brought a massive increase in the people, commodities and services that flow across territorial boundaries. In modernity, citizenship and national belonging have been highly prized, but now it is often said that growing value is attached to mobility itself,[8] and that this may start to undermine the modernist equation of 'ethnic minority' with 'disadvantage'. Rather than simply being a source of stigma, transnational diaspora connections are sometimes capable of providing 'immigrant communities' with substantial economic and social resources, and these connections may be consolidated by the development of cable, satellite, and multi-modal digital media, forms of communication that are themselves increasingly coming to displace print literacy and public broadcasting, the traditional media of the nation-state.[9] In addition, the emergence of global cities provides an environment where multilingualism and cultural hybridity are treated as natural and normal, and this also presents a challenge to the authority of elite cultural canons and national standard languages.[10]

It is hard trying to put precise dates on the emergence of the 'pre-modern', 'modern' and 'post-modern', and exactly how far these shifts reflect really fundamental changes in the way that real people use and experience language, race and ethnicity in their everyday lives is a very difficult empirical question.[11] For this reason, it is often safer to conceive of them as 'perspectives' in Anglo and European discourse than as 'historical eras' and indeed, it would be a serious mistake to assume that the primitive—modern dichotomy is now outdated and no longer influential as an underlying assumption in research and public discourse.

'Perspectives', though, are still crucial both to how we understand the world and to how (and whether) we try to change and influence it, and discussions around late/post-modernity have offered some very consequential shifts in what we think language, ethnicity and race might be. Overall in recent years, rather than imagining that languages, cultures and communities are thing-like entities, relatively clear-cut facts in the world that can be easily identified, described or counted, it has become more common to treat them as ideas and categories that we use to interpret and organise human activity, human activity itself being really far more fluid, ambivalent and indeterminate than any of these categories allow. In line with this, researchers are now often (though by no means always) less concerned about defining the 'essence' of a particular language or culture – its core features or central underlying system – and instead, they are more inclined to attend to the ways in which linguistic and cultural activity as *a highly varied but very general human process* gets divided up and maintained as, for example, 'standard English', or 'black culture'.[12] How do people actually construct and police the boundaries between one way of speaking and another, between one group and another? What's involved when one set of practices is selected, promoted and imposed as an emblematic ideal, and what's been downgraded or excluded, why and how? What are the discourses – the images, representations, practices and events – that hold these divisions and categories in place, giving them a real material presence in the world, impacting in such concrete ways on people's life chances, and what are the discourses that promise/threaten to disrupt them?

We can see the effects of these kinds of shift in perspective if we briefly review some developments in how 'race' and 'ethnicity' themselves have been addressed.

Contemporary academic discussions generally agree that race is a social and cultural construction rather than a biological-scientific fact.[13] But modernity has been inextricably linked with the setting-up of massive systems of slavery and colonial domination,[14] and as a crucial element in the ideological maintenance of these systems, from the late eighteenth century onwards Anglo and European scholars tried to develop elaborate schemes of racial classification, built on biological and genetic foundations, with Europeans invariably placed at the top at the most advanced evolutionary stage, Africans at the bottom and a variety of colonised others in between. These efforts took both written and pictorial form;[15] they often involved comparing races in intricate would-be scientific measurements of body parts like skulls, lips, noses and even buttocks; and this interest in racially based, ranked systems of classification extended to the work of linguistic scholars, evidenced in this volume in casual and unself-conscious references to 'backward races', 'savages' and 'primitive languages'.[16] In the twentieth century, 'scientific' theories of race were discredited in a major way when the claims about race as a biological category propounded by European racists and fascists in the 1930s led to the Holocaust and the general destruction of the Second World War.[17] In addition, the post-1945 period saw independence and liberation movements ending European colonial rule, as well as the civil rights, black power and anti-racist movements, and all of these opposed the depredations associated with biological notions of race. But outside the academic world, pseudo-biological/scientific perspectives are still often felt to fit well with common sense ideas of race. For many people, significant populations around the world can be neatly grouped on the basis of their physical appearance, and this is frequently expressed in (unsatisfactory and inaccurate) colour designations like 'black', 'white' and 'yellow', or in classifications like Asian, Caucasian and African. In fact, one popular way of characterising the racial dimension is to nest it as one of a collection of elements that make up *ethnicity* – a common ancestry, a common language, a common religion and a *distinctive physical appearance*.[18] Counterposed to this, the most recent contemporary challenge to this way of imagining race/ethnicity lies in the post-modern shift of interest away from identifying essences and locating them in classification systems, to analysing practices and the social processes of categorisation themselves. This becomes clearer if we turn to 'ethnicity'.

In everyday discussion, ethnicity is often equated with a 'racially' marked culture. It is assumed that individuals possess (or belong to) cultures that are relatively discrete, homogeneous and static, and that through childhood socialisation and community experience, ethnic culture provides us with tacit but distinctive, ingrained dispositions.[19] This view of ethnicity-as-a-fixed-and-formative-inheritance has, however, been criticised as 'ethnic absolutism' (Gilroy 1987: Ch. 2),[20] and contrasted with an approach in which ethnicity is regarded as something that people can emphasise strategically in a range of different ways, according to their needs and purposes in particular situations.[21] Instead, in this 'strategic' view, ethnicity is viewed more as a relatively flexible resource that individuals and groups use in the negotiation of social boundaries, aligning themselves with some people and institutions, dissociating from others, and this is sometimes described as a 'roUtes' rather than a 'roOts' conception of ethnicity. Compared with its predecessor, this version gives more credit to free will and active agency. However, it is still compatible with ethnicity-as-inheritance if you assume that people are limited by their ethnic-genetic descent to three options: either (a) embracing and cultivating their ethnocultural/linguistic legacy, (b) trying to downplay and drop it as a category that is relevant to them, or (c) drawing attention to the different ethnicities of other people (most often in negative stereotyping). Going one step further, though, a fourth set of possibilities emerges, in which people don't sit contentedly in the group categories that society tries to fix them in, and don't confine themselves only to those identities that they are expected to have legitimate or routine access to: (d) taking on someone else's ethnicity, or creating a new one. This has been a major concern in the most recent work focusing on 'hybridity' and 'new ethnicities',[22] and there is clearly a very complicated range of processes and influences involved – on the one hand, for example, sensitive long-term negotiations about the significance of ethnic identity within close interethnic friendship, and on the other, the commercial marketisation of ethnic forms, products and symbols as commodities, life-style options and art objects. These processes of mixing, blurring and cross-identification – processes that a close look at language can often make really apparent – certainly don't make ethnicity disappear. Indeed, they often provoke intense argument around issues like authenticity, entitlement and expropriation. But they do encourage us even more to problematise the traditional assumption that we are simply responding to clear-cut biological identities when ethnicity and race are salient, inviting us ever more emphatically to treat these two terms as cultural constructs promoted, transgressed, defended or reworked in language, discourse and social activity.

We believe, then, that in pointing to some far-reaching tensions and shifts in the way we understand and experience the world, terms like 'tradition', 'modernity', 'late/post-modernity' are rather important to an understanding of the debates about language, ethnicity and race. In fact, we are using them as a *second* organising principle for the collection. Within each of three major sections (1: 'Colonialism, imperialism and global process'; 2: 'Nation states and minorities'; 3: 'Language, discourse and ethnic style'), extracts are sequenced to suggest a movement of pre-modernity → modernity → post-modernity. Indeed, although we very much hope that as they become more familiar with the material, readers will come to accuse us of gross oversimplification, it may be helpful if, clumsily, tenta-

Table 1   Locating the readings at the interfaces of 'tradition', 'modernity' and 'post-modernity'.

	Tradition ↔ modernity	Modernity ↔ post-modernity
Section 1: Colonialism, imperialism and global process	Jespersen	
	Sapir	
		Ashcroft
	Alleyne	
	Ngũgĩ	
		Mazrui
	Quirk	
		Rampton
Section 2: Nation-states and minorities	Fishman	
		Billig
	Honeyford	
	Rickford	
	Bokhorst-Heng	
	Hill	
		Hewitt
	Urla	
	Heller	
Section 3: Language, discourse and ethnic style	Whorf	
	Philips	
	Gumperz	
	McDermott and Gospodinoff	
	Gumperz and Hernández-Chavez	
	Clark	
		Cutler
		Back

tively and for initial expository and pedagogic purposes, we arrange the readings in Table 1.

This 'sketch map', then, of debates about language, ethnicity and race acknowledges (a) differences in the scale of the social processes addressed, and (b) the tensions and shifts around 'tradition', 'modernity' and 'post-modernity'. But to complete these initial notes of guidance, it's worth introducing just one more set of distinctions, more closely tuned to some of the sharp disagreements between authors that Table 1 might otherwise suggest were rather close to one another.[23] These distinctions are broadly compatible with some of the ideas we have already discussed, but they reckon more explicitly with the issues of power and inequality to which 'ethnicity' and 'race' are so intimately tied.

In debates about the relationship between different races, ethnic and indeed other kinds of social group,[24] three or four general positions on the significance of difference are commonly identified. The first, characterised as the *deficit* position, stresses the inadequacies of subordinate (out)groups and the importance of their being socialised into dominant (in)group norms. In the second, *difference* is the key word and emphasis is given to the integrity and autonomy of the subordinate group's language and culture, and to the need for institutions to be hospitable to diversity. In the third, the focus shifts to larger structures of *domination*, and the need for institutions to combat the institutional processes and ideologies that reproduce the oppression of subordinate groups. The fourth, which can be summarised as a *discourse* perspective, challenges the view (taken by the other three) that communities, cultures and languages are homogeneous and easily defined. Larger social, economic and political systems may play a major part in structuring relations of domination, but they can't be understood outside discourse and interaction, and the complexity of social experience makes it hard to predict the impact on particular groups and individuals. In line with this, there is a lot of emphasis on the cultural politics of imagery and representation. There is obviously a good deal of conflict between these four interpretations of the basic character of diversity, different perspectives have gained ascendancy at different times in different places, and we won't try to plot each of the papers in this collection against this four-fold division. But again, without wanting to overstate its pedigree or its enduring value, we elaborate on these four perspectives in Table 2, hoping that among students, for example, efforts to locate a particular text within the table might generate some interesting discussion. Would it be fair to put e.g. Honeyford in Column 1 and Rickford in Column 2? Do Columns 2 and 4 help to clarify the difference between Philips and McDermott and Gospodinoff? Where would you locate Ngũgĩ and Mazrui? etc. etc.

That is probably sufficient as an introductory pointer to some of the thinking underlying our selection and arrangement of texts in the collection. We should now say something about the more technical aspects of editorial presentation and about how we hope the book might be used.

Table 2 Four orientations to linguistic and cultural diversity.

Interpretation of linguistic and cultural diversity	1 Diversity as deficit	2 Diversity as difference	3 Not diversity, domination	4 Deficit, difference and domination as discourse
View of culture	Culture is equated with the elite canon ('high culture').	Cultures are the sets of values, beliefs and behaviours developed in different settings.	Culture is a reflection of socio-economic relations.	Culture feeds, gets reproduced and emerges in people's activity together – it exists in the processes and resources involved in situated, dialogical, sense-making.
Approach to language	'Prescriptivism': there are norms and standards that should be followed.	'Descriptivism': non-standard forms are actually systematic and authentic.	'Determinism': language is secondary to structures of political and economic domination (and/or it's a distraction from the real issues).	'Constructionism': interpersonal, institutional and collective discourse and interaction are crucial to the processes through which social realities and social identities get reproduced, resisted or created anew.
Descriptive focus	High culture and standard language. The Other's language and culture are unworthy of study.	The language and culture of the Other, which are shown to have autonomy and an integrity of their own.	The linguistic and cultural relationship between self and Other, between 'us' and 'them', in a larger system of domination.	The interaction between global, national and local discourses.
View of research	Research is neutral, objective and informative. It gets us close to the truth.	Research is neutral and objective, but it can also be used on behalf of the people that it studies, to advocate their causes.	Research is either part of the apparatus of hegemonic domination, a form of scientific imperialism, or it can help us see through the mystifications of the dominant ideology.	Research can either be restrictive and controlling with its claims to 'truth', or it can be empowering, giving a voice to types of knowledge that have been silenced or subjugated hitherto.

Table 2 (continued).

Interpretation of linguistic and cultural diversity	1 Diversity as deficit	2 Diversity as difference	3 Not diversity, domination	4 Deficit, difference and domination as discourse
Philosophical perspective	The West is superior, and the linguistic and cultural problems of the Other are their own fault.	Relativism. Cultures and languages are well adapted to the particular settings where they developed, so it makes no sense to say one is 'better' than another.	Power, ideology and capitalist oppression. There is resistance through critical analysis and the mobilisation of oppressed groups.	Power, difference and improvisation in the face of unpredictable contingency. The Other may resist, or see things differently.
Assumptions about the world	There are universals and grand narratives: e.g. development, modernisation, market competitiveness.	There may be grand narratives, but it's the little ones, the subplots, that we want to celebrate.	There are universals and grand narrative: imperialism, exploitation and dependency.	There aren't any universals or grand narratives, and the world is much more chaotic than we have assumed in the past.
Intervention strategy	Assimilation: the Other should learn to become more like us.	Multiculturalism: the different languages and cultures in a society should be recognised, respected and cultivated.	Anti-racism/anti-imperialism: structures of domination need to be critiqued and resisted.	Anti-essentialism: ideas about people having fixed identities, and about groups, cultures and languages being static and homogeneous, are oppressive.
Typical politics	Conservatism.	Liberal pluralism.	Marxism.	Post-modernism.

The editorial presentation of texts

We provide brief introductory notes more closely focused on particular articles at the start of each of the three main sections in the Reader, but we have also inserted quite a few editorial footnotes in each extract, cross-referring to other extracts where the interested reader might like to look next. (These notes are placed at the foot of the page and are referenced with a superscript letter, whereas the author's original notes are placed at the end of each reading, referenced with a superscript number.) With these editorial footnotes, we have generally tried to:

- explain any technical terms from linguistics;
- point to connections with other extracts in the Reader;
- suggest one or two other pieces of further reading relevant to the particular extract on hand.

We have also edited most of the texts themselves, often quite extensively, abbreviating them and also sometimes rewording and adjusting them to make them more accessible to a wider audience. We flag these changes as follows:

- [. . .]: square brackets around three dots show that some of the author's text has been removed;
- [our rewording]: when there are square brackets around some text, this is our rewording.

We apologise to the authors for these alterations, though we still think that each of the extracts makes a substantial argument, and we very much hope that in compensation, the editing may help a little to widen the audience for this work. At the same time, though, we do recommend that if readers want to engage very intensively with particular texts at an advanced level, they should consult the originals – it would be unfair to criticise any given writer for e.g. inadequate exemplification when it has been us as editors who have cut down on the data cited.

Using the Reader

As already indicated, we have organised the volume to bring out arguments and contrasts, and if it's used as a teaching resource, we think that students can learn quite a lot by being asked to compare two or more extracts addressed to a particular theme. Exactly what these themes are will, of course, depend on their course, their tutor, their interests, etc., and it would be very hard to anticipate the lines of connection, similarity and difference that readers themselves construct as they become more familiar with these texts. However, to help readers find a productive route through the articles here, following the paths of particular interest to them:

- Table 1 should provide some initial principles for selecting and sequencing papers;

Table 3 Crude preliminary sub-classification of texts by geographical and institutional focus.

Initial/primary geographical focus[25]

Worldwide	Ashcroft, Jespersen, Sapir, Quirk, Rampton
Africa	Ngũgĩ, Mazrui
Jamaica and the Caribbean	Alleyne
Europe	Fishman
UK	Billig, Honeyford, Hewitt, Gumperz, Back
US	Billig, Rickford, Hill, Whorf, Philips, McDermott and Gospodinoff, Gumperz and Hernández-Chavez, Clark, Cutler
Canada	Heller
Singapore	Bokhorst-Heng
Basque country	Urla

Main institutional focus[26]

Tribes	Jespersen, Whorf, (Sapir), Philips
Literature and academia	Ashcroft, Ngũgĩ
Education	Quirk, Mazrui, (Rampton), Honeyford, Rickford, (Bokhorst-Heng), Heller, Philips, McDermott and Gospodinoff, Gumperz and Hernández-Chavez, Clark
Public media	Billig, Bokhorst-Heng, Urla, Hill, (Cutler), Back
Government	Mazrui, Fishman, Bokhorst-Heng
General/non-specific	Sapir, Alleyne, (Rampton), Hewitt

- there is some more preliminary sub-classification in Table 3 above;
- at the start of each Section, our Introductions provide
  - brief sketches of some of the relationships between the papers there;
  - introductory synopses for each article;
- there are editorial footnotes in each extract, cross-referring to others where the interested reader might like to look next.

If, for example, you wanted to explore the ways in which the language of a subordinate ethnic group acts as a more or less hidden impediment to educational success, the papers by Rickford, Philips, Gumperz, Gumperz and Hernández-Chavez, Honeyford, McDermott and Gospodinoff, and Clark present a lot of issues for discussion. If you were interested in how ethnicity gets cast as a private concern, subordinate to standard language in the public sphere, there are a range of issues presented in the papers by Bokhorst-Heng, Honeyford, Gumperz and Hernández-Chavez, Hill and Clark. For a view of how subordinate ethnic languages become desirable generally, you could see Cutler, Hewitt and Back. And so on.

To go beyond this volume with some of the issues raised in the extracts, we can recommend the following as general starting points:

- *The Cambridge Encyclopedia of Language: 2nd Edition* (D. Crystal Cambridge: Cambridge University Press 1997). For anyone new to linguistics, this is a lucid, accessible, authoritative and affordable introduction to a very wide range of issues in language study.
- *An Introduction to Sociolinguistics: 2nd Edition* (J. Holmes London: Longman 2001). There are a lot of introductory sociolinguistics textbooks, but this is sound and very accessible.

There are a number of edited readers that address language topics relevant to this collection:

- The *Handbook of Language and Ethnic Identity* (J. Fishman (ed.) Oxford University Press 1999) seeks to provide the non-specialist reader with authoritative summaries of the ways in which language and ethnicity have been treated in a range of separate disciplinary and geographical areas (e.g. economics, psychology, sociology; Germany, Sub-Saharan Africa etc.).

Other readers on language in social context require a little more technical involvement with linguistics:

- *Linguistic Anthropology: A Reader* (A. Duranti (ed.) Blackwell 2001).
- *Sociolinguistics: A Reader and Coursebook* (N. Coupland and A. Jaworski (eds) Macmillan 1997).
- *The Discourse Reader* (A. Jaworski and N. Coupland (eds) Routledge 1999).
- *The Bilingualism Reader* (Li Wei (ed.) Routledge 2000).

For readers on ethnicity and race, see

- *Ethnicity* (J. Hutchinson and Smith, A.D. (eds) 1996 Oxford: Oxford University Press).
- *The Ethnicity Reader* (M. Guibernau and J. Rex (eds) Polity, 1997).
- *Theories of Race and Racism* (L. Back and J. Solomos, (eds) Routledge 2000).

Notes

1   In recent academic discussions, 'race' is often put in inverted commas, in order to emphasise that it is a social and cultural idea/construct rather than a valid natural basis for allocating people to different groups. But ethnicities and languages are also cultural ideas (interpretations, categories and inventions), as are most of the things that we refer to in discourse, and so we won't follow this practice of using quotation marks, as it would obviously be extremely cumbersome if we tried to be consistent about it.
2   E.g. (but by no means exclusively) Whorf, Gumperz, Philips in this volume.
3   E.g. (but by no means exclusively) Hill, Gumperz and Hernández-Chavez in this volume.
4   E.g. (but by no means exclusively) Ashcroft, Billig, Back in this volume.
5   E.g. (but by no means exclusively) Ngũgĩ, Mazrui, Honeyford.
6   Cf. Ashcroft, Fishman, Honeyford and Hewitt in this volume.
7   Giddens 1990: 15.

8   Bauman 1998: 2.

9   Anderson 1983, Morley and Robins 1995, Castells 1996.

10   Hannerz 1996, also Harris, Leung and Rampton 2001.

11   See Comaroff and Comaroff 1992 for a powerful critique of the idea that these terms identify fundamental differences in how people live.

12   In different ways in this volume, this shift is discussed in the extracts by e.g. McDermott
and Gospodinoff, Rampton, and elsewhere, it's discussed very effectively in relation to language by Pratt 1987 and Le Page 1988. More generally, the work of Foucault, among others, is an essential reference point (see e.g. Rabinow (ed.) 1991).

13   There is a huge theoretical literature on race and ethnicity which it would be impossible to
review here, but the collections in Back and Solomos (2000) and Hutchinson and Smith
(1996) provide a very useful wide-ranging overview.

14   See Winant 2000.

15   See Pieterse 1992 for an arresting, and convincing, account of this.

16   This is discussed in detail here in the extract by Ashcroft, and it is exemplified in Jespersen.
Schemes of comparative racial-linguistic classification, depicting tribal and ethnic collectivities as homogeneous wholes and contrasting them with Europeans and Anglos, also form
a major background to the extracts by Sapir and Whorf, and even though they argue against
them in very important ways, it is open to question how far they (and indeed others) manage
to escape them

17   See Rex 1983.

18   See Banton 2001.

19   In this volume, see e.g. Whorf, Ngũgĩ, Philips.

20   The idea of ethnicity as an ingrained disposition is problematic in a variety of ways. The
importance and subtlety of the linguistic and cultural dispositions laid down over time at
home and in local networks is undeniable, but what, for example, are the reasons for assuming that these ingrained patterns are to be identified with ethnicity rather than, say, class,
gender, neighbourhood, family etc.?

21   See e.g. Barth 1969 and Moerman 1974. Also in this volume, e.g. Fishman, Bokhorst-Heng
and Gumperz and Hernández-Chavez.

22   See Hewitt 1986, Gilroy 1987, Hall 1988, Mercer 1994. Hewitt 1986 includes a full analysis
of the linguistic dimensions of cross-ethnic identification, as does Rampton 1995. In this
volume, see Cutler and Back.

23   Table 1 captures little of the disagreements between for example, Jespersen and Sapir; Ngũgĩ
and Quirk; Honeyford and Rickford; or Philips and McDermott and Gospodinoff.

24   For a broadly comparable account of political positions in debates about language and
gender, see e.g. Cameron 1996.

25   Of course, imperialism, globalisation and diaspora make the specification of a single
geographic focus seem rather arbitrary.

26   A lot of extracts cover more than one.

References

Anderson, B. 1983. *Imagined Communities: Reflections on the Origin and Spread of Nationalism.*
London: Verso.

Back, L. and Solomos, J. (eds). 2000. *Theories of Race and Racism: A Reader.* London: Routledge.

Banton, M. 2001. Progress in ethnic and racial studies. *Ethnic and Racial Studies* 24 (2) 173–94.

Barth, F. 1969. Introduction. In F. Barth (ed.) *Ethnic Groups and Boundaries.* London: Allen &
Unwin. 9–39.

Bauman, Z. 1998. *Globalisation: The Human Consequences.* Cambridge: Polity Press.

Cameron, D. 1996. The language-gender interface: challenging co-optation. In V. Bergvall, J. Bing and A. Freed (eds) *Rethinking Language and Gender Research*. London: Longman. 31–53.

Castells, M. 1996. *The Rise of the Network Society*. Oxford: Blackwell.

Comaroff, J. and J. Comaroff 1992. *Ethnography and the Historical Imagination*. Boulder: Westview Press.

Giddens, A. 1990. *Social Theory and Modern Sociology*. Cambridge: Polity Press.

Gilroy, P. 1987. *There Ain't no Black in the Union Jack*. London: Hutchinson.

Hall, S. 1988. New ethnicities. *ICA Documents* 7: 27–31.

Hannerz, U. 1996. *Transnational Connections*. London: Routledge.

Harris, R., C. Leung and B. Rampton 2001. Globalisation, diaspora and language education in England. In D. Block and D. Cameron (eds) *Globalisation and Language Teaching*. London: Routledge. 29–46.

Hewitt, R. 1986. *White Talk, Black Talk: Interracial Friendship and Communication among Adolescents*. Cambridge: Cambridge University Press.

Hutchinson, J. and Smith, A.D. (eds) 1996. *Ethnicity*. Oxford: Oxford University Press.

Le Page, R. 1988. Some premises concerning the standardisation of languages, with special reference to Caribbean Creole English. *International Journal of the Sociology of Language* 71: 25–36.

Mercer, K. 1994. *Welcome to the Jungle: New Positions in Black Cultural Studies*. London and New York: Routledge.

Moerman, M. 1974. Accomplishing ethnicity. In R. Turner (ed.) *Ethnomethodology*. Harmondsworth: Penguin. 54–68.

Morley, D. and D. Robins 1995. *Spaces of Identity: Global Media, Electronic Landscapes and Cultural Boundaries*. London: Routledge.

Pieterse, J.N. 1992. *White on Black: Images of Africa and Blacks in Western Popular Culture*. New Haven and London: Yale University Press.

Pratt, M.L. 1987. Linguistic utopias. In N. Fabb, D. Attridge, A. Durant and C. MacCabe (eds) *The Linguistics of Writing*. Manchester: Manchester University Press. 48–66.

Rabinow, P. (ed.) 1991. *The Foucault Reader: An Introduction to Foucault's Thought*. London: Penguin Books.

Rampton, B. 1995. *Crossing: Language and Ethnicity among Adolescents*. London: Longman. (2nd Edition. Manchester: St Jerome Press).

Rex, J. 1983. *Race Relations in Sociological Theory*. London: Routledge & Kegan Paul.

Winant, H. 2000. Race and race theory. *Annual Review of Sociology* 26: 169–85.

SECTION ONE

Colonialism, Imperialism and Global Process

Introduction

THERE ARE THREE major themes running through this Section:

- inequality under colonial and imperial domination;
- the links between language, race, culture and development;
- the global power of English.

The links between language, race and cultural development are at issue in the first three extracts. Jespersen investigates the evolution of language, identifies African, American Indian and other 'savage' languages with earlier stages of human development, and takes it for granted that he, his readers and the 'civilised nations' represent a higher level. Sapir contests the stereotyped associations between language, race and culture that this kind of hierarchy depends on, arguing instead that when 'it comes to linguistic form, Plato walks with the Macedonian swineherd, Confucius with the head-hunting savage of Assam'. Ashcroft situates these debates about language, race and culture in a broader historical context of western thought and imperial scholarship, suggesting that problematic equations of language with culture persist in post-colonial writing.

The next three extracts address the relationship between African languages and English, a language they associate with slavery, colonialism and capitalist globalisation. Alleyne describes what happened to African languages transported to Jamaica, and points to ways in which they have survived under English. Ngũgĩ argues that because peoples, languages and cultures are so strongly connected, African writers should relegate English, while Mazrui shows how the World Bank recognises African languages in its rhetoric while promoting English in its economics.

To some, though, the advantages of English as an internationally intelligible language seem obvious, as does the centrality of its native speakers. This is Quirk's position. For Rampton, though, the idea of the 'native speaker' represents roughly the same kind of conflation of biology, language, ability and identification that Sapir complained of.

To give more detail on each:

- In 'The origin of speech' (1922), Otto Jespersen tries to reconstruct the evolution of language, drawing among other things on accounts of the speech of 'contemporary savages'. On this basis, he argues that linguistic evolution entails progress from emotional, poetic and musical styles of speaking, involving elaborate grammar and inflexible, concrete vocabulary, to language that is more rational, regular, abstract and intellectually flexible, which he associates with a subset of Europeans.

- Edward Sapir's article, 'Language, race and culture' (1921), challenges the 'mystic slogans' of '"race" sentimentalists' who believe that there are inherent and necessary links between a language, a culture and a race. He reviews a range of cases attesting to the lack of correspondence between them, and where they do overlap, he argues that this is the outcome of external history, not a matter of any racial essence. He is prepared to admit that the structure of a language can have an impact on how its speakers think, but even here he advises caution against slip-shod correlations.

- Bill Ashcroft's paper, 'Language and race' (2001) traces the intimate links between notions of 'language' and 'race' in western thought. The idea of 'race' has its roots in colonial domination rather than in nature, and much of the oppressive reality of racialised experience derives from the way it resonates in language with loaded terms like 'black' and 'white'. From the late eighteenth century on, academic study consolidated deterministic equations of race, language, national character and cultural development, and indeed radical twentieth-century thinkers have held to the race-equals-language view, assuming that specific cultures are irrevocably, indissolubly, tied to particular languages. Certainly they are often historically associated, argues Ashcroft, but these links can be reworked, changing the cultural meanings of a language.

- In 'Language in Jamaican Culture' (1989), Mervyn Alleyne examines the African roots of Jamaican language, analysing the ways in which African languages changed, resisted and adapted under slavery and English, the language of (military) domination. He identifies six social, political and linguistic contexts and processes affecting the historical evolution of these languages, and he emphasises the continuity and survival of African linguistic elements, contesting the view that Jamaican language is just a corruption of English.

- Drawing extensively on autobiographical experience in Kenya, 'The language of African literature' (1986) explains Ngũgĩ wa Thiong'o's decision to change from writing in English to Gĩkũyũ. In his analysis of the alienation from African culture produced by education and literature in the languages of

European imperialism, Ngũgĩ argues that the history and values of a people are carried in their language, and that when they abandoned local languages, the educated African bourgeoisie also became isolated from the working class and peasantry, where the national heritages of Africa were really kept alive.

- In 'The World Bank, the language question and the future of African education' (1997), Alamin Mazrui provides a critique of the lip-service that the World Bank pays to the use of African mother-tongues in education. In actuality, its economic policies undercut the institutional infrastructure needed to support local languages, and instead, the use of English in education serves the interests of global capitalism, stratifying the workforce, keeping Africa open to western products and philosophies. Mazrui doesn't believe that English is indissolubly linked to imperialism, but for the moment, it is not conducive to the development of independent African perspectives.

- In 'Language varieties and standard language' (1990), Randolph Quirk discusses the global spread and influence of English. Though he doesn't explore the history of this spread, he insists on the importance of a standard common core closely modelled on the language of its native speakers. He offers a classification of different types of English, and argues that there is no scope for 'liberation linguistics' in education, either in Britain or abroad.

- Ben Rampton's article, 'Displacing the "native speaker": expertise, affiliation and inheritance' (1990) takes issue with the notion of 'native speaker' (and 'mother-tongue'), arguing that this is a pernicious instance of deeply entrenched linguistic essentialism, conflating language, birth, nationality, proficiency and attachment. The extract insists that our relationships with different languages are socially generated, not biologically given, and proposes that 'expertise', 'affiliation' and 'inheritance' provide a better framework for talking about people's linguistic identities.

Chapter 1

Otto Jespersen

1922

THE ORIGIN OF SPEECH[a]

[. . .]

[**W**]E MAY IN SOME INSTANCES take the [languages of contemporary savages] as typical of more primitive languages than those of civilized nations, and therefore as illustrating a linguistic stage that is nearer to that in which speech originated.[b] Still, inferences from such languages should be used with great caution, for it should never be forgotten that even the most backward race has many centuries of linguistic evolution behind it, and that the conditions therefore may, or must, be very different from those of primeval man. [. . .]

[. . .] Sounds

First, as regards the purely phonetic side of language, we observe everywhere the tendency to make pronunciation more easy, so as to lessen the muscular effort; difficult combinations of sounds are discarded, those only being retained which are pronounced with ease. Modern research has shown that the Proto-Aryan[c] sound-system was much more complicated than was imagined in the reconstructions of the middle of the nineteenth century. In most languages now only such sounds are used as are produced by expiration, while inbreathed sounds and clicks or suction-stops are not found in connected speech. In civilized languages we meet with such

---

a From O. Jespersen (1922/64) *Language: Its Nature, Development and Origin*. London: Allen & Unwin pp. 416–42.

b See Ashcroft, this volume, on nineteenth-century ideas about the linguistic development from primitive to modern.

c 'Proto-Aryan' = the language assumed to be the antecedent/parent of Indo-European languages, thought to have been spoken before 3000BC. On the invention of the concept of 'Aryan', see Ashcroft.

sounds only in interjections, as when an inbreathed voiceless *l* (generally with rhythmic variations of strength and corresponding small movements of the tongue) is used to express delight in eating and drinking, or when the click inadequately spelt *tut* is used to express impatience. In some very primitive South African languages, on the other hand, clicks are found as integral parts of words; and Bleek has rendered it probable that in former stages of these languages they were in more extensive use than now. We may perhaps draw the conclusion that primitive languages in general were rich in all kinds of difficult sounds.

The following point is of more far-reaching consequence. In some languages we find a gradual disappearance of tone or pitch accent;[d] this has been the case in Danish, whereas Norwegian and Swedish have kept the old tones; so also in Russian as compared with Serbo-Croatian. In the works of old Indian, Greek and Latin grammarians we have express statements to the effect that pitch accent played a prominent part in those languages, and that the intervals[e] used must have been comparatively greater than is usual in our modern languages. In modern Greek and in the Romanic languages the tone element has been obscured, and now 'stress' is heard on the syllable where the ancients noted only a high or a low tone.[f] About the languages spoken nowadays by savage tribes we have generally very little information, as most of those who have made a first-hand study of such languages have not been trained to observe and to describe these delicate points; still, there is of late years an increasing number of observations of tone accents, for instance in African languages, which may justify us in thinking that tone plays an important part in many primitive languages.[1]

So much for word tones; now for the sentence melody. It is a well-known fact that the modulation of sentences is strongly influenced by the effect of intense emotions in causing stronger and more rapid raisings and sinkings of the tone. "All passionate language does of itself become musical—with a finer music than the mere accent; the speech of a man even in zealous anger becomes a chant, a song" (Carlyle). [. . .]

Now, it is a consequence of advancing civilization that passion, or, at least, the expression of passion, is moderated, and we must therefore conclude that the speech of uncivilized and primitive men was more passionately agitated than ours, more like music or song. This conclusion is borne out by what we hear about the speech of many savages in our own days. European travellers very often record their impression of the speech of different tribes in expressions like these: "pronouncing whatever they spoke in a very singing manner," "the singing tone of voice, in common conversation, was frequent," "the speech is very much modulated and resembles singing," "highly artificial and musical," etc.

These facts and considerations all point to the conclusion that there once was a time when all speech was song, or rather when these two actions were not yet differentiated; but perhaps this inference cannot be established inductively at the

---

d 'Tone or pitch accent' refers to the use of a high or low pitched voice to emphasise/accentuate a particular word or syllable.

e That is the degree of pitch raising and lowering.

f With 'stress', a word (or syllable) is made more prominent by (among other things) increased loudness.

present stage of linguistic science with the same amount of certainty as the statements I am now going to make as to the nature of primitive speech.

[. . . A] great many of the changes going on regularly from century to century,
as well as some of the sudden changes which take place now and then in the history
of each language, result in the shortening of words. This is seen everywhere and
at all times, and in consequence of this universal tendency we find that the ancient
languages of our family, Sanskrit, Zend, etc., abound in very long words [. . .]
We have seen also how the current theory, according to which every language
started with monosyllabic roots, fails at every point to account for actual facts and
breaks down before the established truths of linguistic history. Just as the history
of religion does not pass from the belief in one god to the belief in many gods,
but inversely from polytheism towards monotheism, so language proceeds from
original polysyllabism towards monosyllabism: if the development of language took
the same course in prehistoric as in historic times, we see, by projecting the teaching
of history on a larger scale back into the darkest ages, that early words must have
been to present ones what the plesiosaurus and gigantosaurus are to present-day
reptiles. The outcome of this phonetic section is, therefore, that we must imagine
primitive language as consisting (chiefly at least) of very long words, full of difficult
sounds, and sung rather than spoken. [. . .]

[. . .] Savage tribes

[Among the languages of savage or primitive races nowadays,] there are [. . .] many
different types, even with regard to grammatical structure. But the more these
languages are studied and the more accurately their structure is described, the
more also students perceive intricacies and anomalies in their grammar. Gablentz
(Spr 386)[g] says that the casual observer has no idea how manifold and how nicely
circumscribed grammatical categories can be, even in the seemingly crudest
languages, for ordinary grammars tell us nothing about that. P. W. Schmidt (*Die
Stellung der Pygmäenvölker*, 1910, 129) says that whoever, from the low culture of
the Andamanese, would expect to find their language very simple and poor in
expressions would be strangely deceived, for its mechanism is highly complicated,
with many prefixes and suffixes, which often conceal the root itself. Meinhof (MSA
136)[h] mentions the multiplicity of [ways of forming plurals] in African languages.
Vilhelm Thomsen, in speaking of the Santhal (Khervarian) language, says that its
grammar is capable of expressing a multiplicity of *nuances* which in other languages
must be expressed by clumsy circumlocutions [. . .]; Curr speaks about the erroneous belief in the simplicity of Australian languages, which on the contrary have
a great number of conjugations,[i] etc. The extreme difficulty and complex structure of Eskimo and of many Amerindian languages is so notorious that no words
need be wasted on them here. And the forms of the Basque verb are so manifold
and intricate that we understand how Larramendi, in his legitimate pride at having

---

g Gablentz Spr = G.v.d. Gablentz, *Die Sprachwissenschaft*, Leipzig 1891.
h Meinhof MSA = C. Meinhof, *Die moderne Sprachforschung in Afrika*, Berlin 1910.
i Groups of verbs that can be inflected/internally modified in the same ways.

been the first to reduce them to a system, called his grammar *El Imposible Vencido*, 'The Impossible Overcome.' At Béarn they have the story that the good God, wishing to punish the devil for the temptation of Eve, sent him to the Pays Basque with the command that he should remain there till he had mastered the language. At the end of seven years God relented finding the punishment too severe, and called the devil to him. The devil had no sooner crossed the bridge of Castelondo than he found he had forgotten all that he had so hardly learned.

What is here said about the languages of wild tribes (and of the Basques, who are not exactly savages, but whose language is generally taken to have retained many primeval traits) is in exact keeping with everything that recent study of primitive man has brought to light: the life of the savage is regulated to the minutest details through ceremonies and conventionalities to be observed on every and any occasion; he is restricted in what he may eat and drink and when and how; and all these, to our mind, irrational prescriptions and innumerable prohibitions have to be observed with the most scrupulous, nay religious, care: it is the same with all the meticulous rules of his language. [. . .]

[. . .] Vocabulary

On the lexical side of language we find a development parallel to that noticed in grammar; and, indeed, if we go deep enough into the question, we shall see that it is really the very same movement that has taken place. The more advanced a language is, the more developed is its power of expressing abstract or general ideas.[j] Everywhere language has first attained to expressions for the concrete and special. In accounts of the languages of barbarous races we constantly come across such phrases as these: "The aborigines of Tasmania had no words representing abstract ideas; for each variety of gum-tree and wattle-tree, etc., they had a name; but they had no equivalent for the expression 'a tree'; neither could they express abstract qualities, such as 'hard, soft, warm, cold, long, short, round'"; or, "The Mohicans have words for cutting various objects, but none to convey *cutting* simply." The Zulus have no word for 'cow,' but words for 'red cow,' 'white cow,' etc. [. . .] In Bakaïri (Central Brazil) "each parrot has its special name, and the general idea 'parrot' is totally unknown, as well as the general idea 'palm.' But they know precisely the qualities of each subspecies of parrot and palm, and attach themselves so much to these numerous particular notions that they take no interest in the common characteristics. They are choked in the abundance of the material and cannot manage it economically. They have only small coin, but in that they must be said to be excessively rich rather than poor" (K. v. d. Steinen, *Unter den Naturvölkern Brasiliens*, 1894, 81). The Lithuanians, like many primitive tribes, have many special, but no common names for various colours: one word for gray in speaking about wool and geese, one about horses, one about cattle, one about the hair of men and some animals, and in the same way for other colours (J. Schmidt, *Kritik d. Sonantentheorie* 37). Many languages have no word for 'brother,' but words

---

j Compare Whorf, this volume.

for 'elder brother' and 'younger brother'; others have different words according to whose [. . .] father or brother it is, [. . .] and the same applies in many languages to names for various parts of the body. In Cherokee, instead of one word for 'washing' we find different words, according to what is washed: *kutuwo* 'I wash myself,' *kulestula* 'I wash my head,' *tsestula* 'I wash the head of somebody else,' *kukuswo* 'I wash my face,' *tsekuswo* 'I wash the face of somebody else,' *takasula* 'I wash my hands or feet,' *takunkela* 'I wash my clothes,' *takuteya* 'I wash dishes,' *tsejuwu* 'I wash a child,' *kowela* 'I wash meat' [. . .]. Primitive man did not see the wood for the trees.

In some Amerindian languages there are distinct series of numerals for various classes of objects; thus in Kwakiatl and Tsimoshian (Sapir, *Language and Environment* 239); similarly the Melanesians have special words to denote a definite number of certain objects, e.g. *a buku niu* 'two coconuts,' *a buru* 'ten coconuts,' *a koro* 'a hundred coconuts,' *a selavo* 'a thousand coconuts,' *a uduudu* 'ten canoes,' *a bola* 'ten fishes,' etc. (Gablentz, *Die melan. Spr.* 1. 23). In some languages the numerals are the same for all classes of objects counted, but require after them certain class-denoting words varying according to the character of the objects [. . .]. This reminds one of the systems of weights and measures, which even in civilized countries up to a comparatively recent period varied not only from country to country, sometimes even from district to district, but even in the same country according to the things weighed or measured (in England *stone* and *ton* still vary in this way).

In old Gothonic poetry we find an astonishing abundance of words translated in our dictionaries by 'sea,' 'battle,' 'sword,' 'hero,' and the like: these may certainly be considered as relics of an earlier state of things, in which each of these words had its separate shade of meaning, which was subsequently lost and which it is impossible now to determine with certainty. The nomenclature of a remote past was undoubtedly constructed upon similar principles to those which are still preserved in a word-group like *horse, mare, stallion, foal, colt*, instead of he-horse, she-horse, young horse, etc. This sort of grouping has only survived in a few cases in which a lively interest has been felt in the objects or animals concerned. We may note, however, the different terms employed for essentially the same idea in a *flock* of sheep, a *pack* of wolves, a *herd* of cattle, a *bevy* of larks, a *covey* of partridges, a *shoal* of fish. Primitive language could show a far greater number of instances of this description, and, so far, had a larger vocabulary than later languages, though, of course, it lacked names for a great number of ideas that were outside the sphere of interest of uncivilized people.

There was another reason for the richness of the vocabulary of primitive man: his superstition about words, which made him avoid the use of certain words under certain circumstances—during war, when out fishing, during the time of the great cultic festivals, etc.—because he feared the anger of gods or demons if he did not religiously observe the rules of the linguistic tabu. Accordingly, in many cases he had two or more sets of words for exactly the same notions, of which later generations as a rule preserved only one, unless they differentiated these words by utilizing them to discriminate objects that were similar but not identical.

[. . .] Poetry and Prose

On the whole the development of languages, even in the matter of vocabulary, must be considered to have taken a beneficial course; still, in certain respects one may to some extent regret the consequences of this evolution. While our words are better adapted to express abstract things and to render concrete things with definite precision, they are necessarily comparatively colourless. The old words, on the contrary, spoke more immediately to the senses—they were manifestly more suggestive, more graphic and pictorial: while to express one single thing we are not unfrequently obliged to piece the image together bit by bit, the old concrete words would at once present it to the hearer's mind as a whole; they were, accordingly, better adapted to poetic purposes. Nor is this the only point in which we see a close relationship between primitive words and poetry.

If by a mental effort we transport ourselves to a period in which language consisted solely of such graphic concrete words, we shall discover that, in spite of their number, they would not suffice, taken all together, to cover everything that needed expression; a wealth in such words is not incompatible with a certain poverty. They would accordingly often be required to do service outside of their proper sphere of application. That a figurative or metaphorical use of words is a factor of the utmost importance in the life of all languages is indisputable; but I am probably right in thinking that it played a more prominent part in old times than now. [. . .] The expression of thought therefore tends to become more and more mechanical or prosaic.

Primitive man, however, on account of the nature of his language, was constantly reduced to using words and phrases figuratively: he was forced to express his thoughts in the language of poetry. The speech of modern savages is often spoken of as abounding in similes and all kinds of figurative phrases and allegorical expressions. Just as in the literature transmitted to us poetry is found in every country to precede prose, so poetic language is on the whole older than prosaic language; lyrics and cult songs come before science, [. . .].

[. . .] Emotional songs

If we now try to sum up what has been inferred about primitive speech, we see that by our backward march we arrived at a language whose units had a very meagre substance of thought, and this as specialized and concrete as possible; but at the same time the phonetic body was ample; and the bigger and longer the words, the thinner the thoughts! Much cry and little wool! No period has seen less taciturn people than the first framers of speech; primitive speakers were not reticent and reserved beings, but youthful men and women babbling merrily on, without being so very particular about the meaning of each word. They did not narrowly weigh every syllable—what were a couple of syllables more or less to them? They chattered away for the mere pleasure of chattering, resembling therein many a mother of our own time, who will chatter away to baby without measuring her words or looking too closely into the meaning of each; nay, who is not a bit troubled by the consideration that the little deary does not understand a single word of her affectionate eloquence. But primitive speech—and we return here to an idea thrown out above—still more resembles the speech of little baby himself, before he begins to frame his own language after the pattern of the grownups; the language of our remote forefathers was like that ceaseless humming and crooning with which no thoughts are as yet connected, which merely amuses and delights the little one. Language originated as play, and the organs of speech were first trained in this singing sport of idle hours.

Primitive language had no great store of ideas, and if we consider it as an instrument for expressing thoughts, it was clumsy, unwieldy and ineffectual; but what did that matter? Thoughts were not the first things to press forward and crave for expression; emotions and instincts were more primitive and far more powerful. But what emotions were most powerful in producing germs of speech? To be sure not hunger and that which is connected with hunger: mere individual self-assertion and the struggle for material existence. This prosaic side of life was only capable of calling forth short monosyllabic interjections, howls of pain and grunts of satis-faction or dissatisfaction; but these are isolated and incapable of much further development; they are the most immutable portions of language, and remain now at essentially the same standpoint as thousands of years ago.

[. . . T]he genesis of language is not to be sought in the prosaic, but in the poetic side of life; the source of speech is not gloomy seriousness, but merry play and youthful hilarity. And among the emotions which were most powerful in elic-iting outbursts of music and of song, love must be placed in the front rank. To the feeling of love, which has left traces of its vast influence on countless points in the evolution of organic nature, are due not only, as Darwin has shown, the magnifi-cent colours of birds and flowers, but also many of the things that fill us with joy in human life; it inspired many of the first songs, and through them was instru-mental in bringing about human language. In primitive speech I hear the laughing cries of exultation when lads and lasses vied with one another to attract the atten-tion of the other sex, when everybody sang his merriest and danced his bravest to lure a pair of eyes to throw admiring glances in his direction. Language was born in the courting days of mankind; the first utterances of speech I fancy to myself like something between the nightly love-lyrics of puss upon the tiles and the melodious love-songs of the nightingale.[1]

[. . .] Primitive singing

Love, however, was not the only feeling which tended to call forth primitive songs. Any strong emotion, and more particularly any pleasurable excitement, might result in song. Singing, like any other sort of play, is due to an overflow of energy, which is discharged in "unusual vivacity of every kind, including vocal vivacity." Out of the full heart the mouth sings! Savages will sing whenever they are excited: exploits of war or of the chase, the deeds of their ancestors, the coming of a fat dog, any incident "from the arrival of a stranger to an earthquake" is turned into a song; and most of these songs are composed extempore. "When rowing, the Coast negroes

sing either a description of some love intrigue or the praise of some woman celebrated for her beauty." The Malays beguile all their leisure hours with the repetition
of songs, etc. "In singing, the East African contents himself with improvising a few
words without sense or rime and repeats them till they nauseate." (These quota-
tions, and many others, are found in Herbert Spencer's *Essay on the Origin of Music*,
with his Postscript.) The reader of Karl Bücher's painstaking work *Arbeit und
Rhythmus* (2te aufl. 1899) will know from his numerous examples and illustrations
what an enormous rôle rhythmic singing plays in the daily life of savages all over
the world, how each kind of work, especially if it is done by many jointly, has its
own kind of song, and how nothing is done except to the sound of vocal music.
In many instances savages are mentioned as very expert in adapting the subjects of
their songs to current events. Nor is this sort of singing on every and any occasion
confined to savages; it is found wherever the indoor life of civilization has not killed
all open-air hilarity; formerly in our Western Europe people sang much more than
they do now. The Swedish peasant Jonas Stolt (ab. 1820) writes: "I have known a
time when young people were singing from morning till eve. Then they were
carolling both out- and indoors, behind the plough as well as at the threshing-floor
and at the spinning-wheel. This is all over long ago: nowadays there is silence everywhere; if someone were to try and sing in our days as we did of old, people would
term it bawling."

The first things that were expressed in song were, to be sure, neither deep
nor wise; how could you expect it? Note the frequency with which we are told
that the songs of savages consist of or contain totally meaningless syllables. Thus
we read about American Indians that "the native word which is translated 'song'
does not suggest any use of words. To the Indian, the music is of primal importance; words may or may not accompany the music. When words are used in song,
they are rarely employed as a narrative, the sentences are not apt to be complete"
(Louise Pound, Mod. Lang. Ass. 32. 224), and similarly: "Even where the slightest
vestiges of epic poetry are missing, lyric poetry of one form or another is always
present. It may consist of the musical use of meaningless syllables that sustain the
song or it may consist largely of such syllables, with a few interspersed words
suggesting certain ideas and certain feelings; or it may rise to the expression of
emotions connected with warlike deeds, with religious feeling, love, or even to
the praise of the beauties of nature" (Boas, *International Journ. Amer. Ling.* l. 8). The
magic incantations of the Greenland Eskimo, according to W. Thalbitzer, contain
many incomprehensible words never used outside these songs (but have they ever
been real words?), and the same is said about the mystic religious formulas of
Maoris and African negroes and many other tribes, as well as about the old Roman
hymns of the Arval Brethren. [. . .]

[. . .] Conclusion

Language, then, began with half-musical unanalyzed expressions for individual
beings and solitary events. Languages composed of, and evolved from, such words
and quasi-sentences are clumsy and insufficient instruments of thought, being intricate, capricious and difficult. But from the beginning the tendency has been one of

progress, slow and fitful progress, but still progress towards greater and greater clearness, regularity, ease and pliancy.[k] No one language has arrived at perfection; an ideal language would always express the same thing by the same, and similar things by similar means; any irregularity or ambiguity would be banished; sound and sense would be in perfect harmony; any number of delicate shades of meaning could be expressed with equal ease; poetry and prose, beauty and truth, thinking and feeling would be equally provided for: the human spirit would have found a garment combining freedom and gracefulness, fitting it closely and yet allowing full play to any movement [. . .]

Note

1   From the experience I had with my previous book, *Progress*, from which this chapter has, with some alterations and amplifications, passed into this volume, I feel impelled here to warn those critics who do me the honour to mention my theory of the origin of language, not to look upon it as if it were contained simply in my remarks on primitive love-songs, etc., and as if it were based on *a priori* considerations, like the older speculative theories. What I may perhaps claim as my original contribution to the solution of this question is the *inductive* method based on the three sources of information: [not only the language of primitive races, but also the language of children and especially] the history of language. Some critics think they have demolished my view by simply representing it as a romantic dream of a primitive golden age in which men had no occupation but courting and singing. I have never believed in a far-off golden age, but rather incline to believe in a progressive movement from a very raw and barbarous age to something better, though it must be said that our own age, with its national wars, world wars, and class wars, makes one sometimes ashamed to think how little progress our so-called civilization has made. But primitive ages were probably still worse, and the only thing I have felt bold enough to maintain is that in those days there were some moments consecrated to youthful hilarity, and that this gave rise, among other merriment, to vocal play of such a character as closely to resemble what we may infer from the known facts of linguistic history to have been a stage of language earlier than any of those accessible to us. There is no 'romanticism' (in a bad sense) in such a theory, and it can only be refuted by showing that the view of language and its development on which it is based is erroneous from beginning to end.

Otto Jespersen 1860–1943 was a Danish linguist with an international reputation. He became Professor of English Language and Literature at Copenhagen University and an acknowledged authority on the English language. One of his best known works, first published in 1905, was *Growth and Structure of the English Language* (Oxford: Basil Blackwell, 1982).

---

k Clarity, brevity, ease and regularity were stylistic features promoted in the seventeenth-century European Enlightenment, counterposed to the ornate styles prevalent hitherto (see e.g. R. Scollon and S. Scollon (1995) *Intercultural Communication*. Oxford: Blackwell, Ch. 6). The contrasts between concrete and abstract, emotional and rational etc., used here by Jespersen to distinguish primitive and modern speech, have been recycled elsewhere in discussions of the speech of e.g. the working vs middle classes, and women vs men.

Chapter 2

Edward Sapir

1921

LANGUAGE, RACE AND CULTURE[a]

L ANGUAGE HAS A SETTING. The people that speak it belong to a race (or a number of races), that is, to a group which is set off by physical charac-teristics from other groups. Again, language does not exist apart from culture, that is, from the socially inherited assemblage of practices and beliefs that determines the texture of our lives. Anthropologists have been in the habit of studying man under the three rubrics of race, language, and culture. One of the first things they do with a natural area like Africa or the South Seas is to map it out from this threefold point of view. These maps answer the questions: What and where are the major divisions of the human animal, biologically considered (e.g., Congo Negro, Egyptian White; Australian Black, Polynesian)? What are the most inclusive linguistic groupings, the "linguistic stocks," and what is the distribution of each (e.g., the Hamitic languages of northern Africa, the Bantu languages of the south; the Malayo-Polynesian lan-guages of Indonesia, Melanesia, Micronesia, and Polynesia)? How do the peoples of the given area divide themselves as cultural beings? what are the outstanding "cultural areas" and what are the dominant ideas in each (e.g., the Mohammedan north of Africa; the primitive hunting, non-agricultural culture of the Bushmen in the south; the culture of the Australian natives, poor in physical respects but richly developed in ceremonialism; the more advanced and highly specialized culture of Polynesia)?

The man in the street does not stop to analyze his position in the general scheme of humanity. He feels that he is the representative of some strongly integrated portion of humanity—now thought of as a "nationality," now as a "race"—and that everything that pertains to him as a typical representative of this large group somehow belongs together. If he is an Englishman, he feels himself to be a member of the "Anglo-Saxon" race, the "genius" of which race has fashioned the English

a From E. Sapir (1921/63) *Language: An Introduction to the Study of Speech*. London: Hart-Davis pp. 207–20.

language and the "Anglo-Saxon" culture of which the language is the expression. Science is colder. It inquires if these three types of classification—racial, linguistic, and cultural—are congruent, if their association is an inherently necessary one or is merely a matter of external history. The answer to the inquiry is not encouraging to "race" sentimentalists. Historians and anthropologists find that races, languages, and cultures are not distributed in parallel fashion, that their areas of distribution intercross in the most bewildering fashion, and that the history of each is apt to follow a distinctive course. Races intermingle in a way that languages do not. On the other hand, languages may spread far beyond their original home, invading the territory of new races and of new culture spheres. A language may even die out in its primary area and live on among peoples violently hostile to the persons of its original speakers. Further, the accidents of history are constantly rearranging the borders of culture areas without necessarily effacing the existing linguistic cleavages. If we can once thoroughly convince ourselves that race, in its only intelligible, that is biological, sense, is supremely indifferent to the history of languages and cultures, that these are no more directly explainable on the score of race than on that of the laws of physics and chemistry, we shall have gained a viewpoint that allows a certain interest to such mystic slogans as Slavophilism, Anglo-Saxondom, Teutonism, and the Latin genius[b] but that quite refuses to be taken in by any of them. A careful study of linguistic distributions and of the history of such distributions is one of the driest of commentaries on these sentimental creeds.

That a group of languages need not in the least correspond to a racial group or a culture area is easily demonstrated. We may even show how a single language intercrosses with race and culture lines. The English language is not spoken by a unified race. In the United States there are several millions of negroes who know no other language. It is their mother-tongue, the formal vesture of their inmost thoughts and sentiments. It is as much their property, as inalienably "theirs," as the King of England's. Nor do the English-speaking whites of America constitute a definite race except by way of contrast to the negroes. Of the three fundamental white races in Europe generally recognized by physical anthropologists—the Baltic or North European, the Alpine, and the Mediterranean—each has numerous English-speaking representatives in America. But does not the historical core of English-speaking peoples, those relatively "unmixed" populations that still reside in England and its colonies, represent a race, pure and single? I cannot see that the evidence points that way. The English people are an amalgam of many distinct strains. Besides the old "Anglo-Saxon," in other words North German, element which is conventionally represented as the basic strain, the English blood comprises Norman French,[1] Scandinavian, "Celtic,"[2] and pre-Celtic elements. If by "English" we mean also Scotch and Irish,[3] then the term "Celtic" is loosely used for at least two quite distinct racial elements—the short, dark-complexioned type of Wales and the taller, lighter, often ruddy-haired type of the Highlands and parts of Ireland. Even if we confine ourselves to the Saxon element, which, needless to say, nowhere appears "pure," we are not at the end of our troubles. We may roughly identify this strain with the racial type now predominant in southern Denmark and adjoining

---

b See Ashcroft, this volume, and Rampton on the 'mystique' around the notions of 'native speaker' and 'mother tongue'.

parts of northern Germany. If so, we must content ourselves with the reflection that while the English language is historically most closely affiliated with Frisian, in second degree with the other West Germanic dialects (Low Saxon or "Platt-deutsch," Dutch, High German), only in third degree with Scandinavian, the specific "Saxon" racial type that overran England in the fifth and sixth centuries was largely the same as that now represented by the Danes, who speak a Scandinavian language, while the High German-speaking population of central and southern Germany[4] is markedly distinct.

But what if we ignore these finer distinctions and simply assume that the "Teutonic" or Baltic or North European racial type coincided in its distribution with that of the Germanic languages? Are we not on safe ground then? No, we are now in hotter water than ever. First of all, the mass of the German-speaking popula-tion (central and southern Germany, German Switzerland, German Austria) do not belong to the tall, blond-haired, long-headed "Teutonic" race at all, but to the shorter, darker-complexioned, short-headed Alpine race, of which the central population of France, the French Swiss, and many of the western and northern Slavs (e.g., Bohemians and Poles) are equally good representatives. The distribu-tion of these "Alpine" populations corresponds in part to that of the old continental "Celts," whose language has everywhere given way to Italic, Germanic, and Slavic pressure. We shall do well to avoid speaking of a "Celtic race," but if we were driven to give the term a content, it would probably be more appropriate to apply it to, roughly, the western portion of the Alpine peoples than to the two island types that I referred to before. These latter were certainly "Celticized," in speech and, partly, in blood, precisely as, centuries later, most of England and part of Scotland was "Teutonized" by the Angles and Saxons. Linguistically speaking, the "Celts" of to-day (Irish Gaelic, Manx, Scotch Gaelic, Welsh, Breton) are Celtic and most of the Germans of to-day are Germanic precisely as the American Negro, Americanized Jew, Minnesota Swede, and German-American are "English." But, secondly, the Baltic race was, and is, by no means an exclusively Germanic-speaking people. The northernmost "Celts," such as the Highland Scotch, are in all proba-bility a specialized offshoot of this race. What these people spoke before they were Celticized nobody knows, but there is nothing whatever to indicate that they spoke a Germanic language. Their language may quite well have been as remote from any known Indo-European idiom as are Basque and Turkish to-day. Again, to the east of the Scandinavians are non-Germanic members of the race—the Finns and related peoples, speaking languages that are not definitely known to be related to Indo-European at all.

We cannot stop here. The geographical position of the Germanic languages is such[5] as to make it highly probable that they represent but an outlying transfer of an Indo-European dialect (possibly a Celto-Italic prototype) to a Baltic people speak-ing a language or a group of languages that was alien to Indo-European.[6] Not only, then, is English not spoken by a unified race at present but its prototype, more likely than not, was originally a foreign language to the race with which English is more particularly associated. We need not seriously entertain the idea that English or the group of languages to which it belongs is in any intelligible sense the expression of race, that there are embedded in it qualities that reflect the temperament or "genius" of a particular breed of human beings.

Many other, and more striking, examples of the lack of correspondence between race and language could be given if space permitted. One instance will do for many. The Malayo-Polynesian languages form a well-defined group that takes in the southern end of the Malay Peninsula and the tremendous island world to the south and east (except Australia and the greater part of New Guinea). In this vast region we find represented no less than three distinct races—the Negro-like Papuans of New Guinea and Melanesia, the Malay race of Indonesia, and the Polynesians of the outer islands. The Polynesians and Malays *all* speak languages of the Malayo-Polynesian group, while the languages of the Papuans belong partly to this group (Melanesian), partly to the unrelated languages ("Papuan") of New Guinea.[7] In spite of the fact that the greatest race cleavage in this region lies between the Papuans and the Polynesians, the major linguistic division is of Malayan on the one side, Melanesian and Polynesian on the other.

As with race, so with culture. Particularly in more primitive levels, where the secondarily unifying power of the "national"[8] ideal does not arise to disturb the flow of what we might call natural distributions, it is easy to show that language and culture are not intrinsically associated. Totally unrelated languages share in one culture, closely related languages—even a single language—belong to distinct culture spheres. There are many excellent examples in aboriginal America. The Athabaskan languages form as clearly unified, as structurally specialized, a group as any that I know of. The speakers of these languages belong to four distinct culture areas—the simple hunting culture of western Canada and the interior of Alaska (Loucheux, Chipewyan), the buffalo culture of the Plains (Sarcee), the highly ritualized culture of the southwest (Navaho), and the peculiarly specialized culture of north-western California (Hupa). The cultural adaptability of the Athabaskan-speaking peoples is in the strangest contrast to the inaccessibility to foreign influences of the languages themselves. The Hupa Indians are very typical of the culture area to which they belong. Culturally identical with them are the neighboring Yurok and Karok. There is the liveliest intertribal intercourse between the Hupa, Yurok, and Karok, so much so that all three generally attend an important religious ceremony given by any one of them. It is difficult to say what elements in their combined culture belong in origin to this tribe or that, so much at one are they in communal action, feeling, and thought. But their languages are not merely alien to each other; they belong to three of the major American linguistic groups, each with an immense distribution on the northern continent. Hupa, as we have seen, is Athabaskan and, as such, is also distantly related to Haida (Queen Charlotte Islands) and Tlingit (southern Alaska); Yurok is one of the two isolated Californian languages of the Algonkin stock, the center of gravity of which lies in the region of the Great Lakes; Karok is the northernmost member of the Hokan group, which stretches far to the south beyond the confines of California and has remoter relatives along the Gulf of Mexico.

Returning to English, most of us would readily admit, I believe, that the community of language between Great Britain and the United States is far from arguing a like community of culture. It is customary to say that they possess a common "Anglo-Saxon" cultural heritage, but are not many significant differences in life and feeling obscured by the tendency of the "cultured" to take this common heritage too much for granted? In so far as America is still specifically "English," it is only colonially or vestigially so; its prevailing cultural drift is partly towards autonomous and distinctive developments, partly towards immersion in the larger European culture of which that of England is only a particular facet. We cannot deny that the possession of a common language is still and will long continue to be a smoother of the way to a mutual cultural understanding between England and America, but it is very clear that other factors, some of them rapidly cumulative, are working powerfully to counteract this leveling influence. A common language cannot indefinitely set the seal on a common culture when the geographical, political, and economic determinants of the culture are no longer the same throughout its area.

Language, race, and culture are not necessarily correlated. This does not mean that they never are. There is some tendency, as a matter of fact, for racial and cultural lines of cleavage to correspond to linguistic ones, though in any given case the latter may not be of the same degree of importance as the others. Thus, there is a fairly definite line of cleavage between the Polynesian languages, race, and culture on the one hand and those of the Melanesians on the other, in spite of a considerable amount of overlapping.[9] The racial and cultural division, however, particularly the former, are of major importance, while the linguistic division is of quite minor significance, the Polynesian languages constituting hardly more than a special dialectic subdivision of the combined Melanesian-Polynesian group. Still clearer-cut coincidences of cleavage may be found. The language, race, and culture of the Eskimo are markedly distinct from those of their neighbors;[10] in southern Africa the language, race, and culture of the Bushmen offer an even stronger contrast to those of their Bantu neighbors. Coincidences of this sort are of the greatest significance, of course, but this significance is not one of inherent psychological relation between the three factors of race, language, and culture. The coincidences of cleavage point merely to a readily intelligible historical association. If the Bantu and Bushmen are so sharply differentiated in all respects, the reason is simply that the former are relatively recent arrivals in southern Africa. The two peoples developed in complete isolation from each other; their present propinquity is too recent for the slow process of cultural and racial assimilation to have set in very powerfully. As we go back in time, we shall have to assume that relatively scanty populations occupied large territories for untold generations and that contact with other masses of population was not as insistent and prolonged as it later became. The geographical and historical isolation that brought about race differentiations was naturally favorable also to far-reaching variations in language and culture. The very fact that races and cultures which are brought into historical contact tend to assimilate in the long run, while neighboring languages assimilate each other only casually and in superficial respects,[11] indicates that there is no profound causal relation between the development of language and the specific development of race and of culture.

But surely, the wary reader will object, there must be some relation between language and culture, and between language and at least that intangible aspect of race that we call "temperament."[c] Is it not inconceivable that the particular collective

---

c On language, race and 'temperament', see Jespersen, this volume.

qualities of mind that have fashioned a culture are not precisely the same as were responsible for the growth of a particular linguistic morphology?[d] This question takes us into the heart of the most difficult problems of social psychology. It is doubtful if any one has yet attained to sufficient clarity on the nature of the historical process and on the ultimate psychological factors involved in linguistic and cultural drifts to answer it intelligently. I can only very briefly set forth my own views, or rather my general attitude. It would be very difficult to prove that "temperament," the general emotional disposition of a people,[12] is basically responsible for the slant and drift of a culture, however much it may manifest itself in an individual's handling of the elements of that culture. But granted that temperament has a certain value for the shaping of culture, difficult though it be to say just how, it does not follow that it has the same value for the shaping of language. It is impossible to show that the form of a language has the slightest connection with national temperament. Its line of variation, its drift, runs inexorably in the channel ordained for it by its historic antecedents; it is as regardless of the feelings and sentiments of its speakers as is the course of a river of the atmospheric humors of the landscape. I am convinced that it is futile to look in linguistic structure for differences corresponding to the temperamental variations which are supposed to be correlated with race. In this connection it is well to remember that the emotional aspect of our psychic life is but meagerly expressed in the build of language.

Language and our thought-grooves are inextricably interrelated, are, in a sense, one and the same. As there is nothing to show that there are significant racial differences in the fundamental conformation of thought, it follows that the infinite variability of linguistic form, another name for the infinite variability of the actual process of thought, cannot be an index of such significant racial differences. This is only apparently a paradox. The latent content of all languages is the same—the intuitive *science* of experience. It is the manifest form that is never twice the same, for this form, which we call linguistic morphology, is nothing more nor less than a collective *art* of thought, an art denuded of the irrelevancies of individual sentiment. At last analysis, then, language can no more flow from race as such than can the sonnet form.

Nor can I believe that culture and language are in any true sense causally related. Culture may be defined as *what* a society does and thinks. Language is a particular *how* of thought. It is difficult to see what particular causal relations may be expected to subsist between a selected inventory of experience (culture, a significant selection made by society) and the particular manner in which the society expresses all experience. The drift of culture, another way of saying history, is a complex series of changes in society's selected inventory—additions, losses, changes of emphasis and relation. The drift of language is not properly concerned with changes of content at all, merely with changes in formal expression. It is possible, in thought, to change every sound, word, and concrete concept of a language without changing its inner actuality in the least, just as one can pour into a fixed mold water or plaster or molten gold. If it can be shown that culture has an innate form, a series of contours,

---

d 'Linguistic morphology' = patterning in the way words are formed. In English, for example, present and past are marked in the morphology of verbs ('run', 'ran'; 'opens', 'opened').

quite apart from subject-matter of any description whatsoever, we have a some-thing in culture that may serve as a term of comparison with and possibly a means of relating it to language. But until such purely formal patterns of culture are discov-ered and laid bare, we shall do well to hold the drifts of language and of culture to be non-comparable and unrelated processes.[e] From this it follows that all attempts to connect particular types of linguistic morphology with certain correlated stages of cultural development are vain. Rightly understood, such correlations are rubbish. [. . .] Both simple and complex types of language of an indefinite number of varieties may be found spoken at any desired level of cultural advance.[f] When it comes to linguistic form, Plato walks with the Macedonian swine-herd, Confucius with the head-hunting savage of Assam.

It goes without saying that the mere content of language is intimately related to culture. A society that has no knowledge of theosophy need have no name for it; aborigines that had never seen or heard of a horse were compelled to invent or borrow a word for the animal when they made his acquaintance. In the sense that the vocabulary of a language more or less faithfully reflects the culture whose purposes it serves it is perfectly true that the history of language and the history of culture move along parallel lines. But this superficial and extraneous kind of parallelism is of no real interest to the linguist except in so far as the growth or borrowing of new words incidentally throws light on the formal trends of the language. The linguistic student should never make the mistake of identifying a language with its dictionary.

If [this chapter has] been largely negative in [its] contentions, I believe that [it has] been healthily so. There is perhaps no better way to learn the essential nature of speech than to realize what it is not and what it does not do. Its super-ficial connections with other historic processes are so close that it needs to be shaken free of them if we are to see it in its own right. Everything that we have so far seen to be true of language points to the fact that it is the most sig-nificant and colossal work that the human spirit has evolved—nothing short of a finished form of expression for all communicable experience. This form may be endlessly varied by the individual without thereby losing its distinctive con-tours; and it is constantly reshaping itself as is all art. Language is the most massive and inclusive art we know, a mountainous and anonymous work of unconscious generations.

Notes

1   Itself an amalgam of North "French" and Scandinavian elements.
2   The "Celtic" blood of what is now England and Wales is by no means confined to the Celtic-speaking regions—Wales and, until recently, Cornwall. There is every reason

e Whorf's description of Hopi 'metaphysics' (this volume) represents the kind of underlying cultural pattern that Sapir has in mind here. In fact, there are ambiguities in Sapir's views of the relationship between language, thought and culture, though he is quite clear in his dislike of the kind of broad-brush generalisation evident in e.g. Jespersen (this volume).
f In this volume, compare Jespersen, and Ashcroft's discussion of 'race' and philology.

to believe that the invading Germanic tribes (Angles, Saxons, Jutes) did not exterminate the Brythonic Celts of England nor yet drive them altogether into Wales and Cornwall (there has been far too much "driving" of conquered peoples into mountain fastnesses and land's ends in our histories), but simply intermingled with them and imposed their rule and language upon them.

3   In practice these three peoples can hardly be kept altogether distinct. The terms have rather a local-sentimental than a clearly racial value. Intermarriage has gone on steadily for centuries and it is only in certain outlying regions that we get relatively pure types, e.g., the Highland Scotch of the Hebrides. In America, English, Scotch, and Irish strands have become inextricably interwoven.

4   The High German now spoken in northern Germany is not of great age, but is due to the spread of standardized German, based on Upper Saxon, a High German dialect, at the expense of "Plattdeutsch."

5   By working back from such data as we possess we can make it probable that these languages were originally confined to a comparatively small area in northern Germany and Scandinavia. This area is clearly marginal to the total area of distribution of the Indo-European-speaking peoples. Their center of gravity, say 1000 BC, seems to have lain in southern Russia.

6   While this is only a theory, the technical evidence for it is stronger than one might suppose. There are a surprising number of common and characteristic Germanic words which cannot be connected with known Indo-European radical elements and which may well be survivals of the hypothetical pre-Germanic language; such are *house, stone, sea, wife* (German *Haus, Stein, See, Weib*).

7   Only the easternmost part of this island is occupied by Melanesian-speaking Papuans.

8   A "nationality" is a major, sentimentally unified, group. The historical factors that lead to the feelings of national unity are various—political, cultural, linguistic, geographic, sometimes specifically religious. True racial factors also may enter in, though the accent on "race" has generally a psychological rather than a strictly biological value. In an area dominated by the national sentiment there is a tendency for language and culture to become uniform and specific, so that linguistic and cultural boundaries at least tend to coincide. Even at best, however, the linguistic unification is never absolute, while the cultural unity is apt to be superficial, of a quasi-political nature, rather than deep and far-reaching. (*Editors:* see Fishman and Billig, this volume).

9   The Fijians, for instance, while of Papuan (negroid) race, are Polynesian rather than Melanesian in their cultural and linguistic affinities.

10   Though even here there is some significant overlapping. The southernmost Eskimo of Alaska were assimilated in culture to their Tlingit neighbors. In northeastern Siberia, too, there is no sharp cultural line between the Eskimo and the Chukchi.

11   The supersession of one language by another is of course not truly a matter of linguistic assimilation. (*Editors:* See e.g., Ngũgĩ, Mazrui and Bokhorst-Heng, this volume).

12   "Temperament" is a difficult term to work with. A great deal of what is loosely charged to national "temperament" is really nothing but customary behavior, the effect of traditional ideals of conduct. In a culture, for instance, that does not look kindly upon demonstrativeness, the natural tendency to the display of emotion becomes more than normally inhibited. It would be quite misleading to argue from the customary inhibition, a cultural fact, to the native temperament. But ordinarily we can get at human conduct only as it is culturally modified. Temperament in the raw is a highly elusive thing. (*Editors:* On the ways in which different communicative conventions gets mis-interpreted as temperament/emotional disposition, see Gumperz, this volume.)

Edward Sapir (1884–1939), a founding figure in North American linguistic anthropology, worked at the Universities of California (Berkeley), Pennsylvania, Chicago and Yale, as well as in Ottawa. A good collection of Sapir's writings can be found in Edward Sapir (edited by D. Mandelbaum), *Selected Writings in Language, Culture and Personality* (Berkeley: University of California Press, 1949).

Chapter 3

Bill Ashcroft

2001

LANGUAGE AND RACE[a]

[. . .]

LANGUAGE AND RACE are deeply implicated in Western thought because the rise of language studies not only paralleled the rise in race thinking but they were seen, throughout the nineteenth century, to be virtually synonymous. The link between philology and ethnology[b] provided a powerful foundation for the marriage of linguistic hegemony and racial marginalisation that came to be fundamental to imperial discourse. But, ironically, that spurious link had a powerful residual effect on the thinking of post-colonial writers and intellectuals in the twentieth century, who often saw strategies of resistance in terms of the 'racial' autonomy of mother tongues. The dangerous inheritance of the link between language and race is a model for the problems surrounding all discursive resistance.

There is a case to be made for the assertion that the idea of race exists entirely in language. But to understand the link between language and race, we must go back long before the emergence of race as a category of physiological discrimination, to the uses of language in 'othering' the subjects of Europe's colonial expansion. In 1492 Christopher Columbus' mistaken information that the island of the Canibales was peopled by a fierce tribe who ate intruders, led to the term 'cannibal' usurping 'anthropophagy' for all time as a description of the practice of eating human flesh (Hulme, 1986, p. 19). More importantly, 'cannibal' provided *the* term for the Other, a word for what came to be the absolute abjection of human life, the ultimate other of civilised being.

The proto-racial relationships established by European expansion found one of their most powerful descriptions in Shakespeare's *The Tempest* in which the monster Caliban, whose name is adapted from 'Cannibal' (Carib-Canibal-Caliban), represents

---

a From *Social Identities* 7(3): 311–28.
b Philology = comparative or historical linguistics, and ethnology = 'the science of human races'.

the primitive child of nature in ungrateful rebellion against Prospero's civilising culture. As Prospero's terms of address to Caliban indicate — 'hag-seed', 'lying slave', 'vile race', 'freckled whelp', 'tortoise', — the language of authority and discrimination, which underlies the language of race, need bear no empirical relation to their subject. Indeed the terms deployed during the flourishing of race thinking in the nineteenth century very often bore only the most fanciful relation to the appearance of actual human beings. Race descriptions, like Prospero's terms to Caliban,[1] obtain their power not by verisimilitude, but by the extent to which they embody the epistemic violence of colonialism itself. In this respect the language of race, like all language, is centred in, and generated by, relations of power. [. . .]

'Race' was first used in the English language in 1508 in a poem by William Dunbar, and through the seventeenth and eighteenth centuries it remained essentially a literary word denoting a class of persons or things. It was only in the late eighteenth century that the term came to mean a distinct category of human beings with physical characteristics transmitted by descent. Humans had been categorised in terms of their biological difference from the late 1600s when François Bernier postulated a number of distinctive categories, based largely on facial character and skin colour. Soon a hierarchy of groups (not yet termed races) came to be accepted, with white Europeans at the top. The Negro or black African, or later the Australian Aborigine, was usually relegated to the bottom, in part because of black Africans' colour and allegedly 'primitive' culture, but primarily because they were best known to Europeans as slaves.

Immanuel Kant's use of the German phrase for 'races of mankind' in his *Observations on the Feeling of the Beautiful and Sublime* in 1764 was probably the first explicit use of the term in the sense of biologically or physically distinctive categories of human beings. Kant here elaborates on Hume's 1748 essay 'Of National Characteristics' which makes the familiar claim that there 'never was a civilised nation of any other complexion than white'. Hume averred that 'such a uniform and constant difference' could not happen if it was not a fundamental fact of nature. Clearly then, Kant's use of the term 'race' was based on a deep and pervasive chromatism, a sense that a group's unchangeable physical characteristics — its colour — could be linked in a direct, causal way to psychological nature or intellectual abilities. Kant claims that 'so fundamental is the difference between the races of man . . . it appears to be as great in mental capacities as in colour' (1764, p. 111). The term 'race' was therefore inserted by Kant into a long-standing vocabulary of discrimination, already present in taxonomies such as Bernier's, which were firmly based on colour difference. By the nineteenth century colour had become the unquestioned sign of the relation between external characteristics and inner capacities, despite its complete metaphoricity, arbitrariness and unreliability in describing those external features.

It is in the use of colour terms that the dominance of linguistic tradition over observation comes into play.[c] For the colour terms — 'black', 'white', 'yellow', 'red' — by which racial typology was organised, bear no relation to anything in

---

c See Whorf, this volume, on language shaping perception.

reality. 'Who has seen a black or red person, a white, a yellow, or brown?', asks Henry Louis Gates (1986, p. 6). Nevertheless 'black' and 'white' have become the most powerful significers in the contemporary racial landscape. No two words have had the momentous and catastrophic consequences of the words 'white' and 'black': no two words so completely encompass the binarism [/dualisms] of Western culture, or have such profound cultural ramifications. Yet these two words, which have bound us firmly into a race discourse based on the binary of light and its absence, were not inevitable. Other words, even colour terms, might have been employed to describe the gradation of physical types conceived by François Bernier. But white, black, red, yellow, came to be the markers of racial difference. Would not some other, more specific, less arbitrary words have served better? Or was the distinction between light and darkness, purity and corruption, good and evil an already overdetermined binary into which racial classification slipped effortlessly?

Light has had an importance in Western culture since the Greeks, and the concomitant link between seeing and knowing, the link between light and spiritual illumination have had a profound effect on Western thinking. But why didn't blue, the colour of the sky, or yellow, the colour of the sun and brown, the colour of the earth emerge as the dominant binary? Why this ultimate polarity of white and black? The reason seems to lie in the fascination light had for the western imagi- nation, both in religious and philosophical terms. The ultimate binary — white and black — embodied the distinction between light and its absence. The secret of this stunningly economical binary is the very secret of race, the secret of the persis- tence of this quite spurious category of human identification. But the question remains: what do these terms signify? [. . .]

The English philosopher, David Hume, who came to hold the post of Under Secretary of State, wrote:

> I am apt to suspect the Negroes to be naturally inferior to whites. There scarcely was ever a civilized nation of that complexion, not even any individual eminent in action of speculation. No ingenious manufacturers amongst them, no arts, no sciences. On the other hand, the most rude and barbarous of the whites, such as the ancient GERMANS, the present TARTARS, have still something eminent about them.
>
> (*An Essay on the Nature and Immutability of Truth in Opposition to Sophistry and Skepticism*, cited in Eze, 1997, p. 7)

Here the difference between whites and 'Negroes' (*negre*, black) is a constant, original distinction established in nature. The black race is cast as existing outside 'proper', i.e. white, humanity. 'And', says Emmanuel Eze,

> for the Enlightenment philosophers, European humanity was not only universal, but the embodiment of, and coincident with, humanity *as such*, the framing of the African as being of a different, subhuman species, therefore philosophically and anthropologically sanctioned the exploita- tions of Africans in barbaric ways that were not allowed for Europeans.
>
> (1997, p. 7)

[. . .] Kant's statement, 'This man was black from head to toe, a *clear proof* that what he said was stupid' (1764, p. 113), indicates the core feature of Enlightenment race thinking, that colour was the *self-evident* sign of inherent rational and moral capacities, diminishing as they deviated from the white.

The biological, phrenological, craniological and philological studies which defined, categorised and described racial types in the nineteenth century appear now to be elaborate fictions, invested with an absurd amount of intellectual energy. [. . .] But the experience of race, the 'fact of blackness' as Frantz Fanon put it, is no less real for its empirical fictionality. Language has always 'inscribed' rather than 'described' human difference through such chromatic signifiers. Those signifiers have had an indispensable function in colonial relations and have been notoriously difficult to dislodge. But the paradox of race is that the reality of racial experience centres, not in physical typology, or 'community of blood' or genetic variation, but in language. This occurs in two ways: the development of the concept of linguistic races which saw language and race as inseparable, and the figurative power of language in which chromatic signifiers performed the cultural work of racial 'othering'.

The very term 'black' achieved its connotation in Plato as a sign of lack, of absence. Black came to evoke evil very early in European history, and was allied to concepts of sin, treachery, ugliness, filth and degradation, night and mourning, while 'white' came to be associated with cleanliness, purity, beauty, virginity and peace (Bolt, 1971, p. 131). These terms re-emerged ambivalently in abolitionist literature such as Blake's 'Little Black Boy':

> My mother bore me in the southern wild
> And I am black, but O! my soul is white;
> White as an angel is the English child:
> But I am black as if bereaved of light.

The development of the language of race had its broadest and most influential significance in the emergence of the myth of the 'Dark Continent' shaped by the political and economic pressures of the Victorian period (Brantlinger, 1988, pp. 173–97). The strength of such representation in colonialism arises from the arbitrary adaptability of these signifiers which circulate within the very clear boundaries of imperial binarism, binaries such as: coloniser/colonised; white/non-white; civilised/primitive. Whatever cultural, biological or pseudoscientific terms have been invoked to describe 'racial' variation, the distinction comes down finally to that existing between the imperial powers and their others. Consider the assertion by William Lawrence in 1822:

> the mind of the Negro and the Hottentot, of the Calmuck and the Carib,
> is inferior to that of the European and also their organization is less perfect
> . . . In all particulars . . . the Negro structure approximates unequivo-
> cally to that of the monkey. It not only differs from the Caucasian model;
> but is distinguished from it in two respects; the intellectual characters
> are reduced, the animal features enlarged and exaggerated.
>
> (Stepan, 1982, p. 15)

Here, Lawrence conflates several kinds of non-European together in his racial classification, supported by assertions which, though absurd, had become commonplace because they attempted to explain the biological continuity from ape to *homo sapiens*. This fundamental distinction between white and non-white holds today (by both 'white' and 'black'), as does the unstable and arbitrary nature of racial signifiers. This racial Manicheanism, arising to appease the hegemonic pretensions of imperial powers, was greatly advanced by the invention of the concept of the Aryan race, which itself was the product of the new science of philology. Despite the heavy investment in biological taxonomy in nineteenth century anthropology, it was the link between race and language which most firmly embedded the concept of race in western thought. Curiously, the vagueness and imprecision of racial terms, rather than diminish this fixation, merely served to exacerbate it, by fostering a language that was protean in its application. As Henry Gates points out, race

> is the ultimate trope of difference because it is so very arbitrary in its application . . . The biological difference used to determine 'difference' in sex simply do not hold when applied to 'race'. Yet we carelessly use language in such a way as to *will* this sense of *natural* difference into our formulations.
>
> (1986, p. 5)

For these reasons race has become 'a trope of ultimate, irreducible difference between cultures, linguistic groups, or adherents of specific belief systems'. Paradoxically, in the wake of colonial occupation, with its strongly developed practical racism, race remains the most unstable and misleading, yet strategic focus of representation in post-colonial societies.

Race and philology

Widespread interest in the link between language and race really began in the late eighteenth century with the discovery of the Indo-European family of languages and the subsequent rise of philology — comparative or historical linguistics — which developed out of an interest in the link between language and the essential identity of communities. While the concept of 'race' might exist entirely in language, a convenient and protean trope of Otherness, philology became the major impetus in the myth of the link between language and race as the diversity of languages was used to explain the diversity of races.

Consequently, the English historian Edward Freeman could say with confidence in 1879 that the 'doctrine of race, in its popular form, is the direct offspring of the study of scientific philology' (Freeman, 1879, p. 31). Although 'language is no certain test of race, the men who speak the same tongue are not therefore necessarily men of the same blood', nevertheless 'the natural instinct of mankind connects race and language' (p. 32). Freeman, writing around the height of Britain's own imperial expansion, sums up a century of thinking on the difficult links between language and identity:

> If races and nations, though largely formed by the workings of an arti-
> ficial law, are still real and living things, groups in which the idea of
> kindred is the idea around which everything has grown, how are we to
> define our races and nations? How are we to mark them off from one
> another? . . . I say unhesitatingly that for practical purposes there is one
> test, and one only, and that that test is language.
>
> (p. 33)[d]

Freeman is splendidly vague about how that test may be applied, how language and
race are linked, or even how the communal metaphors of nation and race may be
distinguished. His confidence rested on a century of philological study, but neither
the difficult distinction between nation and race, nor the precise way in which
languages could be said to characterise groups of people had been resolved. Clearly
the establishment of an empire extends the qualities of the (English) nation into
the qualities of the (Anglo-Saxon) race. Although, as J.A. Hobson pointed out at
the turn of the century, imperialism is 'the expansion of nationality' (Hobson, 1902,
p. 6) it was overwhelmingly conceived in terms of the expansion of the British, or
Anglo-Saxon race. Arguably, its major vehicle was neither trade nor war, but the
English language.[e]

Language was only one feature of a broad array of concepts invoked to elaborate the idea of racial grouping and inheritance. Freeman demonstrates something
of the mental gymnastics employed by those determined to propound the link:

> Community of language does not imply community of blood; it might
> be added that diversity of language does not imply diversity of blood.
> But community of language is, in the absence of any evidence to the
> contrary, a presumption of community of blood, and is proof of some-
> thing which for practical purposes is the same as community of blood.
>
> (1879, p. 34).

There is no link between community of language and community of blood yet 'for
practical purposes' we can pretend they are the same thing. [. . .]

Despite the flimsiness of arguments about the essential links between language
and race, the rise of philology was synonymous with the rise of race thinking. The
discovery of the Indo-European family of languages in 1786 by British Orientalist
and jurist William Jones, ushered in a new conception of linguistic history.
However, it was Friedrich Schlegel who gave Jones' statement an anthropological
twist by deducing from the relationship of language a relationship of race (Poliakov,
1977, p. 191). In his enthusiastic prospectus for a science of comparative philology
Schlegel's lasting legacy was to galvanise German youth with the myth of an
Aryan race. 'This linguistic research', says Poliakov, 'produced fateful results in a
field where everything depends on words'. Henceforth, 'the authentic and useful
science of linguistics became absorbed in the crazy doctrine of 'racial anthropology'
(p. 193).

---

d Compare Sapir, this volume.
e For more contemporary views, see Quirk, Mazrui and Ngũgĩ, this volume.

Philology tended to be assimilated to the natural sciences

> because it revealed a natural human capacity expressing itself in a deter-
> ministic manner, beyond the control of individual human will, but
> susceptible to a rigorous systematic study that demonstrated underlying
> laws.
>
> (Poliakov, 1977, p. 24)[f]

Consequently it provided the basis for the study called 'ethnology' or 'the science
of human races'. Philology lent its methodological rigour to

> trace the affinities of all the various 'races' of man, and if possible to
> reduce their present diversity to a primitive unity analogous to that of
> the Indo-European language family.
>
> (p. 24)

The persistent confusion between language and race (underpinned no doubt by the
need of imperial powers to find some basis for defining their dominance over their
colonial populations) was compounded by the developing belief that languages were
species with lives of their own. In 1863 August Schleicher in his *Die Darwinische
Theorie und die Sprachwissenschaft* contended that languages possess 'that succession
of phenomena to which one ordinarily applies the term "life"', from which he
concluded that 'linguistic science is therefore a natural science' (Brew, 1968,
p. 176). The very concept of an Indo-European 'family' of languages and the development of a linguistic family tree[g] inevitably encouraged the perception that
language evolution replicated biological and cultural phylogeny.[h] Although the
organic analogy had many detractors it maintained a hold on popular thinking in a
way that inevitably cemented the link between the racial characteristics of speakers
and the languages they spoke.

Furthermore, a family tree diagram posits a hierarchy of branchings over time
which rests on a view of history as a movement from primitive to ever more highly
developed languages and peoples. This, of course, links the development of
languages to Darwin's theory of species evolution and its associated doctrine of the
survival of the fittest. Influential British anthropologist Edward Tylor held that
although words such as 'savage' and 'barbarous' had come to mean 'such behaviour as is most wild, rough and cruel', 'savage and barbarous tribes often more or
less fairly represent stages of culture through which our own ancestors passed long
ago' (Bolt, 1971, p. 25). The increasing attempt to provide comparative linguistics with a firmly scientific footing parallels the late nineteenth century attempts to

---

f   Much of structural linguistics during the twentieth century has worked with the same view that
language can be analysed as a general system that underlies – and is largely independent of – actual
individuals speaking. Indeed, see Note 2.

g   'Family tree' is a metaphor that linguists have used to explain the historical relationship between
languages. Within the Romance family, for example, Latin is the 'parent' language, and French, Spanish
etc. are 'daughter' languages, French also being 'sister' to Spanish and the others. See D. Crystal 1987
Cambridge Encyclopedia of Language Cambridge: Cambridge University Press, Chapter 50.

h   'Biological and cultural phylogeny' = the biological and cultural development of the human race.

provide a scientific basis for the analysis of race. Both rested on rigid hypotheses which ignored exceptions and bore little relationship to empirical evidence. An example of this was the 'neogrammarian' hypothesis, which provides a telling example of the strong appeal of scientific laws to linguistics analysis.[2] [. . .]

This [assumption about a] deep cultural affinity between language and national character led philologers such as Theodor Waitz to justify the influence of linguistics on two grounds: the characteristics of language are more stable than racial or ethnoracial qualities and thus provided a more reliable guide to historical continuity; and the methods of comparative philology had reached a higher stage of exactitude than those of physical anthropology (Poliakov, 1977, p. 258). Claiming that 'all uncultured nations possess, in comparison with civilised nations, a large mouth and somewhat thick lips' (Whitman, 1984, p. 220), Waitz believed in the influence of intellectual culture on physical form, and asserted that as a primitive community rose to a higher culture, the thick lips would be lost. To develop a sound fundamental understanding of man in his scientifically explicable physiological and psychical aspects, it was necessary to study 'uncivilised nations, man in his primitive state' (1984, p. 221). Cultural scholars had, in effect, created a new academic territory — primitive life [. . .]

The creation of language was the common act of prehistoric communities and the ground of common human existence. But differences in language were held to indicate differences in moral and mental capacities. Humboldt had inspired the doctrine that of the three kinds of languages — the isolating, the agglutinative and the inflected[i] — the inflected languages, such as Indo-European and Semitic, were superior. Consequently for philologers such as Steinthal, because all thought was linguistic, the structure of a language could determine the mental capabilities of its speakers. This notion became developed in Renan's study of the Semitic languages and formed a basis for the link between language and race, because the mental dimension of a particular language could be seen to be analogous to the moral and cultural dimension of a race.

Ernest Renan and linguistic races

The assumption that language is so integral to human life that it determines one's world, or conversely, that the character of one's social and cultural being determines the language one speaks, has been a persistent feature of discourse on language.[j] This assumption has a long history. [. . .] But the philologist-historian who had the most to say about the link between race and language was Ernest Renan. Renan was a voluminously productive and extraordinarily influential Orientalist whose career

---

i In 'isolating' languages, none of the words themselves vary their form, and grammatical relationships are expressed in the word order of the sentence (Chinese is often cited as an example); in 'agglutinative' languages, words are built up out of a sequence of units, with each unit expressing meaning in a one-to-one way, as in e.g. *dis/establish/ment* (see Turkish); and in 'inflected' languages, words change their internal structure, often using one element to signal a number of different meaning (e.g. the *-o* ending of Latin *amo* ('I love') expresses, among other things, the present tense and the first person singular ('I')). See D. Crystal op. cit. p. 293.
j See Whorf, this volume.

spanned three quarters of the nineteenth century. Renan's writing is not so much significant for its originality of thought as it is for the way in which his copious writings reflected the European intellectual milieu of the time, reproducing in distilled form the major Orientalist myths of language, race and culture.

Renan's life work was a monumental description of the Semitic language, religion and history yet his fundamental belief was that this 'race of religions' was destined to give way to the 'Indo-Germanic' race whose inheritance of science and rationality gave them the final responsibility for the philosophical search after truth. The opposition between the Semitic and the Aryan, was, for Renan, incontrovertibly in favour of the latter, being an 'opposition between reason and faith, between truth and revelation, between philosophy (or science) and religion' between Semitic unity and Aryan multiplicity (Todorov, 1993, p. 146).

Renan rejected the notion of biological races, proffering instead the theory of 'linguistic races' which demonstrate a cultural determinism every bit as rigid as [. . .] biological determinism [. . .]. For him there were no pure races, indeed, 'the noblest countries — England, France, Italy — are those in which the blood is most mixed' (Todorov, 1993, p. 140). Renan is adamant that 'race' itself refers to two things: a physical race and a cultural race, and that one must be careful not to confuse the two. Language is the key for Renan, because language plays a dominant role in the formation of a culture.

> Language is thus almost completely substituted for race in the division of humanity into groups, or rather the word 'race' changes meaning. Language, religion, laws, mores brought the race into being much more than blood did.
>
> (Renan, 1887, p. 32)

The Semitic race and the Aryan race, which focus most of Renan's attention, are not physical races but linguistic races.

> As the individuality of the Semitic race has been revealed only by the analysis of language, an analysis particularly well corroborated . . . as this race has been created by philology, there is just one criterion for recognizing Semites, and that is language.
>
> (Renan, 1855, p. 80)

According to Renan, there are five 'documents' which determine a race within the human species: a separate language, a literature with identifiable characteristics, a religion, a history, and a civilisation. Clearly, what he is talking about, without being explicit, is 'culture', but Renan encounters two problems here. First, the concept of a linguistic race is haunted by the presence of biological race. As Todorov observes,

> when he writes in De l'Origine du langage, 'The race that speaks Sanscrit [is] an aristocratic and conquering race, distinguished by its white colour from the darker shades of the former inhabitants [of India]' . . . , we

can attribute the aristocratic and conquering spirit to culture; but can we do the same for light and dark skin?

(1993, p. 143)

Is the mention of skin colour meant to be seen as arbitrary, or does the colour of the skin provide the biological frame for cultural dominance? The concept of linguistic race does not seem to be able to extricate itself from the racialist priority of colour, because linguistic races are, like biological races, situated on a hierarchy of value (indeed the hierarchy of languages is a key feature of Renan's theory).

The second problem is that when positing the deterministic link between language and culture, he must answer the question: which comes first, language or culture?

> The spirit of each people and its language are very closely connected: the spirit creates the language, and the language in turn serves as formula and limit for the spirit.

(p. 96)

On the face of it, this seems to describe the complex interactive relationship between language and culture, but it represents precisely the dilemma we encounter when we attempt to posit, in a deterministic way, that a culture somehow precedes language. As Todorov asks pertinently, 'can the spirit, as a product of the language, really create the language?' (1993, p. 143). Or, does the phrase 'formula and limit of the spirit' let Renan off the hook, by suggesting that the spirit of a people somehow creates its own formula and limit? Either way Renan is caught in a circularity which becomes completely tautologous when he says 'It is in fact in the diversity of races that we must seek the most effective cause of the diversity of idioms'. Either 'race' means a linguistic race in which case the 'diversity of idioms' explains the 'diversity of idioms', or else race retains its 'biological' meaning, in which case physical difference somehow causes linguistic difference. [. . .]

We may examine this problem where Renan becomes more specific about language and race. For at one point he sheets the entire supposed superiority of the Aryan race to its ability to conjugate[k] verbs:

> The Aryan language was highly superior, especially as regards verb conjugations. This marvellous instrument, created by the instinct of primitive men, contained the seeds of all the metaphysics that would be developed later on by the genius of the Hindus, the Greeks or the Germans. The Semitic language, on the contrary, got off to the wrong start where verbs are concerned. The greatest mistake this race ever made (because the most irreparable) was to adopt such a niggardly mechanism for treating verbs that the expression of tenses and moods has always been imperfect and awkward in its language. Even today, the

---

k That is, to vary the form of a verb to express a number of different meanings such as person ('I', 'you', etc.), tense ('past', 'present', etc.), aspect (e.g. simple vs progressive – 'I write' vs 'I am writing') etc.

Arabs are still struggling against the linguistic error committed by their
ancestors ten or fifteen thousand years ago.

(Renan, 1887, p. 35)

This is a racial dichotomy quite breathtaking in its scope and we could hardly
imagine a more explicit example of cultural determinism. [. . .]

The contradictions of the concept of linguistic races are compounded in *Islamism
and Science* where he says, 'All the grammatical processes proceed directly from
the manner in which each race treated ideas' (Renan, 1888, p. 104). Yet the way
a race treats ideas is determined by the grammar of its language. Clearly, the
complexity of the relationship between language and culture requires some other
explanation. Either the linguistic identity of a culture lies in the ways it uses the
language available to it, or the culture can never change, and can never appropriate
that which lies outside it. Since the latter is disproved by history, we must conclude
that the culture of a people does not lie within language as an inherent property,
but in the complex ways in which that people creates, uses, develops, deploys and
engages language. These ways will interact with the historical, geographical,
climatic, religious and material experiences of its speakers and the discourses within
which those experiences emerge. The support such bizarre claims gave to the racial
dichotomies of imperial discourse is clear. If races are primitive today the fault is
in their ancestors who created their languages. Needless to say the European nations
should move in to 'civilise' them.

Sartre and Fanon

If Renan's connection between race and language were simply an anachronistic
element of nineteenth century Orientalism it would remain an historical oddity.
But the assumption, that race is somehow embedded in language, has taken a
tenacious hold on contemporary thinking because the idea of an essential link is an
attractive prospect to both colonisers and colonised. It arises, for instance, as a
foundational aspect of Frantz Fanon's view of race. It is not the purpose of this
essay to try to suggest any causal lineage from nineteenth century philology to
contemporary views of race in language, but rather to point out the paradoxical
connection between them. The assumptions about cultural embodiment emerge in
the earliest post-colonial writing, but there is a strong tradition in French writers
for describing the way in which the French language both dominated and inhibited
the expression of 'black' reality. In most cases the link between language and
race posited by writers such as Sartre and Fanon is an argument about the cultural
specificity of language, although they are not averse to essentialising the situation
at times.

In *Black Orpheus* Jean-Paul Sartre claims that black poetry is essentially a fierce
response to the inadequacy of language: 'this feeling of failure before language . . .
is the source of all poetic expression' (Sartre, 1948, p. xix). Language, for the
black writer was not a neutral, transparent instrument but the determining medium
of thought itself. In his pursuit of self-definition, the black artist saw the inherited
colonial language as a pernicious symbolic system used by the European coloniser

in order to gain total and systematic control of the mind and reality of the colonised world. In the face of Prospero's hubris, his signifying authority (*langue*), the African or Caribbean Caliban deployed his own militant idiom (*langage*).

This is a familiar refrain: language embodies the European culture and represses the reality of the African or Caribbean. It is important to understand the great historical and cultural differences between different languages, such as French and English, and their very different roles in the two different forms of imperialism. But the distinction between *langue* and *langage* is one that holds for all speakers. *Langue* becomes the language of the coloniser by virtue of discriminatory assumptions, such as Renan's belief that such things as verb conjugation are a consequence of racial superiority. All language, in its actual use, is *langage* so there is always in language itself, its amenability to appropriation, its flexibility and malleability, the possibility of transformation, of a self expression which resists the imperial confidence of Prospero. Yet this is not what Sartre, nor Fanon after him, are saying. For them, the language is a discourse firmly demarcated by the cultural boundaries of European civilisation.

But the sense of language embodying culture has been a feature of postcolonial resistance writing for a very long time. When we look for the source of this attitude we do not have to go far past Frantz Fanon. The first chapter of *Black Skins White Masks* is called 'The Negro and Language' and like *Black Orpheus* conflates blackness with culture. For Fanon, to speak means 'above all to assume a culture, to support the weight of a civilisation' (1952, pp. 17–18). But is it the language or the act of using the language, the linguistic tool itself or the fact of one's proficiency in it, which does this cultural work? 'The Negro of the Antilles', claims Fanon, 'will be proportionately whiter — that is, he will come closer to being a real human being — in direct ratio to his mastery of the French language' (p. 18). But surely what Fanon means here is that proficiency in language *represents* civilisation.

When Fanon says 'A man who has a language consequently possesses the world expressed and implied by that language' (1952, p. 18), he is articulating one of the central problems of the question of post-colonial language use. For such a person 'possesses' the language, not as a receptacle of culture, thus making him (or her) white, but as a *signifier*[1] of culture, which, like whiteness, signifies social and cultural dominance. This distinction is in fact crucial to the whole debate over language. The use of language is a signifier of culture, language does not contain that culture:

> The colonized is elevated above his jungle status in proportion to his adoption of the mother country's cultural standards. He becomes whiter as he renounces his blackness, his jungle.
>
> (1952, p. 18)

This sentence is quite correct . . . metaphorically. The problem is that discussion of language such as Fanon's constantly slips between metaphor and literalism.

---

1 'Signifier': as a symbol or an expression of culture. See e.g. Gumperz and Hernández-Chavez, Hill, Cutler, McDermott and Gospodinoff, this volume, and compare e.g. Whorf, Gumperz and Ngũgĩ.

This sentence is preceded by such a conflation, when he says that every colonised people 'finds itself face to face with the language of the civilising nation; that is, with the culture of the mother country'. How effortless it is to slip [. . .] between the figurative and literal.

We can compare this assumption of status through the use of language with the ways in which language operates as a class marker. Speaking in a refined way acts as a class marker, a sign of elevation, and indeed the speaker may be making great pains to change into someone of a different class. But the language will only ever be a signifier of that change. There is no secret formula in a language that effects an inner transformation in its speakers. However, in Fanon's view, the change in behaviour is often so marked that the changed language and the changed person are the same thing:

> The black man who has lived in France for a length of time returns radically changed. To express it in genetic terms, his phenotype undergoes a definitive, an absolute mutation
>
> (1952, p. 19)

but what he means by this is explained in a footnote:

> By that I mean that Negroes who return to their original environments convey the impression that they have completed a cycle, that they have added to themselves something that was lacking. They return literally full of themselves.
>
> (p. 19)

[. . . T]he problem of a slippage between [the metaphorical and the literal] comes about because of the extreme Manicheanism of race. Fanon, discussing Mayotte Capécia's *Je suis Martiniquaise*, says that it would seem 'that for her white and black represent the two poles of a world, two poles in perpetual conflict: a genuinely Manichean concept of the world' (1952, pp. 44–45):

> I am white: that is to say that I possess beauty and virtue, which have never been black. I am the colour of the daylight . . .

> I am black: I am the incarnation of a complete fusion with the world, an intuitive understanding of the earth, an abandonment of my ego in the heart of the cosmos, and no white man, no matter how intelligent he may be, can ever understand Louis Armstrong and the music of the Congo.
>
> (p. 45)

Consequently, for Fanon, 'The Negro enslaved by his inferiority, the white man enslaved by his superiority alike behave in accordance with a neurotic orientation' (1952, p. 60). The tendency to see this enslavement as an enslavement of language denies the post-colonial subject one of the most potent weapons of discursive resistance: an adaptable and transformable language and the readership it brings with it.

Race and writing

The belief, inherited from nineteenth century philology, that language actually embodies cultural difference rather than inscribes or articulates it, is one of the most tenacious in contemporary theory. Far from ending with Fanon this assumption persists to the present day. It extends into an even more impassioned assertion of the embodiment of culture in language in post-colonial writers such as Ngũgĩ wa Thiongo.[m] Although the historical link between language and race has proved difficult to dislodge it is nowhere disrupted more comprehensively than in post-colonial language use, and specifically post-colonial *writing* in English. Ironically, Ngũgĩ's writing itself demonstrates a capacity for resistance that is denied by his theory. The question of language and race goes right to the heart of the problematic character of discursive resistance. Writing on the connection between 'race' and 'writing' Henry Louis Gates voices a widespread disillusionment with the political possibilities of 'black' writing:

> Can writing, with the difference it makes and marks, mask the black-ness of the black face that addresses the text of Western letters, in a voice that speaks English through an idiom which contains the irre-ducible element of cultural difference that will always separate the white voice from the black? Black people, we know, have not been liberated from racism by our writings. We accepted a false premise by assuming that racism would be destroyed once white racists became convinced that we were human, too. Writing stood as a complex 'certificate of humanity', as Paulin Hountondji put it. Black writing, and especially the literature of the slave, served not to obliterate the difference of race; rather the inscription of the black voice in Western literatures has preserved those very cultural differences to be repeated, imitated and revised in a separate Western literary tradition, a tradition of black difference.
>
> (1986, p. 12)

This pessimism has been shared by many writers and critics. But to think that racism would be destroyed by black writing is like assuming that injustice will be destroyed by 'just' writing, or by writing on justice. When we remember the history of these race terms 'black' and 'white' we see how much our problems of race are problems of language. This metaphoric term coined with so little regard for the complexity and diversity of ethnic groups, is now deployed as a universal political identifier. Is there any wonder that the term and 'its' productions should be found wanting?

This is not to belittle the history of very real material suffering and oppression suffered by 'black' peoples. But this suffering has been largely a consequence of a worldwide economic and political adventure — European imperialism. 'Black' and 'white' simply *reverse* the hierarchy of binary terms rather than *erase* the binary. The

---

m See Ngũgĩ, this volume.

broad sweep of post-colonising literatures brings together a much more diverse constituency. But the very use of the terms 'black' and 'white' show that we cannot escape history, nor escape that discourse which constantly attempts to construct us. For many people the question of identity is, as a consequence of that history, overwhelmingly a question of colour, no matter how metaphoric those colour terms may be. And the dominance discourse will continue to construct its others. For both 'black writing' and 'post-colonial writing' (which are not the same thing) the alternative to taking Prospero's voice and speaking back is Caliban's — silence or cursing. [. . .]

[I]t is difficult to see how the concept of 'black' literature and theory, a 'black tradition', can avoid the racialist dynamic it aims to combat. It is not just advisable but crucial that post-colonial intellectuals realise that language has no race, for the consequence of this link — when it leads to the rejection of tools of discursive resistance such as the English language — has been to imprison resistance in an inward looking world. The ultimate consequence of the belief that language embodies race is the deafening silence of a rage that cannot be heard.

Notes

1   The terms by which the play describes Caliban are so inconsistent and of such variety that they represent a virtual crisis of representation in the description of the other. Lacking any clear linguistic framework such as that provided by racial terminology, Caliban has been a role open to every interpretation imaginable. The power of language to 'other' the colonised subject emerges from the arbitrary visual status accorded Caliban. He is 'a strange fish!' (II.ii.27); 'Legg'd like a man! and his fins like arms!' (II.ii.34); 'no fish' (II.ii.36); 'some monster of the isle with four legs' (II,ii.66); 'a plain fish' (V.i.266); and a 'mis-shapen knave' (V.i.268). Morton Luce sums up this contradiction succinctly: 'if all the suggestions as to Caliban's form and features and endowments that are thrown out in the play are collected, it will be found that the one half renders the other half impossible' (Hulme, 1986, p. 107). The apparently confused and ambiguous representation of Caliban comes about because notions of race had not coalesced into clear physiological parameters when Shakespeare wrote, and were not to be so for a century and a half.

2   The hypothesis, that the laws of phonetic [or sound] change admit of no exceptions was first stated by August Leskien in 1876, and again by Herman Paul in 1879: 'Every phonetic law operates with absolute necessity; it as little admits of an exception as a chemical or physical law'. This is an example of a tendency towards the rigid structuration of language which has dogged linguistics. 'On the face of it', says Brew, 'the neogrammarian hypothesis appeared to ignore, and to be flatly contradicted by, the known exceptions to every one of the major regularities of phonetic correspondence between related languages' (1968, p. 177). We see this disturbance of linguistic theory time and again as post-colonial societies appropriate language for their purposes, demonstrating the extreme elasticity of languages. (*Editors:* see also Alleyne, Back, Gumperz and Hernández-Chavez, Hewitt and Urla in this volume.)

References

Ashcroft, B. (1987) 'Language Issues Facing Commonwealth Writers', *Journal of Common-wealth Literature*, XXII (1): 99–118.

—— (1989) 'Constitutive Graphonomy: a Post-colonial Theory of Literary Writing', *Kunapipi*, XI (1): 58–73.

—— (2001) 'Language', *Post-Colonial Transformation*, London: Routledge: 56–81.

Bolt, C. (1971) *Victorian Attitudes to Race*, London: Routledge.

Brantlinger, P. (1988) *Rule of Darkness: British Literature and Imperialism 1830–1914*, Ithaca, NY: Cornell University Press.

Brew, J.O. (ed.) (1968) *One Hundred Years of Anthropology*, Cambridge, Mass: Harvard University Press.

Buffon, Comte de (1968 [1812]) *Natural History General and Particular, by The Count de Buffon: The History of Man and Quadrupeds* (translated by W. Wood), London and New York: T. Cadell Readex Microfilm Reprints.

Eze, E.C. (ed.) (1997) *Postcolonial African Philosophy: a Critical Reader*, Oxford: Blackwell.

Fanon, F. (1968 [1952]) *Black Skin White Masks* (translated by C.L. Markmann) London: Paladin.

Freeman, E.A. (1958 [1879]) 'Race and Language', in E. Thompson and E. Hughes (eds) *Race: Individual and Collective Behaviour*, New York: Free Press.

Gates, H.L. (ed.) (1986) *Race, Writing and Difference*, Chicago: University of Chicago.

Hobson, J.A. (1965 [1902]) *Imperialism* (introduced by P. Siegelman), Ann Arbor: University of Michigan.

Hulme, P. (1986) *Colonial Encounters: Europe and the Native Caribbean 1492–1797*, London and New York: Routledge.

Kant, I. (1960 [1764]) *Observations on the Feeling of the Beautiful and Sublime* (translated by J.T. Goldthwait), Berkeley: California UP.

Poliakov, L. (1977) *The Aryan Myth: A History of Racist and Nationalist Ideas in Europe* (translated by Edmund Howard), New York: New American Library.

Renan, E. (1855) 'Histoire Générale at Systéme Comparé des Langues Sémetiques', *Oeuvres complétes*, Paris: Calmann-Lévy, 1947–1961, 1: 69–97.

—— (1856) 'Lettre a Gobineau' (26 June), *Oeuvres Complétes*, Paris: Calmann-Lévy, 1947–1961, 1: 437–48.

—— (1858) 'De l'Origine du langage', *Oeuvres Complétes*, Paris: Calmann-Lévy, 1947–1961, 8: 9–23, 109–10.

—— (1887) 'Histoire du Peuple Israel', *Oeuvres Complétes*, Paris: Calmann-Lévy, 1947–1961, 6.

—— (1970 [1888]) 'Islamism and Science' in *The Poetry of the Celtic Races and Other Studies* (translated by W.G. Hutchinson), Port Washington, NY: Kennikat Press.

—— (1891) *The Future of Science*, London: Chapman and Hall.

—— (1971 [1896]) *Caliban: a Philosophical Drama Continuing 'The Tempest' of William Shakespeare* (translated by E.G. Vickery), New York: AMS.

Rushdie, S. (1991) *Imaginary Homelands*, London: Granta.

Sartre, J.P. (1972 [1948]) 'Black Orpheus', in L.S. Senghor (ed.) *Anthologie de La Nouvelle Poésie Nègre et Malgache de Langue Française*, Paris: Presses Universitaires de France.

Senna, D. (1998) *Glamour*, New York: Condé Naste.

Stepan, N. (1982) *The Idea of Race in Science: Great Britain, 1800–1960*, London: Macmillan.

Todorov, T. (1993) *On Human Diversity: Nationalism, Racism, and Exoticism in French Thought* (translated by C. Porter), Cambridge, Mass: Harvard.

Whitman, J. (1984) 'From Philology to Anthropology in Mid-Nineteenth Century Germany', in G.W. Stocking (ed.), *Functionalism Historicized: Essays on British Social Anthropology*, Madison: University of Wisconsin.

Bill Ashcroft is Associate Professor in the School of English at the University of New South Wales, Australia. He is the author of *The Empire Writes Back* (London: Routledge, 1989) and *The Post-Colonial Studies Reader* (London: Routledge, 1995).

Chapter 4

Mervyn Alleyne

1989

LANGUAGE IN JAMAICAN CULTURE[a]

AMONG THE MOST WIDESPREAD fallacies about slave societies in the New World is the belief that slaves were unable to communicate with each other because of the wide diversity and mutual non-intelligibility of African languages and dialects and because they (slaves) were systematically separated so that members of the same ethnic/linguistic group would not find themselves on the same plantation. The fact is that African languages were routinely used on slave plantations and have survived in Jamaica up to today. Even if it is true that the military establishment aimed at systematically separating slaves of the same ethnic origin, there is no evidence that this policy was consistently and effectively carried out. Rather there is evidence that in some cases slaves of a particular ethnic-linguistic group were deliberately sought by planters because of certain stereotype characteristics that these slaves were supposed to have. There is also evidence that new slaves were sometimes quartered with people of a similar ethnic origin who would help them to acclimatise and learn the ways of a slave plantation.

So any discussion of the history and evolution of African languages in Jamaica must start out from the recognition that African languages were spoken quite normally on the island. However, the linguistic history of Jamaica shows clearly the significance of social context, and of the period of African migration, for the evolution of African languages. African languages, like African religions and African music, evolved along different paths according to the social context they were used in. As we have seen, the immigration of Africans (mainly Bantu) in the third period of migration (1841–1865) and their settlement in St Thomas were main factors in the persistence of the Kumina religion in that parish. The persistence of the Kikongo language among Kumina worshippers in St Thomas can be similarly explained.

Jamaica was therefore multilingual at the very start of its colonisation by Europeans. If it is true that at first most slaves were Akan in Jamaica (or on the

a From M.C. Alleyne (1989) 'Language' *Roots of Jamaican Culture*. London: Pluto Press pp. 120–48.

Gold Coast, in Barbados, or in Suriname), then the number of languages would be relatively few and most would be closely related; only later would the multiplicity of languages grow and become more complex.

The evolution of African languages in this multilingual setting may be elucidated by a look at the phenomenon of multilingualism in general. Language contact is but one instance of cultural contact. [. . .] In multilingual situations the political dominance of the speakers of one of the languages involved is an important determinant of the nature and direction of language change. In Jamaica, English was the dominant language, that is the language of the military force that kept society together. [. . .] The dominance of English in Jamaica led inevitably to major changes in African languages, while English itself (as spoken by native speakers) changed little. [. . .]

When two languages are mismatched, second language learning is unidirectional: speakers of the subordinate languages learn the dominant language but not vice versa. Speakers of the subordinate languages not only learn the dominant language but surrender their own languages more or less swiftly and more or less completely, depending on the degree of unevenness in the matching of the cultures in contact. The lower languages undergo drastic change as a result of either borrowings from the dominant language or to losses in inner form as a result of growing disuse. The dominant language, however, changes little or not at all when spoken by native speakers, though it changes drastically when acquired as a second language by speakers of the lower languages. It is important to consider whether change in lower languages resulting from borrowings from the dominant language and from losses in inner form is completely distinguishable from the drastic changes that the dominant language undergoes when acquired by speakers of lower languages.[b] Some interpret Jamaican "creole" or "patois" as a product of the continuity of African language structure with loss of inner form and borrowings from English; others as the product of drastic changes introduced into English during its acquisition by Africans. The question is: are these two interpretations mutually irreconcilable? We shall see later that the language of Jamaicans is best understood dynamically, as a "becoming". In its popular contemporary form and in older forms the "continuity" aspect is uppermost; in its modern urbanised "educated" form it is best understood as the product of centuries of approximation to English. This is why it is important to understand the process of language change rather than simply try to classify contemporary forms as genetically or structurally [. . .] related to one or another of the contributory languages. The process may then reveal multiple or changing relationships [. . .]

Dominance is a concept that can be applied not only to relationships between European and African languages but also to relationships among African languages used within the community of Africans. Bilingualism and multilingualism were already common in pre-colonial Africa, and there must have been many polyglots among the enslaved Africans in Jamaica. It is quite likely that Twi-Asante was learned as a second (or third) language by Africans in Jamaica, for as we have seen, the Twi-Asante people were dominant in Jamaica at the start of plantation society,

---

b In other words, whether it is easy to distinguish (a) Kikongo losing some of its grammar and borrowing from English from (b) English learnt as a second language by a native speaker of Kikongo.

when differences between African ethnic groups were still sharp. There is linguistic evidence to support the idea of Twi-Asante dominance. The Maroon language of Jamaica is based almost exclusively on Twi-Asante. Slaves from ethnic groups other than Twi-Asante who joined the Maroons evidently learned the Twi language and surrendered their own. The vast majority of words of African origin in the Jamaican language come from Twi-Asante. This suggests that Twi-Asante, or at least its lexicon, was accepted by Africans of other linguistic groups in Jamaica. Dallas (1703: pp. 31–33) mentions a group that joined Kojo's maroon band,

> distinct in figure, character, language and country. Some of the old people remember that their parents spoke in their own families, a language entirely different from that spoken by the rest of the negroes with whom they had incorporated. They recollected many of the words for things in common use, and declared that in their early years they spoke their mother-tongue. The Coromantee language, however, super-seded the others, and became in time the general one in use.

Given the dominance of Twi-Asante (Coromantee) over other African languages, the factors that characterised contact between English and African languages prob-ably also characterised this intra-African contact. That is to say, acculturation and language learning were probably unidirectional (toward Twi-Asante); "lower" African languages progressively and rapidly decayed until they disappeared completely. Twi-Asante, on the other hand, changed little as a result of contact with these other African languages, which by the end of the eighteenth century were on the point of extinction (just as Twi-Asante is today on the point of extinc-tion in its contact with Jamaican and English). The process that Dallas describes is typical of the general process of language death: reduction in one domain [of activity] after another until the language is spoken only "in their own families" by parents, and subsequent generations recall only "words for things in common use".

The only specifically identifiable traces that these "minor" African languages have left behind are a number of vocabulary items in both the Twi-Asante language of the Maroons and in the Jamaican language as a whole. Twi-Asante in Jamaica now contains, for example, words from Temne and Limba, which are languages of Sierra Leone. The following examples are taken from Dalby (1971: pp. 41–46):

opung	"you dead" cf. Temne *òpong* "he is finished, dead"
katègbè	"?" (apparently uttered to pacify a man in trance) cf. Temne *ketègbè* "calm(ly)"
katègbè yanu	"?" (shouted angrily in response to the above) cf. Temne *ketègbè keyi-èno* "there's no peace here"
akote	"dog" cf. Limba *kuteng* "dog" [. . .]

Social contexts

The different contexts within which African languages were used in Jamaica gave rise to the different evolutionary paths that these languages took. There are six main social and other contexts relevant to the evolution of these languages. They are discussed in the following pages.

1 Expressive genres such as songs and folktales

Songs and folktales differ from the major channel of communication, which is speech. Songs in particular preserve older forms of language, and old songs are sometimes preserved even when they are no longer generally understood. Songs in African languages make religious ceremonies and folk festivals seem more mystical and esoteric.

Sloane (1688) recorded a number of African songs (including "Angola", "Papa", and "Koromanti") during his visit to Jamaica at the beginning of the British colonial period. Roberts (1926), on a visit to Accompong some 200 years later, discovered "that songs still existed and could be sung by some of the Maroons which they designated as Koromanti songs". I myself heard songs during visits to Scotts Hall in the 1960s that were not in English or Spanish or any other language known to me; these too were called "Koromanti songs" by the Maroons. Roberts (ibid.) adds that:

> in addition to their being sung chiefly with words and syllables that are not now understood by the people, they are in other respects markedly different from all others obtained at Accompong or in the vicinity or in other parts of the island . . .

These songs are part of a whole tradition that has been preserved among the Maroons. But this tradition is now weakening as Maroons become more and more indistinguishable from ordinary peasants. It is consistent with the general pattern of the development of "lower" languages in contact situations that these "Koromanti songs" have by now become unintelligible. [. . .]

2 Marronage

This is one of the contexts in which gradual language loss or decay can best be observed. The Maroons set up independent communities separate from the colonial establishment, so they had much less linguistic and cultural contact with Europeans than did slaves. Twi-Asante challenged English for linguistic dominance in the same way as the Maroons challenged the British on the battlefield. Twi-Asante's political and military role as an alternative to English helped preserve it right through until the present, albeit with a reduced structure and fewer functions.

Twi-Asante probably flourished among Maroons during the period of slavery, but after slavery, its military and political role declined as Maroons came into closer contact with other Jamaicans; this accelerated its decay. During slavery, particularly when the Maroons were in a state of war with the British, Twi-Asante was not only tactically indispensable but was a symbol of the African identity of the Maroons, and an anchor of their pride and confidence. Later it lost its active role and became a mere symbol of independence. Today it is no longer a viable means of communication, but Maroons still use it to mark the boundary between them and others.

As we have seen, language loss or decay occurs in two dimensions: loss of inner form (structural), and loss of domains [of use] (functional). Twi-Asante was used in a far fuller form and in many more domains in early Maroon societies than it is today. Dallas (1803: pp. 33, 52–53), for example, records that "Coromantee" was the general language of Maroons in the eighteenth century. Bryan Edwards, the eighteenth century historian, was no doubt referring to Twi-Asante when he mentioned "a barbarous dissonance of the African dialects with a mixture of Spanish and Broken English" spoken by Maroons (see Dalby 1971: pp. 36–37). Today Twi-Asante is almost never used in a referential function,[c] and evidence suggests that it has reached the terminal stage of functional decay typical of contact situations. Maroons no longer know the meaning of many of the words and expressions they remember [. . . and i]t seems never to be used spontaneously, in ordinary everyday communicative contexts. Scott's Hall and Moore Town Maroons can carry on conversations in the old language on request, but they use fixed and stylised expressions,[d] and all creativity is lost. Most of the words and expressions that I have heard are the same as those recorded by Williams (1934). [. . .]

The Maroon Twi-Asante language, like other languages undergoing structural and functional loss as a result of contact, has become laced with importations from English and other languages, and with African words that had become "strange" and are provided with "folk etymologies"[e] that "relate" them to English words. In many cases, the forms imported into Maroon Twi-Asante are relics of the old Jamaican language that have disappeared from contemporary Jamaican. [. . .]

There is very little evidence on which to base a syntactical analysis[f] of Twi-Asante as now used by Jamaican Maroons. [. . .] Africans in Jamaica developed what has come to be known as interlanguage, i.e. utterances that deviate from the norms of both languages in contact. Two processes with which we are already familiar combine to create this interlanguage. These are the gradual decay of the "lower" language through massive loss of structure and its replacement by importations from the "upper language" and special creations that are difficult to interpret historically; and the persistence of "lower" language forms during the acquisition of the "upper" language (that is sometimes called "interference" or "substratum influences"). We have treated these two processes as if they were discrete, but to do so is merely a methodological convenience based on a recognition of two distinct linguistic entities in Jamaica now (i.e. Twi-Asante and the general language of Jamaica). At the beginning of contact, however, when the communicative needs of and pressures on Africans were particularly great, there may have been no way of distinguishing between the transformation of Twi-Asante by loss of forms plus massive importations from English on the one hand and the persistence of Twi-Asante and other African language structures in the process of the acquisition of English on the other.[1] The utterances generated by Africans under pressure to

---

c In its 'referential function', language refers to the world and carries information about it. This is sometimes contrasted with e.g. the 'directive function', which involves language trying to affect the person it's addressed to, or the 'poetic function', where the formal properties of language are manipulated for aesthetic effect.

d See Gumperz and Hernández-Chavez, this volume, on different kinds of mixed speech.

e 'Folk etymologies' = local explanations of the origins of words.

f Analysis of the structure of phrases and sentences.

communicate among themselves and with English speakers were not at first fixed, stable and systematic and could not easily and unequivocably be assigned to an idealised language system such as English or Twi-Asante, but rather belonged to interlanguage.[g] Later, when slaves were more motivated to "speak English" and more aware of the English norm, either the English component in their language increased or the African continuities became more and more diluted (the net result is the same). This has culminated today in the existence of language forms that are still difficult to assign to an idealised language system and that can perhaps best be seen as differential degrees of continuity of African structures in the acquisition of English (plus some forms for which a historical interpretation is difficult). [. . .]

3   Religion and the need for an esoteric means of communication

These are major themes of cultural marronage. Jamaica's Kumina religion has enabled the Kongo language, apparently in the form of the Kikongo dialect, to survive on the island. Warner Lewis (1977: p. 70) says of Kumina that "the control and maintenance of a proper relationship between God and/or the ancestral spirits on the one hand, and men on the other, is a knowledge of the African language (in this case Kikongo) . . . This language is a powerful tool, for without it, the Kuyu i.e. the spirits or duppies, will not hear your summons or invocations."

Among Kumina adepts the African language is better preserved than among the Maroons and there is greater knowledge of its meaning. Even so, there is evidence of severe language change bordering on total language loss. As long as Kumina still has followers some African forms will persist, but they will continue to decay and will become less and less understood. [. . .]

4   Relatively recent migration to Jamaica

This has helped to preserve the Kikongo language in St Thomas and also explains why Kikongo has survived in Trelawny (Freeman's Hall). Kikongo in St Thomas (where it is used in the context of Kumina) is at a far less advanced state of decay than in Trelawny where it does not support the religion. The position of Kikongo in St Thomas demonstrates the role of religion in preserving a language in a situation of bilingual contact, and when St Thomas and Trelawny are compared, we get a picture of how language loss progressively occurs.

Recent migration to Jamaica also explains why fragments of the Yoruba language have survived in Westmoreland and Hanover (Whithorn, Abeokuta).

5   The Jamaican language

African languages have played an extremely important part in the development of the mass language of Jamaica. This language is variously called "creole", "dialect", and "patois", but none of these terms is strictly appropriate. Here this language will be named according to the convention most widely followed in such matters,

---

g For other criticisms of idealised notions of linguistic system, see Ashcroft and Gumperz and Hernández-Chavez, this volume.

that is on the basis of the nationality of its speakers. I will therefore refer to the mass language of Jamaicans as "the Jamaican language", or simply "Jamaican".

The genesis and development of Jamaican is a subject that has attracted widespread interest among linguists working in "creole language studies". I will not specifically discuss these studies here since my concern is not with general theories of language change or creolisation[2] but with the evolution of African languages in Jamaica,[h] where speakers of different African languages needed a medium of communication among themselves and between themselves and speakers of English.

The conditions of contact between English people and Africans in Jamaica inevitably led to the erosion of African languages and to what we shall call the acquisition of English. But the notion of "acquisition" is in reality no more than a descriptive convenience, for the process of language development to which it refers is an extremely complex one involving a varied set of communicative needs. This process is best viewed as a journey starting out from a West African base and moving toward an English target, even if the "target" may not have been a psychological reality for many Africans. [. . .]

The "base" [. . .] has the same surface diversity as religion and music, but, like religion and music, it has a common underlying structure. [. . .] This common underlying structure produced identical or similar continuities in the acquisition of English by Africans of different ethnic subgroups. In the early period members of the Akan group probably set a pattern to which other groups easily accommodated and even contributed (with, for example, vocabulary items), or which they reinforced by virtue of similar or identical patterns in their own speech. Thus Jamaican forms plurals by placing the third person plural pronoun[i] after the noun (*man dem* "men"), even though in Twi-Asante this plural formation is less common than prefixing;[j] however, a number of other Kwa languages (such as Ewe and Yoruba) form plurals by means of the third person plural pronoun, thus reinforcing in Jamaican the less common of the two Twi-Asante plural-forming mechanisms.

The nature of the target [English] toward which African speech in Jamaica moves is extremely complex. [. . .] The shape of the target has changed over the centuries; today it is Jamaican Standard English. However, "target" is in many ways not a psychological reality. Military revolt by Maroons was only one form of resistance to assimilation to the English norm: there was also resistance to cultural assimilation. This cultural resistance took many forms, including both resistance to the adoption of an English language norm and the preservation of language codes incomprehensible to outsiders. Even today many Jamaicans, particularly teenagers whose native dialect is Standard Jamaican English, have turned to other forms of speech far removed from the standard English norm.

But still there has been a movement, sometimes conscious, sometimes unconscious, always inexorable, toward an English more closely approximating what is

---

h See Cassidy, F.G. 1971 (2nd edition) *Jamaica Talk. Three Hundred Years of the English Language in Jamaica* London: Macmillan Education, for a comprehensive account of the evolution of Jamaican language with a strong etymological focus on both English and African language origins.

i In standard English, 'they' and 'them are 3rd person plural pronouns.

j With prefixing, the meaning of a word is changed by an element added to the front (e.g. 'destabilise'), whereas with suffixing, the meanings changed by an element added to the end (e.g. 'fix' to 'fix*ed*').

perceived as the ideal norm. In the past, during slavery, this movement could be explained almost entirely by the need for an instrument of communication between Africans and British. Since emancipation, however, the main driving force behind it has been the realisation by Blacks that command of English is a precondition for upward socioeconomic mobility. Thus two main factors influenced the development of language among the general African population of Jamaica. Both these factors moved the language toward English but at the same time prevented the complete assimilation of Africans to the existing norm of English. The main factor in this process had to do with the objective conditions of the contact situation: the different forms in which, and the different degrees to which, Africans and English interacted in Jamaica. The second important factor was more psychological in character, and had to do with the degree to which Africans were motivated to learn English (or, as the case may be, to assert their identity as Africans and to strive for their political freedom). It is only in this latter sense that the idea of English as a target – to be striven after or to be avoided – was a psychological reality for Africans.[k]

Today this dichotomy between objective conditions of interaction among different groups of Jamaicans (in which the notion of target is not relevant) and the desire by some Jamaicans to "improve" their socioeconomic status by "improving" their English still holds. What is to a large extent new is the role played by schools in promoting an awareness of the target.

My position can therefore be summarised as follows: because Africans speaking different languages and coming from different parts of West Africa needed to communicate both among themselves and (less so) with Europeans (in this case English people, themselves speaking different dialects and coming from different parts of the United Kingdom), their language changed. It is axiomatic that during change caused by language contact of a certain sort elements of the language undergoing change will be transmitted to the new "target". No known community has ever moved from one language to another without such transmissions and continuities. Often, of course, they are eventually discarded and leave no trace whatsoever in the newly adopted language. First the vocabulary is discarded, then the morphology, then the syntax, and finally the phonology;[l] within phonology the old intonation pattern apparently lasts longest.[m]

These continuities and transmissions often become detached from their antecedents. They change in the course of transmission, either because of some degree of fusion with forms from other sources, or to pressures from the new environment, or to weakening of the links with antecedent forms. In the Afro-American case this is so not only for language but also for other forms of culture, including religion (see Herskovits 1947: p. 296).

The presence of African continuities in Jamaican helps to refute the theory that Jamaican is largely derived from English through processes variously described as "corruption", "pathological development", or, more recently, "pidginisation" and

---

k On processes involved in moving to English, see also Ngũgĩ, Mazrui, Bokhorst-Heng and Quirk, this volume.

l Morphology = word structures, syntax = phrase and sentence structures, phonology = pronunciation.

m See Gumperz, this volume, on different intonation patterns within English.

"creolisation". Many language forms explained as corruptions, simplifications, aberrations, pidginisations, and creolisations (whatever these terms may mean) of English can be shown to have very plausible West African antecedents.[n]

Opponents of the theory that African elements persist in Afro-American culture often point to similar elements in cultures in areas of the world where Africans have never been. Opponents of the theory that African "substratum" influences persist in Afro-American languages ("creoles") likewise point to similar linguistic forms in languages scattered throughout the world. But there is no reason why the same linguistic form should not be explained by different factors in different places. "Substratum" influences must of course be substantiated *a fortiori* rather than merely asserted, and explanations in terms of such influences must be weighed against other possible explanations. But they cannot be ruled out just because similar forms exist elsewhere that have different histories. [. . .] In many cases, different substrate languages underlying unrelated new languages born of cultural contact have similar structures, so that structures of the new languages also look similar even though they are unrelated. For example, Peruvian Andean Spanish, Sierra Leone Krio, and Papiamentu (spoken in the Dutch West Indian islands of Curaçao and Aruba) all have the double possessive (e.g. in Andean Spanish *el abuelo su hermano* "the grandfather's brother", i.e. "the grandfather his brother"), but whereas in Peru the source is Quechua, in the case of Krio and Papiamentu[3] it is probably West Africa (cf. Twi *Ata ne na* "Ata's mother", i.e. "Ata his mother"). The Jamaican juxtaposition of two nouns unconnected by a possessive pronoun to express possession as well as the supposed absence of copula[o] are also features of Tok Pisin (Melanesian Pidgin English), but in both Tok Pisin and Jamaican they are adequately explained by formally similar but wholly unrelated substrate influences. Those scholars who build theories about the so-called "universals" of "creole" structure on the basis of similarities between historically unconnected "creoles" tend to ignore these influences. [. . .]

The nature of the contact situation in which the Jamaican language developed, both in towns and trading stations on the West African coast and on the plantations in Jamaica placed Africans in different kinds of contact both with the English language and English culture and with Africans of other ethnic origins. Descriptions of the West African locus (e.g. Lawrence 1963) show how different groups of Africans related differently with the European traders, soldiers, and others. The situation in Jamaica was analogous. Many writers have described occupational stratification in the colonies and shown how it underlies present sociocultural and economic stratification in the West Indies and North America. Although slave society was highly homogeneous, it was also hierarchically structured in terms of occupation, privileges, and access to the culture of the masters. This meant that

---

n See Rickford, this volume, on conflicting views about the origins of Ebonics in the US. For a comprehensive historical review of the development of theories of creolisation see Holm, J. (1988) *Pidgins and Creoles Vol.1*. Cambridge: Cambridge University Press. For some critical comments on such linguistic disputes, see R. Harris and B. Rampton (2002) 'Creole metaphors in cultural analysis: On the possibilities and limits of (socio-)linguistics' *Critique of Anthropology* 22(1): 31–52 (also http://www.kcl.ac.uk/depsta/education/ULL/wpull.html)

o 'De man house' (the man's house) is an example of possession. 'De baby tired' (the baby *is* tired) is an instance of absent copula.

some slaves began to think and behave — and to speak — differently from others. The main occupational difference was between domestic and field slaves; artisans (including "drivers") occupied an intermediate position. Domestics were in close contact with Europeans; their cottages were even white-washed and located near their masters' houses (Settle 1933). The masters favoured their domestics, especially those that bore them children (i.e. mulattoes). The domestics developed forms of language and behaviour appropriate to their occupational needs and status. But though they began to behave more like the Europeans, they still had to maintain links with other slave groups. Patterson (1967: p. 54) notes that the head driver and head cooper lived only two hundred yards from the overseer while the rest of the slaves lived a half a mile away. At the end of one day the head driver got work quotas from the overseer for the following day and had to communicate them to the different classes of slaves. Most slaves worked in the fields. Field slaves were far removed from contact with Europeans, and rarely communicated or had social relations with people other than field slaves. Members of the middle group, chiefly artisans, headmen, "drivers", and perhaps also freedmen doing odd jobs in the developing urban centres and market places, met and communicated with both domestic and field slaves and their speech was therefore influenced by both groups.[p]

During the early years of plantation slavery an important sociocultural distinction emerged between the *bozal* ("slave born in Africa") and the *creole* ("slave born in the colonies"). The *bozal*, regardless of his or her occupation in Jamaica, would pass through all the stages of acculturation: the language of the *bozal* would at first be heavily marked by native speech habits, but in time these habits would be progressively eliminated. The rate at which slaves traversed these stages depended largely on their occupational histories. The creole slaves, on the other hand, learned to speak like members of the group to which they or their parents belonged. Slaves who spent their lives among domestics spoke as domestics and their form of speech differed significantly from that of the field slaves. Many accounts of the time refer to this difference between the *bozal* and the *creole* and look particularly at language differences (cf. Alvarez Nazario 1961).

Not all domestics identified with the group of domestics (some led slave revolts); similarly, not all field slaves identified with field slaves. To the extent that slaves identified with groups to which they did not belong by occupation, they developed forms of behaviour, including speech behaviour, typical of those groups. The wider an individual's range of contacts and the more complex his or her self-image and identification, the more styles and levels of language he or she acquired.

Economic changes after emancipation brought new influences into play in Jamaica. In Barbados, most emancipated slaves stayed on the sugar plantations. The plantation as a social institution afforded little opportunity for primary social contact between master and slave or between manager and field worker. Even so, Blacks and Whites interacted more on the plantations than they did in Jamaica, where former slaves left the plantations in large numbers after emancipation and set up communities of smallholders in the remote hills.

---

p See also Ngũgĩ and Mazrui, this volume, on language contact and class stratification.

In Jamaica Blacks have acculturated less to Whites than in Barbados. In Jamaica the form of speech – mainly rural – commonly called "creole" still shows clear links to field slave speech, of which it is the modern representative. Today there are other levels of speech alongside "creole" in Jamaica that show fewer links with the earliest period and are modern representatives of the speech of drivers, artisans, and domestics. Taken together, these levels form what is called Jamaica's linguistic continuum. Any variable – phonological, morpho-syntactical, or lexico-semantic[q] – may appear in forms identified or identifiable with the basic "creole" variety, with the standard dialect, or with any one of a number of intermediate bands in the continuum. These intermediate variants can generally be ranged, in terms of their formal characteristics and grammatical structure and in terms of speakers' reaction to them,[4] along a scale of degrees of approximation either to the "target" (Standard English) or to the base ("creole"). This scale may also be calibrated in terms of the degree of continuity (or loss) of West African features. West African features prevail at the "creole" end of the continuum and are progressively replaced by forms approximating more and more to Standard English.

The term "decreolisation" is sometimes used in connection with intermediate speech varieties in Jamaica (as well as in Antigua and in Guyana, and in connection with the non-standard English dialect of Trinidad and Barbados). Decreolisation refers to the process by which a "creole" dialect is modified in the direction of the standard dialect. Even the basic "creole" dialect of Jamaica (or of Antigua or Guyana) can therefore be analysed as an instance of decreolisation, since the contemporary "creole" form is much closer to Standard English than its seventeenth, eighteenth, and nineteenth century forms. My own argument up to now has been that what is here called creolisation (preceded, according to most of those who uphold the theory, by an initial stage of pidginisation[r]) is in reality an initial phase (or rather, series of phases) in bilingual contact in which large numbers of West African linguistic features persist but are subsequently eliminated as contact with English grows and endures. This progressive elimination of African features and their replacement by Standard-like forms, or forms typically representing intermediate approximations to the Standard dialect, is apparently what is meant by the term "decreolisation". However, the process thus understood is not just a uniform and unilinear succession of chronological stages, but a complex reflection of different types of social and cultural relationships both among Africans and between Africans and Europeans. Intermediate varieties of speech have existed for as long as "creole" varieties, though they were at first demographically less important and less frequently used and acknowledged.

Speech variation is very intense in Jamaica, and speakers command a series of levels or registers through which they shift without any necessarily apparent motivation. Jamaican intuitions about grammaticality[s] are based largely on prescriptive

---

q 'Lexico-semantic' = related to word meaning.

r In Rickford's terms (this volume): 'Native to none of its speakers, a pidgin is a mixed language, incorporating elements of its users' native languages but with less complex grammar and fewer words than either parent language. A pidgin language emerges to facilitate communication between speakers who do not share a language; it becomes a creole language when it takes root and becomes the primary tongue among its users. This often occurs among the children of pidgin speakers'.

s That is, their intuitions about how grammatically acceptable or correct particular sentences are.

norms set by the schools or by the elite. [. . .] In the past field slaves, who formed the majority of the population in Jamaica, had few if any social relations outside their own group. Their "creole" grammar remained highly homogeneous, stable, and consistent for as long as they were numerically strong, directed mainly or exclusively toward their own group, and isolated from other groups.[5] Since slaves were not socially mobile, there was no pressure on them to adopt speech behaviour typical of other groups. This changed with the emancipation of slaves and other social reforms, particularly the introduction of public education. These reforms made social mobility possible and created strong pressures on people to modify their speech in the direction of the prestige norm. This led not so much to the mixing of "creole" forms with "standard" forms as to the rejection of a number of features seen as deviating most from English and the adoption by people of speech characteristics of the social group immediately above them. [. . .]

Lexico-semantics

There were obviously far more West African words in the Jamaican language in the past than there are now. Many such words have now become archaic; they are used infrequently and only by older country people. African words disappeared from Jamaican either because they came to be stigmatised in the course of the general pejoration of "folk" culture by urban culture or because they referred to West African artifacts that themselves fell out of use in Jamaica. Things like the *benta* (a musical instrument) and *dukunu* (a sort of food) no longer exist actively in Jamaican culture, so the African words that designate them have become (or are becoming) archaic or obsolete. Other African words for things still used, such as the names of various yams (*afu*, *pumpum*, *taya* and *bayere*) and words like *bankra* "basket" and *ackee* remain vibrant.

A number of African words referring to objects, actions and concepts of a very general nature, not specific to any particular culture, have also persisted in the Jamaican language, showing how tenacious are the African roots of its vocabulary. In most cases they exist side by side with English derived words, e.g. *unu* "you", *nyam* "eat", *juk* "stab", *poto-poto* "mud", *dopi* "spirit", *doti* "earth".

West African semantic structures are also present in the Jamaican language, though they have changed somewhat in the course of time. Gender and generation are expressed by affixing words meaning "male", "female", "mother", "father", or "child" to a neutral stem. Thus *man cow* means "bull", *woman cow* means "heifer", and *cow pikni* means "calf". This device is related to another that forms names by juxtaposing the names of two primary objects. A finite set of central concepts is used to form the names of an infinite set of objects. Such naming is definitional rather than arbitrary. Thus *eye water* means "tears", *mouth water* "saliva", *nose hole* "nostril", *head back* "nape", and *hand middle* "palm". Some of these words have by now given way to arbitrary names derived from English. At one time Jamaicans probably used expressions such as *bobi mofo* "nipple" (lit. "breast mouth"), *ago futu* "heel" (lit. "knot foot"), and *ago mau* "ankle" (lit. "knot hand"), still found today in Suriname. This method of labelling is common in West African languages, e.g. *ana miri* "eye water" and *òno miri* "mouth water" in Igbo and *bar bu sèt* "day clean" ("dawn") in Wolof. Jamaican has also preserved with little change a pattern of associating abstract concepts with parts of the body. Niger-Congo languages are full of lexico-semantic units such as *hard ears* "stubbornness", e.g. *ano kware* "truth" ("mouth true"), *aso oden* "disobedience" ("ear hard"), *ano yede* "flattery" ("mouth sweet") in Yoruba; and *kanga ntima* "stubbornness" ("tie heart") in Kikongo. Saramaccan (a language of Suriname) contains many such forms; and Russell (1868) cites a number (used adjectivally) in Jamaican though they are no longer used today: *pick mouth* "troublesome", *strong eye* "domineering", *strong physic* "hot-tempered", and *strong head* "stubbornness", *big eye* "greed", *dry eye* "boldness", *hard ears* "stubbornness", and *cut eye* "scorn" are the forms most often heard.

6   New twentieth-century philosophies and ideologies: Black Nationalism and Rastafarianism

It is well known that philosophical, political and intellectual movements shape languages. The lexicon of French, for example, changed greatly at the time of the French revolution. Special interest groups in a society often "create" a new "language", chiefly in the lexical field. Halliday (1978: pp. 164–5) refers to an "anti-society", i.e. "a society that is set up within another society as a conscious alternative to it. It is a mode of resistance, resistance which may take the form either of passive symbiosis or of active hostility and even destruction." Halliday also speaks of an "antilanguage" generated by the antisociety.

If we ignore the pathological connotations of Halliday's analysis, his observations about "antilanguage" and the role of philosophical and ideological movements in language evolution can be applied to the language of Rastafarianism. This language is an excellent example of the impact of social forces on cultural institutions. Even so, the form and function of Rastafari language can best be analysed in terms of a theory of African continuity.

Rastafari language differs from the "antilanguages" mentioned by Halliday in one important way. Languages of antisocial groups are strongly influenced by the need for secrecy and for an esoteric form of communication. But Rastafari language has no such motivation or intent, for Rastafarianism is universalistic. Rastafari language flows directly from Rastafari philosophy and expresses a fundamental relationship of humans to nature and the universe. The Rastafari goal is not to restrict communication but to widen it by removing internal inconsistencies in the semantic structure of the language, reducing incompatibilities between language form and function, and reducing the arbitrariness of the linguistic sign.

These aims are related to a philosophical view of language and of the word as well as to an aesthetic view of language that leads to the cultivation of various forms of verbal art. Rastas believe in the "evocative power of the word", i.e. the power of the word to evoke and, in a sense, to be the thing meant. According to Yawney (1972: p. 30), "to the Rastas, words are seals of the mind, words have power and they must not be abused but rather used with awareness." Pollard (1980: p. 6) mentions "changes in the lexicon to reflect the philosophical position of the speaker". Nettleford (1978: p. 201) talks of the "small but pointedly relevant lexicon of normative/descriptive word-symbols" and (in Owens 1976: p. ix) of "a means of communication that would faithfully reflect the specificities of [Rastafari] experience and perception of self, life and the world". [. . .]

There is little in the historical record to prove a continuous link between the word philosophies of Africa and of modern Rastafarianism, but Barry Chevannes (cited in Pollard 1980) suggests such a link when he claims that Rastafari young men who had come together in or around 1949 under the name "Youth Black Faith" initiated the "jargon presently attributed to the Rastafari as a whole" by "carrying further" the tradition mentioned by Martha Beckwith, that is the "facility with which Jamaicans pun" and the "easy loquacity of the Jamaican peasant". True, "pre-literate" societies tend to develop high verbal skills, and the alienation of the Rastafari from Jamaican society was a main cause of the emergence of the Rastafari "antilanguage". But beyond this there is evidence that the Rastafari belief in the power of the word is an African continuity upon which Rastas successfully built.

The Rastafari language is an off-shoot from Jamaican. The main modifications have been in the lexicon, in forms of greeting and address, and in the pronoun system.[t] [. . .]

Notes

1   The same kind of dual interpretation suggests itself for other aspects of culture: Is Pukumina an African religion with massive importations from Christianity and loss of some of its original inner form, or is it a degree of African religious continuity during the acquisition of Christianity?

2   See Alleyne 1980 (Chapter 4).

3   Colloquial Dutch, however, which has heavily influenced Papiamentu, also used the double possessive: *vader z'n hoed* "father his hat".

4   As a general rule, reactions to "creole"-like forms are the most negative. For example, *nyam* and *eat* [mean the same thing]. The use of *nyam*, which is "creole" and West African in origin, is discouraged except when referring to animals or to grotesque or inelegant ways of eating by humans.

5   There were of course ways in which individual slaves could gain prestige and leadership within the community of slaves, and these ways would be very important to study. But they are not the same as social mobility.

References

Alleyne, Mervyn C. 1980 *Comparative Afro-American*. Ann Arbor: Karoma.

Alvarez Nazario, Manuel 1961 *Elemento Afronegroide en el Español de Puerto Rico*. San Juan: Instituto de Cultura Puertorriqueña.

Dalby, David 1971 "Ashanti survivals in the language of the Maroons". *African Language Studies* XII: pp. 31–51.

Dallas, R.C. 1803 *The History of the Maroons*. 2 vols. London: Frank Cass.

Halliday, M.A.K. 1978 *Language as Social Semiotic*. London: Arnold.

Herskovits, Melville 1947 *Trinidad Village*. New York: Octagon and W. Bascom.

Lawrence, Arnold 1963 *Trade Castles and Forts of West Africa*. London: Jonathan Cape.

Lewis, Maureen Warner 1977 *The Nikuyu: Spirit Messengers of the Kumina*. Savacou Publications, Mona. Pamphlet No. 3.

---

t For a further discussion of Rastafarian language see Pollard, V. (2000) *Dread Talk: The Language of Rastafari*. Kingston, Jamaica. Canoe Press University of the West Indies/McGill-Queen's University Press.

Nettleford, Rex 1978 *Caribbean Cultural Identity: The Case of Jamaica*. Kingston: Institute of Jamaica.

Owens, J. 1976 *Dread: The Rastafarians of Jamaica*. Kingston: Sangster.

Patterson, Orlando H. 1967 *The Sociology of Slavery*. London: McGibbon and Kee.

Pollard, Velma 1980 "Dread talk, the speech of the Rastafarian in Jamaica". *Caribbean Quarterly* 26(4): pp. 32–41.

Roberts, Helen 1926 "A study of folksong variants based on field work in Jamaica". *Journal of American Folklore* 38: pp. 149–216.

Russell, Thomas 1868 *The Etymology of Jamaica Grammar*. Kingston: McDougall.

Settle, E. Ophelia 1933 "Social Attitudes during the slave regime: Household servants versus field hands". In *Racial Contacts and Social Research. Publications of the American Sociological Society* XXVIII: pp. 95–98.

Sloane, Hans 1688/1707 *A Voyage to the Islands: Madeira, Barbados, Nieves, St. Christopher, and Jamaica*. London.

Williams, Joseph 1934/38 *The Maroons of Jamaica*. Chestnut Hill, Mass: Boston College Press.

Yawney, Carole 1972/79 Lions in Babylon: The Rastafarians of Jamaica as a Divisionary Movement. PhD dissertation, University of McGill.

———————————

Mervyn Alleyne is Emeritus Professor of Linguistics at the University of the West Indies at Mona, Jamaica. He is the author of *Comparative Afro-American: An Historical-comparative Study of English-based Afro-American Dialects of the New World* (Ann Arbor: Karoma, 1980).

Chapter 5

Ngũgĩ wa Thiong'o

1986

THE LANGUAGE OF
AFRICAN LITERATURE[a]

I

THE LANGUAGE OF AFRICAN literature cannot be discussed meaningfully outside the context of those social forces which have made it both an issue demanding our attention and a problem calling for a resolution.

On the one hand is imperialism in its colonial and neo-colonial phases, [. . .] continu[ing] to control the economy, politics, and cultures of Africa. [. . . O]n the other, and pitted against it, are the ceaseless struggles of African peoples to liberate their economy, politics and culture from that Euro-American-based stranglehold to usher a new era of true communal self-regulation and self-determination. [. . .] The choice of language and the use to which language is put is central to a people's definition of themselves in relation to their natural and social environment, indeed in relation to the entire universe. Hence language has always been at the heart of the two contending social forces in the Africa of the twentieth century.

The contention started a hundred years ago when in 1884 the capitalist powers of Europe sat in Berlin and carved an entire continent with a multiplicity of peoples, cultures, and languages into different colonies. It seems it is the fate of Africa to have her destiny always decided around conference tables in the metropolises of the western world: her submergence from self-governing communities into colonies was decided in Berlin; her more recent transition into neo-colonies along the same boundaries was negotiated around the same tables in London, Paris, Brussels and Lisbon. The Berlin-drawn division under which Africa is still living was obviously economic and political, despite the claims of bible-wielding diplomats, but it was also cultural. Berlin in 1884 saw the division of Africa into the different languages of the European powers. African countries, as colonies and even

---

a From Ngũgĩ wa Thiong'o (1981) *Decolonising the Mind*. London: Heinemann pp. 4–33.

today as neo-colonies, came to be defined and to define themselves in terms of the languages of Europe: English-speaking, French-speaking or Portuguese-speaking African countries.

Unfortunately writers who should have been mapping paths out of that linguistic encirclement of their continent also came to be defined and to define themselves in terms of the languages of imperialist imposition. Even at their most radical and pro-African position in their sentiments and articulation of problems they still took it as axiomatic that the renaissance of African cultures lay in the languages of Europe.

I should know!

II

In 1962 I was invited to that historic meeting of African writers at Makerere University College, Kampala, Uganda. The list of participants contained most of the names which have now become the subject of scholarly dissertations in universities all over the world. The title? 'A Conference of *African Writers of English Expression*'.[1]

I was then a student of *English* at Makerere, an overseas college of the University of London. The main attraction for me was the certain possibility of meeting Chinua Achebe. I had with me a rough typescript of a novel in progress, *Weep Not, Child*, and I wanted him to read it. In the previous year, 1961, I had completed *The River Between*, my first-ever attempt at a novel, and entered it for a writing competition organised by the East African Literature Bureau. [. . .].

The title, 'A Conference of African Writers of English Expression', automatically excluded those who wrote in African languages. Now on looking back from the self-questioning heights of 1986, I can see this contained absurd anomalies. I, a student, could qualify for the meeting on the basis of only two published short stories, 'The Fig Tree (Mũgumo)' in a student journal, *Penpoint*, and 'The Return' in a new journal, *Transition*. But neither Shabaan Robert, then the greatest living East African poet with several works of poetry and prose to his credit in Kiswahili, nor Chief Fagunwa, the great Nigerian writer with several published titles in Yoruba, could possibly qualify.

The discussions on the novel, the short story, poetry, and drama were based on extracts from works in English and hence they excluded the main body of work in Swahili, Zulu, Yoruba, Arabic, Amharic, and other African languages. Yet, despite this exclusion of writers and literature in African languages, no sooner were the introductory preliminaries over than this Conference of 'African Writers of English Expression' sat down to the first item on the agenda: 'What is African Literature?'

The debate which followed was animated: Was it literature about Africa or about the African experience? Was it literature written by Africans? What about a non-African who wrote about Africa: did his work qualify as African literature? What if an African set his work in Greenland: did that qualify as African literature? Or were African languages the criteria? OK: what about Arabic, was it not foreign to Africa? What about French and English, which had become African languages? What if an European wrote about Europe in an African language? If . . . if . . .

if . . . this or that, except the issue: the domination of our languages and cultures by those of imperialist Europe:[b] in any case there was no Fagunwa or Shabaan Robert or any writer in African languages to bring the conference down from the realms of evasive abstractions. The question was never seriously asked: did what we wrote qualify as African literature? The whole area of literature and audience, and hence of language as a determinant of both the national and class audience, did not really figure: the debate was more about the subject matter and the racial origins and geographical habitation of the writer.

English, like French and Portuguese, was assumed to be the natural language of literary and even political mediation between African people in the same nation and between nations in Africa and other continents. In some instances these European languages were seen as having a capacity to unite African peoples against divisive tendencies inherent in the multiplicity of African languages within the same geographic state. Thus Ezekiel Mphahlele later could write, in a letter to *Transition* number 11, that English and French have become the common language with which to present a nationalist front against white oppressors, and even 'where the whiteman has already retreated, as in the independent states, these two languages are still a unifying force'.[c] In the literary sphere they were often seen as coming to save African languages against themselves. Writing a foreword to Birago Diop's book *Contes d'Amadou Koumba* Sédar Senghor commends him for using French to rescue the spirit and style of old African fables and tales. 'However while rendering them into French he renews them with an art which, while it respects the genius of the French language, that language of gentleness and honesty, preserves at the same time all the virtues of the negro-african languages.'[2] English, French and Portuguese had come to our rescue and we accepted the unsolicited gift with gratitude. Thus in 1964, Chinua Achebe, in a speech entitled 'The African Writer and the English Language', said:

> Is it right that a man should abandon his mother tongue for someone
> else's? It looks like a dreadful betrayal and produces a guilty feeling.
> But for me there is no other choice. I have been given the language and
> I intend to use it.[3]

See the paradox: the possibility of using mother-tongues provokes a tone of levity in phrases like 'a dreadful betrayal' and 'a guilty feeling'; but that of foreign languages produces a categorical positive embrace, what Achebe himself, ten years later, was to describe as this 'fatalistic logic of the unassailable position of English in our literature'.[4]

The fact is that all of us who opted for European languages – the conference participants and the generation that followed them – accepted that fatalistic logic to a greater or lesser degree. We were guided by it and the only question which preoccupied us was how best to make the borrowed tongues carry the weight of our African experience by, for instance, making them 'prey' on African proverbs and other peculiarities of African speech and folklore. [. . .]

---

b Compare Mazrui, this volume.
c Compare Bokhorst-Heng and Quirk, this volume.

Why, we may ask, should an African writer, or any writer, become so obsessed by taking from his mother-tongue to enrich other tongues? Why should he see it as his particular mission? We never asked ourselves: how can we enrich our languages? How can we 'prey' on the rich humanist and democratic heritage in the struggles of other peoples in other times and other places to enrich our own? Why not have Balzac, Tolstoy, Sholokov, Brecht, Lu Hsun, Pablo Neruda, H.C. Anderson, Kim Chi Ha, Marx, Lenin, Albert Einstein, Galileo, Aeschylus, Aristotle, and Plato in African languages? And why not create literary monuments in our own languages? [. . .] What was our responsibility to the struggles of African peoples? No, these questions were not asked. What seemed to worry us more was this: after all the literary gymnastics of preying on our languages to add life and vigour to English and other foreign languages, would the result be accepted as good English or good French? Will the owner of the language criticise our usage? Here we were more assertive of our rights! Chinua Achebe wrote:

> I feel that the English language will be able to carry the weight of my African experience. But it will have to be a new English, still in full communion with its ancestral home but altered to suit new African surroundings.[5]

Gabriel Okara's position on this was representative of our generation:

> Some may regard this way of writing English as a desecration of the language. This is of course not true. Living languages grow like living things, and English is far from a dead language. There are American, West Indian, Australian, Canadian and New Zealand versions of English. All of them add life and vigour to the language while reflecting their own respective cultures. Why shouldn't there be a Nigerian or West African English which we can use to express our own ideas, thinking and philosophy in our own way?[6]

How did we arrive at this acceptance of 'the fatalistic logic of the unassailable position of English in our literature', in our culture and in our politics? What was the route from the Berlin of 1884 via the Makerere of 1962 to what is still the prevailing and dominant logic a hundred years later? How did we, as African writers, come to be so feeble towards the claims of our languages on us and so aggressive in our claims on other languages, particularly the languages of our colonization? [. . .]

III

I was born into a large peasant family: father, four wives and about twenty-eight children. I also belonged, as we all did in those days, to a wider extended family and to the community as a whole.

We spoke Gĩkũyũ as we worked in the fields. We spoke Gĩkũyũ in and outside the home. I can vividly recall those evenings of story-telling around the fireside.

It was mostly the grown-ups telling the children but everybody was interested and involved. We children would re-tell the stories the following day to other children who worked in the fields picking the pyrethrum flowers, tea-leaves, or coffee beans of our European and African landlords. [. . .]

We [. . .] learnt to value words for their meaning and nuances. Language was not a mere string of words. It had a suggestive power well beyond the immediate and lexical meaning. Our appreciation of the suggestive magical power of language was reinforced by the games we played with words through riddles, proverbs, transpositions of syllables, or through nonsensical but musically arranged words. So we learnt the music of our language on top of the content. The language, through images and symbols, gave us a view of the world, but it had a beauty of its own. The home and the field were then our pre-primary school but what is important, for this discussion, is that the language of our evening teach-ins, and the language of our immediate and wider community, and the language of our work in the fields were one.

And then I went to school, a colonial school, and this harmony was broken. The language of my education was no longer the language of my culture. [. . .]

It was after the declaration of a state of emergency over Kenya in 1952 that all the schools run by patriotic nationalists were taken over by the colonial regime and were placed under District Education Boards chaired by Englishmen. English became the language of my formal education. In Kenya, English became more than a language: it was *the* language, and all the others had to bow before it in deference.

Thus one of the most humiliating experiences was to be caught speaking Gĩkũyũ in the vicinity of the school. The culprit was given corporal punishment – three to five strokes of the cane on bare buttocks – or was made to carry a metal plate around the neck with inscriptions such as I AM STUPID or I AM A DONKEY. Sometimes the culprits were fined money they could hardly afford. And how did the teachers catch the culprits? A button was initially given to one pupil who was supposed to hand it over to whoever was caught speaking his mother tongue. Whoever had the button at the end of the day would sing who had given it to him and the ensuing process would bring out all the culprits of the day. Thus children were turned into witch-hunters and in the process were being taught the lucrative value of being a traitor to one's immediate community.

The attitude to English was the exact opposite: any achievement in spoken or written English was highly rewarded; prizes, prestige, applause; the ticket to higher realms. English became the measure of intelligence and ability in the arts, the sciences, and all the other branches of learning. English became *the* main determinant of a child's progress up the ladder of formal education.

As you may know, the colonial system of education in addition to its apartheid racial demarcation had the structure of a pyramid: a broad primary base, a narrowing secondary middle, and an even narrower university apex. Selections from primary into secondary were through an examination [. . .], in which one had to pass six subjects ranging from Maths to Nature Study and Kiswahili. All the papers were written in English. Nobody could pass the exam who failed the English language paper no matter how brilliantly he had done in the other subjects. I remember one boy in my class of 1954 who had distinctions in all subjects except English, which he had failed. He was made to fail the entire exam. He went on to become a turn boy in a bus company. I who had only passes but a credit in English got a place at the Alliance High School, one of the most elitist institutions for Africans in colonial Kenya. The requirements for a place at [. . .] Makerere University College were broadly the same: nobody could go on to wear the undergraduate red gown, no matter how brilliantly they had performed in all the other subjects unless they had a credit – not even a simple pass! – in English. Thus the most coveted place in the pyramid and in the system was only available to the holder of an English language credit card. English was the official vehicle and the magic formula to colonial elitedom.

Literary education was now determined by the dominant language while also reinforcing that dominance. Orature (oral literature) in Kenyan languages stopped. In primary school I now read simplified Dickens and Stevenson alongside Rider Haggard. Jim Hawkins, Oliver Twist, Tom Brown – not Hare, Leopard and Lion – were now my daily companions in the world of imagination. In secondary school, Scott and G.B. Shaw vied with more Rider Haggard, John Buchan, Alan Paton, Captain W.E. Johns. At Makerere I read English: from Chaucer to T.S. Eliot with a touch of Graham Greene.

Thus language and literature were taking us further and further from ourselves to other selves, from our world to other worlds.

What was the colonial system doing to us Kenyan children? [. . .] To answer [this . . .], let me first examine the relationship of language to human experience, human culture, and the human perception of reality.

IV

Language, any language, has a dual character: it is both a means of communication and a carrier of culture.[d] Take English. It is spoken in Britain and in Sweden and Denmark. But for Swedish and Danish people English is only a means of communication with non-Scandinavians. It is not a carrier of their culture. For the British, and particularly the English, it is additionally, and inseparably from its use as a tool of communication, a carrier of their culture and history. Or take Swahili in East and Central Africa. It is widely used as a means of communication across many nationalities. But it is not the carrier of a culture and history of many of those nationalities. However in parts of Kenya and Tanzania, and particularly in Zanzibar, Swahili is inseparably both a means of communication and a carrier of the culture of those people to whom it is a mother-tongue.

Language as communication has three aspects or elements. There is first what Karl Marx once called the language of real life,[7] the element basic to the whole notion of language, its origins and development: that is, the relations people enter into with one another in the labour process, the links they necessarily establish among themselves in the act of a people, a community of human beings, producing wealth

---

d For a range of views on language as a carrier of culture in this volume, see e.g. Ashcroft, Sapir and Whorf (and others). On the ways in which contradictory views about language being culture-free or culture-laden can figure in political ideology, see Bokhorst-Heng, this volume.

or means of life like food, clothing, houses. [. . .] Production is co-operation, is communication, is language, is expression of a relation between human beings and it is specifically human.

The second aspect of language as communication is speech and it imitates the language of real life, that is communication in production. The verbal signposts both reflect and aid communication or the relations established between human beings in the production of their means of life. [. . .]

The third aspect is the written signs. The written word imitates the spoken. Where the first two aspects of language as communication through the hand and the spoken word historically evolved more or less simultaneously, the written aspect is a much later historical development. [. . .]

In most societies the written and the spoken languages are the same, in that they represent each other: what is on paper can be read to another person and be received as that language which the recipient has grown up speaking. In such a society there is broad harmony for a child between the three aspects of language as communication. His interaction with nature and with other men is expressed in written and spoken symbols or signs which are both a result of that double inter-action and a reflection of it. The association of the child's sensibility is with the language of his experience of life.

But there is more to it: communication between human beings is also the basis and process of evolving culture. In doing similar kinds of things and actions over and over again under similar circumstances, similar even in their mutability, certain patterns, moves, rhythms, habits, attitudes, experiences and knowledge emerge. Those experiences are handed over to the next generation and become the inher-ited basis for their further actions on nature and on themselves. There is a gradual accumulation of values which in time become almost self-evident truths governing their conception of what is right and wrong, good and bad, beautiful and ugly, courageous and cowardly, generous and mean in their internal and external rela-tions. Over a time this becomes a way of life distinguishable from other ways of life. They develop a distinctive culture and history. Culture embodies those moral, ethical and aesthetic values, the set of spiritual eyeglasses, through which they come to view themselves and their place in the universe. Values are the basis of a people's identity, their sense of particularity as members of the human race. All this is carried by language. Language as culture is the collective memory bank of a people's experience in history. Culture is almost indistinguishable from the language that makes possible its genesis, growth, banking, articulation and indeed its transmission from one generation to the next.

Language as culture also has three important aspects. Culture is a product of the history which it in turn reflects. Culture in other words is a product and a reflection of human beings communicating with one another in the very struggle to create wealth and to control it. But culture does not merely reflect that history, or rather it does so by actually forming images or pictures of the world of nature and nurture. Thus the second aspect of language as culture is as an image-forming agent in the mind of a child. Our whole conception of ourselves as a people, indi-vidually and collectively, is based on those pictures and images which may or may not correctly correspond to the actual reality of the struggles with nature and nurture which produced them in the first place. But our capacity to confront the world creatively is dependent on how those images correspond or not to that reality, how they distort or clarify the reality of our struggles. Language as culture is thus mediating between me and my own self; between my own self and other selves; between me and nature. Language is mediating in my very being. And this brings us to the third aspect of language as culture. Culture transmits or imparts those images of the world and reality through the spoken and the written language, that is through a specific language. In other words, the capacity to speak, the capacity to order sounds in a manner that makes for mutual comprehension between human beings is universal. This is the universality of language, a quality specific to human beings. It corresponds to the universality of the struggle against nature and that between human beings. But the particularity of the sounds, the words, the word order into phrases and sentences, and the specific manner, or laws, of their ordering is what distinguishes one language from another. Written literature and orature are the main means by which a particular language transmits the images of the world contained in the culture it carries. [. . .]

V

So what was the colonialist imposition of a foreign language doing to us children?

The real aim of colonialism was to control the people's wealth: what they produced, how they produced it, and how it was distributed; to control, in other words, the entire realm of the language of real life. Colonialism imposed its control of the social production of wealth through military conquest and subsequent political dictatorship. But its most important area of domination was the mental universe of the colonised, the control, through culture, of how people perceived themselves and their relationship to the world. Economic and political control can never be complete or effective without mental control. To control a people's culture is to control their tools of self-definition in relationship to others.

For colonialism this involved two aspects of the same process: the destruction or the deliberate undervaluing of a people's culture, their art, dances, religions, history, geography, education, orature and literature, and the conscious elevation of the language of the coloniser. The domination of a people's language by the languages of the colonising nations was crucial to the domination of the mental universe of the colonised.

Take language as communication. Imposing a foreign language, and suppressing the native languages as spoken and written, were already breaking the harmony previously existing between the African child and the three aspects of language. Since the new language as a means of communication was a product of and was reflecting the 'real language of life' elsewhere, it could never as spoken or written properly reflect or imitate the real life of that community. [. . .] Learning, for a colonial child, became a cerebral activity and not an emotionally felt experience.

But since the new, imposed languages could never completely break the native languages as spoken, their most effective area of domination was the third aspect of language as communication, the written. The language of an African child's formal education was foreign. The language of the books he read was foreign.

The language of his conceptualisation was foreign. Thought, in him, took the visible form of a foreign language. So the written language of a child's upbringing in the school (even his spoken language within the school compound) became divorced from his spoken language at home. There was often not the slightest relationship between the child's written world, which was also the language of his schooling, and the world of his immediate environment in the family and the community. For a colonial child, the harmony existing between the three aspects of language as communication was irrevocably broken. This resulted in the disassociation of the sensibility of that child from his natural and social environment, what we might call colonial alienation. The alienation became reinforced in the teaching of history, geography, music, where bourgeois Europe was always the centre of the universe.

This disassociation, divorce, or alienation from the immediate environment becomes clearer when you look at colonial language as a carrier of culture.

Since culture is a product of the history of a people which it in turn reflects, the child was now being exposed exclusively to a culture that was a product of a world external to himself. He was being made to stand outside himself to look at himself. [. . .] The images of this world and his place in it implanted in a child take years to eradicate, if they ever can be.

Since culture does not just reflect the world in images but actually, through those very images, conditions a child to see that world in a certain way, the colonial child was made to see the world and where he stands in it as seen and defined by or reflected in the culture of the language of imposition.

And since those images are mostly passed on through orature and literature it meant the child would now only see the world as seen in the literature of his language of adoption. From the point of view of alienation, that is of seeing oneself from outside oneself as if one was another self, it does not matter that the imported literature carried the great humanist tradition of the best in Shakespeare, Goethe, Balzac, Tolstoy, Gorky, Brecht, Sholokhov, Dickens. The location of this great mirror of imagination was necessarily Europe and its history and culture and the rest of the universe was seen from that centre.

But obviously it was worse when the colonial child was exposed to images of his world as mirrored in the written languages of his coloniser. Where his own native languages were associated in his impressionable mind with low status, humiliation, corporal punishment, slow-footed intelligence and ability or downright stupidity, non-intelligibility and barbarism, this was reinforced by the world he met in the works of such geniuses of racism as a Rider Haggard or a Nicholas Monsarrat; not to mention the pronouncement of some of the giants of western intellectual and political establishment, such as Hume ('. . . the negro is naturally inferior to the whites . . .'),[8] Thomas Jefferson ('. . . the blacks . . . are inferior to the whites on the endowments of both body and mind . . .'),[9] or Hegel with his Africa comparable to a land of childhood still enveloped in the dark mantle of the night as far as the development of self-conscious history was concerned. Hegel's statement that there was nothing harmonious with humanity to be found in the African character is representative of the racist images of Africans and Africa such a colonial child was bound to encounter in the literature of the colonial languages.[10] The results could be disastrous. [. . . For most children,] the negative image becomes internalised and it affects their cultural and even political choices in ordinary living. [. . .]

Thus the 1962 conference of 'African Writers of English expression' was only recognising, with approval and pride of course, what through all the years of selective education and rigorous tutelage, we had already been led to accept: the 'fatalistic logic of the unassailable position of English in our literature'. The logic was embodied deep in imperialism; and it was imperialism and its effects that we did not examine at Makerere. It is the final triumph of a system of domination when the dominated start singing its virtues.

VI

The twenty years that followed the Makerere conference gave the world a unique literature – novels, stories, poems, plays written by Africans in European languages – which soon consolidated itself into a tradition with companion studies and a scholarly industry.

Right from its conception it was the literature of the petty-bourgeoisie born of the colonial schools and universities. It could not be otherwise, given the linguistic medium of its message. Its rise and development reflected the gradual accession of this class to political and even economic dominance. But the petty-bourgeoisie in Africa was a large class with different strands in it. It ranged from that section which looked forward to a permanent alliance with imperialism in which it played the role of an intermediary between the bourgeoisie of the western metropolis and the people of the colonies – the section which in my book *Detained: A Writer's Prison Diary* I have described as the comprador bourgeoisie – to that section which saw the future in terms of a vigorous independent national economy in African capitalism or in some kind of socialism, what I shall here call the nationalistic or patriotic bourgeoisie. This literature by Africans in European languages was specifically that of the nationalistic bourgeoisie in its creators, its thematic concerns and its consumption.[e]

Internationally the literature helped this class, which in politics, business, and education, was assuming leadership of the countries newly emergent from colonialism, or of those struggling to so emerge, to explain Africa to the world: Africa had a past and a culture of dignity and human complexity.

Internally the literature gave this class a cohesive tradition and a common literary frame of references, which it otherwise lacked with its uneasy roots in the culture of the peasantry and in the culture of the metropolitan bourgeoisie. The literature added confidence to the class: the petty-bourgeoisie now had a past, a culture and a literature with which to confront the racist bigotry of Europe. This confidence – manifested in the tone of the writing, its sharp critique of European bourgeois civilisation, its implications, particularly in its negritude mould, that Africa had something new to give to the world – reflects the political ascendancy of the patriotic nationalistic section of the petty-bourgeoisie before and immediately after independence.

---

e Compare Urla, this volume.

So initially this literature – in the post-war world of national democratic revo-lutionary and anti-colonial liberation in China and India, armed uprisings in Kenya and Algeria, the independence of Ghana and Nigeria with others impending – was part of that great anti-colonial and anti-imperialist upheaval in Asia, Africa, Latin America and Caribbean islands. It was inspired by the general political awakening; it drew its stamina and even form from the peasantry: their proverbs, fables, stories, riddles, and wise sayings. It was shot through and through with optimism. But later, when the comprador section assumed political ascendancy and strengthened rather than weakened the economic links with imperialism in what was clearly a neo-colonial arrangement, this literature became more and more critical, cynical, disillusioned, bitter and denunciatory in tone. It was almost unanimous in its portrayal, with varying degrees of detail, emphasis, and clarity of vision, of the post-independence betrayal of hope. But to whom was it directing its list of mistakes made, crimes and wrongs committed, complaints unheeded, or its call for a change of moral direction? The imperialist bourgeoisie? The petty-bourgeoisie in power? The military, itself part and parcel of that class? It sought another audience, prin-cipally the peasantry and the working class or what was generally conceived as the people. The search for new audience and new directions was reflected in the quest for simpler forms, in the adoption of a more direct tone, and often in a direct call for action. It was also reflected in the content. Instead of seeing Africa as one undif-ferentiated mass of historically wronged blackness, it now attempted some sort of class analysis and evaluation of neo-colonial societies. But this search was still within the confines of the languages of Europe whose use it now defended with less vigour and confidence. So its quest was hampered by the very language choice, and in its movement toward the people, it could only go up to that section of the petty-bourgeoisie – the students, teachers, secretaries for instance – still in closest touch with the people. It settled there, marking time, caged within the linguistic fence of its colonial inheritance.[f] [. . .]

VII

But African languages refused to die. They would not simply go the way of Latin to become the fossils for linguistic archaeology to dig up, classify, and argue about the international conferences.

These languages, these national heritages of Africa, were kept alive by the peas-antry. The peasantry saw no contradiction between speaking their own mother-tongues and belonging to a larger national or continental geography. They saw no necessary antagonistic contradiction between belonging to their immediate nation-ality, to their multinational state along the Berlin-drawn boundaries, and to Africa as a whole. These people happily spoke Wolof, Hausa, Yoruba, Ibo, Arabic, Amharic, Kiswahili, Gĩkũyũ, Luo, Luhya, Shona, Ndebele, Kimbundu, Zulu, or Lingala without this fact tearing the multinational states apart. During the anti-colonial struggle they showed an unlimited capacity to unite around whatever leader or party best and most consistently articulated an anti-imperialist position.

---

f See also Mazrui, this volume, on English determining the lines of communication.

If anything it was the petty-bourgeoisie, particularly the compradors, with their French and English and Portuguese, with their petty rivalries, their ethnic chauvinism, which encouraged these vertical divisions to the point of war at times. No, the peasantry had no complexes about their languages and the cultures they carried!

In fact when the peasantry and the working class were compelled by necessity or history to adopt the language of the master, they Africanised it without any of the respect for its ancestry shown by Senghor and Achebe, so totally as to have created new African languages, like Krio in Sierra Leone or Pidgin in Nigeria, that owed their identities to the syntax and rhythms of African languages. All these languages were kept alive in the daily speech, in the ceremonies, in political struggles, above all in the rich store of orature – proverbs, stories, poems, and riddles.[g]

The peasantry and the urban working class threw up singers. These sang the old songs or composed new ones incorporating the new experiences in industries and urban life and in working-class struggle and organisations. These singers pushed the languages to new limits, renewing and reinvigorating them by coining new words and new expressions, and in generally expanding their capacity to incorporate new happenings in Africa and the world.

The peasantry and the working class threw up their own writers, or attracted to their ranks and concern intellectuals from among the petty-bourgeoisie, who all wrote in African languages. It is these writers like Heruy Wäldä Sellassie, Germacäw Takla Hawaryat, Shabaan Robert, Abdullatif Abdalla, Ebrahim Hussein, Euphrase Kezilahabi, B.H. Vilakazi, Okot p'Bitek, A.C. Jordan, P. Mboya, D.O. Fagunwa, Mazisi Kunene and many others rightly celebrated in Albert Gérard's pioneering survey of literature in African languages from the tenth century to the present, called *African Language Literatures* (1981), who have given our languages a written literature. Thus the immortality of our languages in print has been ensured despite the internal and external pressures for their extinction. [. . .]

And finally from among the European-language-speaking African petty-bourgeoisie, there emerged a few who refused to join the chorus of those who had accepted the 'fatalistic logic' of the position of European languages in our literary being. It was one of these, Obi Wali, who pulled the carpet from under the literary feet of those who gathered at Makerere in 1962 by declaring in an article published in *Transition* (10 September 1963), 'that the whole uncritical acceptance of English and French as the inevitable medium for educated African writing is misdirected, and has no chance of advancing African literature and culture', and that until African writers accepted that any true African literature must be written in African languages, they would merely be pursuing a dead end. [. . .]

VIII

The question is this: we as African writers have always complained about the neo-colonial economic and political relationship to Euro-America. Right. But by our

---

g Compare Alleyne, this volume.

continuing to write in foreign languages, paying homage to them, are we not on the cultural level continuing that neo-colonial slavish and cringing spirit? What is the difference between a politician who says Africa cannot do without imperialism and the writer who says Africa cannot do without European languages?

While we were busy haranguing the ruling circles in a language which automatically excluded the participation of the peasantry and the working class in the debate, imperialist culture and African reactionary forces had a field day: the Christian bible is available in unlimited quantities in even the tiniest African language. The comprador ruling cliques are also quite happy to have the peasantry and the working class all to themselves: distortions, dictatorial directives, decrees, museum-type fossils paraded as African culture, feudalistic ideologies, superstitions, lies, all these backward elements and more are communicated to the African masses in their own languages without any challenges from those with alternative visions of tomorrow who have deliberately cocooned themselves in English, French, and Portuguese. It is ironic that the most reactionary African politician, the one who believes in selling Africa to Europe, is often a master of African languages; that the most zealous of European missionaries who believed in rescuing Africa from itself, even from the paganism of its languages, were nevertheless masters of African languages, which they often reduced to writing. The European missionary believed too much in his mission of conquest not to communicate it in the languages most readily available to the people: the African writer believes too much in 'African literature' to write it in those ethnic, divisive and underdeveloped languages of the peasantry!

The added irony is that what they have produced, despite any claims to the contrary, is not African literature. The editors of the Pelican Guides to English literature in their latest volume were right to include a discussion of this literature as part of twentieth-century English literature, just as the French Academy was right to honour Senghor for his genuine and talented contribution to French literature and language. What we have created is another hybrid tradition, a tradition in transition, a minority tradition that can only be termed as Afro-European literature; that is, the literature written by Africans in European languages. It has produced many writers and works of genuine talent: Chinua Achebe, Wole Soyinka, Ayi Kwei Armah, Sembene Ousmane, Agostino Neto, Sédar Senghor, and many others. Who can deny their talent? The light in the products of their fertile imaginations has certainly illuminated important aspects of the African being in its continuous struggle against the political and economic consequences of Berlin and after. However we cannot have our cake and eat it! Their work belongs to an Afro-European literary tradition which is likely to last for as long as Africa is under this rule of European capital in a neo-colonial set-up. So Afro-European literature can be defined as literature written by Africans in European languages in the era of imperialism.

But some are coming round to the inescapable conclusion articulated by Obi Wali with such polemical vigour twenty years ago: African literature can only be written in African languages, that is, the languages of the African peasantry and working class, the major alliance of classes in each of our nationalities and the agency for the coming inevitable revolutionary break with neo-colonialism.

IX

I started writing in Gĩkũyũ language in 1977 after seventeen years of involvement in Afro-European literature, in my case Afro-English literature. [. . .] Wherever I have gone, particularly in Europe, I have been confronted with the question: why are you now writing in Gĩkũyũ? Why do you now write in an African language? In some academic quarters I have been confronted with the rebuke, 'Why have you abandoned us?' It was almost as if, in choosing to write in Gĩkũyũ, I was doing something abnormal. But Gĩkũyũ is my mother tongue! The very fact that what common sense dictates in the literary practice of other cultures is being questioned in an African writer is a measure of how far imperialism has distorted the view of African realities. It has turned reality upside down: the abnormal is viewed as normal and the normal is viewed as abnormal. [. . .] Africa even produces intellectuals who now rationalise this upside-down way of looking at Africa.

I believe that my writing in Gĩkũyũ language, a Kenyan language, an African language, is part and parcel of the anti-imperialist struggles of Kenyan and African peoples. [. . .] So I would like to contribute towards the restoration of the harmony between all the aspects and divisions of language so as to restore the Kenyan child to his environment, understand it fully so as to be in a position to change it for his collective good. I would like to see Kenya peoples' mother-tongues (our national languages!) carry a literature reflecting not only the rhythms of a child's spoken expression, but also his struggle with nature and his social nature. With that harmony between himself, his language and his environment as his starting point, he can learn other languages and even enjoy the positive humanistic, democratic and revolutionary elements in other people's literatures and cultures without any complexes about his own language, his own self, his environment. The all-Kenya national language (i.e. Kiswahili); the other national languages (i.e. the languages of the nationalities like Luo, Gĩkũyũ, Maasai, Luhya, Kallenjin, Kamba, Mijikenda, Somali, Galla, Turkana, Arabic-speaking people, etc.); other African languages like Hausa, Wolof, Yoruba, Ibo, Zulu, Nyanja, Lingala, Kimbundu; and foreign languages – that is foreign to Africa – like English, French, German, Russian, Chinese, Japanese, Portuguese, Spanish will fall into their proper perspective in the lives of Kenyan children. [. . .]

We African writers are bound by our calling to do for our languages what Spencer, Milton, and Shakespeare did for English; what Pushkin and Tolstoy did for Russian; indeed what all writers in world history have done for their languages by meeting the challenge of creating a literature in them, which process later opens the languages for philosophy, science, technology, and all the other areas of human creative endeavours.

But writing in our languages per se – although a necessary first step in the correct direction – will not itself bring about the renaissance in African cultures if that literature does not carry the content of our people's anti-imperialist struggles to liberate their productive forces from foreign control; the content of the need for unity among the workers and peasants of all the nationalities in their struggle to control the wealth they produce and to free it from internal and external parasites. [. . .]

But it is precisely when writers open out African languages to the real links in the struggles of peasants and workers that they will meet their biggest challenge. For to the comprador-ruling regimes, their real enemy is an awakened peasantry and working class. A writer who tries to communicate the message of revolutionary unity and hope in the languages of the people becomes a subversive character. It is then that writing in African languages becomes a subversive or treasonable offence with such a writer facing possibilities of prison, exile or even death. For him there are no 'national' accolades, no new year honours, only abuse and slander and innumerable lies from the mouths of the armed power of a ruling minority – ruling, that is, on behalf of U.S.-led imperialism – and who see in democracy a real threat. A democratic participation of the people in the shaping of their own lives or in discussing their own lives in languages that allow for mutual comprehension is seen as being dangerous to the good government of a country and its institutions. African languages addressing themselves to the lives of the people become the enemy of a neo-colonial state.

Notes

1   The conference was organised by the anti-Communist Paris-based but American-inspired and financed Society for Cultural Freedom which was later discovered actually to have been financed by the CIA. It shows how certain directions in our cultural, political, and economic choices can be masterminded from the metropolitan centres of imperialism.

2   The English title is *Tales of Amadou Koumba*, published by Oxford University Press. [. . .]

3   The paper is now in Achebe's collection of essays *Morning Yet on Creation Day*, London: 1975.

4   [C. Achebe 1975. 'Introduction' to *Morning Yet on Creation Day*, London.]

5   Chinua Achebe 'The African writer and the English language', in *Morning Yet on Creation Day*.

6   *Transition* No. 10, September 1963 (*Editors:* Compare Quirk, this volume).

7   Marx and Engels, German Ideology, the first part published under the title, *Feuerbach: Opposition of the Materialist and Idealist Outlooks*, London: 1973, p. 8.

8   Quoted in Eric Williams *A History of the People of Trinidad and Tobago*, London 1964, p. 32.

9   Eric Williams, ibid. p. 31

10 In references to Africa in the introduction to his lectures in *The Philosophy of History*, Hegel gives historical, philosophical, rational expression and legitimacy to every conceivable European racist myth about Africa. Africa is even denied her own geography where it does not correspond to the myth. Thus Egypt is not part of Africa; and North Africa is part of Europe. Africa proper is the especial home of ravenous beasts, snakes of all kinds. The African is not part of humanity. Only slavery to Europe can raise him, possibly, to the lower ranks of humanity. Slavery is good for the African. 'Slavery is in and for itself *injustice*, for the essence of humanity is *freedom*; but for this man must be matured. The gradual abolition of slavery is therefore wiser and more equitable than its sudden removal.' (Hegel *The Philosophy of History*, Dover edition, New York: 1956, pp. 91–9.) Hegel clearly reveals himself as the nineteenth-century Hitler of the intellect. (*Editors:* On racist representation in nineteenth-century thoughts, see also Ashcroft, this volume).

Ngūgī wa Thiong'o was born in Kenya and became a celebrated novelist, a play-wright and an academic. His many famous novels include *A Grain of Wheat* (London: Heinemann, 1967) and *Petals of Blood* (London: Heinemann, 1977). His radical stance on culture and politics, which included writing in his native language as well as English, led to his removal from his Professorship at the University of Nairobi by the Kenyan Government and his detention in 1977. Since 1978 he has been in exile in the UK and the US. He is Erich Maria Remarque Professor of Comparative Literature and Performance Studies at New York University.

Chapter 6

Alamin Mazrui

1997

THE WORLD BANK, THE LANGUAGE QUESTION AND THE FUTURE OF AFRICAN EDUCATION[a]

THERE IS A CONTEST going on in African education between English, primarily, as a medium of instruction, and the indigenous languages. It is a contest in which the World Bank is playing a role ostensibly at odds with its expressed position. The process of colonial education had the general effect of marginalising most African languages in favour of Euro-languages, creating an imperialist linguistic configuration that came to legitimise and reproduce the unequal division of power and resources between the speakers of Euro-languages and speakers of African languages. The overwhelming majority of post-colonial African governments inherited educational systems with Euro-languages as the predominant media of instruction. To date, only a tiny minority of sub-Saharan African nations – like Somalia, Ethiopia, Tanzania and the Sudan – have succeeded in extending instruction in African languages beyond the lower primary levels, and, even in these anomalous cases, post-primary education has remained the exclusive preserve of Euro-languages.

The linguistic set-up in African education that was bequeathed to the continent by the colonial dispensation has prompted two kinds of responses over the years. There is, first, the functionalist response which stresses the inevitability and even usefulness of English, suggesting that, because of its global status, because of its wealth of publications, because of its 'affinity' with the inherited school system, English is a natural choice as the medium of African education. As soon as Kenya became independent in 1963, for example, the Ominde Commission (set up specifically to advise the government on issues of educational policy) recommended that English be used from the first grade of elementary education on the grounds that it would expedite learning in all subjects – partly by avoiding what was presumed to be a difficult transition from the 'vernaculars', and partly because of

a From *Race and Class* 38(3): 35–48.

the language's own 'intrinsic' resourcefulness.[1] The Commission's report thus gave further impetus to the growing momentum for the introduction of English as a medium of instruction at an earlier phase in education than even under the British. The Kenya government is a prime example of a regime that has continued to be influenced by functionalist ideology concerning the place of English in African education.[b]

At the other extreme is the nationalist response which advocates the re-centring of African languages in African educational instruction. This school of thought has been influenced principally by the views of the United Nation's Educational, Scientific and Cultural Organisation (UNESCO) on the use of so-called vernacular languages in education. Since the 1950s, it has been UNESCO's position that (a) the 'vernaculars' are superior to the foreign languages in enhancing cognitive skills in a child's early education, and (b) as media of instruction, 'vernaculars' may promote linguistic skills that facilitate, rather than inhibit, the acquisition of the imperial language at a later stage in the educational process.[2]

This controversy about which linguistic medium of educational instruction accords the child the best learning facility has led to several experimental projects, both in Africa and elsewhere. The results of some of these experiments have, seemingly, vindicated the functionalists, while others have vindicated the nationalists.

In Uganda, for example, the 1968 Iganga experiment, based on the teaching of geography, concluded in favour of English-medium instruction. The Six Year Primary (Experimental) Project at Ile-Ife, Nigeria, which was launched in 1970, on the other hand, arrived at the opposite conclusion: that instruction in a first language greatly facilitates learning.[3] These conflicting experimental results do not necessarily demonstrate that one approach is as good as the other; rather, they may reflect the ideological biases of the experimenters themselves which have influenced the premises of their investigations. In spite of these uncertainties about the real effects that a medium of instruction can have on learning, however, the World Bank has enunciated its own position which is outlined below.

But, before that, it is worth making a few points about the imperial language that is the focus of much of my discussion here, English, the most global of all imperial languages. In the words of David Crystal:

> English is used as an official or semi-official language in over 60 coun-
> tries, and has a prominent place in a further 20. It is either dominant
> or well established in all six continents. It is the main language of
> books, newspapers, airports and air-traffic control, international business
> and academic conferences, science, technology, medicine, diplomacy,
> sports, international competitions, pop music and advertising. Over
> two-thirds of the world's scientists write in English. Three quarters of
> the world's mail is written in English. Of all the information in the
> world's electronic retrieval systems, 80% is stored in English. English
> radio programmes are received by over 150 million in 120 countries.

---

b See Ngũgĩ, this volume.

Over 50 million children study English as an additional language at primary level; over 80 million study it at secondary level (these figures exclude China).[4]

Moreover, the World Bank and its sister Bretton Woods institution, the International Monetary Fund (IMF), are located in, and exist under the control of, the single largest – both geographically and demographically – English-speaking country in the world, the United States of America. From its very location and source of control, therefore, one would expect the World Bank to have a particular Anglo-linguistic bias in its attempts to determine the destiny of the world we share. Is this expectation borne out by World Bank policies and practices in Africa?

The World Bank and 'mother tongues'

On the surface, the World Bank has generally identified itself with the more nationalist school of thought that encourages the use of African 'mother tongues' as media of instruction, at least in the lower levels of elementary education. In spite of the rhetorical commitment of several African governments to the promotion of African languages as instructional media, the World Bank has compiled data demonstrating that, in the overwhelming majority of cases, the imperial languages – English, French and Portuguese especially – continue to predominate from the earliest levels of the educational pyramid almost throughout the continent.[5] And, by all indications, European languages are becoming increasingly consolidated in African education as in other domains of African society. The present trend in Africa, then, is towards maximum convergence between Euro-languages and secular education, and maximum divergence between Afro-ethnic languages and school. This is a picture that obviously portends a gloomy future for the 'development' of African languages, and explains, to some extent, the persistent calls of some nationalists for policies that will assist in re-centring African languages in education and in the lives of African people more generally.

Like many functionalists who tend to argue that English in Africa, and in the so-called Third World in general, has become useful and vital in its own right, in spite of its colonial roots, the World Bank recognises that fluency in imperial languages 'may help promote political stability and build national unity as well as serve economic purposes'. In contradistinction to the functionalists, however, the World Bank tries to project an image of being genuinely sensitive to the advantages of the more familiar tongues of the average African pupil as media of educational instruction. It notes that:

Current research suggests that (a) the acquisition both of oral fluency and of literacy in a second language is most successful when there is a strong foundation in the first language; (b) conversational skills in a second language are learned earlier than is the ability to use the language for academic learning, and (c) academic skills learned in school transfer readily from one language to the other.[6]

For the World Bank, the most effective educational approach is to begin instruction in a local language and switch to the second language – almost invariably the European colonial tongue – at a later stage.

In a more recent World Bank publication on strategies and priorities for education, the pedagogic merits of instruction in a language that is most familiar to the child are expressed once again. 'Learning is more effective', it is claimed, 'if instruction in the first several grades is in the child's native language. This approach allows for mastery of the first language and promotes cognitive development needed for learning a second language.'[7] Clearly, the World Bank's view seems to conform with the linguistic position espoused by UNESCO concerning educational instruction, a position which continues to influence some African pedagogists and language nationalists.

The World Bank, however, goes further to accept an even more radical proposition. Not only does instruction in a student's first language enhance learning and the development of certain basic cognitive skills, but instruction in a less familiar, second or foreign language is actually detrimental to the educational progress of the child. 'Children who speak a language other than the language of instruction [which here refers to the European languages] confront a substantial barrier to learning. In the crucial, early grades when children are trying to acquire basic literacy as well as adjust to the demands of the school setting, not speaking the language of instruction can make the difference between succeeding and failing in school, between remaining in school and dropping out'.[8] In view of such serious consequences for the educational future of African children arising from instruction in 'foreign' linguistic media, finding ways of centring African languages in education would be expected to be a high priority for any institution that claims to have the educational welfare of the continent at heart.

In spite of its proclaimed conviction about the pedagogic and educational value of 'mother-tongue' instruction, however, the World Bank claims that it cannot impose an educational language policy on any African country. Each country, we are told, has the freedom to determine a language policy that is commensurate with its own unique political, economic, cultural and linguistic peculiarities. This same institution that has been coercing African governments into overhauling their educational structures virtually overnight, has suddenly become mindful of the national sovereignty of these countries and of their right to linguistic self-determination. And so, the World Bank perfectly 'understands' that there are many instances when early immersion – that is, instruction in the European languages, in an all-European language environment, from day one of schooling – is more appropriate than instruction in local languages, and that such immersion may be the only pragmatic option available to a nation.[9]

With this seemingly democratic – albeit patronising – disposition, the World Bank's real position begins to be unmasked. We begin to see a view that encourages the consolidation of the imperial languages in Africa. The World Bank's own pronouncements in favour of education in local languages in the earlier phases now become suspect – are they a ploy intended to establish a firmer foundation for a higher level of proficiency in the imperial language at a later stage? Not that the World Bank believes that this is a workable formula for Africa, but even if it did, its interest in 'vernacular' instruction may lie only in the transitional benefits towards the acquisition of the Euro-languages. This is, perhaps, why the World Bank never raises the possibility of using African languages beyond the first few years of elementary education. UNESCO has campaigned for a shift to local languages in the earlier years of a child's education, and it has also recommended, on educational grounds, 'that the use of the mother-tongue be extended to as late a stage in education as possible'.[10] But the World Bank does not seem to regard the linguistic Africanisation of the whole of primary education and beyond as an effort that is worth its consideration. Its publication on strategies for stabilising and revitalising universities, for example, makes absolutely no mention of the place of language at this tertiary level of African education.[11]

The World Bank's structural adjustment prescriptions for African education may be a further betrayal of the institution's Euro-linguistic agenda. The shortage of instructional materials in local African languages is, in many instances, probably as true today as it was in the 1950s when UNESCO carried out its survey on 'vernacular' instruction. According to the UNESCO document:

> One of the most important and difficult problems connected with the use of vernacular languages in education is that of providing reading materials. It will often happen that even a language which is quite capable of being used as a medium of instruction will be almost entirely without books or other materials. The difficulty is . . . above all to find the money.[12]

At least in the initial stages, then, establishing the necessary conditions for sustainable instruction in the local languages — which, in the World Bank's opinion quoted above, is crucial to the uninterrupted educational progress of a child — requires substantial government investments in generating educational resources. Yet, the World Bank's prescriptions continue to place heavy emphasis on the reduction of government subsidies in education, though such subsidies are indispensable to the promotion of instruction in the local languages. In effect, the vaunted freedom of choice over education allowed to African nations by the democrats of the World Bank is no choice at all! For, under World Bank-IMF structural adjustment programmes, the only path open to African nations is the adoption of the imperial languages from the very outset of a child's education.

The World Bank's structural adjustment programmes also contribute to the consolidation of imperial languages in education in a different demographic sense. In its attempts to justify its pressure on African governments to cut down on educational expenditure and force students to assume part of the cost of higher education, the World Bank has sometimes argued that the majority of students can actually afford to pay for themselves because they supposedly come from relatively affluent backgrounds. Subsidies to public universities, in particular, are considered not only inefficient educational investment, but also regressive social spending because students enrolled in universities are disproportionately from the upper end of the scale of income distribution.[13]

In absolute terms, however, the World Bank figures are unequivocal that the majority of students in Africa — an average of about 60 per cent — come from the ranks of the peasantry, workers and small traders who are not likely to have the means to meet the increasing cost of university education. The natural outcome would be an increase in drop-out rates among students from poorer family backgrounds. In Kenya's Moi and Egerton Universities, for example, with a combined population of about 6,000 students, over 2,000 students were deregistered in early May 1996 over non-payment of fees and tuition.[14] These tuition 'defaulters' are more likely to have come from lower- than upper-class families. The net effect of the World Bank's structural adjustment programmes in education, therefore, is increasingly to transform the African university into a 'white collar' institution in terms of the parental background of its student population.[c]

This population shift in African universities has certain linguistic consequences. The imperial languages in Africa have their strongest demographic base among the children of white collar families. In some African cities, the English language is increasingly becoming the tongue with which middle- and upper-class children feel most comfortable in virtually all conversational situations and domains. As Abdulaziz has observed with regard to Kenya, for instance, there is a growing

> number of high cost private and international schools where many of the teachers are expatriate native speakers of English. Children who go to these expensive schools come from rich, western educated elite families, normally with both wife and husband possessing high competence in the English language . . . The children live in exclusive and expensive multinational suburbs where the primary language of the playground, shopping centres, schools, places of entertainment, churches and hospitals is English.[15]

In essence, then, the exclusionary effect that the World Bank's prescriptions will necessarily have on the children of the lower classes will give further impetus to the consolidation of the imperial languages in African education.

The World Bank's linguistic Eurocentrism in the educational arena is further demonstrated by its views on educational achievements in Tanzania. Outside 'Arabophone' Africa, Tanzania is one of the very few African countries which, after 1967, managed to completely replace the imperial language, English, with a widely spoken indigenous lingua franca, Kiswahili, in all the seven years of elementary education – even as English continued to be maintained as a school subject. It was further envisaged that a time would come when Kiswahili would be the sole medium of instruction from the earliest to the latest stages of education in Tanzania. In a 1982 report from the Presidential Commission on Education, set up by the then president of the country, Mwalimu Julius Nyerere, it was recommended that the teaching of both English and Kiswahili be strengthened, while the use of Kiswahili as a medium of instruction be extended to post-primary education. In the words of the report:

> In order that the nation be able to develop its culture and ease the understanding of most of the populace at the different stages of education without the encumbrance of a foreign language, it is recommended

---

c See Ngũgĩ, this volume.

that . . . plans be made to enable all schools and colleges in the country
to teach all subjects in Kiswahili beginning with Form I in January 1985
and the University beginning 1992.[16]

By all indications, however, this pressure for linguistic change in favour of Kiswahili
in Tanzania's school system was brought to an abrupt end after the country
capitulated to the IMF and its draconian conditionalities which forced it to reduce
its subsidies in education and other social spheres. Prior to this, 'donors had
accepted certain conditions put forth by the Tanzanian government, especially
with respect to its autonomy in the area of educational planning . . . [But] by
the beginning of the 1980s, the Tanzanian government had embarked on intense
negotiations with international donor agencies, in particular the International
Monetary Fund. The negotiations were driven by food shortages resulting from
drought, and severe problems with financial resources to purchase petroleum
products and other inputs needed for the maintenance of its economic sector.'[17]
All this dealt a blow to Tanzania's own independence in determining its educational destiny. Nonetheless, the country has continued to use Kiswahili as its main
medium of instruction in public schools and even in those colleges that train teachers
of primary education.

The World Bank, however, does not seem to be comfortable with the Tanzanian
model. In its comparative analysis of high school students' performance between
Kenya and Tanzania, for example, it casts doubt on the prudence of Tanzania's
educational language policy. It suggests that Tanzania's high school education is
qualitatively inferior to that of Kenya, and that this educational inferiority is attrib-
utable, in part, to the exclusive emphasis on Kiswahili as a medium of instruction
at the primary level. In the words of the World Bank document on education in
sub-Saharan Africa:

> The Tanzanian system also greatly emphasised the use of Swahili at the
> primary level, which may have made it more difficult for students to
> learn in English in secondary school. Research indicates that for any
> given combination of inputs of individual ability and years of secondary
> schooling in the two countries, cognitive output (as measured by scores
> on academic achievement tests) are substantially higher in Kenya than
> in Tanzania.[18]

The basis of this cross-country comparison and the conclusion drawn from it is, of
course, of questionable merit on purely methodological grounds. But that aside,
we are suddenly told to believe that, empirically speaking, basic educational instruction in a more familiar indigenous language is not, after all, the academic asset that
it has been claimed to be by some educational theorists, but a cognitive liability.
The Kenyan model, which uses English from the first year of primary school, and
sometimes as early as the kindergarten, to the complete exclusion of more indigenous languages, is now upheld as the more effective and superior instructional
arrangement.

From the above examples, it is clear that the World Bank is speaking with two
voices. It is engaged in an exercise of deception, giving the impression of being

philosophically in sympathy with educational instruction in local languages, but pursuing pro-imperial language policies in practice. Indeed, it is no coincidence that soon after Tanzania had completely submitted to the clutches of the World Bank and the IMF in the 1980s, the British Overseas Development Agency (ODA) moved in, in full force, to launch the multi-million dollar English Language Teaching Support Project in 1987.

Virtually throughout Africa there have been alarm bells about declining academic standards. Yet, neither the World Bank/IMF, nor the British Overseas Development Agency have attempted to question the wisdom of educational instruction in European languages. But, in the one country, Tanzania, that has dared to challenge the hegemony of the imperial language by replacing it with Kiswahili in the primary school, the educational language policy has quickly been seized upon as the culprit for supposedly poor academic standards. The double standards here are quite clear, and behind them may be the World Bank's hidden agenda for its linguistic Eurocentrism in African education.

Language, education and development

What, then, could be the World Bank's motives for its camouflaged advocacy of European language instruction in Africa? The World Bank and the IMF have become the principal organisations through which the capitalist West seeks to control the destiny of the rest of the world. In this respect, the establishment and reconstitution of structural inequalities (in institutional set-ups and financial allocations) and cultural inequalities (including attitudes, pedagogic principles, etc.), between the imperial European languages and other languages become indispensable strategies towards that attempted control.[19] The question, then, is how a specific language policy – overt or covert – comes to serve as an instrument of imperialist control.

Some nationalists have sought to explain linguistic imperialism in deterministic terms. In accordance with the ideas of Benjamin Lee Whorf, they have sometimes argued that there is a culturally-bound 'tyranny of language' such that the semantic structure of one's language, as well as the language habits it fosters, come to determine one's perception of the social world.[20] And, if Whorf was interested in explaining the cognitive impact of language purely on its native speakers, the nationalists have made a cross-cultural leap, claiming that the world view inherent in any particular language can actually be transposed to speakers of other unrelated languages. When western countries and institutions seek to impose their languages on Africa, therefore, the quasi-Whorfian interpretation of the African nationalists is that the West intends to imbue the collective mental universe of the African people with a European world view. This perspective, however, is one that I do not find wholly tenable, and, as I have tried to demonstrate elsewhere, it has weaknesses and limitations which render it less than adequate in explaining the imperialist role of European languages in Africa.[21]

The other way of viewing the place of language in imperialist control is to consider the economic imperative, which has both a labour side and a market side to it. With regard to the labour dimension, in particular, the World Bank's language 'policy' on educational instruction in Africa can be seen as part of a wider economic agenda intended to meet the labour requirements of foreign capital. Here the language question goes hand-in-hand with the World Bank's recommended restructuring of African university education into regional polytechnics for the production of mental and manual labour, of graduates who supposedly have the practical skills needed by African economies.[22] Expectedly, European languages will continue to be the media of instruction in these institutions, and the development of technical and vocational Euro-linguistic skills will be an essential part of this labour policy.

The labour needs of foreign capital in several African countries usually operate at three interdependent levels. These include: (a) the level of workers qualified for unskilled or semi-technical jobs in light manufacturing and assembly plants; (b) the level of technical maintenance and other 'support' services for foreign and other businesses, hotels and so forth; and (c) the level of middle management, mainly for corporations investing in Africa. May the language of instruction in Africa have some bearing on the creation or reproduction of this labour hierarchy?

Remember one of the World Bank's own documents quoted earlier, that using an instructional language that is alien to the student 'can make the difference between succeeding and failing, between remaining in school and dropping out.' If this claim is true, relatively poor performance and high drop out rates resulting from the convergence between Euro-languages and educational instruction is likely to affect the children of poorer families most acutely – for it is they, rather than the children of the rich, who are least familiar with the European languages of instruction. And it is ultimately these poor students who will have been conditioned to constitute the 'modernised' unskilled and semi-skilled labour pool. The children of upper-class families whose familiarity with the European languages is much greater, on the other hand, may be expected to end up in universities and, eventually, in managerial positions. Thus, a system of educational instruction is put in place in which those who are expected to succeed, and those who are expected to fail and drop out, is closely class-bound; can be seen, indeed, as part of a wider capitalist design. In essence, the World Bank's proposed educational configuration in Africa demonstrates the continued role of instruction in Euro-languages in creating and maintaining social divisions that serve an economy dominated primarily by foreign economic interests and, secondarily, by a small aspiring African bourgeoisie.[d]

The market motive of the World Bank's Euro-linguistic bias, on the other hand, has more to do with the role of the English language as a medium of global capitalism. [. . .] If international capitalism helped the fortunes of English, [. . .] the consolidation of that capitalism on a global scale has now, to a certain extent, become dependent on the language. According to Naysmith, the role of English in the production and reproduction of global inequalities has a lot to do with the central place it has assumed as the language of international capitalism.[23] Within this international context, the capitalist centre has virtually been serving as the 'proprietor' and the periphery as its 'labourer' and 'consumer'. And it is the English language which allows the proprietor nations of the centre to have contact with each and every consumer nation in the periphery in a way that leads to the increasing consolidation of the global capitalist market. As leading institutional representatives

---

d Compare Alleyne's account of language and social stratification in slave society.

of international capitalism, the World Bank and the IMF naturally have a vested interest in this interplay between linguistics and economics.

Finally, imperialist control can also be approached from the point of view of language, not as a reservoir of culturally-bound world views, but as an instrument for the communication of ideas. The global hegemony of the English language, in particular, facilitates World Bank-IMF attempts to force Africa, for example, into a state of intellectual dependence on the West. Quoting a publication of the Civil Liberties Organisation, George Caffentzis has noted that:

> SAPs [Structural Adjustment Programmes] often require the hiring of foreign experts as part of the conditionalities attached to IMF-WB loans. For example, a $120 million loan to the Nigerian university system puts the control of the importation of books and journals as well as expatriate staff in the hands of the Bank and its agents – hence foreign agents must be used to determine the very imports to be paid for by loans.[24]

Had the medium of instruction in Nigeria been Hausa, Igbo or Yoruba, this degree of determination of the country's academic and intellectual orientation by the World Bank-IMF pair would certainly have been more difficult.[e]

To take another example, a World Bank loan to the Central African Republic, supposedly intended to improve the quality and accessibility of elementary education, came with a package of conditions that required the nation to import its textbooks (and even French language charts) directly from France and Canada. This stringency was justified on the grounds that printing in these western countries is cheaper than in the Central African Republic, making their publications more affordable to the average African child.[25] It has been estimated that, due to similar World Bank projects and linkages, over 80 per cent of school books in 'Francophone' Africa are now produced directly in France.[26] In the process, the World Bank has not only empowered the West to control further the intellectual destiny of African children, but has also continued to weaken and destroy infrastructural facilities, primarily publishing houses, for the technical production of knowledge locally. In terms of sheer cost effectiveness, French and Canadian publishers would have found it far more difficult to participate in this World Bank agenda had the language of instruction in the Central African Republic been one of the local languages instead of French.[f]

The European languages in which Africans are taught are, therefore, important sources of intellectual control. They aid the World Bank's efforts to enable Africans to learn only that which promotes the agenda of international capitalism. Partly because of this Euro-linguistic policy, intellectual self-determination in Africa has become more difficult. And, for the time-being, the prospects of a genuine intellectual revolution in Africa may depend in no small measure on a genuine educational revolution that involves, at the same time, a widespread use of African languages as media of instruction.

---

e For another angle on how English has determined lines of communication, see Ngũgĩ this volume.
f See also Heller, this volume.

Elsewhere I have had occasion to argue that while Euro-languages have historically been carriers of imperialist discourse, they can and sometimes have been transmuted to serve as instruments of resistance against imperialist discourse.[27] Similar sentiments have been expressed by Alastair Pennycook, who has called for all applied linguists and English teachers around the world to 'become political actors engaged in a critical pedagogical project to use English to oppose the dominant discourses of the West and to help the articulation of counter-discourses in English'.[28]

But to use English to create counter-discourses and counter-ideologies does not necessarily amount to undermining the language's role in consolidating the global capitalist market, in stratifying labour for the benefit of international capital, or in reducing dependency on the West in the educational sphere. Furthermore, counter-discourse is not the same thing as independent discourse. Counter-discourse is often a reactive process to the terms of discourse established by the 'other'. The African quest for intellectual independence must be based on independent terms of reference that can guide the continent towards a more organic path. Under the present global configuration of power relations, the English language is not likely to allow Africans the politico-economic space for this kind of intellectual independence. African languages may fare better, for the very act of re-centring them sets in motion new dynamics that may provide some room for intellectual manoeuvre, at least in the short run. But the struggle to recentre these languages naturally demands our engagement in a wider struggle – against imperialism, and against organisations like the World Bank and IMF and what they represent – to create a new world order.

Notes

1   Republic of Kenya, *Kenya Education Commission Report, Part I* (Nairobi, Government Printers, 1964), p. 60.

2   UNESCO, *The Use of Vernacular Languages in Education* (Paris, UNESCO, 1953), pp. 47–9.

3   Ayo Bamgbose, *Language and the Nation: the language question in sub-Saharan Africa* (Edinburgh, Edinburgh University Press, 1991).

4   David Crystal, *The Cambridge Encyclopaedia of Language* (Cambridge, Cambridge University Press, 1987).

5   See World Bank, *Education in Sub-Saharan Africa: policies for adjustment, revitalisation and expansion* (Washington, World Bank, 1988).

6   Ibid., p. 44. (*Editors:* for a review of research on bilingualism and education, see C. Baker 1996 *Foundations of Bilingual Education and Bilingualism: 2nd Edition* Clevedon: Multilingual Matters.)

7   World Bank, *Priorities and Strategies for Education* (Washington, World Bank, 1995), p. 79.

8   M.E. Lockheed and A.M. Verspoor, *Improving Primary Education in Developing Countries* (New York, OUP for World Bank, 1991), p. 153. (*Editors:* See also Honeyford, this volume, on multilingualism and education in a 'developed' country.)

9   Ibid., p. 167.

10   UNESCO, op. cit., p. 47.

11   W.S. Saint, *Universities in Africa: strategies for stabilisation and revitalisation* (Washington, World Bank, 1993).

12   UNESCO, op. cit., pp. 50–1.

13   World Bank, *Higher Education: the lessons of experience* (Washington, World Bank, 1994), p. 3.

14   *Daily Nation* (Nairobi, 4 May 1996), p. 18.

15   Mohamed H. Abdulaziz, 'East Africa', in J. Chesire (ed.), *English Around the World: the social contexts* (Cambridge, Cambridge University Press, 1991), p. 397.

16   Zaline M. Roy-Campbell, *Power and Pedagogy: choosing the medium of instruction in Tanzania* (University of Wisconsin-Madison, PhD thesis, 1992), p. 178.

17   Ibid.

18   *Education in Sub-Saharan Africa*, op.cit., p. 56.

19   R. Phillipson, *Linguistic Imperialism* (Oxford, Oxford University Press, 1992), p. 47.

20   Benjamin L. Whorf, *Language, Thought and Reality*, edited by J.B. Carrol (Cambridge, Mass., MIT Press, 1987). (*Editors:* See the extract by Whorf in this volume, and also Ngũgĩ).

21   Alamin Mazrui, 'African languages and European linguistic imperialism', in S. Federici (ed.), *Enduring Western Civilisation: the construction of the concept of western civilisation and its 'others'* (Westport, Praeger, 1995), pp. 161–74. (*Editors:* See also Ashcroft, this volume.)

22   *Higher Education: the lessons of experience*, op. cit.

23   J. Naysmith, 'English as imperialism', *Language Issues* (vol. 1. no. 2, 1987), p. 3.

24   C.G. Caffentzis, 'The World Bank's African capacity building initiative: a critique', *Newsletter of the Committee for Academic Freedom in Africa* (No. 6, Spring 1994). p. 17.

25   Jean-Clotaire Hymbound, 'La logique de la Banque Mondiale', *Afrique Education* (September 1995), p. 4.

26   Marie-Claire Nnana, 'Livres scolaires: vers une guerre nord-sud?', ibid., p. 17.

27   Alamin Mazrui, 'Language and the quest for liberation in Africa: the legacy of Frantz Fanon', *Third World Quarterly* (vol. 14, no. 2, 1993), pp. 351–63. (*Editors:* See also Ashcroft, this volume.)

28   A. Pennycook, 'English in the world/the world in English', in J.W. Tollefson (ed.), *Power and Inequality in Language Education* (Cambridge, Cambridge University Press, 1995), p. 55.

Alamin Mazrui is Associate Professor in the Department of African American and African Studies, Ohio State University, US.

Chapter 7

Randolph Quirk

1990

LANGUAGE VARIETIES AND STANDARD LANGUAGE[a]

A FEW MONTHS AGO, the Department of Education and Science in London published a very important document on the teaching of English [. . .] in Britain (Kingman, 1988). [. . . O]ur Secretary of State, Mr Kenneth Baker, decide[d] to set up a distinguished committee of inquiry on this subject [. . . b]ecause [he] and many others in Britain have been dissatisfied with the teaching of English in British schools: dissatisfied with *what* is taught, *how* it is taught, and *the results* of the teaching as they show in the capabilities of school leavers. I would like to invite you to consider to what extent – if any – this report has relevance for the teaching of English *outside* Britain: specifically, in countries such as Japan and Germany, Senegal and India – countries where English is not a native language. [. . .]

Varieties of English

The conclusions of the Kingman Committee strike most people as wholly sensible. It is the duty of British schools, says the report, "to enable children to acquire Standard English, which is their right" (p. 14) – a statement which may seem so obvious and unsurprising that the only *surprise* is why it needs to be stated.

The very first page of the report explains: the committee found that teachers were distracted by the belief that children's capacity to use English effectively "can and should be fostered only by exposure to varieties[b] of the English language".[c] It is not of course that the committee deny the interest and importance of the variation within English – still less that such variation exists. They would agree, I am sure, that our ability to vary our language according to our social and regional

---

a From *English Today* 21: 3–10.
b That is, different types and dialects of English.
c See Honeyford, Rickford as well as Gumperz and Hernández-Chavez, all in this volume.

backgrounds, our professional careers, and indeed our creative urges as individuals, is at the very heart of the gift that human language bestows. [. . .] No, what they are saying is that the interest in varieties of English has got out of hand and has started blinding both teachers and taught to the central linguistic structure from which the varieties might be seen as varying.

This may well be true, but I think there is a more serious issue that I would like to address, and that is the profusion and (I believe) *confusion* of *types* of linguistic variety that are freely referred to in educational, linguistic, sociolinguistic, and literary critical discussion. Let me give some recent examples where the word *English* is preceded by an adjective or noun to designate a specific "variety":

American English
Legal English
Working-class English
Computer English
BBC English
Black English
South Asian English
Queensland Kanaka English
Liturgical English
Ashkenazic English
Scientific English
Chicago English
Chicano English

Some of these you'll have come across, others you may not, but it will take only a moment's reflection to convince you that – whether familiar or not – these varieties are on desperately different taxonomic bases. For example, *legal English* refers to a style that may be used equally (and perhaps indistinguishably) in American English and British English. *Ashkenazic English* is a term which has been used to characterise the usage of Ashkenazi Jews in the United States, but whether it holds for Ashkenazim living in Britain or Australia or indeed Israel, I don't know.

When Braj Kachru (1982) talks about *South Asian English*, he is referring to audible similarities in the way Indians, Pakistanis, Bangladeshis and Sri Lankans speak English; but when E. G. Bokamba (1982) refers to *African English*, he seems not to be claiming linguistic similarities but only the common ground that the work so labelled was written in Africa by black Africans. Fernando Peñalosa (1980) applies the term *Chicano English* to the English used by those of Mexican Spanish origin in the U.S.A. and he contrasts it with *Anglo English* – not presumably a synonym for *American English* since it would doubtless exclude both the English of black Americans and perhaps equally the *Anglo-English* of Britain. [. . .]

[. . .] Let me try to find a path through this maze of varieties and supervarieties by attempting a taxonomy (see [the] panel [Figure 7.1]).

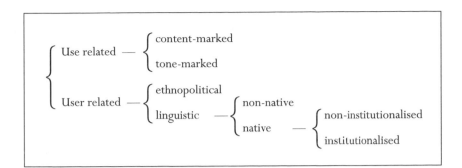

Figure 7.1   A taxonomy of varieties of English.

Use-related and user-related varieties

The first distinction we need to make is between those varieties that are *use*-related and those that are *user*-related. The former concerns varieties that an individual assumes along with a relevant role: and a given individual may have a mastery of several such varieties. A woman who is a lawyer must express herself in *legal English* in drafting an agreement, in *tennis English* when she confesses that her friend beat her "in straight sets"; she may write articles for the [UK] *Sunday Times* in *literary English*, and her word-processor makes her feel the need to master a little *computer English*.

From such *use*-related varieties, we distinguish *user*-related varieties, where in general an individual is tied to one only: Americans, for example, express themselves only in *American English*, the British only in *British English* – and they know that they sound phony if they try to switch between varieties. But two lawyers corresponding on a case across the Atlantic both switch into *legal English*, however much each colours his or her legal English with the user-related American or British variety of the language.

Within the user-related varieties, however, we must distinguish between varieties identified on ethnopolitical grounds and those identified on linguistic grounds. [. . .] This is an important distinction and it is one that should be confronted by those who speak about *Taiwanese English* and *Hong Kong English*, for example, since on linguistic grounds there are similarities that relate not to the political labels *Hong Kong* and *Taiwanese* but to the Chinese that is spoken in both areas. The distinction also reveals the ambiguity in the term *Chinese English* itself: English as used in the People's Republic *or* features of English influenced by a Chinese L1 (whether in China, Taiwan, Singapore or Malaysia). One must seek analogous clarification about the variety called *Black English*: if it covers all the blacks in North America, any linguistic basis becomes rather broad; and if it is extended to include the English of blacks in Britain, a linguistic basis becomes almost incredible – especially since the term *Black* is assumed not only by Britons of Afro-Caribbean origin but equally by many who are of Pakistani and Indian origin as well.[d]

---

d Compare Back, this volume.

Keeping to the linguistic branch from this node, we face another distinction: that between non-native varieties of English and native varieties, the former including long-recognised types like *Indian English* (in Kachru's sense), *Nigerian English, East African English*. [. . . Presumably, non-native varieties also include varieties in] which one can sometimes recognise the ethnic background of a person by his or her English: *Russian English, French English, Japanese English*. The problem with varieties in this branch is that they are inherently unstable, ranged along a qualitative cline, with each speaker seeking to move to a point where the varietal characteristics reach vanishing point, and where thus, ironically, each variety is best manifest in those who by commonsense measure speak it worst. (cf. Quirk, 1988).[e]

The other branch from this node is the native varieties – *American English, Australian English, British English, New Zealand English, South African English, New England English, Yorkshire English* and so on. And within these we make our final distinction: between *non-institutionalised* varieties and those varieties that are *institutionalised* in the sense of being fully described and with defined standards observed by the institutions of state. Of the latter, there are two: *American English* and *British English*; and there are one or two others with standards rather informally established, notably *Australian English*. But most native varieties are not institutionalised and while sharing a notable stability as compared with non-native varieties, they resemble these to a slight extent in being on a socioeconomic cline, such that the features marking an individual as being a speaker of Yorkshire English or New York English tend to disappear the higher up the socioeconomic scale he or she happens to be.

Native and non-native

Now, of all the distinctions I've made, the one that seems to be of the greatest importance educationally and linguistically is that between native and non-native: it is the distinction that is probably also the most controversial.[f] Indeed, I have made it the more controversial by implicitly excluding from the non-native branch a node which permits the *institutionalised-non-institutionalised* distinction to apply to them. I exclude the possibility only because I am not aware of there being any institutionalised non-native varieties, a point to which I shall return later.

Let me just refer, however, to some recent psycholinguistic work by René Coppieters (1987) which strikingly underscores the *native/non-native* distinction. Coppieters worked with a group of about twenty native speakers of French and with a similar-sized group of non-native speakers – all of whom with a high level of performance, all of them resident in France for at least five years and using French as their working language. Indeed the mean residence level was 17 years and many of the group were believed by French people to be native speakers.

Yet in a range of interesting and sophisticated elicitation tests, the success rate of the non-natives fell not merely *below* but *outside* the range of native success to a statistically significant degree [. . .]. For example, in judging and exploring the

---

e Compare McDermott and Gospodinoff, this volume.
f See Rampton, this volume.

semantics of paired sentences involving the imperfect tense and the passé composé, what we may call the 'failure' rate of the natives was 2%, that of the non-natives 41.5%. For example:

> Il a soupçonné quelque chose, j'en suis sûr.
> Il soupçonnait quelque chose, j'en suis sûr.

The difference in the sets of scores was reflected in the comments by the non-natives. Though they always managed to understand and make themselves understood fairly well through the linguistic and situational context, they said repeatedly that they had developed no intuitions about the distinction between the imperfect and the passé composé: and two who said just this had worked in important professional positions in France for 15 and 21 years respectively. It would be interesting to see similar controlled experiments for English with such pairs as "The spacecraft is now 1000 km from (+/– the) earth", "She (+/– has) lived there for three years."

The implications for foreign language teaching are clear: the need for native teacher support and the need for non-native teachers to be in constant touch with the native language. And since the research suggests that natives have radically different internalisations, the implications for attempting the institutionalisation of non-native varieties of any language are too obvious for me to mention.[g]

Standard English

Instead, let me return to the broader issue of language varieties as it concerned the Kingman Committee, since they saw this as bound up with uncertain attitudes to *standards*, noting that some teachers of English believed "that any notion of correct or incorrect use of language is an affront to personal liberty".

It would take me too far from the subject of this lecture to examine why so many teachers should have turned away from concentrating on Standard English, from criticising a student's poor usage as incorrect, and should have preferred to explore the variety of language that students bring to their classrooms from very different social and regional backgrounds. Suffice it to say that the reasons have been idealistic, humanitarian, democratic and highly reputable, reasons which honourably motivated student teachers. And why not, indeed? If recent history has given us a "liberation theology", why not also a "liberation linguistics"?

The trouble, as the Kingman Committee sees it, is that such an educational fashion went too far, grossly undervaluing the baby of Standard English while *over-valuing* the undoubtedly important bathwater of regional, social and ethnic varieties: giving the impression that any kind of English was as good as any other, and that in denying this, nothing less was at stake than "personal liberty" itself. By contrast,

---

g On cultural and economic dynamics affecting English in Africa, see Ngũgĩ and Mazrui, this volume. For critical discussion of English as a world language (beyond the references in this article), see R. Phillipson 1992 *Linguistic Imperialism* Oxford: Oxford University Press, and A. Pennycook 1994 *The Cultural Politics of English as an International Language* London: Longman.

the Kingman Report sees such an educational ethos as trapping students in their present social and ethnic sectors and as creating a barrier to their educational progress, their career prospects, their social and geographical mobility. Command of Standard English, says the Report, so far from inhibiting personal freedom, "is more likely to increase the freedom of the individual than diminish it" (Kingman, 1988, p. 3).

English in non-English-speaking countries

Let me now turn from the fairly parochial issue of teaching English in Britain to the teaching of English in non-English speaking countries – where overwhelmingly greater numbers of students are involved. Most of the Kingman Report should surely have no bearing upon *them*. Since students in the Soviet Union or Japan bring little English of their own to the classroom, there can be no question of the teacher performing his or her task by merely exposing them to the "varieties of English language" around them. They come to learn a totally unfamiliar language, so there can be no question of the teacher rejecting the "notion of correct or incorrect" use of English. And all the students know perfectly well that, as Kingman says, their command of Standard English is likely to increase their freedom and their career prospects. So of course they – teachers and taught alike – accept the basic conclusion that it is the institution's duty to teach Standard English.

At any rate, that is what one would *expect* to be the position with teaching English as a foreign language, and it is the position that is assumed by most foreign ministries of education and by most foreign students – and their parents.[h]

But the contrast between teaching English to English boys and girls in Leeds and teaching English to Japanese boys and girls in Kobe is not as neat and absolute as I have made it seem. Some schools in London and New York, for instance, have so many pupils from a non-English speaking background that the techniques and approaches of teaching English as a foreign language have to be adopted – in precisely the same schools and often by the same teachers as those where the ideals of what I've called "liberation linguistics" are still enthusiastically served up, however much they are just stale leftovers from the 1960s.

Let me give you a New York example. A well-respected educationist wrote an article a year or so ago on the teaching of English to the many thousands of New York children who come from Spanish-speaking homes (Goldstein, 1987). These children, she said, identify far more with the black children in the streets around them than with white children, and for that reason the English they should be taught is not Standard English but what she calls Black English. This is the English that will help them to relate to their peers outside the classroom; and after all, she pointed out, a sentence like "I don't have none" shows "a correct use of Black English negation" (p. 432).

Now, that article was published in one of the best known international journals, read by teachers of English not only in the United States but in Italy, Greece, China, and Japan – by the most professionally-minded, in fact, of English language

---

h See Bokhorst-Heng, this volume.

teachers throughout the world. The context in which the article was *written* of course is clear enough, but what about attempts to adapt its message in the very different contexts in which it is *read*?

We must not forget that many Japanese teachers, Malaysian teachers, Indian teachers have done postgraduate training in Britain and the United States, eager to absorb what they felt were the latest ideas in English teaching. Where better, after all, to get the latest ideas on this than in the leading English-speaking countries? The interest in "varieties of English language", called in question on the first page of the Kingman report, has in fact been widely stimulated, as we know from university theses being written in a whole host of countries: with titles like *Malaysian English*, *Filipino English*, *Hong Kong English*, *Nigerian English*, *Indian English*.

The countries last mentioned here, of course, are chiefly those where English has had an *internal* role over a long period for historical reasons. English was indeed the language used by men like Gandhi and Nehru in the movement to liberate India from the British raj and it is not surprising that "liberation linguistics" should have a very special place in relation to such countries. Put at its simplest, the argument is this: many Indians speak English; one can often guess that a person is Indian from the way he or she speaks English; India is a free and independent country as Britain is or as America is. Therefore, just as there is an *American English* (as recorded, for example, in the Webster Collegiate Dictionary), and a *British English* (as recorded, for example, in the Concise Oxford), so there is an *Indian English* on precisely the same equal footing (and of course a *Nigerian English*, a *Ghanaian English*, a *Singaporean English*, a *Filipino English*, etc., etc.).

No one would quarrel with any of this provided there was agreement within each such country that it was *true*, or even that there was a determined policy to *make* it true. So far as I can see, neither of these conditions obtains, and most of those with authority in education and the media in these countries tend to protest that the so-called national variety of English is an attempt to justify inability to acquire what they persist in seeing as 'real' English. [. . .]

No one should underestimate the problem of teaching English in such countries as India and Nigeria, where the English of the teachers themselves inevitably bears the stamp of locally acquired deviation from the standard language ("You are knowing my father, isn't it?"). The temptation is great to accept the situation and even to justify it in euphemistically sociolinguistic terms. [. . .][i]

Half-baked quackery

When we turn from the [. . .] problems of countries like India and the Philippines to countries like Spain and Japan which have little or no legacy of localised English on the streets, in offices, or in markets, we would surely expect to find no such conflicts about teaching Standard English. And so it is for the most part, no doubt. But not entirely. Ill-considered reflexes of liberation linguistics and a preoccupation with what the Kingman Report calls "exposure to varieties of English language" intrude even here. And this in two respects.

---

i Compare Ngũgĩ, this volume.

First, the buoyant demand for native-speaking English teachers means that one occasionally finds, in Tokyo or Madrid, young men and women teaching English with only a minimal teacher training, indeed with little specialised education: they're employed because, through accident of birth in Leeds or Los Angeles, they are native speakers of English. Not merely may their own English be far from standard but they may have little respect for it and may well have absorbed (at second or third hand) the linguistic ethos that is simplified into the tenet that any English is as good as any other.

One such young Englishman approached me after a lecture I'd given in Madrid a few months ago. Why, he asked, had I distinguished between the nouns *message* and *information* as countable and uncountable?[j] His students often wrote phrases like *several informations* and since he understood what was meant, how could they be wrong? In some wonderment that I was actually talking to a British teacher of English, I gently explained about Standard English being the norm by which we taught and made judgments. He flatly disagreed and went on to claim that he could not bring himself to correct a Spanish pupil for using a form that had currency in an English dialect – *any* English dialect. "She catched a cold" is as good as "She caught a cold", he ended triumphantly and strode away.

Let's hope that such half-baked quackery is rare because the *other* respect in which "exposure to varieties" is ill-used is not all that rare, I fear. This is where academic linguists from Britain or America, sometimes with little experience of foreign language teaching, are invited to advise on teaching English abroad. If by training or personal interest they share the language ethos that the Kingman Report criticises, their advice – merely a bit controversial in its original British or American educational context – is likely to be flagrantly misleading when exported with minimal adaptation to, say, Japan. Indeed, it can even happen with consultants who have years of hands-on ELT experience.

An example. A year or so ago, the Japan Association of Language Teachers invited a British educationist to address their annual convention. I learned about this from a worried Japanese official who drew my attention to the text of this British expert's address published in Tokyo. It warned teachers not to make "overly hasty judgments about the language performance of learners", and particular emphasis was given by the expert to the following statement: "Language behaviour which at first sight appears to be flawed may in fact be a manifestation of a new – though as yet unrecognised – variety of English." (Coleman, 1987, p. 13). I was also asked about the *Four Seasons Composition Book* (Pereira and O'Reilly, 1988) in which Japanese students are told that "if you can make yourself understood . . . that is good enough" since their attempts constitute "a respectable variety of English".

The implications of this, if hard-working Japanese teachers took such advice seriously, are quite horrendous. Students, "liberally" permitted to think their "new variety" of English was acceptable, would be defenceless before the harsher but

---

j In UK standard English, 'countable' nouns treat things as separable entities – 'a cat', 'four biscuits' – while 'uncountable' nouns treat them as continuous – 'some milk', 'too much energy'. In Nigerian English, 'luggages' and 'furnitures' are acceptable as countable nouns, whereas in UK standard English, these words are uncountable (so the Nigerian forms are unacceptable).

more realistic judgment of those with authority to employ or promote them. They have in effect been denied the command of Standard English which, to quote the Kingman Report yet again, "is more likely to increase the freedom of the individual than diminish it" (p. 3).

Standard English alive and well

Certainly, if I were a foreign student paying good money in Tokyo or Madrid to be taught English, I would feel cheated by such a tolerant pluralism. My goal would be to acquire English precisely because of its power as an instrument of international communication. I would be annoyed at the equivocation over English since it seemed to be unparalleled in the teaching of French, German, Russian or Chinese.[k]

I would be particularly annoyed at irrelevant emphasis on the different varieties of English when I came to realise they mattered so little to native speakers of English – to those who effortlessly read the novels of Saul Bellow, Iris Murdoch and Patrick White, perceiving no linguistic frontier to match the passports (American, British and Australian) of these writers. And when I came to realise that the best grammars and dictionaries similarly related to a Standard English that was freely current throughout the world.[l]

Indeed, the widespread approval of the Kingman Report confirms that the mass of ordinary native-English speakers have never lost their respect for Standard English, and it needs to be understood abroad too (cf. Hao, 1988; Yashiro, 1988) that Standard English is alive and well, its existence and its value alike clearly recognised. This needs to be understood in foreign capitals, by education ministries, and media authorities: and understood too by those from the U.K. and the U.S.A. who teach English abroad.

Of course, it is not easy to eradicate once-fashionable educational theories, but the effort is worthwhile for those of us who believe that the world needs an international language and that English is the best candidate at present on offer. Moreover, the need to make the effort is something for which we must bear a certain responsibility – and in which we have a certain interest.

References

Bokamba, E. G. (1982). The Africanization of English. In B. B. Kachru (ed.), *The other tongue: English across cultures* (pp. 77–98). Urbana, IL: University of Illinois Press.

Coleman, H. (1987). Is the "false beginner" a false concept? *The Language Teacher*, *11*(14), 11–17.

Coppieters, R. (1987). Competence differences between native and near-native speakers. *Language*, *63*, 544–573.

---

k Compare Heller, this volume.

l Quirk was himself the lead author in the huge, and hugely authoritative, *Comprehensive Grammar of the English Language* (with S. Greenbaum, G. Leech and J. Svartvik, Longman 1985).

Goldstein, L. M. (1987). Standard English: The only target for nonnative speakers of English? *TESOL Quarterly*, *21*, 417–436.

Hao, K. (1988). The view from China. *English Today*, *13*, 50–52.

Kachru, B. B. (ed.). (1982). *The other tongue: English across cultures*. Urbana, IL: University of Illinois Press.

Kachru, B. B. (1983). *The Indianization of English: The English language in India*. New York: Oxford University Press.

Kingman, J. (Chairman). (1988). *Report of the committee of inquiry into the teaching of English language* [The Kingman Report]. London: Her Majesty's Stationery Office.

Peñalosa, F. (1980). *Chicano sociolinguistics*. Cambridge, MA: Newbury House.

Pereira, J., and O'Reilly, E. (1988). *Four seasons composition book*. Kyoto: City Press.

Quirk, R. (1981). International communication and the concept of nuclear English. In L. E. Smith (ed.), *English for cross-cultural communication* (pp. 151–165). London: Macmillan.

Quirk, R. (1988). The question of standards in the international use of English. In P. H. Lowenberg (ed.), *Language spread and language policy*. Washington, DC: Georgetown University Press.

Yashiro, K. (1988). Sociolinguistic considerations for teaching English as an international language in Japan. *The Language Teacher*, *12*(4), 14–16.

Lord Professor Randolph Quirk was Professor of English Language and Literature at University College London, and founded the Survey of English Usage.

Chapter 8

Ben Rampton

1990

DISPLACING THE 'NATIVE SPEAKER'

Expertise, affiliation and inheritance[a]

Mystique and myth

> The whole mystique of the native speaker and the mother tongue should probably be quietly dropped from the linguist's set of professional myths about language.
>
> (Ferguson 1982: vii)

[. . .]

CHARLES FERGUSON [is] not alone in this observation, and dissatisfaction with the terms *native speaker* and *mother tongue* is now very widespread. At the same time, these terms seem to be very resilient, and efforts to modify them just end up testifying indirectly to their power. For example, a good deal of effort is now being made to show the independent legitimacy of Englishes worldwide (e.g. Kachru 1982), but when these are described as *the other tongue* or *nativized varieties*, the English of the ethnic Anglos is still there in the background as the central reference point. There is a need for new terms and this article suggests some.

The trouble with the native speaker

It is important first of all to be clear about what the problems actually are. Otherwise, alterations may be simply cosmetic. In an educational context, the idea of being the native speaker of a language and having it as your mother tongue tends to imply at least five things:

---

a From *ELT Journal* 44(2): 97–101. A fuller version appears in Rampton, B. (1995) *Crossing: Language and Ethnicity among Adolescents.* London: Longman: Chapter 13.

1   A particular language is inherited, either through genetic endowment or through birth into the social group stereotypically associated with it.
2   Inheriting a language means being able to speak it well.
3   People either are or are not native/mother-tongue speakers.
4   Being a native speaker involves the comprehensive grasp of a language.
5   Just as people are usually citizens of one country, people are native speakers of one mother tongue.

All these connotations are now strongly contested by many people. The capacity for language itself may be genetically endowed, but *particular* languages are acquired in social settings. It is sociolinguistically inaccurate to think of people belonging to only one social group, once and for all. People participate in many groups (the family, the peer group, and groups defined by class, region, age, ethnicity, gender, etc.): membership changes over time and so does language.[b] Being born into a group does not mean that you automatically speak its language well—many native speakers of English can't write or tell stories, while many non-native speakers can. Nobody's functional command is total: users of a language are more proficient in some areas than others. And most countries are multilingual: from an early age children normally encounter two or more languages. Yet despite the criticisms, the terms native speaker and mother tongue remain in circulation, continuously insinuating their assumptions.

There are always ideological issues involved in discussions about who speaks what in education, and political interests often have a stake in maintaining the use of these concepts. Thus the supremacy of the native speaker keeps the UK and the US at the centre of ELT (Naysmith 1986/7):[c] at the opposite end of the scale, governments may use the notion of mother tongue to imply that certain languages are of interest only to particular minority groups, thereby denying either a language or its speakers full involvement in mainstream education (Skutnabb-Kangas 1981). On its own, altering terminology does little to change this state of affairs, but by inserting or removing particular assumptions, alteration can clarify or usefully redirect our understanding.

As concepts, mother tongue and native speaker link together several ideas which it is vital to separate. Summarizing the problem with these concepts, we can say that:

1   They spuriously emphasize the biological at the expense of the social. Biological factors doubtless do count in language learning, but they never make themselves felt in a direct and absolute way. Their influence is only ever interpreted in social context, and so to a considerable extent, they are only as important as society chooses to make them.
2   They mix up language as an instrument of communication with language as a symbol of social identification (Weinreich 1953; Edwards 1977).

Recognition of the first difficulty helps to direct our search for alternative terms. Our selections must acknowledge the social nature of the processes which link

---

b See Sapir, this volume, for a critique of essentialist ideas about language, culture and race.
c Compare Quirk, Ngũgĩ and Mazrui, this volume.

people to particular languages. They must be able to connect productively with our wider understanding of society. With that requirement in mind, we can then begin to address the second difficulty.

Language expertise

When educationalists have the communicative aspects of language in mind, they should speak of accomplished users as *expert* rather than as *native* speakers. Expertise has the following advantages over nativeness as a metaphor for considering language proficiency:

1   Although they often do, experts do not have to feel close to what they know a lot about. Expertise is different from identification.
2   Expertise is learned, not fixed or innate.
3   Expertise is relative. One person's expert is another person's fool.
4   Expertise is partial. People can be expert in several fields, but they are never omniscient.
5   To achieve expertise, one goes through processes of certification, in which one is judged by other people. Their standards of assessment can be reviewed and disputed. There is also a healthy tradition of challenging 'experts'.

The notion of expertise overcomes at least some of the problems. It is also fairer to both learners and teachers. Firstly, if native-speaker competence is used to set targets and define proficiency, the learner is left playing a game in which the goal-posts are being perpetually moved by people they cannot often challenge. But if you talk about expertise, then you commit yourself to specifying much more closely the body of knowledge that students have to aim at. Learning and teaching become much more accountable. In addition, the notion of expert shifts the emphasis from 'who you are' to 'what you know', and this has to be a more just basis for the recruitment of teachers.

Expertise does not, however, cover the ways in which language can stand as a symbol of social group identification. This is a very important issue in education, and it is also strongly connoted in the terms native language and mother tongue. To emphasize that symbolic value, a term like *language loyalty* (or *language allegiance*) needs to be added alongside language expertise.

Language loyalty

Inheritance and affiliation

In fact, two aspects of language loyalty are worth distinguishing: *inheritance* and *affiliation*. It is particularly important to use a specific term to stake out the claims of the second (language affiliation) in order to make sure that the shadowy authority of notions like native language don't lead us to give pride of place to the first (inheritance).

Both affiliation *and* inheritance are negotiated. This is fairly self-evident with affiliation, which we commonly think of in terms of the social processes that it involves (requesting, applying, granting, agreeing, breaking off, etc.). But it is also true in the case of inheritance. Governments make laws about it; people try to decide what cultural and material items to include in their legacies; while others accept, claim, reject, and contest them. The crucial difference between them is that affiliation refers to a connection between people and groups that are considered to be separate or different, whereas inheritance is concerned with the continuity between people and groups who are felt to be closely linked. Inheritance occurs *within* social boundaries, while affiliation takes place *across* them.

Because both inheritance and affiliation are matters of social negotiation and conflict, the relationship between them is always flexible, subtle, and responsive to the wider context.[d] It would be very hard to assert definitively that X is a language of inheritance and Y is a language of affiliation—indeed in doing so, you would have to recognize that you were taking up a stance in social debate. People belong to many groups, feelings of group-belonging change, and so do the definitions of groups themselves. New but valued inheritances can emerge from powerful affiliations, while cherished inheritances can lose their value and be disowned. Wherever language inheritance is involved, there tends to be a sense of the permanent, ancient, or historic. It is important, however, to underline the fact that affiliation can involve a stronger sense of attachment, just as the bond between lovers may be more powerful than the link between parents and children.

Inheritance and affiliation compared with other terms

There are a great many terms other than mother tongue and native language which are used to describe the ties between speakers and languages. What is the particular value of thinking about language loyalty in terms of inheritance and affiliation? The value of these terms lies in the way they draw attention to language policy and language education as social activities in which efforts are made to manage continuity, change, and the relationship between social groups.

There are, of course, many definitions of languages in terms of when, where, and how much they are learnt and used—*first, second, primary, home, school*, etc. But these do not go to the heart of language allegiance: it is perfectly possible for someone to regard a language learned at age 35 in college as a part of his or her group inheritance. Other terms focus more directly on group relations—for example, *majority* and *minority* language, or *ethnic, national*, and *community* language. But, for the three reasons below, these terms are not as incisive or as generally applicable as the notions of language inheritance and language affiliation.

1   Whereas the terms mentioned can all be valuable concepts in *particular* settings, inheritance and affiliation point to aspects of loyalty that are relevant to *all* group situations, however they are defined (by family, class, gender, race, region, profession, etc.).

---

d In this volume, compare Hewitt, Back, Cutler, Bokhorst-Heng and Fishman.

2 There is a tendency to think only of inheritance when terms like ethnic or community language are used, and as a result speakers may get fixed in language categories.[e]

3 Affiliation and inheritance can be used to discuss the position of individuals as well as groups, and this is useful in discussion of education, which generally has to consider both.

Conclusion

Sociolinguistic situations are always very complicated, and it is important to have a number of ways of thinking about the links between people and language. For many purposes, the concepts *expertise, inheritance*, and *affiliation* will be inappropriate, and they obviously leave out certain issues that are relevant to language and inter-group relations (for example, as they stand, they don't treat linguistic enmity). Nevertheless, they help us to think about individual cases and about general situations more clearly than do the concepts *native speaker* and *mother tongue*. They tell us to inspect each 'native speaker's' credentials closely, and they insist that we do not assume that nationality and ethnicity are the same as language ability and language allegiance.[f] They also remind us to keep our eyes on social affairs. It is not hard to think of governments which talk about reward according to expertise ('equality of opportunity'), require smaller groups to relinquish their inheritances, but then only concede them affiliate status. The *native speaker* and the *mother tongue* clutter perception of these and other situations.

References

Edwards, J. R. (1977) 'Ethnic Identity and Bilingual Education', in H. Giles (ed.) *Language, Ethnicity and Intergroup Relations*. New York Academic Press.

Ferguson, C. 1982 'Foreword', in B. Kachru (ed.) *The Other Tongue: English Across Cultures*. Oxford: Pergamon. vii–xi.

Kachru, B. (ed.) (1982) *The Other Tongue: English Across Cultures*. Oxford: Pergamon.

Naysmith, J. H. (1986/7) 'English as Imperialism'. *Language Issues* 1/2: 3–5.

Skutnabb-Kangas, T. (1981) 'Guest Worker or Immigrant–Different Ways of Reproducing an Underclass'. *Journal of Multilingual and Multicultural Development* 2/2: 89–115.

Weinreich, U. (1953) *Languages in Contact*. The Hague: Mouton.

Ben Rampton is Professor in the School of Social Science and Public Policy at King's College, London.

---

e See Honeyford, this volume.

f See Sapir, this volume.

Nation-states and Minorities

Introduction

I N   P U B L I C   D I S C U S S I O N about ethnic minorities, the nation-state quite often stands in the background, treated as the essentially unproblematic, larger context that 'awkward' minorities need to come to terms with. To counteract this tendency, the first two extracts spotlight the linguistic, cultural and political processes involved in the assertion of dominant/majority nationalisms. Fishman discusses the way language and society are imagined and shaped in the development of nation-states, and Billig focuses on the routine maintenance of a sense of national identity in nation-states that are well-established. The next two extracts debate the status of linguistic minorities in state education systems – Honeyford argues against multicultural language education policy, while Rickford explains some of the reasons for giving official recognition to non-standard minority speech varieties. After that, three extracts reflect on the ways in which language and ethnic identity are conceptualised, perceived and represented – Bokhorst-Heng focuses on policy directives within a multilingual state, Hewitt theorises the processes of mixing and hybridisation that emerge through everyday experience in contemporary cities, and Hill describes covert racism in public discourse. The last two extracts address the strategies and processes involved in language revival and language maintenance in indigenous minority contexts – Urla describes the alternative to purist language politics articulated in low-cost community radio, and Heller addresses the way in which a minority language gets repositioned as the nation-state starts to lose its authority within a late modern global economy.

Between them, these extracts refer to France, Turkey, US, UK, Singapore, the Basque country and Canada. The focus of each can be summarised as follows:

- Joshua Fishman's extract, 'The impact of nationalism on language planning' (1972), looks at the cultural and political dynamics involved in the emergence of the modern nation-state, identifying three, often contradictory imperatives – 'unification', 'authentification', 'modernisation'. He discusses the relationship between government (broadly conceived) and the construction of nationhood, and looks at two concrete examples of the role that language policy plays in this relationship (France and Turkey).

- In the extract from his book, *Banal Nationalism* (1995), Michael Billig focuses on the ways in which people in well-established nation-states are continuously provided with low-key reminders of national identity. They hardly notice this, and tend to see 'hot nationalism' as something that happens elsewhere, but these banal, routine remindings keep the ground fertile for outbreaks of nationalist fervour. Billig discusses examples of this tendency in the US, and provides a case-study of how this low-level awareness of nationality is maintained in the discourse of the British press.

- Ray Honeyford's chapter on 'The language issue in multi-ethnic English schools' (1988) discusses multicultural education policy in England. He argues against the idea that there should be full bilingual education for pupils with South Asian language backgrounds, and articulates concern about the position of majority white children in ethnically mixed schools. Turning to the linguistic situation of children of African Caribbean descent, he stresses the importance of standard English, and criticises academic linguists for their relativism about creoles and other languages.

- John Rickford's essay, 'Suite for ebony and phonics' (1997) is a contribution to the fierce debate that followed the decision of the Oakland School Board (California, US) to recognise African American Vernacular English in its district schools. Rickford seeks to clarify the relationship between research and educational practice, and explains how academic linguists approach their object of study differently from most other people. He describes some of the linguistic rules which make Ebonics distinctive, and outlines three possible explanations of its origins, characterising them as Afrocentric, Eurocentric and Creolist.

- The article by Wendy Bokhorst-Heng, 'Singapore's *Speak Mandarin Campaign*: Language ideological debates and the imagining of a nation' (1999), provides a detailed case study of political efforts to standardise the language used by Chinese speakers in a linguistically diverse nation-state, where government has strong beliefs about the cultural significance of language and also assumes that ethnic sub-groups should be linguistically homogenous. Bokhorst-Heng looks at how political rhetoric seeks to reconcile ethnic subgroup homogeneity within an overarching national multiculturalism, and identifies key points of resistance.

- Roger Hewitt's article, 'Language, youth and the destabilisation of ethnicity' (1992), opens with a critique of ideas about unified ethnic cultures, and suggests that to do justice to the contemporary cultural processes of unequal, dialogical mixing and hybridisation, a term like 'polyculture' would be better than 'multicultural'. He discusses the findings of research on language in urban England showing how young people from notionally separate ethnic groups influence each other's language use, producing new forms of English. He also argues that sociolinguistic work needs to develop a deeper sense of the meaning of identity.

- What's accepted in private speech is often unacceptable in public, but the distinction between private and public is actually fluid, and in 'Mock Spanish, covert racism and the (leaky) boundary between public and private spheres' (1995), Jane H. Hill shows how public speech often carries 'light' elements, designed to make it seem more down-to-earth and democratic. Derogatory stereotypes, however, are often slipped in here, where any challenge can be dismissed as humourless political correctness. Hill describes these mechanisms at work in the racist exploitation of Spanish in white public discourse in the US.

- Jacqueline Urla's extract, 'Outlaw language: Creating alternative public spheres in Basque free radio' (1995), describes a form of minority language activism that is radically different from the primarily bourgeois language movements most commonly discussed. Instead of wanting to develop a unified literate standard language, low-tech, low-cost radio in the Basque country articulates a democratic, anti-authoritarian ethos in which youth express their solidarity with Basque/Euskera in mixed and irreverent speech.

- Monica Heller's article, 'Alternative ideologies of *la francophonie*' (1999), focuses on French-speakers in Ontario, Canada. Envisaging it as a shift from modernity to high modernity, she analyses the conflict between nationalist ideologies of authenticity and the commodification of French within global markets. At the same time, these global markets both encourage the standardisation of French as a language of international communication and give value to its local distinctiveness in the tourist and culture economies. Heller describes how the tensions between nationalist, multicultural, market and hip hop philosophies are played out in the dynamics of class and ethnicity in a French-language high school.

Chapter 9

Joshua Fishman

1972

THE IMPACT OF NATIONALISM ON LANGUAGE PLANNING[a]

[. . .]

IT IS THE PURPOSE of this chapter to indicate the major similarities and differences between earlier European manifestations of nationalism and its impact on European language planning.

Nationalism

Three broad emphases characterize the manifestations of modern mass nationalism in Europe since the days of the French Revolution and its Napoleonic aftermath:

Unification

Nationalism as an integrative movement seeks to go beyond the primordial ties to family and locality (which defined the affiliative horizon of the common man in predominantly pre-industrial and pre-urban times) and to forge wider bonds that can draw the rural, the urban, and the regional into a broader unity: the nationality. In its birth throes nationalism stresses the inherent unity of populations that have never been aware of such unity before. In its further development nationalism may stress uniformation rather than unification alone.

Authentification

Nationalism is uniqueness-oriented. The avowed rationale for the unification of hitherto particularistic and diverse subgroups and the manifest dynamism both for

---

a From J.A. Fishman (1972) *Language in Sociocultural Change*. California: Stanford University Press pp. 224–43.

the unificatory as well as for the purposive goals of nationalism are the ethnic uniqueness and cultural greatness of the nationality. This uniqueness, it is claimed, was, in the past, responsible for glorious attainments. If it can be recaptured in all of its authenticity, then, it is predicted, surely greatness will once again be achieved and, this time, permanently retained.

Modernization

Nationalism is a response to the problems and opportunities of modernity. Under the leadership of new proto-elites[1] [. . .] nationalism [. . .] links] the weight of unified numbers and the dynamism of convictions of uniqueness [to] the pursuit of organized cultural self-preservation, [to] the attainment of political independence, [to] the improvement of material circumstances, or [to] the attainment of whatever other purpose will enhance the position of the nationality in a world in which social change is markedly rapid and conflictive.

All three [of these] ingredients [. . .] are essential for differentiating between nationalism and other social movements.[2] Without recognizing the ingredient of broader unification, nationalism cannot be differentiated from millenial sectarianisms, which, though alienated from most of their contemporaries, nevertheless, stress uniqueness as a response to the corruptions of modern life. Without recognizing the stress on ethnic or indigenous uniqueness, nationalism cannot be differentiated from cross-national movements for political, economic, or cultural planning, including international socialism and various regional confederations. Without recognizing the stress on accepting and overcoming the obstacles of modernization, nationalism cannot be differentiated from nativistic and traditionalistic movements that seek a genuine return to the ways of the past rather than (as in the case of nationalism) a selective and purposive orientation thereto.[3]

Dialectic

It is quite apparent from the foregoing that there is a built-in dialectic within nationalism, a quite inevitable tension between its major components. Most obvious is the tension between the requirements of modernization and those of authentification. The one emphasizes the instrumental uniformities required by modern politico-operational integration[b] and is constantly straining toward newer, more rational, more efficient solutions to the problems of today and tomorrow. The other emphasizes the sentimental uniformities required by continuity based on socio-cultural integration and is constantly straining towards purer, more genuine expressions of the heritage of yesterday and of long ago.

A potential conflict also exists between the goal of authentification and that of unification since, in reality, pre-nationalist authenticity is highly localized. As a result, the supralocal authenticity sought by nationalism must, to a large extent, be elaborated and interpreted rather than merely returned to or discovered ready made. The more stress on real authenticity, therefore, the more danger

---

b Integration of political-operational institutions such as royal houses, government traditions, education systems etc. (see pp. 119ff.).

of regionalism and ultimate secessionism.[c] The more stress on unification/uniformation, the less genuine authentification.

Even unification/uniformation and modernization are frequently at odds with each other. Some modern goals might well be more fully or easily attained through the encouragement of diversity (e.g., relations with important neighboring sources of supply might well be improved if ethnic minorities speaking the same languages as those used in the sources of supply were encouraged to maintain their distinctiveness), while some pre-existing uniformities are actually weakened rather than strengthened by industrialization, urbanization, and other modernity tendencies (e.g., the weakening of religious bonds).

It is part and parcel of the essence of nationalism to incorporate these potentially conflicting themes in its basic ideology. Similarly, it is part and parcel of the essence of nationalism to engage the dialectic that is caused by the tension between these themes and to derive from this dialectic a constant procession of solutions to the problems engendered by its own ideological commitments. It is this dialectic between potentially conflicting elements that constantly recharges the dynamism of nationalist causes. Their business is always unfinished because none of the goals of nationalist ideology is ever fully attained or even substantially assured, not only because of possible outside opposition, but also because of the internal instability of any resolution between its own contending components.

Types of European nationalism

Modern European nationalisms were generally responses to the same co-occurrences that prompted other major mass modernization movements of the past two centuries (widespread dislocations and disorganization of recently urbanized populations brought on by the impact of industrialization, the appearance of proto-elites offering action-oriented solutions to mass problems related to social change, and the massification of political and cultural participation in response to the pressures exerted by both the masses and elites referred to). [Perhaps due to the similarity of their origins, . . .], nationalism proved to be combinable with all major co-occurring ideologies (*viz.*, democratic nationalism, socialist nationalism, facist nationalism, etc.), [but] it contributed a very special emphasis of its own: *its stress on the ethnic authenticity of the nationality*. This stress appears to have been recognized in two different (but interrelated) fashions throughout the course of the nineteenth century.

The state into nationality process

Nationality in the older and more firmly established European states was considered to be a by-product of the common political-operational institutions that had evolved in these states over the centuries. By the early nineteenth century, these states had already gone through lengthy and successive processes of expansion and unification,

---

c On mundane processes of both unification and 'supra-local authentification', see Billig in this collection.

which, on the one hand, had produced a rather widespread sentiment of common nationality among their urban upper and middle classes and which, on the other hand, made it easier for them to cope with the problems of continued social change. These were the so-called (and self-called) historic nations of Europe who could claim in the nineteenth century that their primary institutions (their royal houses, their governmental traditions, their educational systems, their well established commercial and industrial patterns, and, above all, their centuries of "shared experiences") had produced the unified and authentic nationalities that populated them. Common nationality, therefore, was a derivative, a by-product, of common institutions rather than anything that could exist prior to or without such institutions. The "historic nations" of Europe were, by consensus, England, France, Spain, Portugal, Holland, Denmark, and Sweden and, at least potentially, also the Russian, Austro-Hungarian, and Ottoman empires. The fact that these latter three were still digesting various ethnic groups was well recognized, but it was assumed not only that they would succeed in doing so but also that it was only natural and proper that they continue to do so. Had not England digested the Welsh, the Scots, and the Irish? Had not France digested the Bretons, the Normans, the Gascons, the Occitans; and Spain the Galicians, the Catalans, the Basques, and the like? The same process of unification and re-authentification on a broader base would doubtlessly occur in the still multiethnic empires as well, given time and the improvement of their primary institutions. This then became the target of nationalism in the "historic nations" of nineteenth century Europe: the institutional liberalization and modernization of the established states, for only such liberalization and modernization could alleviate the suffering of the masses, could further the unity of states, and could constructively harness the genius of nationalities that the common institutions had created. The nationalism of the "historic nations" of the early nineteenth century was, therefore, liberal nationalism. It was the nationalism of those who already had their own historically evolved and recognized states and state institutions. It was also the nationalism of the colonizers, for the "historic nations" of Europe were, simultaneously, the nations that held, and were to continue to seek, political and economic colonies, both close at hand as well as in new territories beyond the seas, in the Americas, in Asia, and in Africa. It was this supralocal brand of nationalism (with its stress on the integrative capacity of political-operational institutions [. . .]) that they exported willy-nilly to their far-flung outposts.

Nationality into state processes

The Napoleonic wars and the widespread but successful revolutions of 1830 and 1848 increased the awareness of European liberal intellectuals that there *were* apparently *some* nationalities who *were* [*nationalities*] even in the absence of states of their own. Could anyone deny that the Greeks, the Poles, the Germans, the Italians, the Hungarians, and the Irish were nationalities? Although they had no states of their own at the time, and, therefore, no integrating state institutions under their own control, they nevertheless once had had them, long ago; and these, it was believed, had left such an imprint on the life of the people that they had continued as nationalities, as "defeated historic nationalities" on the strength of their common past memories. [. . .]

Down to the very end of the nineteenth century and even into the twentieth, the intellectuals and spokesmen of the "historic nations" of the Atlantic coastline of Europe continued to argue, and then to plead, on behalf of the validity and the morality of the primacy of state-into-nationality process. Their efforts, however, were largely in vain because the very populations whom they sought to contain (and, in contrast, with whom they had termed themselves "historic nations") could not be contained.

The outmoded political-operational institutions of the multiethnic [Austro-Hungarian, Russian and Ottoman] empires in Central, Eastern, and Southern Europe could not begin to fashion sufficiently integrative sociocultural bonds to compensate for the severe dislocation of their ethnically variegated rural populations. [It was along ethnic lines that p]roto-elites, trained in Western Europe, incessantly appeared to organize the mass demand for material improvement and for popular participation [. . .]. In organizing, in activating, and in focusing the masses, the proto-elites proceeded not only to capitalize and elaborate upon widespread [. . .] integrative themes of prior stability, justice, glory, and independence but also to fashion from them a view of nationality that was particularly appropriate for their own needs.

Among the submerged peoples of Europe [— the Greeks, Poles, Germans, Italians etc. —], nationality was espoused as a primary, natural phenomenon, which, in turn, gave rise to the state as a secondary, instrumental by-product. Nationalities represented God-given demarcations or unities, and, as such, their uniqueness deserved to be prized, defended, liberated, and enhanced. These uniquenesses— and first and foremost among them, their respective vernaculars—were not only reflections of the limitless ingenuity and bounty of the Divine Force but also, each in its own right, directly responsible for the past period of greatness and glory that each submerged nationality had at one time experienced. The nationalist mission, therefore, was to recover or reconstruct the authentic uniqueness of the nationality (which had been contaminated by foreign models) and, thereby, to recover for the *present* as well as establish for the future the greatness that had existed in the *past*.

By means of this interpretation of nationality, the peoples of Central, Eastern, and Southern Europe sought to attain two goals. They did not want to be "peoples without histories" or even new nationalities; rather, they wanted to view themselves as continuations of old and once-illustrious traditions. However, neither they nor their leaders wanted to return to the past. Therefore, their slogan was "We must be —— and Europeans." The past was a key to the spirit of greatness, but, once unlocked, this spirit was to be used to overcome current hardships and to gain the good things of the world today. Thus, more recent European nationalism emphasized the ethnic uniqueness and authenticity of the nationality. Nationalities created states for their own protection and enhancement—for the recovery, cultivation, and enhancement of linguistic and cultural treasures. The nationality is primary and eternal. The state is derivative and unstable.[4]

Although their nationality-into-state view of nationalism contributed mightily to the trials and tribulations that destroyed the multiethnic empires of the Hapsburgs, the Czars, and the Sultans, it had but faint echoes throughout most of Africa and Asia. Between the two of them, however, the state-into-nationality processes and nationality-into-state processes reflect the two kinds of integrative bonds upon which all nations depend and which constantly reinforce each other, converge with each other, and give birth to each other. Just as the state-into-nationality nations stress(ed) their common sociocultural bonds, particularly in times of stress, so did (and do) the nationality-into-state nations stress politico-operational institutions as soon as they gain(ed) independence and face(d) the functional problems of modern nationhood.[5]

Two examples of language planning in Europe

[Defining it in relatively restrictive terms . . . , language planning involves the implementation of language policy decisions and the elaboration and codification of linguistic varieties, putting them] to newer and "higher" purposes than those to which they hitherto had normally been put.[6] [W]e [. . .] find ample illustrations of such planning in each of the two types of European nationalisms that we have reviewed.

In France

The classical example of language planning in the context of state-into-nationality processes is that of the French Academy. Founded in 1635—i.e., at a time well in advance of the major impact of industrialization and urbanization—the Academy, nevertheless, came after the political frontiers of France had long since approximated their current limits. Nevertheless, sociocultural integration was still far from attained at that time, as witnessed by the facts that in 1644 the ladies of Marseilles Society were unable to communicate with Mlle. de Scudéry in French; that in 1660 Racine had to use Spanish and Italian to make himself understood in Uzès; and that even as late as 1789 half of the population of the South did not understand French. The unparalleled literary creativity in French under the patronage of Louis XIV [1661–1715] could aim, at most, at a maximal audience of two million literates (out of a total estimated population of twenty million). However, actually, no more than two hundred thousand participated in the intellectual life of the country, and many of these considered Italian, Spanish, and Occitan far more fitting vehicles for cultured conversation, whereas for publications Latin, too, was a common rival. All in all, the French Academy assumed an unenviable task—and one much ridiculed throughout the centuries—when it presumed to codify French vocabulary, grammar, and spelling to perfect refined conversation and written usage.[7]

Several aspects of the Academy's approach show [that it was not aiming for modernization]. Far from seeking to provide technical [terms] for industrial, commercial, and other applied pursuits, the Academy steadfastly refused to be concerned with such "uncultured" and "unrefined" concerns. Instead of attempting to reach the masses with its products, the Academy studiously aimed its publications (at least for three centuries, if not longer) at those already learned in the French language. Finally, instead of appealing to anything essentially French in "spirit," in "genius," in "essence," or in "tradition," it defended its recommendations via appeals to such purportedly objective criteria as euphonia, clarity, and necessity (redundancy). More than two hundred years after its founding, when the Academy's continued lack of concern for the technical vocabulary of modernization had come to be accompanied by attacks on *anglomania* and the tendency to *angliciser*, the worst that was said about overly frequent English borrowings was that they were unnecessary rather than that they were un-French.

From the point of view of its members, the Academy was an institution—one of several—whose goal was to fashion and reinforce French nationality. The Academy existed prior to, and independently of, the French nationality. Indeed, French nationality was but a by-product of the work of the Academy and of similar institutions and, therefore, logically could not and morally should not be invoked to carry out the Academy's goals. A similar disinclination to appeal to nationalist authenticity mark[ed] the largely informal efforts on behalf of language planning in England and the much more formal efforts of the (Royal) Academy in Spain.

[In contrast to the state-into-nationality processes illustrated in France, i]n the nationality-into-state context, the links between the authenticity component of nationalism and language planning on the one hand, and the modernization-unification components of nationalism and language planning on the other hand, are much more prominent and much more conscious. As a result, institutions and guidelines for language planning come into being very early in the mobilization process and remain in the foreground at least until authenticity, modernization, and unification seem reasonably assured. Here we are dealing with more highly pressured situations in which language planning is of high priority not only because of ideological considerations but also because without it, the new elites can neither communicate with each other about specialized elitist concerns while remaining within the limits of authenticity, nor move the masses towards greater unification, authentification, and modernization.

In Turkey

The case of Turkish language planning[8] is justifiably well known for the speed and the thoroughness with which it pursued modernization. As part of its over-all post World War I program of seeking a *new* Turkish identity (in contrast with its old Ottoman-Islamic identity), governmentally sponsored language planning conscientiously and vigorously moved to attain script reform (Roman in place of Arabic script), to attain Europeanization of specialized nomenclatures (rather than the Arabic and Persian loan words hitherto used for learned or cultured purposes), and to attain vernacularization or simplification of vocabulary, grammar, and phraseology for everyday conversational use (discarding the little understood and ornate flourishes patterned on Arabic or Persian).

Obviously, Turkish language planning was a part of Atatürk's over-all program of modernization. No nationalist movement, however, can continue to push modernization without regard for authenticity. Thus the break with the holy Arabic script soon came to be defended on the ground that it was unsuited for the requirements of authentic Turkish [pronunciation]. Since even the prophet had clearly been an Arab before he was a Mohammedan, he could hardly dispute the desire of Turks to put the needs of their Turkish authenticity first. The vast Europeanization of Turkish technical vocabulary had to be rationalized on the basis of the Great Sun Language theory. On the basis of this authenticity-stressing theory, it was claimed that all European languages were initially derived from Turkish. In that case, all recent borrowings could be regarded as no more than reincorporations into the Turkish language of words or morphs that it had originally possessed but lost under the foreign impact of Arabic and Persian. Thus, the process of borrowing from European sources was ultimately not rationalized as a modernizing step, but, rather as an authenticating step! So, too, and even more clearly, was the vernacularization and simplification of non-technical Turkish. Here the language of the Anatolian peasant was held up as a model of purity and authenticity on the ground that it had been least contaminated by foreign influences and least corrupted by foreign fads.

Thus, on every front, decisions about language modernization in Turkey were finally rationalized and legitimatized through sentiments of authenticity and a way was found for these two components of nationalist ideology to reinforce common nationalist goals rather than to conflict with them or with each other. Such dialectic skill is by no means rare in the annals of language planning within highly nationalist contexts. On occasion, modernization may appear to have the upper hand and, on other occasions, authentification is stressed. In the longer run, however, what needs to be grasped is not so much the seesawing back-and-forth as the need to retain both components (actually all three components since uniformation, too, must not be lost); and what needs to be found is a *modus vivendi* between them. Many examples of arriving at resolutions to the contradictory pressures built into nationalist language planning are to be found in the Estonian, Czech, Ukrainian, Greek, Turkish, and other relatively recent European language-planning experiences. These examples deserve at least as much attention as do those drawn from more uncompromising periods in which one or another component of the "holy trinity"[d] was stressed. [. . .]

Notes

1   *Proto-elites*: the leadership of nationalist groups in their early and formative period, before they are fully and formally organized. *Elites*: the leadership of later, more organized periods in the history of nationalist movements.

2   Of the huge literature on (European) nationalism the major presentations which devote some attention to all three of these components are Deutsch (1966), Gellner (1964), and Znaniecki (1952). (*Editors:* In the present collection, Fishman's account of nationalism can be compared with the papers by Ngũgĩ and Bokhorst-Heng, as well as with the accounts of globalisation and imperialism in Heller and Mazrui.)

3   Nationalism shares with all of the foregoing the characteristic of being a protest movement related to social change and the dislocation resulting therefrom. It is illustrated by Despres (1967).

4   [See Jaszi (1929), Kolarz (1946), and Kahn (1950).]

d   That is, unification, authentification, modernization.

5   [See Zangwill (1917), Talmon (1965), Pflanze (1966), Rustow (1968), and Fishman et al. (1968)].
6   For a brief but enlightening introduction to language planning, given these very restrictions, see Ferguson et al. (1968). The basic references are Haugen (1966a and 1966b). (*Editors:* More recent treatments can be found in e.g. R. L. Cooper 1989 *Language Planning and Social Change* Cambridge: Cambridge University Press; and, at a very introductory level, in J. Holmes 2001 *Introduction to Sociolinguistics: 2nd Edition,* Part 2 London: Longman.
7   [See Robertson (1910), Brunot, Gache (1969)].
8   [See Heyd (1950, 1954)].

References

Bright, William, ed. 1966. *Sociolinguistics. Proceedings of the UCLA Sociolinguistics Conference, 1964.* Janua Linguarum, Series Major, 20. The Hague: Mouton.

Brunot, Ferdinand. 1924–53. *Histoire de la Langue Française des Origines à nos Jours.* 1–9 (in 14 pts.). Paris: A. Colin.

Despres, Leo A. 1967. *Cultural Pluralism and Nationalist Politics in British Guiana.* Chicago: Rand McNally.

Deutsch, Karl W. 1966. *Nationalism and Social Communication: An Inquiry into the Foundations of Nationality.* 2nd edn (revised tabular and bibliographic material). Cambridge, Mass.: MIT Press.

Ferguson, Charles A. 1968. Language development, in Fishman, Ferguson, and Das Gupta, 27–36.

Fishman, Joshua A.; Ferguson, Charles A.; and Das Gupta, Jyotirindra, eds. 1968. *Language Problems of Developing Nations.* New York: John Wiley and Sons.

Gache, Paul. 1969. Language française et langue issue de l'Angleterre. *Le Travailleur,* 39:15:1, 5.

Gellner, Ernest. 1964. *Thought and Change.* Chicago: University of Chicago Press.

Haugen, Einar. 1966a. *Language Conflict and Language Planning: The Case of Modern Norwegian.* Cambridge: Harvard University Press.

—— . 1966b. Linguistics and language planning, in Bright, 50–71.

Heyd, Uriel. 1950. *Foundations of Turkish Nationalism: The Life and Teachings of Ziya Gökalp.* London: Luzac and Harvill.

—— . 1954. *Language Reform in Modern Turkey.* Oriental Notes and Studies, 5. Jerusalem: Israel Oriental Society.

India. Ministry of Scientific Research and Cultural Affairs. 1963. *A Common Script for Indian Languages.* Delhi: Republic of India.

Jazsi, Oscar. 1929. *The Dissolution of the Habsburg Monarchy.* Chicago: University of Chicago Press.

Kahn, Robert A. 1950. *The Multinational Empire: Nationalism and National Reform in the Habsburg Monarchy, 1848–1918,* 2 vols. New York: Columbia University Press. (Also note his one vol. Abridgement, 1957. *The Habsburg Empire: A Study in Integration and Disintegration.* New York: Praeger.)

Kolarz, Walter. 1946. *Myths and Realities in Eastern Europe.* London: Lindsay Drummond.

Pflanze, Otto. 1966. Characteristics of nationalism in Europe, 1848–1871. *Review of Politics,* 28:129–43.

—— . 1958. *Reform of the Chinese Written Language.* Peking: Foreign Languages Press.

Robertson, D. Maclaren. 1910. *A History of the French Academy 1635 [1634]–1910.* New York: Dillingham.

Rustow, Dankwart. 1968. Language, modernization and nationhood, in Fishman, Ferguson, and Das Gupta, 87–106.

Talmon, J. L. 1965. *The Unique and the Universal*. London: Secker and Warburg.

Zangwill, Israel. 1917. *The Principle of Nationalities*. London: Watts.

Znaniecki, Florian. 1952. *Modern Nationalities*. Urbana: University of Illinois Press.

Joshua Fishman is Emeritus Professor at Yeshiva University in New York, and has written books such as *Bilingualism in the Barrio* (with R. L. Cooper and R. Ma) (New York: Yeshiva University, 1968) and *Reversing Language Shift* (Clevedon: Multilingual Matters, 1991). He is one of the founding figures in macro-sociolinguistics and the sociology of language.

Chapter 10

Michael Billig

1995

BANAL NATIONALISM[a]

[. . .]

ROLAND BARTHES CLAIMED that ideology speaks with "the Voice of Nature" (1977, p. 47). As others have pointed out, ideology comprises the habits of behaviour and belief which combine to make any social world appear to those, who inhabit it, as the natural world (Billig, 1991; Eagleton, 1991; Fairclough, 1992 [. . .]). By this reckoning, ideology operates to make people forget that their world has been historically constructed. Thus, nationalism is the ideology by which the world of nations has come to seem the natural world – as if there could not possibly be a world without nations. Ernest Gellner has written that, in today's world, "a man (sic) must have a nationality as he must have a nose and two ears" (1983, p. 6). It seems 'natural' to have such an identity. In the established nations, people do not generally forget their national identity. If asked 'who are you?', people may not respond by first giving their national identity (Zavalloni, 1993 [. . .]). Rarely, if asked which is their nationality, do they respond 'I've forgotten', although their answers may be not be quite straightforward [. . .]. National identity is not only something which is thought to be natural to possess, but also something natural to remember.

This remembering, nevertheless, involves a forgetting, or rather there is a complex dialectic of remembering and forgetting. As will be seen, this dialectic is important in the banal reproduction of nationalism in established nations. Over a hundred years ago, Ernest Renan claimed that forgetting was "a crucial element in the creation of nations" (1990, p. 11).[b] Every nation must have its history, its own collective memory. This remembering is simultaneously a collective forgetting: the nation, which celebrates its antiquity, forgets its historical recency. Moreover,

---

a Extracts from M. Billig (1995) *Banal Nationalism*. London: Sage pp. 37–40, 43–46, 55–59, 109–25.
b See Ashcroft on Renan, this volume.

nations forget the violence which brought them into existence, for, as Renan pointed out, national unity "is always effected by means of brutality" (p. 11).

Renan's insight is an important one: once a nation is established, it depends for its continued existence upon a collective amnesia. The dialectic, however, is more complex than Renan implied. Not only is the past forgotten, as it is ostensibly being recalled, but so there is a parallel forgetting of the present. As will be suggested, national identity in established nations is remembered because it is embedded in routines of life, which constantly remind, or 'flag', nationhood. However, these reminders, or 'flaggings', are so numerous and they are such a familiar part of the social environment, that they operate mindlessly, rather than mindfully (Langer, 1989). The remembering, not being experienced as remembering, is, in effect, forgotten. The national flag, hanging outside a public building or decorating a filling-station forecourt, illustrates this forgotten reminding. Thousands upon thousands of such flags each day hang limply in public places. These reminders of nationhood hardly register in the flow of daily attention, as citizens rush past on their daily business.

There is a double neglect. Renan implied that intellectuals are involved in the creation of amnesia. Historians creatively remember ideologically convenient facts of the past, while overlooking what is discomfiting. Today, social scientists frequently forget the national present. The banal episodes, in which nationhood is mindlessly and countlessly flagged, tend to be ignored by sociologists. They, too, have failed to notice the flag on the forecourt. Thus, Renan's insight can be expanded: historians might forget their nation's past, whilst social scientists can forget its present reproduction.

Th[is] . . . sociological forgetting is not fortuitous; nor is it to be blamed on the absent-mindedness of particular scholars. Instead, it fits an ideological pattern in which 'our' nationalism (that of established nations, including the United States of America) is forgotten: it ceases to appear as nationalism, disappearing into the 'natural' environment of 'societies'. At the same time, nationalism is defined as something dangerously emotional and irrational: it is conceived as a problem, or a condition, which is surplus to the world of nations. The irrationality of nationalism is projected on to 'others'.

Complex habits of thought naturalize, and thereby overlook, 'our' nationalism, whilst projecting nationalism, as an irrational whole, on to others. At the core of this intellectual amnesia lies a restricted concept of 'nationalism', which confines 'nationalism' to particular social movements rather than to nation-states. Only the passionately waved flags are conventionally considered to be exemplars of nationalism. Routine flags – the flags of 'our' environment – slip from the category of 'nationalism'. And having slipped through the categorical net, they get lost. [. . .]

Waved and unwaved flags

[. . .] The uncounted millions of flags which mark the homeland of the United States do not demand immediate, obedient attention. On their flagpoles by the street and stitched on to the uniforms of public officials, they are unwaved, unsaluted and unnoticed. These are mindless flags. Perhaps if all the unwaved flags which decorate the familiar environment were to be removed, they would suddenly be noticed, rather like the clock that stops ticking. If the reds and blues were changed into greens and oranges, there would be close, scandalized scrutiny, as well as criminal charges to follow.

One can ask what are all these unwaved flags doing, not just in the USA but around the world? In an obvious sense, they are providing banal reminders of nationhood: they are 'flagging' it unflaggingly. The reminding, involved in the routine business of flagging, is not a conscious activity; it differs from the collective remembering of a commemoration. The remembering is mindless, occurring as other activities are being consciously engaged in.

These routine flags are different from those that seem to call attention to themselves and their symbolic message. Belfast in Northern Ireland is divided into mutually suspicious Catholic and Protestant districts. In the former, the Irish tricolor is widely displayed as a gesture of defiance against British sovereignty. In the backstreets of Protestant neighbourhoods, the kerb-stones are often painted with the pattern of the Union Jack (Beattie, 1993). These are not mindless symbols, for each side is consciously displaying its position and distancing itself from its neighbour. The tricolors, in this respect, differ from those hanging on public buildings south of the border. One might predict that, as a nation-state becomes established in its sovereignty, and if it faces little internal challenge, then the symbols of nationhood, which might once have been consciously displayed, do not disappear from sight, but instead become absorbed into the environment of the established homeland. There is, then, a movement from symbolic mindfulness to mindlessness. [. . .]

Hot and banal nationalism

[. . .] The standard definitions of nationalism tend to locate nationalism as something beyond, or prior to, the established nation-state. In this respect, the social scientific definitions follow wider patterns of thinking. For example, Ronald Rogowski (1985) defines nationalism as "the striving" by members of nations "for territorial autonomy, unity and independence". He claims that this definition matches "everyday discourse", adding that "we routinely and properly speak of Welsh, Quebecquois and Arab nationalism" (pp. 88–9). [. . .] Rogowski is correct in stating that this is the way that 'nationalism' is used routinely – but whether more 'properly' is another matter. The definition, in concentrating on the striving for autonomy, unity and independence, ignores how these things are maintained once they have been achieved.[c] No alternative term is offered for the ideological complex, which maintains the autonomous nation-state.

Nationalism, thus, is typically seen as the force which creates nation-states or which threatens the stability of existing states. In the latter case, nationalism can take the guise of separatist movements or extreme fascistic ones. Nationalism can appear as a developmental stage, which mature societies (or nations) have outgrown once they are fully established. This assumption is to be found in Karl Deutsch's (1966)

---

c Compare the article by Fishman in this collection.

classic study *Nationalism and Social Communication*. More recently, it underlies Hroch's (1985) valuable study *Social Preconditions of National Revival in Europe*. Hroch postulates three stages of nationalism. The first two stages describe how interest in the national idea is awakened by intellectuals and, then, how it is diffused; and the final stage occurs when a mass movement seeks to translate the national idea into the nation-state. There are no further stages to describe what happens to nationalism once the nation-state is established. It is as if nationalism suddenly disappears.

Nationalism, however, does not entirely disappear, according to this view: it becomes something surplus to everyday life. It threatens the established state and its established routines, or it returns when those orderly routines have broken down. Ordinary life in the normal state (the sort of state which the analysts tend to inhabit) is assumed to be banal, unexciting politically and non-nationalist. Nationalism, by contrast, is extraordinary, politically charged and emotionally driven.

Anthony Giddens describes nationalism as "a phenomenon that is primarily psychological" (1985, p. 116 [. . .]). Nationalist sentiments rise up when the "sense of ontological security is put in jeopardy by the disruption of routines" (1985, p. 218). In these circumstances, "regressive forms of object-identification tend to occur", with the result that individuals invest great emotional energy in the symbols of nationhood and in the promise of strong leadership (p. 218). Nationalism, according to Giddens, occurs when ordinary life is disrupted: it is the exception, rather than the rule. Nationalist feelings "are not so much a part of regular day-to-day social life" (1985, p. 215), but "tend to be fairly remote from most of the activities of day-to-day social life". Ordinary life is affected by nationalist senti-ments only "in fairly unusual and often relatively transitory conditions" (p. 218). Thus, the psychology of nationalism is that of an extraordinary, emotional mood striking at extraordinary times. Banal routines, far from being bearers of nation-alism, are barriers against nationalism.

Analysts, such as Giddens, are reserving the term 'nationalism' for outbreaks of 'hot' nationalist passion, which arise in times of social disruption and which are reflected in extreme social movements. In so doing, they are pointing to a recog-nizable phenomenon – indeed, one which is all too familiar in the contemporary world. The problem is not what such theories describe as nationalist, but what they omit. If the term 'nationalism' is applied only to forceful social movements, some-thing slips from theoretical awareness. It is as if the flags on those filling-station forecourts do not exist. [. . .]

Certainly, each nation has its national days, which disrupt the normal routines. There are independence day parades, thanksgiving days and coronations, when a nation's citizenry commemorates, or jointly remembers, itself and its history [. . .]. It could be argued that these occasions are sufficient to flag nationhood, so that it is remembered during the rest of the year, when the banal routines of private life predominate. Certainly, great national days are often experienced as being 'memorable'. The participants are aware that the day of celebration, on which the nation is collectively remembered, is itself a moment which is to be remembered (Billig, 1990; Billig and Edwards, 1994). Afterwards, individuals and families will have their stories to tell about what they did on the day the prince and princess married, or the queen was crowned (Billig, 1992). [. . .]

The great days of national celebration are patterned so that the national flag can be consciously waved both metaphorically and literally. However, these are by no means the only social forms which sustain what is loosely called national identity. In between times, citizens of the state still remain citizens and the state does not wither away. The privately waved flags may be wrapped up and put back in the attic, ready for next year's independence day, but that is not the end of flagging. All over the world, nations display their flags, day after day. Unlike the flags on the great days, these flags are largely unwaved, unsaluted, unnoticed. Indeed, it seems strange to suppose that occasional events, bracketed off from ordinary life, are sufficient to sustain a continuingly remembered national identity. It would seem more likely that the identity is part of a more banal way of life in the nation-state. [. . .]

Our patriotism – their nationalism

[. . . S]ome social scientists insist that patriotism and nationalism represent two very different states of mind. The distinction would be convincing if there were clear, unambiguous criteria, beyond an ideological requirement to distinguish 'us' from 'them'. Walker Connor, one of today's leading specialists on nationalism, claims that nationalism and patriotism "should not be confused through the careless use of language" (1993, p. 376 [. . .]). According to Connor, nationalism is an irrational, primordial force, "an emotional attachment to one's people" (1993, p. 374). Nationalists often appeal to 'blood ties', in order to tap into these irrational forces. Nationalism, argues Connor, arises in ethnic groups, which claim common origins of blood. Connor cites the rhetoric of Hitler, Bismark and Mao to illustrate the dangerously irrational force of such appeals. Because nationalism is based upon a sense of the nation's ethnic unity, the national loyalties of 'immigrant' nations should not be described as 'nationalist': "I wish to make it clear that my comments do not refer . . . to immigrant societies such as those within Australia, the United States and non-Quebec Canada" (1993, p. 374).

If the loyalties, engendered in the United States, are not properly called nationalist, then they should be called 'patriotic'. Connor writes of his school days in the United States, when he and fellow pupils were taught to sing 'America' and to think of Washington and Jefferson as the founders of the nation. The United States might have adopted some of the ideas of 'nationalism', but still this was not nationalism proper. It did not possess the emotional depth and irrational force of nationalism. Politically, this puts patriotism at a disadvantage, when competing with the (alien) forces of nationalism:

> Despite the many advantages that the state has for politically socializing its citizens in patriotic values, patriotism – as evident from the multitude of separatist movements pockmarking the globe – cannot muster the level of emotional commitment that nationalism can.
>
> (Connor, 1993, p. 387)

The rhetoric tells its story. American loyalties, inculcated in school, are constructed as being 'patriotic'; they do not constitute a problematic irruption of the irrational psyche, unlike nationalism, which provokes "countless fanatical sacrifices" (1993, p. 385). The words 'fanatical', 'irrational', 'instinct' attach themselves to 'nationalism' in Connor's text. 'Patriotic values' (the term has a comforting rhetoric) are threatened by the nationalist movements, which 'pockmark the globe' (and, here, the rhetoric of disfigurement is used). 'Their' emotional bonds, so different from 'ours', are the problem and the threat.

The language is psychological, yet there is no direct psychological evidence to distinguish the rational state of patriotism from the irrational force of nationalism (see also the arguments of Eller and Coughlan, 1993). The evidence lies in the social events themselves: mass movements of nationalism are deemed irrational. The analysis, with its dire warnings, soothingly reassures. So much can be forgotten, as 'we' recall 'their' nationalism with horror. The wars waged by US troops; the bombings in Vietnam and Iraq; the bombast of successive US presidents; and the endless display of the revered flag: all these are removed from the problems of over-heated nationalism. If required, they can be transmuted into the warm glow of patriotism, the healthy necessity rather than the dangerous surplus. [. . .]

The claim that nationalism and patriotism are psychologically distinct needs to be backed by evidence about different states of mind or underlying motivations. Often the force of the claim is stronger than the empirical data cited in support. Kosterman and Feshbach (1989) claim to have found empirical evidence that patriotic attitudes about one's own country are unrelated to negative attitudes about foreign nations. Their claims and their evidence are worth examining: they reveal, not so much an objective difference between nationalism and patriotism, but the readiness to claim such a difference.

Kosterman and Feshbach gave samples of US residents questionnaires, asking them about their views of America. Having factor-analysed the replies, Kosterman and Feshbach argued that patriotism and nationalism formed separate dimensions, which can be assessed by independent scales. The patriotic scale included items such as 'I love my country' or 'When I see the American flag flying, I feel great.' The nationalist items compared America with other countries (i.e. 'generally, the more influence America has on other nations, the better off they are'). The mean scores of the patriotism scale were generally high (significantly higher than the nationalist scale), indicating that the patriotic statements about being emotionally committed to America attracted general assent. Despite Kosterman and Feshbach's claims about the independence of the patriotism and nationalism scales, the data, in fact, showed the two scales to be significantly correlated (1989, Table VII, p. 268). Also both scales correlated with other variables in similar ways: for example, on both scales Republican supporters scored more highly than Democratic supporters (Table X, p. 270).

Kosterman and Feshbach draw wide-ranging conclusions from their data. They claim that their results supported "a sharp discrimination between nationalism and patriotism" (p. 273). They warn against nationalism: "one cannot help but be concerned" by nationalism, which encourages "belligerent actions". By contrast, patriotism is valuable because it is as "important to the well-being of a nation as high self-esteem is to the well-being of an individual"; patriotism, far from causing wars, may actually be a means "of *reducing* international belligerence" (p. 273, emphasis in original). This conclusion comes after evidence that those with higher nationalist scores tend to have higher patriotic scores. Thus, the sentiments, which supposedly reduce international belligerence, tend to accompany those which promote it, despite the protestation that the two should be sharply distinguished. It would seem that something other than the empirical results was pushing the authors to their praise of patriotism and their criticism of nationalism.

Underlying such arguments is the assumption that hatred of the outgroup (rather than love of the ingroup) provides the motivation for nationalist warfare. This is almost certainly an oversimplification. In an important analysis, Jean Bethke Elshtain (1993) argues that, in the past century, young men have gone to war in their millions motivated not primarily by hatred of the enemy, but by a 'will-to-sacrifice'. The willingness to die in the cause of the homeland precedes a motive to kill. The elements of this will-to-sacrifice in the cause of the nation are upper-most in the items on the 'patriotism scale': the love of the flag, the 'great pride in that land that is our America', the importance 'for me to serve my country' and so on. As Kosterman and Feshbach's study shows, such sentiments are widely held in the United States by men and women. Arguably, these shared sentiments provide the background for nationally united responses, should some other nation appear to threaten the pride, politics or economics of 'our' great America.

This is the context for those doubly forgotten flags. Contrary to what respondents claimed in response to the questionnaire item, they do not feel great whenever they see the American flag flying. They see it far too often to feel that way each time. They see it too frequently even to notice that they are seeing it. Those flags, together with other routine signs of nationhood, act as unmindful reminders, preventing the danger of collective amnesia. The citizens, however, do not forget their appropriate responses, when the social occasions demand: they know to declare that the flag gives them a great feeling. All the while, the forgetting is doubled. Social scientists have probed the most intimate parts of modern life. They have calculated the number of sexual fantasies the average adult American is likely to have per day. But a census of flags has not been undertaken. No one asks how many stars and stripes the average American is likely to encounter in the course of the day. Nor what is the effect of all this flagging. [. . .]

The Day Survey

[. . . B]anal flaggings of nationhood are neither unusual, nor confined to politics. If nationalism is banally enhabited, then such flaggings should be continually made in the media, not just when the words of politicians are repeated.

To demonstrate this systematically, it would be necessary to sample the various forms of mass media and mass culture over a lengthy period in a number of countries. Of particular interest would be the quotient of flagging on 'ordinary' days, which are not days of national celebration or intense electoral campaigning. In lieu of such systematic evidence, an illustrative Day Survey is offered here. This looks at flagging in one country, in one medium, on one day: British national newspapers on 28 June 1993.

No times – indeed no places – can be called wholly 'ordinary'. Throughout the United Kingdom during the early 1990s, the issue of national identity was very much a political issue. John Major's Conservative government was continuing Margaret Thatcher's mixture of free market economics and popular, national authoritarianism (see Hall, 1988 [. . .]; Jessop et al., 1988, for analyses of Thatcherism). Quite apart from the continuing conflict in Northern Ireland, and the steady political support for the separatist Scottish Nationalist Party, Britain's uneasy relations with the European Community were dividing the Conservatives. To appease the anti-European wing, Major [. . .] frequently played the patriotic card, but with little effect on the wider audience. During 1993 and the following year, opinion polls showed the British government's popularity, and the personal standing of its leader, slumping to record lows. On the other hand, there is some suggestive evidence that the patriotic card – in the form of scares about immigrants and 'others' from Europe – might have helped the Conservatives to secure their fourth successive General Election victory in 1992 (Billig and Golding 1992 [. . .]). In a general sense, a number of issues concerning sovereignty were current within the British political context of June 1993.

Historically, Britain has the second highest newspaper readership in the world (Bairstow, 1985). According to the British National Attitudes Survey, roughly two-thirds of the population read a newspaper at least three times a week, although this has been declining [. . .]. As in other countries, newspapers are a main source of news for significant numbers of the population [. . .]. The morning press is basically national, although the evening papers are local. The ten major daily, national newspapers were chosen for this survey. They are conventionally divided into three market groups: the 'sensational tabloids' – *Daily Star, Daily Mirror* and *Sun*, aimed principally at working-class readers; the 'respectable' tabloids – *Daily Mail, Daily Express* and *Today*; and the 'heavies' or broadsheets – *The Times, Guardian, Daily Telegraph* and *Independent*, addressed at a middle-class audience.

The terms 'tabloid' and 'broadsheet' refer to more than the size of the newspaper's page: they refer to the paper's own sense of its readership. The distinction between tabloid and broadsheet is not a political one, for it cuts across editorial commitments. Politically, the *Mirror* has a tradition of supporting the Labour Party. *Today*, the *Guardian*, and the *Independent* can also be described as left-of-centre. The rest, which constitute the majority both in terms of the number of papers and in terms of readership, support the Conservative Party. Ownership cuts across the tabloid/broadsheet distinction. Rupert Murdoch's News International owns the tabloid *Sun* and *Today*, together with *The Times*. [. . .]

Choosing a day for the survey was always going to be somewhat arbitrary. The day had to be selected in advance to avoid electoral campaigns and planned national celebrations. I chose Monday 28 June 1993 for the Day Survey, fixing on that day a week in advance. No general election, international summit or royal birth was in the offing. I could not predict the topics for the major headlines of that day: whether they would report a political speech, savage crime or royal scandal. Otherwise, there was no particular justification for choosing that date, as compared with others, except, most importantly, that it was convenient for me.

Flagging the daily news

In the event, the main news story of the day was presented as a sudden, unforeseen event, although, taken over time, it was an event which fitted a predictable, long-established pattern. All but two of the newspapers led their front pages with the bombing of Baghdad by American war-planes, acting on the orders of President Clinton. The *Star* featured a story about pop fans wilting in the heat of an open air concert in London. The *Sun*, on the morning after the Baghdad raid, used its banner headlines to announce: 'Rock Star's Mum of 70 Has a Toyboy, 29'. The US bombing made an appearance on the fourth page of the *Sun*, following bare-chested young women who, as is customary, could be viewed on page three [. . .].

The bombing of Baghdad was a story which flagged nationhood in a direct manner. At first sight, however, some of the headlines seemed to suggest the story of a personal quarrel between Presidents Clinton and Hussein. *The Times* declared: "Clinton warns Saddam: don't try to hit us back". The *Star* had a similar headline: "Fight back and we smash you, warns Clinton". Its first sentence declared: "President Clinton last night threatened to 'finish off' evil Saddam Hussein", thereby indicating the quarrel to be one between good and bad, and signalling its own stance [. . .]. The individuals, nevertheless, are not mere individuals, for they personify nations. The pronominal plural is in evidence: 'we' smash you; don't hit 'us' back. The deixis[d] of reported speech was being used: the national 'us' is not that of the paper and its readers but that of the quoted Clinton [. . .]. The *Star* completed its opening sentence by locating the individual actors in a world of nations: Saddam Hussein will be finished off "if the Iraqi despot dares a revenge attack for America's missile attack on Baghdad". The attack was not merely Clinton's: it was America's. The target was not merely Baghdad or Hussein: it was Iraq, a nation: "Clinton acclaims Iraqi strike", headlined the *Independent*. The civilian casualties were unfortunate by-products of this attack on a nation: "Six dead as missiles miss Iraqi target" subheadlined the *Guardian*.

America and Iraq may have been the main characters, but the papers depicted a chorus of nations reacting to the episode. Typically, nations and their governments were presented as single actors, often metonymically represented by the capital city. "Britain, Russia and other American allies expressed firm support", stated *The Times*. "French reaction struck an equivocal note", declared the *Independent*, "Paris said it understood the reasons for the strike . . .". The style was conventional. There was

---

d Making sense of an utterance involves more than just comprehending the words and grammar – we also need to have an idea of who's speaking to whom, when and where. 'Deixis' and 'deictic' are terms that linguists use to cover the way in which linguistic meaning relies on our interpretation of the situation and moment when a text (or utterance) is produced. Words like 'I/you', 'this/that', 'now/then' and 'here/there' are obvious examples of deictic language – with any particular utterance, you obviously need to know who's speaking to work out who 'I', for example, refers to. But as Billig goes on to argue, deixis is much more pervasive than this: whenever we make sense of a piece of discourse, we're working with some idea of a context around it. For a brief introductory account of deixis and related issues, see Hanks, W. (2001) 'Indexicality' in A. Duranti (ed.) *Key Terms in Language and Culture*. Oxford: Blackwell pp. 119–21. For another analysis in this collection of what 'we' can mean in public discourse, see the article by Bokhorst-Heng.

much talk about what 'Washington' and other capital places were saying and doing. The semantic conventions depict a world of national actors, in which nations, courtesy of their governmental leaders, speak and act. [. . .]

The papers, in covering the story of the attack, gave particular prominence to British dimensions. Papers supporting the British government conveyed an image of Britain at the head of the international chorus: "John Major led international support for the raid", wrote the *Daily Mail*, perennially loyal to the Conservative Party. One particular British angle was accorded special attention: the plight of three British citizens imprisoned in Iraq. *The Times*, on its front page, headlined this story "Hopes for prisoners dashed". *Today*, which editorially was critical of the raid, led with the story. "What hope for them now" was its headline, with "Families of jailed Brits slam Iraq raid" as the subheading. The opening paragraph stated that the "Families of Britons imprisoned by Saddam Hussein say their men have been condemned to more years in jail by the US attack on Iraq." Again, there is a mixture of personal and national actors: Saddam Hussein and the United States. But there is more. The story implies a national audience. This audience is assumed to be British, hoping for the release of fellow Britons. Moreover, this audience is also presented simultaneously as if it were a 'universal audience' (Perelman, 1979 [. . .]). The 'hopes' of the headlines are not attributed to any particular persons: they are not even 'our hopes'. They are disembodied, universal hopes, which all of 'us' – all reasonable readers – are invited to share with the paper. These (reasonable) hopes are for the future of three British men, not for the injured citizenry of Baghdad.

Perhaps it is hardly surprising that the news of the world's most powerful nation bombing the capital city of another nation should capture such attention. Nor is it surprising that the news should be presented in a framework of nationhood. If nationhood were only flagged in this particular story, then the Day Survey would have provided poor evidence for the thesis of banal nationalism. However, the headline flagging of nationhood was by no means confined to the Baghdad bombing. All papers on that day carried other stories, whose headlines or first lines outwardly flagged Britishness: "Britain got a triple dose of good news yesterday" (*Sun*); "Britain basked in 79° temperatures yesterday" (*Sun*); "Britain's highest bungee jump" (*Star*); "Britain's latest cult heroes" (*Today*); "Brits in passport scam" (*Today*); "Is the British teenager dead or just resting a lot?" (*Today*); "A new eating fad is about to hit Britain" (*Mirror*); "Britain's Best Cartoons" (*Mirror*); "British Scrabble champion" (*Mail*); "the Blue-Print for Britain" (*Express*); "Britain's super-saviours" (*Express*); "Billions spent 'needlessly' by Britain on Black Wednesday" (*Guardian*); "worst places in Britain to be without a job" (*Guardian*); Concorde and "the British Aerospace industry" (*Independent*); "Britain's first gene transplant" (*Telegraph*); "Britain's timekeepers" and "the last minute of Wednesday, June 30" (*Telegraph*); "Martin Hoyle on a new British voice" (*Times*); and lastly, and least snappily, there was "Britain's most successful and widely publicised community-led urban renewal project" (*Times*). [. . .]

[T]he eye of the reader, whether of tabloid or quality paper, will have seen 'Britain' draped around a variety of [. . .] stories on [the 28th of June]. Some of the headlines and opening sentences may have caught the attention, but this attention will, as likely as not, have been only momentary, before becoming lost in the collective forgetfulness which accompanies each daily presentation of news. [. . .] The memory of specific items is not what matters. Beyond, the specifics lies a pattern, or what Stuart Hall (1975) called a "context of awareness". The frequency of nations being mentioned suggests that, in the context of awareness, flagging plays an important part.

Newspapers and the deictics of homeland-making

The context of awareness employs a complex deixis of 'here' and 'now'. The 'now' is to be routinely understood as the 'now' of up-to-date news. The 'here' is more complex. The papers, like the television, are giving 'us' today's news from the world. Baghdad, Washington, Paris are 'here' on the page. But where are 'we', the receivers, and where are 'we', the writers? Routinely, newspapers, like politicians, claim to stand in the eye of the country. Particularly in their opinion and editorial columns, they use the nationalized syntax of hegemony, simultaneously speaking to and for the nation, and representing the nation in both senses of 'representation'. They evoke a national 'we', which includes the 'we' of reader and writer, as well as the 'we' of the universal audience [. . .].[e]

The *Sun*, in its editorial, complained that the European Community had taken "our money". 'Our' did not refer to the finances of the paper, nor to the vast resources of its proprietor. It was to be read as 'us' the nation. *Today*'s regular columnist ended his piece with a ringing declaration: "Time we changed Government. Certainly time we changed Prime Minister." The 'we' was not the 'we' of writer and *Today* readers; nor was it the 'we' of the proprietor which *Today* shares with the *Sun*. Nor was it the 'we' of the whole world. A national 'we' was being invoked, comprising the 'reasonable people' of the nation, who were being represented as the whole nation. This 'we' included non-readers of the paper, whilst the readers were being addressed as nationals.

Lest it be thought that the national 'we', with its presumed internal identity of identities, represents a style of journalism, which is confined to the popular press, the same address is used in the 'serious' papers – on their most serious of pages. The *Daily Telegraph*, in its Business News, headlined an article: "Why our taxes need never rise again". [. . .]

Roger Fowler (1991), in his book *Language in the News*, has suggested that deixis does not occur commonly in newspapers, as compared with ordinary conversation. That might be true if deixis is identified overtly with the use of words like 'this', 'here' and 'us'. Editorial writers, feature-columnists and even reporters on the business pages may, from time to time, address the readers as a national 'us'. But in the news sections, 'we' are not evoked so often. Nevertheless, there are other routine forms of deixis, especially the deixis of homeland-making, which presents *the* national home as the context of utterance. *The* nation becomes *the* place, as the centre of the universe contracts to the national borders. Three examples

---

e See also Bokhorst-Heng's discussion in this volume of how 'we' is used in political speeches.

of homeland-making deixis can be given: the nation, the weather and the home news. Detailed analysis would doubtless reveal many other instances.[f]

The nation

Examples from the Day Survey suggest that the phrase 'the nation' is commonly used by journalists, as well as politicians (see also Achard, 1993). The *Mail* wrote about "one of the nation's most wanted men"; a British tennis player was "the centre of the nation's sporting focus". The *Express* discussed medium-sized companies which "contribute nearly £4 billion to the nation's wealth". The *Guardian* cited a politician referring to "the nation's interest and love of music". *Today*, using a quoted deixis, reported that "a group of backbenchers are set to tear apart defence policies claiming the Prime Minister is risking the nation's security". Britain is *the* nation; and, in the last example and elsewhere, the British Prime Minister is *the* Prime Minister.

Readers, unless informed to the contrary by headline or first paragraph, can usually assume that a story is being set in the homeland. *The Times* had a special 'focus' on the nuclear industry. The items referred to the British nuclear industry, except when they contained specific markers of foreignness. The unqualified definite article could be used to indicate the homeland: "*the* industry wants *the* government to think long-term, looking to energy needs in the 21st century" (emphases added). The stories in the *Telegraph*'s Business News likewise indicated a British scene, unless otherwise specified: "Unemployment is on course to fall further as key regions . . .": 'key regions' were to be understood as regions within Britain. By contrast a foreign scene was specified, particularly in the first sentence: "Two American software entrepreneurs . . ."; "A £500 m offer of shares in French pharmaceuticals company Roussel-Uclaf . . .". In these cases, 'we' know immediately that 'we' are not 'here', in 'this', 'our' country. Otherwise, 'we' can relax at home.

The weather

The weather can often be a topic of news in the press. On the day of the survey, the *Star* led with a 'sizzling-heat' story about hundreds of fans collapsing at a pop concert. The opening paragraphs provided no geographic location. Without the setting being specified, readers could assume correctly that the drama had occurred 'here', in Britain. Hot weather abroad would not have been newsworthy.

The very notion of 'the weather' implies a national deixis, which is routinely repeated. The papers regularly carry small, unobtrusive weather reports, typically labelled 'Weather'. The *Mirror* has 'Today's Weather' and the *Sun*, with obscure individuality, puts its weather information beneath the sign 'Newsdesk'. The reports tend to be similar. They contain a map of Britain, which is not actually labelled as Britain: the shape of the national geography is presumed to be recognizable. The *Telegraph*, *Guardian*, *Independent* and *The Times* have a longer report, accompanied

---

f Fowler's 1991 book is a useful introduction to the analysis of ideology in news and media discourse. On 'critical discourse analysis' more generally, see e.g. N. Fairclough (1989) *Language and Power*. London: Longman.

by a further map showing Europe and the north Atlantic. In these maps, the British Isles happen to be placed in a central location. [. . .]

A homeland-making move transforms meteorology into *the* weather. And *the* weather – with its 'other places', its 'elsewheres' and its 'around the country's – must be understood to have its deictic centre within the homeland. 'The weather' appears as an objective, physical category, yet it is contained within national boundaries. At the same time, it is known that the universe of weather is larger than the nation. There is 'abroad'; there is 'around the world'. These are elsewheres beyond 'our' elsewheres. The national homeland is set deictically in the central place, syntactically replicating the maps of the North Atlantic. All this is reproduced in the newspapers; and all this, in its small way, helps to reproduce the homeland as the place in which 'we' are at home, 'here' at the habitual centre of 'our' daily universe.

The home news

The deixis of homeland-making is not confined to the little words, such as 'the', 'this' or 'us'. There is a further element built into the organization of many newspapers, especially the broadsheets. It is a truism that, in the British press, national news predominates over international items. Fowler refers to the 'homocentrism' of the press, which is "a preoccupation with countries, societies and individuals perceived to be like oneself" (1991, p. 16). An international story, such as the bombing of Baghdad, can force its way on to the front pages of most papers, but even so, the British angle is not to be denied. The *Sun* resisted the pressure of international crises. The 'Rock star' and his 'mum', who dominated its headlines, were both British: the 'toyboy', adding spice to the story, was Spanish, and a 'jobless waiter' to boot. The *Star*'s weather story was set in Britain. The *Guardian* writer Martin Kettle wrote several days later about "the old Fleet Street slide rule for the news value of death and disaster stories – six Brits, 60 Frogs,[g] 600 more remote aliens" (*Guardian*, 17 July 1993). He was, of course, writing about Fleet Street and British journalism, criticizing 'our' biased interest in 'ourselves'. [. . .]

The *Express*, in common with most tabloids, mixes foreign and domestic items on its news pages, with domestic stories generally outnumbering the foreign ones. By contrast, the broadsheets, on their inside pages, separate foreign from domestic news, reserving different pages for each. At the top of each page is a signpost informing readers where they are. *The Times* signposts 'Home News' and 'Overseas News'; the *Telegraph* uses 'News' and 'Foreign News', as if all news is homeland news, unless otherwise specified; the *Independent* distinguishes between 'Home', 'Europe' and 'International', whilst the *Guardian* has a similar tri-partite division into 'Home News', 'European News' and 'International News'. Thus, all the broadsheets, whatever their politics, maintain a principle of news *apartheid*, keeping 'home' news and foreign news paginally separate. All, except the *Telegraph*, use the term 'home' to signpost events taking place within the national boundaries. [. . .]

---

g A mildly derogatory term for French people, used in Britain.

The broadsheets habitually organize their news so that nationhood operates, to use Hall's phrase, as a context for awareness. [. . .] The signposts are not merely page headings. 'Home' indicates more than the contents of the particular page: it flags the home of the newspaper and of the assumed, addressed readers. Daily, we, the regular readers, flick our eyes over the directing signs. Without conscious awareness, we find our way around the familiar territory of our newspaper. As we do so, we are habitually at home in a textual structure, which uses the homeland's national boundaries, dividing the world into 'homeland' and 'foreign', *Heimat* and *Ausland*. Thus, we readers, find ourselves at home in the homeland and in a world of homelands.

Masculine arms waving the flags of sport

Through the routine deictics of homeland-making, the press may flag nationhood across its pages. This does not mean, however, that those flags are waved. Some right-wing papers, like the *Mail*, *Express*, *Sun* and *Telegraph*, are known for supporting the right-wing players of patriotic cards, at least in British politics. Nevertheless, all the papers, whatever their politics, have a section in which the flag is waved with regular enthusiasm. This is the sports section. These sections are aimed at men. As Sparks and Campbell have written, "the reader inscribed in the sports pages is overwhelmingly masculine" (1987, p. 462). [. . .]

Sport may have its own separate ghetto in the newspapers, but sport is never merely sport, as C.L.R. James, the profoundest analyst of the subject, repeatedly stressed. [. . .] Modern sport has a social and political significance, extending through the media beyond the player and the spectator. James observed of [cricket], which he loved and dissected intellectually, that "far more people scan the cricket news in the morning paper" than read books (1989, p. xi). Not least of this significance is that the sporting pages repeat the commonplace stereotypes of nation, place and race, not to mention those of masculinity (O'Donnell, 1994).

On the Monday of the Survey, a swirling flurry of flags was waving for 'us', 'our victories' and 'our heroes'. That day marked the start of the second week of the annual tennis tournament at Wimbledon, in which the top professional players from around the world compete in gendered competition. The *Sun* had actually hoisted the flag for Britain, presenting, at the start of the tournament, the "*Sun* Sport's Union Jack", flying at the top of a flag-pole. The idea was to lower the flag one notch each time a British competitor was eliminated from the competition. On past form, a quick lowering of the national flag could be expected, followed by semi-ironic articles bemoaning the national plight. Against predicted expectations, a British player still remained in the competition; and the national flag still could be depicted to flutter across the *Sun*'s sporting pages, albeit not far up the pole. Under the headline 'Battler Brits' (in red type against a blue and white background), the paper proclaimed: "We've done it! *Sun* Sport's Union Jack is still with us as the second week of Wimbledon gets underway today – thanks to Andrew Foster the only surviving Brit in the singles competition." There was much more about "our new star", whom 'we', the readers and the nation, were invited to praise.

The *Sun* was not alone in celebrating British success, or, rather, British avoidance of quick defeat in the tennis. If the *Star* wrote of "Britain's new Wimbledon hero" and the *Mirror* praised "British tennis hero Andrew Foster" who carried "British tennis hopes", then the broadsheets, using wordier phrases, bore the same message. *The Times*, under the headline "Battling Britons enjoy joke at critics' expense", declared that "Brit after Brit has been brave enough to win". The *Guardian*'s tennis correspondent argued that Wimbledon's first week had been particularly "memorable" because of "the contributions made by British players against the odds and expectations". Here, the flag was being waved tastefully. 'We' were not praising 'ourselves' with brazen, outward ostentation, raising and lowering iconographic flags. The celebration was objectified: the event simply was 'memorable', as if being memorable were an objective characteristic. The particular collective memory – 'our memory' – was elided with an implied universal memory. Everyone, or all reasonable people, would remember the British avoidance of defeat. [. . .]

That day offered a whole range of sporting options for flag-waving. [. . .]

Sport, war and masculinity

One has to ask what is the significance of the daily flag-waving, such as that revealed in the Day Survey? The issue of masculinity is clearly important. The sports pages are men's pages, although they are not presented as such. They appear as pages for all the nation, like the British pub was presented as an institution for all the British. On foreign fields, the men win their trophies, or lose their honour, doing battle on the nation's behalf. The readers, mainly men, are invited to see these male exploits in terms of the whole homeland, and, thus, men's concerns are presented as if defining the whole national honour.

The parallel between sport and warfare seems obvious, yet it is difficult to specify precisely the nature of the connection. At first sight, it might appear that sport is a benign reproduction of war. It is easy – all too easy – to see the regular circuses of international sport as substitutes for warfare. Where nations once fought for real, now they sublimate their aggressive energies into struggles for ascendancy on the playing field (Eriksen, 1993, p. 111). The sports pages, in inviting us readers to wave flags, echo the language of warfare. Frequently, the metaphors of weaponry (firing, shooting, attacking) are employed [. . .]. If sport is a sublimation, then the flag-waving is a safety-valve, draining away masculine, aggressive energies and making the world a more peaceable place.

However, one should be sceptical of such a comforting thought. [. . .] [S]port does not confine itself to the playing field and its marked territory in the newspapers. It intrudes upon political discourse. Politicians frequently use sporting metaphors, including those which echo warfare (Shapiro, 1990). Nixon was particularly fond of boxing analogies (Beattie, 1988). Margaret Thatcher preferred the language of cricket, often declaring that she was "batting for Britain", and claiming during the last days of her premiership that she "was still at the crease, though the bowling has been pretty hostile of late" (Young, 1993 [. . .]). The US President traditionally opens the baseball season, throwing the first pitch.

Politicians can, when waving the national flag, advocate sporting policies, so that the flag-waving of sport itself becomes another flag to be waved. John Major, [British prime minister], addressing his party's conference in 1994, announced a policy to put competitive sport "back at the heart of school life": he declared sport to be "part of the British instinct, part of our character" (p. 7, text of speech issued by Conservative Central Office, 14 October 1994). Also, as Eco implied, sport can replace political debate within politics, thereby contributing to a dangerous politics of 'us' and 'them', which seems beyond the scope of debate. In Italy, Silvio Berlusconi, the media entrepreneur and owner of Italy's most successful professional football side, campaigned successfully for the presidency, using the symbols associated with support for the national football team. His television commercials culminated in the football chant 'Forza Italia'. Having triumphed in the election, the new president introduced fascists into his coalition government.

Sport does not merely echo warfare, but it can provide the symbolic models for the understanding of war. When the British troops returned victoriously from the Falklands War, they were met at the harbour by crowds, swaying, chanting and waving flags, as if they were celebrating a football team returning with a silver trophy. During the war, cartoonists had frequently depicted the contest as a football match (Aulich, 1992). Those engaged in fighting, such as the US pilots in the Vietnamese War, often use the metaphors of the playing field to make sense of their experience (Rosenberg, 1993). In this way, war is understood in terms of something more familiar.

Of course, the issue of gender cannot be ignored. It is men who largely read the daily flag-waving accounts of the sports pages. Although the creation of the nation-state may have brought women into political life on a scale hitherto unknown (Colley, 1992, chapter 6), citizenship still is often gendered in the details of its entitlements and duties (Williams, 1987; Yuval-Davies, 1993 [. . .]). Above all, it is men who are expected to answer the state's ultimate call to arms; they are the ones who will pursue the conduct of the war, shooting and being shot, raping, but not being raped, in the cause of the homeland [. . .]. As Jane Bethke Elshtain argues, the compelling theme driving young men to the battlefield is sacrifice, rather than aggression: "The young man goes to war not so much to kill as to die, to forfeit his particular body for that of the larger body, the body politic" (1993, p. 160).

The political crisis which leads to the war can be quickly created, but the willingness to sacrifice cannot be. There must be prior rehearsals and reminders so that, when the fateful occasion arises, men, and women, know how they are expected to behave. Daily, there is a banal preparation. On the sporting pages, as men scan for the results of the favoured team, they read of the deeds of other men doing battle, in the cause of that larger body, the team. And often the team is the nation, battling for honour against foreigners. Then, an unspecifiable added value of honour is at stake.

In the Day Survey, personal sacrifice in the cause of the nation was applauded on the sports pages. An athlete (described as a "reluctant hero", and male, of course) is reported as saying "when your country needs you . . . how can you say No" (*Mail*). The same paper reported the rugby hero, who, despite pain and injury, carried on to fight for the cause of national honour against New Zealand. The

"Anglicised Welshman at the heart of the Wellington campaign" (a description which itself echoes military history), appeared afterwards with "one eye blackened, one knee strapped, hand and cheekbone swollen". He declared: "This was a do-or-die situation. The tour had to be saved."

Scanning the cricket, football or baseball results is not like reading the speech of a finance minister or of 'Tokyo's reaction' to a raid on Baghdad. No sense of duty attends the reading of sports reports. The sporting pages are, to adapt a phrase from Barthes (1975), texts of pleasure. Day after day, millions of men seek their pleasures on these pages, admiring heroism in the national cause, enjoying prose which intertextually echoes warfare. Such pleasures cannot be innocent. If nationhood is being flagged, then the routine reminders might also be rehearsals; the echoes of the past cannot be discounted as preparations for future time. Perhaps we – or our sons, nephews or grandsons – might respond one day, with ready enthusiasm, or with dutiful regret, on hearing that our country needs us to do-or-die. The call will already be familiar; the obligations have been primed; their words have long been installed in the territory of our pleasure. [. . .]

References

Achard, P. 1993. Discourse and social praxis in the construction of nation and state. *Discourse and Society*. 4: 75–98.

Aulich, J. 1992. Wildlife in the South Atlantic: graphic satire, patriotism and the Fourth Estate. In J. Aulich (ed.) *Framing the Falklands War*. Buckingham: Open University Press.

Bairstow, T. 1985. *Fourth-Rate Estate*. London: Comedia.

Barthes, R. 1975. *The Pleasure of the Text*. New York: Farrar, Strauss and Giroux.

Barthes, R. 1977. *Roland Barthes*. Basingstoke: Macmillan.

Beattie, G. 1988. *All Talk*. London: Weidenfeld & Nicolson.

Beattie, G. 1993. *We Are the People*. London: Mandarin.

Billig, M. 1990. Collective memory, ideology and the British royal family. In D. Middleton and D. Edwards (eds) *Collective Remembering*. London: Sage.

Billig, M. 1991. *Ideology and Opinions: Studies in Rhetorical Psychology*. London: Sage.

Billig, M. 1992. *Talking of the Royal Family*. London: Routledge.

Billig, M. and D. Edwards 1994. La construction sociale de la mémoire. *La Recherche*. 25: 742–5.

Billig, M. and P. Golding 1992. The hidden factor: Race, the news media and the 1992 election. *Representation*. 31: 36–8.

Colley, L. 1992. *Britons*. New Haven CT: Yale University Press.

Connor, W. 1993. Beyond reason: The nature of the ethno-national bond. *Ethnic and Racial Studies*. 16: 373–89.

Deutsch, K. 1966. *Nationalism and Social Communication*. Cambridge MA: MIT Press.

Eagleton, T. 1991. *Ideology: An Introduction*. London: Verso.

Eller, J. D. and R. M. Coughlan. 1993. The poverty of primordialism: The demystification of ethnic attachments. *Ethnic and Racial Studies*. 16: 181–202.

Elshtain, J. 1993. Sovereignty, identity, sacrifice. In M. Ringrose and A. Lerner (eds) *Reimagining the Nation*. Buckingham: Open University Press.

Eriksen, T. 1993. *Ethnicity and Nationalism*. London: Pluto Press.

Fairclough, N. 1992. *Discourse and Social Change*. Cambridge: Polity.

Fowler, R. 1991. *Language in the News*. London: Routledge.

Gellner, E. 1983. *Nations and Nationalism*. Oxford: Blackwell.

Giddens, A. 1985. *The Nation State and Violence*. Cambridge: Polity Press

Hall, S. 1975. Introduction. In A. C. H. Smith *Paper Voices*. London: Chatto & Windus.

Hall, S. 1988. Authoritarian populism. In B. Jessop, K. Bonnett, S. Bromley and T. Ling (eds) *Thatcherism*. Cambridge: Polity Press.

Hroch, M. 1985. *Social Preconditions of National Revival in Europe*. Cambridge: Cambridge University Press.

James, C. L. R. 1989. *Cricket*. London: Allison and Busby.

Jessop, B., K. Bonnett, S. Bromley and T. Ling (eds) 1988. *Thatcherism*. Cambridge: Polity Press.

Kosterman, R. and S. Feshbach 1989. Toward a measure of patriotic and nationalistic attitudes. *Political Psychology*. 10: 257–74.

Langer, E. 1989. *Mindfulness*. Reading MA: Addison Wesley.

O'Donnell, H. 1994. Mapping the mythical: A geopolitics of national sporting stereotypes. *Discourse and Society*. 5: 345–80.

Perelman, C. 1979. *The New Rhetoric and the Humanities*. Dordrecht: D. Reidel.

Renan, E. 1990. What is a nation? In H. Bhabha (ed.) *Nation and Narration*. London: Routledge.

Rogowski, R. 1985. Causes and varieties of nationalism. In E. Tiryakian and R. Rogowski (eds) *New Nationalisms in the Developed West*. Boston MA: Allen & Unwin.

Rosenberg, S. 1993. The threshold of the thrill. In M. Cooke and A. Woollacott (eds) *Gendering War Talk*. Princeton NJ: Princeton University Press.

Shapiro, M. J. 1990. Representing world politics: The sport/war intertext. In J. Der Derian and M. Shapiro (eds) *International/Intertextual Relations*. Lexington MA: Lexington Books.

Sparks, C. and M. Campbell 1987. The inscribed reader of the British quality press. *European Journal of Communication*. 2: 455–72.

Williams, F. 1987. Racism and the discipline of social policy: A critique of welfare theory. *Critical Social Policy*. 20: 4–29.

Young, H. 1993. *One of Us: A Biography of Margaret Thatcher*. London: Pan Books.

Yuval-Davies, N. 1993. Gender and nation. *Ethnic and Racial Studies*. 16: 621–32.

Zavalloni, M. 1993. Identity and hyperidentities: The representational foundation of self and culture. *Papers on Social Representations*. 2: 218–35.

Michael Billig is Professor of Social Science at the University of Loughborough in England. He has played a leading role developing discourse perspectives in psychology.

Chapter 11

Ray Honeyford

1988

THE LANGUAGE ISSUE IN MULTI-ETHNIC ENGLISH SCHOOLS[a]

WHEN A NATION BECOMES multi-ethnic the question of language assumes new importance. The place of languages spoken by minority groups in the public affairs and education systems always gets onto the political agenda. Since language is central to the individual's and the group's identity, history and traditions, the debate is often fierce and sometimes acrimonious. In recent years there have been heated controversies surrounding language in many parts of the world. Canada, Belgium, Wales, Sri lanka, Israel and the USA are all examples of where contentious debates about minority languages have taken place. In a democracy, where head-counting is the determining process in elections, the size of the minority population is a crucial factor. The place of Spanish in the USA, for instance, did not become a significant issue until ethnic quotas were removed from the USA's immigration policies in 1965. New arrivals of Latinos increased from 21 to 41 per cent, and that excluded the sizeable illegal entries. This meant greatly increased electoral powers to Spanish-speaking groups, which was rapidly expressed as demands for separate language rights. This movement succeeded.[b] An historic, Supreme Court decision in 1967 granted parents the right to have their children educated in the mother-language. This tendency to demand language rights appears to be an inevitable development in multi-ethnic societies. Such rights appear to function to reassure the minority group that it has a place in the world, that its demands are taken seriously and that its culture is respected by the world at large.

A debate about 'mother-tongue' provision is now taking place in Britain. Demands for official forms, information leaflets and notices in 'mother-languages' have been successfully made in many of the local authority areas. The sizeable and

---

a From R. Honeyford (1988) 'The Language Issue', *Integration or Disintegration: Towards a Non-racist Society*. London: The Claridge Press, pp. 211–39.

b See Hill (this volume) on the Official English Movement, which subsequently developed in reaction to this.

rapidly increasing Asian population in Britain represents an enormous linguistic diversity. In Bradford alone there are 14,201 schoolchildren who, between them, speak 64 different non-English languages; in Haringey the figures are 7,407 and 87.[1] [. . . A]n [Inner London Education Authority] survey recently discovered 146 different languages and dialects in its schools, and this phenomenon is growing. [. . .]

The flavour of the demands being made can be judged from an article in the [Commission for Racial Equality]'s *Education Journal* for March 1981 by an Asian senior lecturer in a college of education:[2]

> Shouldn't they [Asian parents] as British parents, campaign for a rightful place of mother tongue in the mainstream schooling of their children: . . . If schools at Infant and Primary stage continue to function as mono-lingual and monocultural entities they will miserably fail in the education of bilingual children.

As we shall see, there is no convincing empirical evidence to support this assertion, but it is one frequently made by protagonists in the debates.[c]

Although I am specifically concerned here about the minority-language debate in education it is important to stress that the issue has important consequences for our multi-ethnic identity as a nation. If rights regarding language are granted to minorities in Britain, as they have been in the USA, then a crucial decision regarding our whole character as a polyglot nation will also have been taken. The concept of integration, with all citizens loyal to one national ideal—with 'mother-culture's' maintenance and transmission being regarded as an essentially private responsi-bility—is undermined by the granting of separate language rights to minorities. There is increasing anxiety in the USA regarding the 'melting-pot' theory, which enables a large, diverse society to function as a stable coherent nation. There is a fear that this is being progressively undermined by the creation, for instance, of a separate and publicly funded Spanish-speaking community, unable and unwilling effectively to become part of the wider, dominant English-speaking community. Just as a national, generally accepted language can function to bind disparate communities together, so the granting of separate language rights can carry the danger of division and acrimony.[d] We need to be aware that language and politics are inseparable. [. . .]

Mother-tongue and practicalities

[. . .] It is true that, according to the Education Act 1944, the providers of educa-tion are enjoined to educate the child according to his or her age, ability and

---

c On the complex issues involved, see e.g. C. Baker (1996) *Foundations of Bilingual Education and Bilingualism: 2nd Edition.* Clevedon: Multilingual Matters. For a review of research on bilingualism in the UK written at around the same time as Honeyford's extract, see M. Taylor and S. Hegarty (1987) *The Best of Both Worlds . . . ?* Berkshire: NFER Nelson. Also, see Mazrui (this volume) on the World Bank.

d Compare Bokhorst-Heng and Heller in this volume.

aptitude. It is equally clear that an ethnic minority child will have an aptitude for the language of his or her home and country.[e] However, legislative edicts are always to be understood in terms of the age in which they are promulgated. In 1944 the concept of aptitudes could not have had any connection with the notion of mother-tongue preference. When the Act was put on the Statute Book Britain was essentially a monolingual society—at least in terms of there being an unquestioned national language in which the school had always taught. There could have been no way in which the authors of the Act could have predicted the incredible growth of foreign languages used as mother-tongues in Britain today. The mother-tongue issue is the product of large-scale immigration which came some years after the 1944 Act. [. . .]

Sometimes the argument is bolstered by references to the Welsh experience. It is argued that since, *de facto*, in many parts of Wales children are taught in Welsh, does this not set a precedent for mother-tongues in English schools? This point was put very strongly, for instance, at a conference organised in 1976 by the [Commission for Racial Equality (CRE)] and the Centre for Bilingual and Language Education at Aberystwyth. After all, if Welsh pupils are compelled to use Welsh to learn with, or take Welsh to appreciate the culture and history of Wales, why should not Urdu-speaking children in Bradford schools do the same with regard to Pakistani culture? This has a superficial plausibility, as well as touching on liberal sentiments about civil rights and the defence of the underdog. It suffers, however, from a number of false assumptions. First, it ignores the fact that rights have to do with time. There is a sense in which rights have to be earned—instant conferring of rights on immigrants (apart, of course, from those general civil rights that all British citizens automatically enjoy) is not possible. For one thing, there has to be a lengthy time lag before the indigenous community can be convinced that immigrants intend to form a permanent community, whose special demands can be considered: there is much more likelihood of Welsh people remaining in Wales than of Asians or, indeed, of West Indians staying in England.[f] Second, Wales is the historic homeland of the Welsh. They are not an immigrant community at all in the sense that England's ethnic minorities are. If the analogy is to convince it would have to run along the lines of Welsh children living and going to school in England, having the right to be taught in Welsh in their English schools, and no-one has suggested that. Most people, including Welsh parents, would consider it bizarre. Moreover, no previous immigrant community has made such mother-tongue demands—the Jews and central Europeans, for instance, have never proposed such 'rights'. In addition, the argument ignores the sheer number of mother-languages now in Britain. If the right to one mother-language in schools is granted, then that same right must clearly be given to all mother-languages. The costs involved would, of course, be colossal, unacceptable to public opinion and almost certainly prohibitive.

Promoting a pride in the minority culture certainly appears a perfectly worthy objective for teachers to pursue. After all, the culture of the home is a decisive influence in the child's identity and his sense of personal worth. In terms of

---

e Compare Rampton, this volume.
f Compare Hewitt, this volume.

emotional and social development it is generally agreed that the culture of the home is more influential than formal schooling. However, the notion that the school either should or can be involved in this process, to the extent of actually teaching in the language of the home, is by no means established. There is little evidence to suggest that children are in any sense damaged by functioning in two languages. No-one now seriously suggests, for instance, that the West Indian child's exposure to the standard English of the classroom as opposed to the Creole spoken in his home threatens his self-concept—although some have advanced the notion that his intellectual progress might be impaired. Moreover, no-one has suggested, again, that previous immigrant communities have suffered in this respect. Are Jewish children any less proud of their Jewish heritage and culture because they are bilingual? The contrary view might be easier to support; the consciousness of living in a world foreign to one's origins often reinforces attachment to the original mother-culture. Moreover, even if it could be held that the school ought to teach in the mother-culture, there would be formidable practical problems. The following are just some of these:

(1)   How would the principle apply to multi-lingual schools? Many of Britain's inner-city schools now contain children who speak many *different* mother-languages, and these children are often in the same class. How, apart from linguistic Apartheid, could each child be taught in its mother-tongue? (Advocates of mother-tongue teaching often speak as if Britain were the linguistic equivalent of Canada, where just two major languages are fighting for supremacy.)

(2)   Even within Britain's linguistic diversity there are local variations of dialect. Moreover, many minority parents, although they speak one language, will prefer for historical and status reasons to see their children taught in a different tongue. For instance, some of the sizeable Italian community in Britain speak Sicilian Italian, but the parents concerned would prefer standard Italian, since this carries more status. The Sylheti Bengali-speaking father might well follow the Italian parents in Britain, and for much the same reasons. Punjabi-speaking children would prefer perhaps to be taught in Urdu since that is the national language of learning for their parents; while East Punjabis might well prefer Hindi for religious reasons. Some Cantonese-speaking parents might choose Mandarin Chinese as the medium of instruction for their children, since this is the national language of China and Taiwan. In short, even the definition of what constitutes the 'mother-language' is problematic. Even if the problem of definition could be overcome, where would the many teachers required come from? One difficulty here is that there is some evidence that Asian parents have little desire to encourage their children to go into teaching. They, perhaps correctly, perceive it as a low-level occupation and much prefer their offspring to enter 'real' professions, such as medicine and the law. So the potential supply of, say, Asian-speaking teachers may be far too small to meet the demand. Moreover, would public opinion accept the very large costs involved?

Attempting to preserve and promote the child's 'mother-culture' may seem an attractive liberal principle but implementing it in linguistic terms could be a recipe for educational chaos.

What of linguistic links with the mother-country? Embedded in this notion is an assumption about the concept of 'mother-country'. It is as if we are here assuming that successive generations of minority people will always regard the country of family origins as the 'mother-country'. Now clearly, original first-generation immigrants will tend to do so, but is that the case for their children and grandchildren? Does a British–Asian child born in Bradford have the same relationship to Pakistan as his immigrant parents? Is there not a natural tendency for such links to be weakened over time and for future generations to come to regard Britain as their 'mother-country'?[g] How many of Britain's Polish-speaking pupils in school now regard Poland as their mother-country? Even if this natural process were not to take place, how far is the state, through the school system, responsible for maintaining immigrants' links with their country of origin? Is that process not a naturally and inevitably private one? If the state were to accept this line of argument, then again there would be a very large expenditure involved, since *all* immigrants and their descendants would share in the benefits. Since Britain [. . .] is never likely to have more than 6 per cent of its population from the minorities, it is very unlikely that public opinion would support this position. [. . .]

However, increasing a nation's linguistic resources certainly seems a defensible objective. Trade, diplomacy and defence are all linked to foreign policy and multilingual negotiations. All may benefit from having a population proficient in a range of languages. In this sense, Britain can clearly benefit from its multi-ethnic character. However, this is not an argument for bilingual education but for putting minority languages on the timetable at the secondary level.[h] Urdu, for instance, might well be set beside French and German as part of the school's foreign-language programme—always, of course, assuming that the necessary resources exist and there is a genuine parental demand. It cannot be assumed that Asian parents, for instance, necessarily want their mother-languages on the school curriculum. There is good evidence to suggest that they do not perceive it as a priority; the demand in Britain has not come from parents so much as Asian intellectuals, educators and professional race relations personnel. An HMI[i] report in 1984 found, after looking at the mother-tongue in four [Local Education Authories (LEAs)], only moderate parental support. For instance, of 950 pupils speaking Punjabi only 71 (7.4 per cent) opted for Punjabi lessons; 25 per cent of the relevant community opted for Bengali; 17 per cent supported Cantonese; 10 per cent Turkish; and 22 per cent Greek. Minority parents had a no-nonsense, instrumental view of their children's educational needs. They opted for the mother-tongue only when it did not conflict with vocationally more valuable subjects or with those that had more

---

g See Back, this volume.

h Honeyford's argument tuned with official government policy from the late 1980s onwards, and a number of minority languages have been available as options with the modern foreign languages curriculum at secondary level. For reviews of language education policy in England, see Harris, Leung and Rampton (2001) 'Globalisation, diaspora and language education in England'. *Working Papers in Urban Language and Literacies* 17, and Rampton, Harris and Leung (2001) 'Education in England and speakers of languages other than English', *Working Papers in Urban Language and Literacies* 18 (both accessible on-line at http://www.kcl.ac.uk/depsta/education/ULL/wpull.html)

i Her Majesty's Inspectorate – the top inspectors of UK schools.

status.[3] This same attitude was discovered by CRC researchers in 1977. They interviewed 700 parents for whom Urdu, Hindi, Gujerati, Punjabi and Greek were the mother-tongues and found an average demand of 16 per cent.[4] Moreover, if the mother-tongue is to be placed on the school timetable there are two vital conditions involved. First, the placing of, say, Gujerati on the timetable should not involve compulsion; it should, like many other school subjects, be optional. As I write, there is considerable public resentment being expressed about a school in Wolverhampton compelling its pupils to take Punjabi. That kind of approach is insensitive and will not improve race relations. Second, a school considering this move needs to liaise very carefully with its parents. If the school is multilingual there is a very real danger that the selection of, say, one Asian language (more would be impracticable) might well create objections from parents who speak one of those languages not selected. The great value of choosing the traditional European languages, of course, is that this danger is avoided. There are no sizeable French, German or Spanish groups in Britain. Putting an Asian language on the curriculum might be fully justified but, handled wrongly, the process could create inter-communal conflict. It should never be forgotten that there is historic animosity among many of Britain's minority groups, and history is a very powerful influence in pupils' behaviour and relationships.

The case, then, for using the 'mother-language' as the medium of instruction has not been made and there are obvious and important reasons why the proposal should be rejected. However, there are acceptable grounds for placing an ethnic-minority language on the timetable—subject to certain safeguards.

The multilingual classroom and achievement

A question which has caused much debate is 'If a disproportionate number of pupils are using English as a second language will academic standards decline'? This is a difficult issue, not only because it raises complex empirical problems but because of the current emotional and political climate surrounding questions involving ethnicity. Any attempt even to propose a question whose resolution might reflect adversely on the ethnic minorities tends to be met with strident opposition and imputations of ill-will from the very influential anti-racist lobby. [. . . I]t is an issue which does cause concern both to parents and teachers, including, in my own direct experience, some ethnic-minority parents themselves. One of the key problems here is that the term 'ethnic-minority pupil' has always been applied to children of overseas origin. However, as we now know, there are many schools where the minority children are white and indigenous. In a very real sense *they* are, within the context of the school, ethnic-minority children. Although it is not possible to provide objective information about the relationship between proportions of ethnic-minority children and average levels of achievement, there is little doubt that there is much intuitive belief that the relationship is problematic.

Although we find this concern dismissed in the literature of anti-racism as belonging to the 'assimilationalist' phase of race relations, that concern continues, rightly or wrongly. It was first officially acknowledged in 1963, when a group of parents in Southall protested about their anxieties regarding this problem. The then

Minister of Education expressed the following view in the House of Commons: 'If possible, it is desirable on *educational grounds* [my emphasis] that no one school should have more than 30 per cent of immigrants.' This was echoed in [Department for Education and Science] Circular 7/65, which emphasised the need to reassure white parents about their children's schooling: 'It will be helpful if the parents of non-immigrant children can see that practical measures have been taken to deal with the problem in school and that the progress of their own children is not being restricted by the undue preoccupation of the teaching staff with the linguistic and other difficulties of immigrant children' [. . .]. Although the label 'immigrant' applied progressively to a decreasing proportion of ethnic children, anxiety continued. According to the CRC's survey of teacher opinion in multi-ethnic schools there was widespread concern about the educational problems faced by the minority children. The following typical quotes give the source of the problems: 'Language problems with both Asians and West Indians.' 'If their mothers don't speak English and can't help with their books and reading this can be hard on the children.'[j] 'Quite often a child born here will know a little English before it starts school.' 'Children born abroad do not necessarily have greater difficulties. A Greek Cypriot child born here to a non-English speaking mum can still enter primary school knowing no English.' It is difficult to see how a disproportionate number (a term which, in the present state of knowledge, must necessarily carry an intuitive definition) of such children in the classroom can fail to depress the overall academic atmosphere and average levels of achievement.

A press report in 1980 makes clear the kind of anxiety this problem can evoke in a head teacher. A small Church of England primary school in London's Tower Hamlets (an area with a very large Bengali community) had an ethnic-minority pupil population of 40 per cent. The head teacher insisted on having no more than 50 per cent of such children in any one class, for purely educational reasons:[5]

> Both the Authority and the Church have refused to grasp this nettle and we want it brought out into the open for informed debate. At present we have over 50 per cent non-English speaking children in our infant class and we simply cannot take any more and do our job properly . . . My policy is not racial in any way.

A not-dissimilar anxiety is to be found in a Schools Council pamphlet.[6] This was a survey of 94 LEAs divided into areas with high, medium and low concentrations of ethnic-minority pupils[, . . . a] substantial and statistically representative [sample]. It is worth quoting the relevant passage in full [. . .]

> Several authorities reported concern about the situation of white children in schools with high proportions of ethnic minorities . . . in schools of very high proportions of ethnic minorities the situation of white children (usually of economically and socially depressed families) is greatly ignored and deserves further detailed research.

---

j On language use in Asian homes up until 1987, see Taylor and Hegarty (op. cit.) pp. 169–75 for a fuller and more differentiated account of research.

Fifty-four per cent of head teachers (who replied to the questionnaire) in schools with 30 per cent or more pupils from ethnic minority groups drew attention to the 'special' needs of their white pupils, many stressing that the needs of this group tended to be ignored:

> We have to be careful that children with language problems who are not truly remedial, do not swamp the remedial teachers who should be coping with truly remedial problems . . . We are not acting in a positive way on this need of which we have long been aware.

Seventy-eight per cent of schools said that in-service courses on multi-ethnic education should cover the needs of white children in these schools and 60 per cent considered that present in-service courses do not do so—'this is a neglected aspect'. [. . .][k]

A complicating factor here is that in terms of performance in public examinations Asian children—on average—do surprisingly well. However, this countervailing evidence needs to take account of the following relevant factors:

1   We do not know how far the pupils concerned have attended schools with high, medium or low concentrations of children using English as a second language. The high average Asian performance could reflect the results of a disproportionate number of Asian children from schools with low proportions of such pupils.

2   We do know that Bangladeshi children are, by any criteria, low achievers at the moment.

3   If we include West Indian pupils on the grounds of dialect problems (a judgement for which there is much support) then we have a further group whose average educational performance is significantly lower on a national scale than the general average—and possibly for reasons to do with language.

4   Detailed surveys of examination results on a national scale for 1981[7] reveal that examination results are lower per pupil in LEAs with:

   a   More teachers per pupil;
   b   Higher expenditure per pupil;
   c   Higher proportions of pupils who are non-white or born abroad.

5   Similar surveys for 1982[8] reveal that examination results are lower per pupil in LEAs with:
   a   Higher expenditure per pupil;
   b   Higher proportions of pupils who are non-white or born abroad;
   c   Higher proportions of inexperienced teachers.

Although these factors are intercorrelated—making simple judgements inadmissible—there does appear to be evidence for more detailed study of the effects of ethnic-

---

k   For a discussion of the encounter between white working class youngsters and multicultural education policies, see Hewitt, R. (1996) *Routes of Racism: the Social Basis of Racist Action*. Stoke-on-Trent: Trentham Books.

minority proportions on levels of white achievement. It is important to stress that this issue has nothing whatsoever to do with race, genetics or colour but with competence in the English language; and if the concerns noted above are valid, then the effects are as damaging for ethnic-minority as for white children. However, it seems very unlikely that the necessary research could be carried out unless there is a considerable change in the climate surrounding race relations—the present one is far too prescriptive and narrow. Moreover, really reliable correlations between proportions of pupils using English as a second language and school achievement could not be established until national, academic benchmarks at key ages of, say, seven, eleven, fifteen and eighteen were available. However, it is important for educational planning—particularly the question of dispersal policies—and for good race relations.

The West Indian language issue

> Language—even West Indian children don't have the same vocabulary or background knowledge that you might take for granted.

> West Indian difficulties are more severe. Patois is often not recognised as being a language on its own.

> A higher percentage of West Indian children fail than those of other ethnic groups—this may be a communication failure.

> We also realise that the West Indian pupils who appeared to speak English in fact had difficulty with the language.

Those are the opinions of teachers experienced in teaching [black] West Indian children in English schools and are reported in a survey carried out by the Community Relations Council.[9] My own extensive experience of teaching West Indian youngsters suggests that most teachers would support this view of the language difficulties such children experience in the classroom. In looking at the educational performance and experience of British–West Indian children one thing is immediately apparent: as a group they perform less well on average than Asians or white pupils. This is widely recognised with regard to public examinations results [at age 16 . . .] However, it also appears to be the case with other age levels [. . .]

This pattern is reflected in the judgement of Tomlinson,[10] who reviewed the extensive literature up to 1982:

> The conclusion reached after a study of research into the educational performance of West Indian children is that in general these pupils do underperform and underachieve in comparison with white and Asian minority groups . . . The optimistic assumption that 'immigrant' performance would improve with length of schooling in Britain and that black British children's performance would come up to or at least equal that of inner city white children does not appear to have come about.

Now in discussing the question of educational achievement we have constantly to bear in mind that the issues are complex. What causes an individual child or group of children to perform at a particular level constitutes a perennial—not to say controversial—debate among educators of all kinds. Indeed, so complex is this question that experts in the field tend not to talk about causes at all but rather about 'factors associated with' particular outcomes. We now know, for instance, that such factors as age, sex, motivation, social class, the school, the teacher, the head teacher, parental attitudes and basic ability can all be shown to be connected with achievement in school, and in recent years there has been intense interest in the role of language. Although there is general agreement about the link between language and educability, there are many unresolved and contentious questions surrounding that relationship. For instance, what is the nature of the link between language and thought? How is language acquired? How does language develop in the growing child? What is the relationship between spoken and written language? How do children best learn to read? Is there a specific language ability? Do the different school subjects generate their own distinctive discourse? How does the teacher's use of language link with pupil understanding and progress? Can we postulate a typical working-class as opposed to middle-class language—and if we can, what is the significance of the difference for educability? There is continuing debate about these and many other language issues, but if this phenomenon is in general intrinsically contentious, the particular question of how far the language of West Indian children accounts for their performance in schools is very much more so. [. . .]

The basic issue

At the heart of the debate lies the question: Are some forms of language superior to others? Alternatively, within this context can we say that the standard English of the classroom is superior to the non-standard variants used by West Indian families? If the answer to that question is no, then there would appear to be little reason to assume that the poorer academic achievement of West Indian pupils is associated with language. However, since there *is* among educationists and theoreticians a consensus that language and education are connected, we surely have to accept the need to examine the question. This is far from easy. A dominant theme in educational circles in Britain over the last 30 years has been cultural relativism.[1] The notion that one culture is the equal of all others has been a virtually unquestioned assumption. Even to raise the question with which I began this paragraph would be considered improper by many intellectuals. Pointing to possible qualitative differences is forbidden, and this is as true of language as any other cultural product. I will not pause to examine the mental gyrations that this position requires for its maintenance. Suffice it to say that the climate to which it gives rise has created a major stumbling-block. However, if we capitulate to received wisdom then we may well be denying ourselves access to truths which could be of benefit to a significant group of children.

---

1 See also Quirk (this volume).

The striking feature of the debate is the contrast between the views of teachers and parents, on the one hand, and those of linguistic experts, on the other. I have already indicated the conviction of teachers that West Indian children do have specific language difficulties. Their parents, too, are emphatic about the importance of standard English to progress in schools. Tomlinson says: 'West Indian parents are also anxious that their children should become fluent in standard English as early as possible.' This does not, of course, indicate that West Indian parents regard standard English as being superior in general to the family Creole. Nor does it preclude the possibility that such parents correctly perceive the higher status accorded to standard English in our society. However, the crucial thing here is that West Indian parents accept that standard English is more *appropriate* to progress in an English school. This parent–teacher consensus finds no echo among those who generate influential theories about comparative linguistics.

Professor John Honey[11] has provided a set of questions which encapsulate the dominant egalitarian traditions among linguists. For example: 'It is an established fact that no language or dialect is superior to another . . . There is virtually unanimous recognition among linguists that one language or dialect is as good as another.' The strength of this tradition and the immense influence it has had in education[m] can be gained from this comment in the Rampton Report on the education of black children: 'From the evidence we have received . . . we do not accept that for the vast majority of British-born [West Indian] children language factors play a part in underachievement.' This view has been widely condemned by both teachers and researchers, and its genesis has been suggested by Bald:[12] 'Its contradiction of the evidence and the "mental gymnastics" it involves can only be explained in terms of the political and social climate surrounding the debate about black school achievements.'

Just how convincing is the 'all languages are equally good' school of thought? Intuitively we suspect its validity. This is particularly so when comparing the language of societies markedly unequal in terms of intellectual and scientific development. In this context, how does West Indian Creole compare with standard English? There is no doubt that Creole is a developed language with its own rule-governed systems and extensive vocabulary.[n] Is it, however, as rich, complex and powerful as the standard English in which, say, nuclear physics, Western philosophy and literary criticism are expressed? Is it as likely to encapsulate and transmit abstract thoughts and to tolerate irony, ambiguity and conceptual complexity? The answer may well be yes to all these questions. In raising them I may simply be reflecting my own parochialism. I do not know West Indian Creole, but I do know that the cultural history of the two languages and of the language populations concerned have been markedly different. The people of the West Indies have a tradition of poverty, economic exploitation and educational denial. They have traditionally had to work all the hours God sent them to keep body and soul together. They have not enjoyed that substantial leisure and economic security which are the prerequisites of cultural and technical advance. On the other hand, Britain has

---

m For a valuable review of this controversy and its educational ramifications, see D. Cameron (1995) *Verbal Hygiene*. London: Routledge.
n See Alleyne and Rickford, this volume.

always had a cultivated leisured class, with a tradition of exposure to both abstract thought and empirical enquiry, and it is they who have created the standard English of the classroom. Are these two groups likely to have produced languages with equal capacities for producing the educated person in the generally accepted sense, i.e. in the context of the culturally diverse and technically complex Britain in which British black children now live out their lives? This seems intrinsically unlikely. Those West Indian parents who complained to the Rampton Committee that language differences ought not to be used as an excuse for their children's educational failure were not pointing to the equality of Creole and standard English. They were complaining about those teachers who had effectively failed to convey that standard English which is the basis of progress in school.

However, is there more available than intuition to guide our response to this question? A further factor in assessing the validity of the linguistic relativity theory is the character of educational controversy. The educational establishment has a noted tendency to sustain its hegemony by using theory and research in self-interested ways. Interpretation of findings in research and their application to educational practice tends to reinforce current fashions. [. . .] One wonders how far this process has distorted the work of linguists. The dominant egalitarianism has certainly endorsed what it sees as support for its ideology, but how far is this interpretation correct? There appear to be two strands in modern linguistics. First, there are those who argue for the essential equality of all languages—what might be termed a pure form of the theory. However, there are also those who argue for the adequacy of language for the purpose of those using it. These are clearly different ideas, but they are often lumped together as one coherent body of opinion by those with an intellectual vested interest. Again I draw on Honey's work to illustrate. Consider the following:

> Every language has sufficiently rich vocabulary for the expression of all the distinctions that are important in the society using it.
> (Lyons, *Chomsky*, 1970/77, p. 21)

> All varieties of a language are structured, complex, rule governed systems which are *entirely adequate* for the needs of their speakers.
> (Trudgill, *Sociolinguistics*, 1974, p. 20)

Each of these writers has been frequently quoted as being a supporter of linguistic relativity,° but are they actually saying that all languages are equally good or are they suggesting that language serves the needs of the group which exists in a distinctive context? That existing human need can be effectively discharged by using the available language? It may well be that, as Lyons says, every language is adequate for expressing relevant distinctions in a given society, but what if the inhabitants of a society choose to change their social context? Suppose they decide to live in another and more complex society. Will their original language still be adequate? Alternatively, in order to survive and then flourish in the new society, might they not require a different form of language? Again, although Trudgill asserts

---

o See Whorf, this volume.

the essential complexity of all variety of language, he does not refer to equality but rather to adequacy to needs. A very simple example illustrates this. In Britain we have one word for snow; [Inuit] have seven. We have no need to make a fine distinction of this natural phenomenon since it plays little part in our lives. However, [Inuit] live in a more complex environment in this respect, and require a more discriminating language to reflect this. At least some of the linguists who are quoted by egalitarian theorists appear to accept this. Might this notion of linguistic adequacy to a given context be of significance to West Indian children struggling with the complex demand of formal education? Is it entirely fortuitous that the medium of instruction in Jamaican schools is standard English?

However, what of the concept that I have called the pure form of linguistic egalitarianism? If indeed there are no qualitative differences between languages, if they are all equally appropriate to very different cultural environments, where does this leave West Indian children in English schools? Can we ensure that they will make the transition from the home to the school without any particular linguistic difficulty? Or should we, for reasons of identity and cultural pride, teach in Creole? There are indeed those who would advocate the latter course, and there are those who, while not going that far, believe that the English school ought to devote at least part of the timetable teaching Creole[p] [. . .]. Or should we, in view of the continued relative failure of West Indian children in English schools, question the whole argument? At least such an enterprise could have the merit of settling whether language plays a significant part.

The pure form of linguistic relativism

A very significant attack on this position has been produced by Honey. In *The Language Trap* he has examined critically the pretensions of this school of thought, and his judgement is unequivocal: 'What is especially noteworthy about these theorists is that they offer no proofs for their rulings nor even any empirical evidence.' The basis of their position is in fact an *a priori* commitment to a naive cultural relativism. Honey supports his own view that there *are* qualitative differences between languages and within variants of the same language by showing that different cultures function at different levels of complexity, create different needs and produce languages which vary in richness and density. The notion of 'needs' is crucial here. The relativists argue that if a given language group lacks the vocabulary and grammar to handle, say, modern medicine, technology or communications this proves that they have no *need* of these things. While it could be argued that the impact of these on non-Western societies has not been an unmixed blessing, the state of their languages cannot be used as evidence to support the idea that they do not need them—that involves a value judgement on Western culture, and is not a description of a non-Western language. Moreover, the notion that languages and social development are synchronised—that words and culture advance in step, as it were—is very questionable. While language may reflect the current *general* needs of its users, this does not account for the time lag before innovations can occur

p Compare Rickford, this volume.

and be named, nor for the fact that *individual* members of a language group may well be in advance of their community in perceiving a new phenonemon and borrowing it from another society. However, such an individual would have no means of describing this new phenomenon in the existing form of the language. In short, unless we reject the notion of cultural development, it is difficult to see how this can be facilitated without corresponding changes in the language.

This has a particular relevance for black youngsters in British schools. For many years, teachers have been led to believe in what might be termed the 'Labov factor'. Labov, an American linguist of considerable influence over the past 15 years or so, has argued that the non-standard speech of the American negro is the equal of standard English as a vehicle for complex thought.[q] In this he has been in opposition to those psychologists [. . .] who have argued for a theory of linguistic deprivation to explain variations in educational performance. Honey examined the basis of Labov's theory in detail, paying particular attention to his crucial empirical work. His conclusion is emphatic:

> The widely publicised attempt to prove that one specific, non-standard variety of English (i.e. Black English Vernacular), which has hitherto been regarded as subject to limitations as a vehicle for the expression of logic or of the finer points of philosophical argument, is, in fact, entirely equal to standard English for all these intellectual tasks *and may even be superior to it* has been shown to be what we could charitably describe in scientific terms as bunk. So the fact is that the possibility that speakers of certain languages and dialects suffer a 'verbal deficit' which in turn may entail an intellectual deficit is still an open question and it has to be recognised that there is at least some evidence in support of that possibility.

In short, those of us who are teachers but not professional linguists may have been misled. What has for so long been presented as an established consensus is nothing of the kind. It is clear from Honey's work that there is considerable conflict among professionals on this issue. It may well be that in our proper attempts not to give offence to minorities and their culture we have been misled by inadequate and fashionable theory. Perhaps our fear of upsetting the egalitarian establishment (and latterly its multicultural education offshoot) has caused us to underestimate the language problems of West Indian children. It *may* be of some significance that, whereas considerable efforts have been made to teach Asian children English (and they have done surprisingly well in schools) we have tended to ignore the language problems of the West Indian children on the grounds that they have none. The English as a foreign language policies of many LEAs have been the almost exclusive preserve of Asian children. Since they initially speak a markedly different language from English, we have, in general, tended to assume that West Indian Creole is so like standard English that West Indian pupils can be more or less ignored in this respect. [. . .] A further problem here is the role of Caribbean dialect

---

q See W. Labov (1969) 'The logic of nonstandard English'. *Georgetown Monographs on Language and Linguistics* 22. Washington: Georgetown University Press.

in establishing and maintaining group identities. Bald has claimed that West Indian pupils may deliberately engage in Creole in order to express an anti-authority stance. There is dispute about why so many West Indian youngsters adopt a confrontational attitude in schools, but that it happens is indubitable. Brook[13] has described their dialect as 'An anti-language, hidden, subversive and hostile'. Clearly, this kind of language is hardly appropriate for educational purposes. [. . .]

Conclusion

Language is a central issue in multi-ethnic societies. While the mother-tongue is deeply significant for minorities, the wisdom of a state that grants separate language rights to minorities is questionable—assuming that harmonious integration is the ideal. If loyalty to a national ideal is thought to be desirable, the concept of a single national language has a crucial role to play. Apart from the political aspect, there are formidable practical problems standing in the way of granting language rights to minorities. The central arena in which the debate about language is to be held is the school. [. . .]

Notes

1   *Linguistic Minorities in England*, Linguistic Minorities Project, University of London Institute of Education (1983).

2   R. Kaushall 1981 'Mother Tongue as an Issue of Importance', *Education Journal*. Commission for Racial Equality. March.

3   *Mother Tongue Teaching in Four Local Education Authorities: An HMI Enquiry*, DES, HMSO, London (1984).

4   *The Education of Ethnic Minority Children*, Community Relations Council (1977). (*Editors:* Taylor and Hegarty (op. cit) pp. 214–30 provide a comprehensive review of research on Asian parents' attitudes to mother-tongue teaching up until 1987).

5   *Daily Telegraph*, 29 December 1980.

6   A. Little and R. Willey, *Multi-ethnic Education: The Way Forward*, Schools Pamphlet No. 18 (1981).

7   J. Marks, C. Cox and M. Pomian-Srzednicki, *Standards in English Schools*, Report No. 1, National Council for Educational Standards, London (1983).

8   J. Marks and M. Pomian-Srzednicki, *Standards in English Schools: Second Report*, National Council for Educational Standards, London (1985).

9   *The Education of Ethnic Minority Children,* Community Relations Council 1977. (*Editors:* for a review of research on the West Indian language issue up until about 1980, see M. Taylor 1981 *Caught Between* Berkshire: NFER-Nelson 68–103.)

10 S. Tomlinson, *Ethnic Minorities in British Schools*, Heinemann Educational, London (1983) p. 44.

11 J. Honey, *The Language Trap*, National Council for Educational Standards, London (1983).

12 J. Bald, 'Ignoring the Evidence', *The Times Educational Supplement*, 2 October 1981.

13 M. R. M. Brook 1980 'The Mother Tongue Issue in Britain' *British Journal of the Sociology of Education* Vol 1, No. 1.

In the early 1980s Ray Honeyford was a white headteacher of middle school (for children aged 8–13) in Bradford, a city in the north of England. A very significant number of his pupils were from migrant families of South Asian (mainly Pakistani) and Caribbean descent. But in 1984 he published an article, opposing multicultural education, in a right-wing journal. After many months of public, media-led controversy and debate, he resigned from his post.

Chapter 12

John Rickford

1997

SUITE FOR EBONY
AND PHONICS[a]

1   What is Ebonics?

TO JAMES BALDWIN, writing in 1979, it was "this passion, this skill . . .
this incredible music." Toni Morrison, two years later, was impressed by its
"five present tenses" and felt that "the worst of all possible things that could happen
would be to lose that language." What these novelists were talking about was
Ebonics, the informal speech of many African Americans, which rocketed to public
attention a year ago this month after the Oakland School Board approved a resolution
recognizing it as the primary language of African American students.

The reaction of most people across the country – in the media, at holiday
gatherings, and on electronic bulletin boards – was overwhelmingly negative.
In the flash flood of e-mail on America Online, Ebonics was described as "lazy
English," "bastardized English," "poor grammar," and "fractured slang." Oakland's
decision to recognize Ebonics and use it to facilitate mastery of Standard English
also elicited superlatives of negativity: "ridiculous, ludicrous, *very, very stupid*,"
"a terrible mistake."

However, linguists – who study the sounds, words, and grammars of languages
and dialects – though less rhapsodic about Ebonics than the novelists, were much
more positive than the general public. Last January, at the annual meeting of the
Linguistic Society of America, my colleagues and I unanimously approved a resolution describing Ebonics as "systematic and rule-governed like all natural speech
varieties." Moreover, we agreed that the Oakland resolution was "linguistically and
pedagogically sound."

Why do we linguists see the issue so differently from most other people?[b]
A founding principle of our science is that we describe *how* people talk; we don't

a From *Discover* 18: 2 (1997). Republished with other of Rickford's articles in J. Rickford (1999)
African American Vernacular English. Oxford: Blackwell pp. 320–28.
b Compare Honeyford, this volume.

judge how language should or should not be used. A second principle is that all languages, if they have enough speakers, have dialects – regional or social varieties that develop when people are separated by geographic or social barriers. And a third principle, vital for understanding linguists' reactions to the Ebonics controversy, is that all languages and dialects are systematic and rule-governed. Every human language and dialect that we have studied to date – and we have studied thousands – obeys distinct rules of grammar and pronunciation.

What this means, first of all, is that Ebonics is not slang. Slang refers just to a small set of new and usually short-lived words in the vocabulary of a dialect or language. Although Ebonics certainly has slang words – such as *chillin* ("relaxing") or *homey* ("close friend"), to pick two that have found wide dissemination by the media – its linguistic identity is described by distinctive patterns of pronunciation and grammar.

But is Ebonics a different language from English or a different dialect of English? Linguists tend to sidestep such questions, noting that the answers can depend on historical and political considerations. For instance, spoken Cantonese and Mandarin are mutually unintelligible, but they are usually regarded as "dialects" of Chinese because their speakers use the same writing system and see themselves as part of a common Chinese tradition. By contrast, although Norwegian and Swedish are so similar that their speakers can generally understand each other, they are usually regarded as different languages because their speakers are citizens of different countries. As for Ebonics, most linguists agree that Ebonics is more of a dialect of English than a separate language, because it shares many words and other features with other informal varieties of American English. And its speakers can easily communicate with speakers of other American English dialects.

Yet Ebonics is one of the most distinctive varieties of American English, differing from Standard English – the educated standard – in several ways. Consider, for instance, its verb tenses and aspects. ("Tense" refers to *when* an event occurs, "aspect" to *how* it occurs, whether habitual or ongoing.) When Toni Morrison referred to the "five present tenses" of Ebonics, she probably had usages like these – each one different from Standard English – in mind:

1   He runnin. ("He is running.")
2   He be runnin. ("He is usually running.")
3   He be steady runnin. ("He is usually running in an intensive, sustained manner.")
4   He bin runnin. ("He has been running.")
5   He BIN runnin. ("He has been running for a long time and still is.")

In Standard English, the distinction between habitual or non-habitual events can be expressed only with adverbs like "usually." Of course, there are also simple present tense forms, such as "he runs," for habitual events, but they do not carry the meaning of an ongoing action, because they lack the "-ing" suffix. Note too that "bin" in example 4 is unstressed, while "BIN" in example 5 is stressed. The former can usually be understood by non-Ebonics speakers as equivalent to "has been" with the "has" deleted, but the stressed BIN form can be badly misunderstood. Years ago, I presented the Ebonics sentence "She BIN married" to 25 Whites and

25 African Americans from various parts of the United States and asked them if they understood the speaker to be still married or not. While 23 of the African Americans said yes, only 8 of the Whites gave the correct answer. [. . .]

Word pronunciation is another distinctive aspect of dialects, and the regularity of these differences can be very subtle. Most of the "rules" we follow when speaking Standard English are obeyed unconsciously. Take for instance English plurals. Although grammar books tell us that we add "s" to a word to form a regular English plural, as in "cats" and "dogs," that's true only for writing. In speech, what we actually add in the case of "cat" is an *s* sound; in the case of "dog" we add *z*. The difference is that *s* is voiceless, with the vocal cords spread apart, while *z* is voiced, with the vocal cords held closely together and noisily vibrating.

Now, how do you know whether to add *s* or *z* to form a plural when you're speaking? Easy. If the word ends in a voiceless consonant, like "t," add voiceless *s*. If the word ends in a voiced consonant, like "g," add voiced *z*. Since all vowels are voiced, if the word ends in a vowel, like "tree," add *z*. Because we spell both plural endings with "s," we're not aware that English speakers make this systematic difference every day, and I'll bet your English teacher never told you about voiced and voiceless plurals. But you follow the "rules" for using them anyway, and anyone who doesn't – for instance, someone who says "book*z*" – strikes an English speaker as sounding funny.

One reason people might regard Ebonics as "lazy English" is its tendency to omit consonants at the ends of words – especially if they come after another consonant, as in "tes(t)" and "han(d)." But if one were just being lazy or cussed, or both, why not also leave out the final consonant in a word like "pant"? This is not permitted in Ebonics; the "rules" of the dialect do not allow the deletion of the second consonant at the end of a word unless both consonants are either voiceless, as with "st," or voiced, as with "nd." In the case of "pant," the final "t" is voiceless, but the preceding "n" is voiced, so the consonants are both spoken. In short, the manner in which Ebonics differs from Standard English is highly ordered; it is no more lazy English than Italian is lazy Latin. Only by carefully analyzing each dialect can we appreciate the complex rules that native speakers follow effortlessly and unconsciously in their daily lives.

2 Who speaks Ebonics?

If we made a list of all the ways in which the pronunciation and grammar of Ebonics differ from Standard English, we probably couldn't find anyone who always uses all of them. While its features are found most commonly among African Americans (*Ebonics* is itself derived from "ebony" and "phonics," meaning "black sounds"), not all African Americans speak it. The features of Ebonics, especially the distinctive tenses, are more common among working-class than among middle-class speakers, among adolescents than among the middle-aged, and in informal contexts (a conversation on the street) rather than formal ones (a sermon at church) or writing.

The genesis of Ebonics lies in the distinctive cultural background and relative isolation of African Americans, which originated in the slaveholding South. But contemporary social networks, too, influence who uses Ebonics. For example, lawyers and doctors and their families are more likely to have more contact with Standard English speakers – in schools, work, and neighborhoods – than do blue-collar workers and the unemployed. Language can also be used to reinforce a sense of community. Working-class speakers, and adolescents in particular, often embrace Ebonics features as markers of African American identity, while middle-class speakers (in public at least) tend to eschew them.[c]

Some Ebonics features are shared with other vernacular varieties of English, especially Southern white dialects, many of which have been influenced by the heavy concentration of African Americans in the South. And a lot of African American slang has "crossed over" to white and other ethnic groups.[d] Expressions like "givin five" ("slapping palms in agreement or congratulation") and "Whassup?" are so widespread in American culture that many people don't realize they originated in the African American community. Older, non-slang words have also originated in imported African words. *Tote*, for example, comes from the Kikongo word for "carry," *tota*, and *hip* comes from the Wolof word *hipi*, to "be aware." However, some of the distinctive verb forms in Ebonics – he runnin, he be runnin, he BIN runnin – are rarer or non-existent in white vernaculars.

3   How did Ebonics arise?

The Oakland School Board's proposal alluded to the Niger-Congo roots of Ebonics, but the extent of that contribution is not at all clear. What we do know is that the ancestors of most African Americans came to this country as slaves. They first arrived in Jamestown in 1619, and a steady stream continued to arrive until at least 1808, when the slave trade ended, at least officially. Like the forebears of many other Americans, these waves of African "immigrants" spoke languages other than English. Their languages were from the Niger-Congo language family, especially the West Atlantic, Mande, and Kwa sub-group spoken from Senegal and Gambia to the Cameroons, and the Bantu sub-group spoken farther south. Arriving in an American milieu in which English was dominant, the slaves learned English. But how quickly and completely they did so and with how much influence from their African languages are matters of dispute among linguists.

3.1   The Afrocentric view

The Afrocentric view is that most of the distinctive features of Ebonics represent imports from Africa. As West African slaves acquired English, they restructured it according to the patterns of Niger-Congo languages.[e] In this view, Ebonics simplifies consonant clusters at the ends of words and doesn't use linking verbs like "is" and "are" – as in, for example, "he happy" – because these features are generally absent from Niger-Congo languages. Verbal forms like habitual "be" and BIN, referring to a remote past, it is argued, crop up in Ebonics because these kinds of tenses occur in Niger-Congo languages.

c See Clark, this volume.
d See Cutler, and also Hewitt in this volume.
e See Alleyne, this volume.

Most Afrocentrists, however, don't cite a particular West African language source. Languages in the Niger-Congo family vary enormously, and some historically significant Niger-Congo languages don't show these forms. For instance, while Yoruba, a major language for many West Africans sold into slavery, does indeed lack a linking verb like "is" for some adjectival constructions, it has another linking verb for other adjectives. And it has *six* other linking verbs for non-adjectival constructions, where English would use "is" or "are." Moreover, features like dropping final consonants can be found in some vernaculars in England that had little or no West African influence. Although many linguists acknowledge continuing African influences in some Ebonics and American English words, [. . .] they want more proof of its influence on Ebonics pronunciation and grammar.

3.2   The Eurocentric view

A second view, the Eurocentric – or dialectologist – view, is that African slaves learned English from white settlers, and that they did so relatively quickly and successfully, retaining little trace of their African linguistic heritage. Vernacular, or non-Standard features of Ebonics, including omitting final consonants and habitual "be," are seen as imports from dialects spoken by colonial English, Irish, or Scotch-Irish settlers, many of whom were indentured servants. Or they may be features that emerged in the twentieth century, after African Americans became more isolated in urban ghettos. (Use of habitual "be," for example, is more common in urban than in rural areas.) However, as with Afrocentric arguments, we still don't have enough historical details to settle the question. Crucial Ebonics features, such as the absence of linking "is," appear to be rare or non-existent in these early settler dialects, so they're unlikely to have been the source. Furthermore, although the scenario posited by this view is possible, it seems unlikely. Yes, African American slaves and Whites sometimes worked alongside each other in households and fields. And yes, the number of African slaves was so low, especially in the early colonial period, that distinctive African American dialects may not have formed. But the assumption that slaves rapidly and successfully acquired the dialects of the Whites around them requires a rosier view of their relationship than the historical record and contemporary evidence suggest.

3.3   The creolist view

A third view, the creolist view, is that many African slaves, in acquiring English, developed a pidgin language – a simplified fusion of English and African languages – from which Ebonics evolved. Native to none of its speakers, a pidgin is a mixed language, incorporating elements of its users' native languages but with less complex grammar and fewer words than either parent language. A pidgin language emerges to facilitate communication between speakers who do not share a language; it becomes a creole language when it takes root and becomes the primary tongue among its users. This often occurs among the children of pidgin speakers – the vocabulary of the language expands, and the simple grammar is fleshed out. But the creole still remains simpler in some aspects than the original languages. Most creoles, for instance, don't use suffixes to mark tense ("he walk*ed*"), plurals ("boy*s*"), or possession ("John*'s* house").

Creole languages are particularly common on the islands of the Caribbean and the Pacific, where large plantations brought together huge groups of slaves or indentured laborers. The native languages of these workers were radically different from the native tongues of the small groups of European colonizers and settlers, and under such conditions, with minimal access to European speakers, new, restructured varieties like Haitian Creole French and Jamaican Creole English arose. These languages do show African influence, as the Afrocentric theory would predict, but their speakers may have simplified existing patterns in African languages by eliminating more complex alternatives, like the seven linking verbs of Yoruba I mentioned earlier.

Within the United States African Americans speak one well-established English creole, Gullah. It is spoken on the Sea Islands off the coast of South Carolina and Georgia, where African Americans at one time constituted 80 to 90 percent of the local population in places. When I researched one of the South Carolina Sea Islands some years ago, I recorded the following creole sentences. They sound much like Caribbean Creole English today:

1   E. M. run an gone to Suzie house. ("E. M. went running to Suzie's house.")
2   But I does go to see people when they sick. ("But I usually go to see people when they are sick.")
3   De mill bin to Bluffton dem time. ("The mill was in Bluffton in those days.")

Note the creole traits: the first sentence lacks the past tense and the possessive form; the second sentence lacks the linking verb "are" and includes the habitual "does"; the last sentence uses unstressed "bin" for past tense and "dem time" to refer to a plural without using an *s*.

What about creole origins for Ebonics? Creole speech might have been introduced to the American colonies through the large numbers of slaves imported from the colonies of Jamaica and Barbados, where creoles were common. In these regions the percentage of Africans ran from 65 to 90 percent. And some slaves who came directly from Africa may have brought with them pidgins or creoles that developed around West African trading forts. It's also possible that some creole varieties – apart from well-known cases like Gullah – might have developed on American soil.

This would have been less likely in the northern colonies, where Blacks were a very small percentage of the population. But Blacks were much more concentrated in the South, making up 61 percent of the population in South Carolina and 40 percent overall in the South. Observations by travelers and commentators in the eighteenth and nineteenth centuries record creole-like features in African American speech. Even today, certain features of Ebonics, such as the absence of the linking verbs "is" and "are," are widespread in Gullah and Caribbean English creoles but rare or non-existent in British dialects.

My own view is that the creolist hypothesis incorporates the strengths of the other hypotheses and avoids their weaknesses.[f] But we linguists may never be able to settle that particular issue one way or another. What we can settle on is the unique identity of Ebonics as an English dialect.

---

f For a survey of creoles and of theories of their origins, see J. Holm (1988 and 1989) *Pidgins and Creoles: Volumes 1 and 2.* Cambridge: Cambridge University Press.

4   The Oakland School Board proposal

So what does all this scholarship have to do with the Oakland School Board's proposal? Some readers might be fuming that it's one thing to identify Ebonics as a dialect and quite another to promote its usage.[g] Don't linguists realize that non-standard dialects are stigmatized in the larger society, and that Ebonics speakers who cannot shift to Standard English are less likely to do well in school and on the job front? Well, yes. The resolution we put forward last January in fact stated that "there are benefits in acquiring Standard English." But there is experimental evidence both from the United States and Europe that mastering the standard language might be easier if the differences in the student vernacular and Standard English were made explicit rather than entirely ignored.

To give only one example: at Aurora University, outside Chicago, inner-city African American students were taught by an approach that contrasted Standard English and Ebonics features through explicit instruction and drills. After eleven weeks, this group showed a 59 percent reduction in their use of Ebonics features in their Standard English writing. But a control group taught by conventional methods showed an 8.5 percent increase in such features.

This is the technique the Oakland School Board was promoting in its resolution last December. The approach is not new; it is part of the 16-year old Standard English Proficiency Program, which is being used in some 300 California schools. Since the media uproar over its original proposal, the Oakland School Board has clarified its intent: the point is not to teach Ebonics as a distinct language but to use it as a tool to increase mastery of Standard English among Ebonics speakers. The support of linguists for this approach may strike nonlinguists as unorthodox, but that is where our principles – and the evidence – lead us.

John Rickford is Martin Luther King Centennial Professor in Linguistics and African and Afro-American Studies at Stanford University in the US.

---

g See Honeyford and Quirk, this volume.

Chapter 13

Wendy Bokhorst-Heng

1999

SINGAPORE'S *SPEAK MANDARIN CAMPAIGN*

Language ideological debates and the imagining of the nation[a]

1 Introduction

ACCORDING TO BENEDICT ANDERSON, "Communities are to be distinguished, not by their falsity/genuineness, but by the style in which they are imagined" (1991: 6). I take this notion of "imagined communities" as my starting point in this chapter because of the focus it implicitly puts on language. Imagining requires language. But also, around the world, nationalist leaders have used the meanings of language to define this imagining. What is meant by the meanings of language is more than the symbolic use of language, as one might use a national flag or national anthem, in the rallying call of nationalism. Rather, the focus is on how [debates about language—"language ideological debates"—occur within] the larger discourses of imagining the nation, how they participate in that process and inform each other.

In this chapter, I will consider the production and reproduction of language meanings within the context of imagining Singapore. [. . .] Ever since independence, the government in Singapore has imagined a nation that is disciplined, orderly, rugged, efficient, and controlled. Individuality and alternative expressions of national and personal identity are discouraged (Chua 1995). Within this framework, former Prime Minister Lee Kuan Yew has personally developed very particular ideas about language and about how these meanings of language further his view of what is a good society and how that society is to be understood. In particular, while being imagined as multi-ethnic and multilingual, this discourse is more about homogeneity within each ethnic community rather than heterogeneity within the nation.

a This extract originally appeared in J. Blommaert (ed.) (1999) *Language Ideological Debates*. Berlin: Mouton de Gruyter pp. 235–66. On language planning more generally, see e.g. Kaplan, R.B. and R.B. Baldauf Jr. (1997) *Language Planning From Practice To Theory*. Clevedon: Multilingual Matters.

The production and reproduction of these language ideologies find their nexus in the annual *Speak Mandarin Campaign* (henceforth *SMC*). The *SMC* is aimed at the largest ethnic community in Singapore, the Chinese, and its goal is to stimulate the use of one standardized language variety—Mandarin Chinese—rather than the many Chinese dialects spoken by members of that community in Singapore. Thus, the ultimate effect of the *SMC* is one of homogenizing the Chinese community, in itself seen as a necessary building block for building a multicultural, pluralist Singaporean nation. [. . .]

2   Singapore: some background

The Singaporean population comprises three major ethnic groups: 77.5 percent Chinese, 14.2 percent Malays, and 7.1 percent Indians (and 1.2% "Others"). Of these groups, the Chinese community is the most heterogeneous. In the 1957 census, 11 Chinese dialects were identified as mother-tongues: 39.8 percent claimed Hokkien to be their mother-tongue, 22.6 percent Teowchew, 20 percent Cantonese, 6.8 percent Hainanese, 6.1 percent Hakka, and the remaining 4.7 percent other Chinese and Malaysian dialects. As put by Lee Kuan Yew recently in a book commemorating the 50th anniversary of the British Council in Singapore, "We were a Tower of Babel, trying to find a common tongue" (*Strait Times (ST)* 18 April 1997). Since Independence in 1965, the People's Action Party (PAP) government has attempted to reduce this linguistic diversity and to homogenize the Chinese community. Following familiar nationalist rhetoric, the government leaders (and particularly Lee Kuan Yew) have fervently argued that this linguistic diversity is incompatible with the goals of nation-building and have developed policies specifically aimed to solve the problems that such diversity posed for the nation. In part because the Chinese community is particularly divided in its heterogeneity, the government has especially targeted this community. As will be discussed later in this paper, the argument has been that a divided Chinese community would not only be detrimental to the survival of that particular community, but also detrimental to the survival of the nation.

However, it is precisely Singapore's linguistic and cultural diversity that has hindered such arguments from appearing alone. In the first place, the basis of the PAP government's platform at Independence was that the party stood for *all* Singaporeans [. . .]. Thus, "multiracialism" has systematically formed the basis of its political and nationalist agenda. Furthermore, given the fact that Singapore is physically surrounded by Indonesia and Malaysia—two predominantly Malay and Islamic nations—Singapore has had to carefully manage its image. With a predominantly Chinese population, the leaders had to assure their neighbors that Singapore was not an extension of China (and more importantly in the earlier days, of Communism), but was first of all devoted to its position as a Southeast Asian nation.

Thus, for these and other reasons, all efforts to unite the Chinese community have been couched within the larger policies of multiracialism and multilingualism.[b]

---

b For an overview of comparable tensions within nationalism, see Fishman, this volume.

Revamping the education system was one of the first policy actions of the PAP leaders. Rather than allowing different language-stream schools to continue as had been the practice under British colonialism (Wilson 1978), they introduced bilingualism as a way to unify and nationalize the education system. All students in Malay-, Tamil- and Mandarin-medium schools would learn English as a second language (mostly for Math and Science). All those in English-medium schools would learn the language associated with their ethnicity as a second language (mostly for Civics and History). In effect, this form of bilingualism made English the lingua franca of Singapore, giving the policy the name among local academics "English-knowing bilingualism" (Kachru 1983). Like in most postcolonial African countries, the former colonial language (in this case English) was seen as an ethnically neutral language and thus (among other reasons) introduced for the purposes of national unity and for economic development [. . .] But in contrast to the way in which, for instance, Mozambique has adopted Portuguese (Stroud 1999), Singapore's leaders have very carefully excluded English from the realm of nationalist discourse and denied it any status as a mother-tongue in Singapore. I will return to this later [. . .].

Not only did this definition of bilingualism make English the lingua franca, but it also prescribed for each person their "mother-tongue." For all ethnic groups, in a curious twist, "mother-tongue" is defined according to one's father's ethnicity (and which thus may not be the language spoken in the home). If your father is ethnically Chinese, your mother-tongue is Mandarin, if Indian then Tamil, and if Malay then Bahasa Malay. So, even though Mandarin was identified as "mother-tongue" for only 0.1 percent of the Chinese community in the 1957 census, Mandarin was prescribed as such for all ethnic Chinese within the bilingual policy. Within this framework, English cannot be a mother-tongue. The proscriptive definition of bilingualism has thus made bilingualism more a policy about homogenization than heterogeneity, and more about linguistic purism than diversity.

The government's efforts to entrench these three mother-tongues in the various communities were particularly intense in the late 1970s after the bilingual policy received its first official evaluation. In 1978, then Prime Minister [. . .] Lee Kuan Yew appointed Defence Minister Dr. Goh Keng Swee and the "education team" to evaluate the bilingual policy as it pertained to the Chinese community. In their final report, the committee declared the policy a failure. Less than 40 percent of the students attained the minimum competency level in two languages. The committee saw the continued use of dialects in the home as the main reason for this failure. Because about 85 percent of the students spoke only dialects at home, they were in effect having to learn two languages at school. As well, what they were learning at school was thus not being reinforced at home. On the basis of these findings, and in a rare case of admitting failure, the government concluded that not all children were able to cope with the demands of becoming fully bilingual. However, this is not to say that the policy of bilingualism was to be abandoned. Rather, major changes were made in the education system such that language became the very basis of society. Language-based streaming was introduced, whereby the educational system was stratified according to the different language abilities of the students. The weakest students would receive monolingual education; the best students would receive intensive bilingual training. For all children in Primary school, more than 50 percent of curriculum time would be devoted to language learning. Thus, "effective bilingualism" has become closely aligned with academic, and hence social and economic, success. Since 1987, all schools are now English-medium with "mother-tongue" taught as a second language.

Going by the most recent census conducted in 1990, it appears that the use of "mother-tongue" in the home is taking hold. 29.8 percent of Chinese households use Mandarin as their predominant household language, 50.6 percent one of the dialects, and 19.2 percent English (Tham 1996: 27). While a question on mother-tongue (which appeared only in the 1957 census) cannot be compared on a par with questions on language use, these figures do suggest that there has been a pattern of remarkable language shift away from the use of dialects to Mandarin and English.

While there were real pedagogical and academic concerns motivating the government to make such radical changes in the education system, what the government leaders had to say about language suggests a deeper concern. Furthermore, the fact that these changes coincided with the launching of the first *Speak Mandarin Campaign* also suggests that these policies were entwined in the larger language ideological debates gripping the imagining of the nation. Why Lee Kuan Yew and his government were so concerned about the failure of the bilingual policy has to do with their view of language meanings, with their assumptions of what a "good" society is, and with how they understood the role of language and especially the bilingual policy in the imagining of that society. [. . .] To these meanings I now turn.

3 English-knowing bilingualism: crisis management

The bilingual policy has been premised on what Pendley (1983) calls the "functional polarization" of language, or, as Kuo and Jernudd (1994) describe it, the "division of labor between languages." In his 1972 speech at a Singapore Teachers' Union Dinner, Lee Kuan Yew established the parameters of this polarization (*The Mirror*, 20 November 1972):

> When I speak of bilingualism, I do not mean just the facility of speaking two languages. It is more basic than that, first we understand ourselves . . . then the facility of the English language gives us access to the science and technology of the West. It also provides a convenient common ground on which . . . everybody competes in a neutral medium.
>
> With the language [mother-tongue] go the fables and proverbs. It is the learning of a whole value system, a whole philosophy of life, that can maintain the fabric of our society intact, in spite of exposure to all the current madnesses around the world.

On the one side of this polarization is English, the language needed for instrumental and pragmatic purposes. Professor Jayakumar, then Minister of State (Law and Home Affairs), outlined three pragmatic functions for English (*ST*, 19 August 1982). First, at the national level, "English is the major international language for trade, science and technology and proficiency in the language is essential as Singapore becomes a leading financial and banking centre." [. . .] Second, at the individual level, "education in English is the key to the productivity concept. With increasing modernization, skilled workers who know English will be in greater demand . . . it is the key to acquisition of skills and training and career advancement." [. . .] Finally, at the community level, when English "is the common language here, it will enable all Singaporeans—regardless of race—to communicate with one another." In this pragmatic view, then, the English language is seen as neutral and culture-less.[c]

Positioned on the other side of this polarization are the three "mother-tongues," Malay, Tamil and Mandarin. As mother-tongues, they are the languages of identity, of ethnicity and of culture. They are the languages of good values, and, in Lee Kuan Yew's words, of a "whole philosophy of life." They are the languages of national cohesion. As put another way by Lee Kuan Yew, while English is for *new knowledge*, to support the development of a modern industrial nation, mother-tongue is for *old knowledge*, to keep the people anchored and focused amidst the changes around them (*ST*, 24 November 1979).

What we see in this polarization is a very selective (and often paradoxical) understanding of language. With respect to English, the view is that the language can be separated from culture and technology so that it is possible to adopt the technology accessed through English without necessarily accepting its culture. In contrast, the mother-tongue is seen to somehow inherently embody one's ethnically defined culture. Through mother-tongue education, children would be "inculcated with good eastern values and cultures . . . These values will be thus programmed like a computer in the children and form their basic principles in dealing with society and with problems" (Choo Wee Khiang, *Parliamentary Debates*, 17 January 1989, Vol. 52, Prt 1, Col. 152). Unlike English, it is impossible to separate one's mother-tongue from culture.

While the lines demarcating language meanings within this structure of functional polarization have been presented by Lee Kuan Yew as rational and unproblematic, in practice the model has been very difficult to sustain. [. . .]

During the 1970s, government leaders began to express concern about the increase of individualism, consumerism and liberalism among the people. [. . .] Dr. Tay Eng Soon (Minister of State, Education) noted [. . .] that there was an increase of such undesirable qualities as "hippyism, a libertine pre-occupation with self-gratification, the cult of living for today and for myself and to hell with others" among the youth (*ST*, 13 December 1982). In the context of this discourse, the meanings of English took on added elements. English, the leaders argued, actually posed a threat to the imagining of the nation. The threat of English came in two ways. In the first place, because English is seen as being neutral and mother-tongue to embody one's culture, to learn English at the expense of the mother-tongue would leave a person "deculturalized." In his 1972 speech to the teachers, Lee Kuan Yew explained what he meant by deculturalization in his reference to the Caribbean. It is a "calypso-type society . . . speaking pidgin English, mindlessly aping the Americans or British with no basic values or cultures" of their own, and leading a

---

c   Ngũgĩ and Mazrui also discuss English in the global economy.

"steel-beating and rum-brewing-and-drinking, happy go lucky life," he said. Frankly, "I do not believe this [kind of society] is worth the building . . . worth the preserving" (*The Mirror*, 20 November 1972). What Lee Kuan Yew seems to be suggesting is that to be monolingual in English would invite the danger of having no culture at all. One would be reduced to mindless imitation of the West, not being Asian and not being Western either, with no identity to call one's own.

But there is another (and very contradictory) element to English. [. . . R]ather than being neutral, English carries cultural meaning as well. Only, the cultural values associated with English are debased and decadent. C. V. Devan Nair (then National Trade Union Congress Secretary General), put it this way: "Through the English language we are enabled to absorb all that modern science and technology can offer us." However, at the same time, most younger Singaporeans also imbibe "the mindless pop culture of the West." This culture and way of life, he says, is one "in which the centres of cognition, perception and feeling are not located in the cerebral cortex, or even in the heart and its cultured emotions. On the contrary, they are located below the waist, and primarily in what may be called the lower vital centres" (*ST*, 15 January 1979). [. . .] Instead of exploring the social changes as associated with concurrent changes in Singapore's economic and political conditions, these were labeled as alien, brought in through the non mother-tongue. A tension is thus created between the pragmatic needs for English in the imagining of the nation and the potential threat it carries to that imagining.

The answer to this quandary lies in reinforcing the boundaries of the functional polarization of language through what has come to be called the "Asianizing" of Singapore. Because English could potentially lead to deculturalization, Singaporeans needed to be "re-culturalized", they needed to have their Chineseness, Indianness and Malayness restored to them. Because English carried the threat of decadent Westernization, Singaporeans needed a cultural ballast to ground them and protect them. And so, since the late 1970s, through various measures such as moral education programs in the school, the institution of a set of "core" national values, and the creation of different self-help groups for the different communities, the government has sought to re-Asianize the people. Greater emphasis was placed on the prescription of mother-tongues, in the belief that "a race = a culture = a language". [. . .]

Although all three communities are the focus of this Asianizing effort, special attention has been given to the Chinese. [. . .] MP Dr. Ow Chin Hock explained the reasons for this focus: "Unlike the Malay community, Chinese Singaporeans do not have such uniting factors as a common language and religion." In fact, he argued, there is no such thing as *a* Chinese community in Singapore. Rather, "there are three sub-communities: the English educated Chinese, the Chinese educated, and the less educated, dialect-speaking Chinese" (*ST*, 16 October 1990). Thus, the newspaper caption read, "Chinese Singaporeans face crisis in values and culture." Because there was nothing within the community to unite them, the re-ethnification of the Chinese community was paramount. It was in this context of crisis intervention that Lee Kuan Yew launched in 1979 what has become an annual *Speak Mandarin Campaign*.

4   The *Speak Mandarin Campaign*

Three key official arguments have been appealed to by the government in support of the *Speak Mandarin Campaign*. First, there is the *educational* argument: because the continued use of dialects created a burden for children having to learn two languages at school, the use of dialects at home must be restricted and replaced by Mandarin. Second, there is the *cultural* argument: because of the dominance of English, and the threat of deculturalization and Western decadence that came with it, Chinese Singaporeans needed to be re-ethnicized through Mandarin, which would also then provide them with a cultural ballast. And through this re-ethnicization, they would also be united to form *a* Chinese community. Finally, there is the *communicative* argument: Chinese Singaporeans need a lingua franca other than English. The most logical choice was Mandarin, as it was neutral to all dialect groups. While these arguments structure much of the campaign's discourse, the issues are in fact much more complex, and have to do with very specific views of language and how language meanings figure into the imagining of the nation. After first considering the *SMC* as a campaign, I will try to unpack some of these meanings.

4.1   The campaign

Given the fact that imagining the nation in Singapore occurs through very centralized planning, it is perhaps not surprising that the "national campaign" has become the most common genre of government-to-people communication. In his analysis of campaigns in Singapore, Tham Kok Wing (1983) identified sixty-six national campaigns between 1958 and 1982. National campaigns are all planned by the Prime Minister's Office. They have been used to direct and influence public awareness of certain issues, to encourage people to behave in specific desired ways, to control the spread of certain "undesirable" practices or values, as an instrument for policy implementation, to consolidate mass support, and ultimately to psychologically build up the citizenry for the task of nation-building. They have had a wide scope, including Anti-Spitting, Courtesy, and more recently (1996/1997), a Smile campaign. While diverse in their messages, nonetheless the campaigns exhibit a certain stable and generic form [. . .] The general framework is that of crisis management: a crisis is presented, and the government's answer to that crisis is rationalized as being the only answer to that crisis. [. . .]

While the *SMC* has been meant for only the Chinese community, it has been presented in the [style] of a national campaign, having its precedents in the pre-Independence national language campaigns. It has been intensely prescriptive in its concerted effort to alter the language behavior of Chinese Singaporeans, to convince them to abandon their use of dialects for the sake of their community and the nation. The *SMC* speeches are almost messianic in their warning of impending crisis should the Chinese fail to unite through the use of Mandarin. In many ways, the *SMC* has been even *larger* than the national campaigns. In terms of duration, it has been by far the longest running campaign. In terms of organization, it has its own secretariat. The campaign involves a completely comprehensive effort, drawing in members of education, mass media, grassroots, the Singapore Chinese Chamber of Commerce and Industry (SCCCI), government leaders, and even the Prime Minister. And its visibility is far greater than any other campaign. As put succinctly by Harrison, "The campaigning for Mandarin has not, as far as can be established, used sky-writing. To find such an omission has been difficult" (1980: 177). Banners, posters, and stickers with campaign slogans encouraging the Chinese to speak Mandarin are displayed in public places. T-shirts with the same slogans are worn by students. Advertisements supporting the campaign appear on television, radio and in the cinemas. Numerous activities have been generated in support of the campaign including Mandarin classes (even via telephone and the Internet) and various contests and workshops. No other campaign has seen such a sustained and extensive presence in Singapore. [. . .]

4.2 The crystallization of language meanings: a speech by Goh Chok Tong

[. . . T]he *SMC* is part of the overall objective of restoring to the Chinese their Chineseness, to *make* Mandarin the mother-tongue of all Chinese Singaporeans. This effort is based on the belief that "a race = a language = a culture", and translated into campaign slogans such as "*hua ren hua yu*" (literally "Chinese people, Chinese language") and, "If you are Chinese, make a statement—in Mandarin." Two key arguments have been presented to support this goal, both couched within the overall framework of a crisis leading to the inevitable conclusion that Mandarin must be the mother-tongue for all Chinese Singaporeans. The first is the *Mandarin versus Dialect* argument, and the second is the *Mandarin versus English* argument. Throughout the campaign, these two debates can be seen weaving in and out of each other, [. . . and] leaders frequently play these two debates against each other, using their contradiction to both create a tension and then to resolve that tension.

To examine the crystallization of language meanings within these two debates, and their role within the imagining of the nation, I will draw primarily from Goh Chok Tong's speech delivered at the launching ceremony of the 1991 *Speak Mandarin Campaign*. [. . .] While the PAP has held a clear majority of voters' support since Independence, there had been a steady decline throughout the decade of the 1980s: 75.5 percent in 1980, 61.8 percent in 1988, and 61 percent in 1991. The 1991 results were particularly upsetting for the party as the election marked the beginning of Goh Chok Tong's leadership as Prime Minister [. . .] The declining support caused the PAP leaders to re-examine their ideology and administration. In their post-election analysis, they attributed their losses to the fact that the opposition candidates had used dialects in their campaigning to win the support of the Chinese community (*ST*, 14 December 1991). They were forced to acknowledge the voice of resistance in the defining of language meanings. Thus, in some ways, 1991 is a watershed in language meanings, a time when the voice of the people was heard. It is in this context that Goh's 1991 *SMC* speech was given. I will now give the full text of the speech:

"Mandarin is more than a language"

Mr Goh Chok Tong, The Prime Minister
30 September 1991

A nation is "a single people traditionally fixed on a well-defined territory, speaking the same language and preferably a language all its own, possessing a distinct culture, and shaped to a common mould by many generations of shared historical experience." [Rupert Emerson in *From Empire to Nation*]. By this definition, Singapore is not yet a nation. We do not speak the same language, and we do not yet possess the many generations of shared historical experience.

Within the same family, it is still very common to find that grandparents, parents and children do not share the same primary language —the language they are most comfortable in. For the grandparents the language they use is very often dialect, for the parents Mandarin; and for the children English. Of course, the three generations do still converse with one another through a combination of dialect, Mandarin and English. But their common vocabulary is unlikely to go beyond 500 words. They will have difficulty discussing any subject in depth. Their conversation will be shallow, limited by each other's command of the other generation's primary language.

I speak Hokkien to my mother. My children speak to me and my wife in English, and Mandarin to their grandmother, my mother. They have dropped dialect. It will take another generation in my family for three generations to share the same one primary language.

Heterogeneous community

In Singapore, communication across families is even more complicated for the older generation. It is not unusual to find two Chinese together who are unable to talk to one another. One may speak Hokkien only while the other Cantonese. How can we ever build a nation if the Chinese community is unable even to speak the same language, be it dialect, Mandarin or English?

You will discover how heterogeneous Singapore is when you go campaigning in an election. No political leader in Singapore can reach out on his own to every Singaporean. No matter how good a linguist he is, he cannot be expected to master the four official languages plus over 20 Chinese and Indian dialects.

It is in our national interest to move into a situation where all Singaporeans can speak to one another in a common language, i.e. English, and to members of his own community in his mother-tongue. For the Chinese, the common mother-tongue should be Mandarin rather than dialect. Unlike Hong Kong, where Cantonese predominates, it will not be politically acceptable if we replace the teaching of Mandarin with any of the major dialects. I do not think we can agree on which dialect to be taught. If we do not succeed in forging Mandarin as the common mother-tongue, the link language for future generations of Chinese Singaporeans will be English only.

Already English is becoming the dominant language among Chinese households. Its use had increased from 10 per cent in 1980 to 21 per cent in 1990.

Language and values

The question is whether with the greater use of English, we may lose some aspects of our identity. These are the traditional values of our forefathers.

Values and language cannot be easily separated. They are intrinsically linked to each other. Values get into our minds and hearts through folklore. For the Chinese these stories and beliefs are preserved in their literature or passed on by word of mouth. Although Chinese literature, idioms and proverbs can be translated into English, their full meaning may be lost in the process.

A Chinese Singaporean who does not know Chinese—either Mandarin or dialect—runs the risk of losing the collective wisdom of the Chinese civilization. This year's campaign slogan is apt. Mandarin is more than a language. Mandarin not only allows the Chinese to communicate with one another but also opens up many chests of treasures—Chinese literature, music, operas, paintings, calligraphy, ceramics and so on. When we can appreciate them, we will feel proud to be part of that rich history which is Chinese.

A sense of history

Having a sense of history is important. It gives us our bearing and makes us understand what we are today. As a country, Singapore's history is short. But if we know Mandarin, we can identify with a 5000 year old civilization.

Last month, the Chinese Chamber of Commerce and Industry organized a congress of Chinese businessmen from all over the world. These were successful men and women. One would expect them to prefer using English, which is the language of trade and business. But I was told that that was not the case. Although the official language of the congress was English, the moment someone spoke in Mandarin, the atmosphere changed. It became more intimate. The use of Mandarin brought out immediately a common understanding among the Chinese businessmen of different nationalities. They felt a common bond. They felt they belonged together.

Making Mandarin popular

Our problem is how to make Mandarin popular with our students. Many parents have voiced the concern that their children may not be able to cope with the learning of Mandarin in schools. I believe we should make

learning the language lively and enjoyable. We should put fun and humor
to soften the serious task of teaching Chinese.

Last year's "Speak Mandarin Campaign" made some Singaporeans
uncomfortable. I fully understand their concerns. Let me assure non-
Chinese Singaporeans that the government is not promoting the Chinese
language or culture at the expense of the others. In fact, the Ministry
of Information and the Arts is working together with the Malay Language
Committee to promote standard Malay. The Ministry has also asked the
Indian community if it needs help to promote the use of Tamil. We
want all the ethnic communities to preserve their language, culture and
values. We aim to be a harmonious multi-racial nation.

For the Chinese community, our aim should be a single people,
speaking the same primary language, that is Mandarin, possessing a
distinct culture and a shared past, and sharing a common destiny for
the future.

Such a Chinese community will then be tightly-knit. Provided it is
also tolerant and appreciative of the other communities' heritage, able
to communicate with them in English, and work with them for a
common future, Singapore will grow to become a nation.

[. . . Prime Minister Goh's] speech follows the argumentation structure common
in many of the national campaigns: one which propounds a problem and then
provides a solution to that problem. [. . .] At the very outset of the speech, [he]
establishes the premise of "the problem": [Rupert Emerson's timeless assertion of
what a nation is. T] his definition [is then taken] as common-sense knowledge, and
used to measure the degree of nationhood [that Singapore has] achieved so far.
Singapore is not yet a nation. It does not have a *common language* and it does not
have a *common history*. [Emerson's] definition establishes what Singapore is not, and
provides a direction for what Singapore should work towards.

[So linguistic diversity is identified first as a challenge to] Singapore's achievement of nationhood. [. . .] What is interesting in Goh [. . .]'s speech is that he
frames the problem as a *national* problem. Singapore is not yet a nation because it
does not have a common language. Yet, in the rest of his speech, he concentrates
on the problems of linguistic diversity within just the Chinese community. Thus
he uses a *national* framework to address community issues. Providing factual
evidence, he problematizes Singapore's linguistic diversity at all levels of society:
from the smallest unit, the family, including his own; to the Chinese community,
where dialects hinder intra-ethnic communication; and to government, where no
political leader "can reach out on his own to every Singaporean." [. . .]

At this point, Goh introduces the inevitable solution[, . . .] linguistic uniformity: "It is in our national interest," he argues, "to move into a situation where all
Singaporeans can speak to one another in a common language, i.e., English, and
to members of his own community in his mother-tongue." For the Chinese, this
common mother-tongue was to be, or become, Mandarin, rather than any dialect.
Goh quickly dismisses dialect as being not even a viable consideration: "I do not
think we can agree on which dialect to be taught." He then goes on to imply that
if linguistic (dialect) diversity were to continue, Mandarin would not take hold as

the common mother-tongue. And in that event, English, he predicted, would become the intra-ethnic link language. He then constructs the rest of his argument using the Mandarin versus English dichotomy. But before I turn to this part of his argument, the Mandarin versus Dialects dichotomy needs to be considered a bit more, as it is crucial to understanding the making of a mother-tongue.

4.2.1 MANDARIN VERSUS DIALECTS

The 1979 campaign was launched with the call to "*Speak more Mandarin and less dialect*" and "*No dialect, more Mandarin.*" While they agreed with the promotion of Mandarin, many members of the Chinese community took strong offence to this overt call to eliminate the use of dialects. Traditionally, it was dialect-speaking parents and grandparents that played an active role in the transmission of culture and values. And dialects, not Mandarin, were seen as necessary for intimacy, for culture and roots, for family and clan identity, and as the true mother-tongue. And so the campaign slogans were softened to read "*From now on, speak Mandarin, please*" and "*Let's speak Mandarin.*" However, while the slogans were softened, the objective to eliminate the use of dialects remained central to the campaign. This was [carried out by asserting a number of contrasts between Mandarin and dialects in campaign and government speeches:]

- Dialects are vulgar, polluting, and associated with the uneducated; Mandarin is refined and part of the literary culture. [(e.g. *ST*, 11 July 1980)]. [. . .]
- Dialects are divisive, fragmentary, and a major cause of miscommunication and misunderstanding; Mandarin is the language of unity, cohesion, and a bridge between the different members of the Chinese community. [(e.g. *ST*, 9 June 1981; *ST*, 2 October 1985)]. [. . .]
- Dialects are a burden on the young, forcing them to learn two languages when they go to school; Mandarin facilitates academic success. [(e.g. *ST*, 26 October 1981; *ST*, 17 November 1980)]. [. . .]
- Dialects have no value, neither culturally nor economically; Mandarin is linked to a 5,000-year old history, rich in culture, and bears immense economic potential with the opening up of China's markets. [(e.g. *ST*, 17 October 1980)]. [. . .]
- Dialects represent the past and are primitive; Mandarin is the future. [(e.g. *ST*, 15 June 1980; *ST*, 10 January 1980)]. [. . .]

By contrasting the meanings of dialects with Mandarin, dialects are [. . .] denied validity in the imagining of the nation and community, and even in the home. [. . . A]lthough in 1979 Lee Kuan Yew had assured parents that the choice was theirs as to what language they wanted their children to speak in the home, it is clear what that choice should be. In this dicho[tomous] structuring of language meanings, then, the government simultaneously created a void by banishing dialects from nation, community, and home, leaving the Chinese community and individual with no mother-tongue, and then filled that void by prescribing Mandarin as their mother-tongue.

4.2.2. MANDARIN VERSUS ENGLISH

In his call for linguistic uniformity, it is significant that Goh [argues . . .] in his speech for linguistic uniformity through [. . .] English plus mother-tongue. In fact, he presents the increasing dominance of English among the Chinese as problematic [. . .] The increasing presence of English in the homes of Chinese Singaporeans relates to the second element of nationhood lacking in Singapore: the lack of shared historical experiences and culture. [. . .] As [he] put it, "The question is whether with the greater use of English, we may lose some aspects of our identity. These are the traditional values of our forefathers." At the individual level, a person would lose "the collective wisdom of the Chinese civilization" and would lose his/her bearings; he/she would be deculturalized. English cannot become a mother-tongue.[1] [. . .]

Goh spends the rest of his speech establishing the merits of Mandarin over English in the imagining of the nation. In the first place, he presents the *cultural argument*: Mandarin is "more than just a language . . . it also opens up many chests of treasures—Chinese literature, music, operas, paintings, calligraphy, ceramics, and so on." He then offers the *pragmatic argument*, bringing Mandarin out of the context of culture to that of business and commerce in his example of the use of Mandarin at the SCCCI Congress. With the more recent focus of the *SMC* on the English-educated Chinese, the business appeal of Mandarin has grown even stronger. Mandarin has given Singaporeans an edge over its predominantly Malay neighbors in establishing commercial ties with China. However, this pragmatic argument rarely appears alone, and indeed, cannot. For Mandarin to become the established mother-tongue of the Chinese community (especially the English-medium educated), it must go beyond the neutrality and pragmatism of English. In Goh's account of the SCCCI congress, he uses the device of contrast to take Mandarin there. The moment someone switched from English to Mandarin, "the atmosphere changed." There was intimacy, brotherhood, a common understanding. [. . . N]ot only does Mandarin hold a place in the commercial sector, but [. . . i]t could unite this group of nationally diverse, but ethnically homogeneous, Chinese members, whereas English could not. [. . .]

The validity of Mandarin in the nationalist agenda is thus established. Now we come to the climax, the proposed solution. Goh began his speech with a discussion concerning the definition of a nation. The problem is that Singapore is not yet a nation—it does not have a common language and it does not have shared historical experiences. In his speech, he demonstrated how the use of Mandarin can fill both needs. Because of the link between Mandarin and values, and between Mandarin and history, because Mandarin has a place in the commercial sector, and because all Chinese can unite through the use of Mandarin, Chinese Singaporeans must embrace Mandarin. Only then will they become a community, "a single people, speaking the same language, that is Mandarin, possessing a distinct culture and a shared past, and sharing a common destiny for the future". Such a Chinese community, he argues, "will then be tightly-knit;" only then will they be able to contribute to the task of nation building; then "Singapore will grow to become a nation." While Goh does give a disclaimer that this will only be possible if the Chinese community is sensitive to the non-Chinese communities, he does seem to nonetheless suggest that nationhood is contingent on the unity of the Chinese community. There is thus a blurring of the lines between nation and community [. . .]

4.3   The voices of resistance

[This slippage between nation and community is the first of two key paradoxes . . .] created by the use of a national campaign for the promotion of Mandarin. [. . .] The second has to do with the slippage between public and private created by the use of the *public* genre of the national campaign to make Mandarin a mother-tongue, an issue located in the *private* domain of the home. These two paradoxes have translated into areas of resistance, the former mainly voiced by the non-Chinese communities, and the latter by the members of the Chinese community. These are by no means the only voices of resistance; however, they do demonstrate how such resistance has contributed to language ideological debates in Singapore.

4.3.1   MANDARIN FOR NATION? FOR COMMUNITY?

The multiracialist discourse in the "Asianizing of Singapore" paints a picture of Singapore as being a multiethnic nation with three homogenous ethnic communities unproblematically coexisting in equilibrious relation to each other. Singapore has rejected the "melting pot" model in favor of retaining the cultural heritage of the different ethnic communities. The multi-racialist discourse also contends that cultural and ethnic identity coexists harmoniously with political loyalty at the national level. Goh Chok Tong captured this harmony in the phrase: "Unity in diversity" (*ST*, 14 August 1988). The continuance of ethnic identity has allowed the government to be absolved of many of the responsibilities of cultural main-tenance and social welfare, making them the responsibility of the individual communities (Chua Beng Huat 1995).

However, there are a number of problems with this model. In the first place, the sheer disproportionate size of the Chinese community constantly threatens the balance of equilibrium between the different ethnic communities. Chinese-related issues often dominate the agenda, and the non-Chinese communities frequently feel overwhelmed and marginalized (Puru Shotam 1987; Tan Su Hwi 1996). There is often considerable slippage in the government's discourse between nation and community. It is not always clear which is being referenced. A look at the use of pronouns in Goh Chok Tong's 1991 *SMC* speech demonstrates this ambiguity.

In this speech, Goh is clearly attempting to develop a sense of inclusiveness and community, particularly in his frequent use of "we" and "us", together used 18 times.[d] Not only does the choice of pronouns evoke a sense of community, but it also brings everyone into the problem. Together they will work towards solving the problem of nationhood—which is "our problem," "our aim" and in "our national interest." Such inclusive pronouns also evoke a strong sense of Goh's presence in the text, which is made even more visible by his use of "I" (5X) and "me" (2X). In contrast to the use of inclusive pronouns, "they" is used only 8 times—

---

d Compare Billig's discussion of pronouns and 'deixis', this volume.

in reference to a family, to his own family, to language and values, and to the Chinese businessmen. Not once was "they" used to refer to an outgroup, or to separate "us" from "them".

It is instructive to note in this context when Goh does *not* use inclusive pronouns. After drawing his audience into the problem with "we" and "us," when it comes to working out the solution in the last paragraph, he retreats. In the last paragraph, he lapses into the traditional community-based rhetoric whereby each community is responsible for its own welfare. In order to remove himself, it seems he needs to extract the human element that had been so present in his text. For the first time, the Chinese community is de-humanized as an "it." If Singapore is to become a nation, it requires not the efforts of "we" or "us," but rather, it requires the efforts of an inanimate Chinese community.

However, while Goh's use of inclusive pronouns create a sense of community and bonding, a closer analysis reveals considerable ambiguity. The use of "we" in some cases clearly refers to Singaporeans (e.g. "We do not yet speak the same language, and we do not yet possess the many generations of shared historical experience"), and in other cases to the Chinese community (e.g. "When we can appreciate them, we will feel proud to be part of that rich history which is Chinese"). But the other references are not so clear. At least the following patterns of reference can be found in the text:

1   "we" = Singaporeans? Chinese Community? Government?
E.g.: "How can we ever build a nation if the Chinese community is unable even to speak the same language, be it dialect, Mandarin or English?" [. . .]

2   "we" = Chinese Singaporeans (presumably)
E.g.: "I do not think we can agree on which dialect to be taught. If we do not succeed in forging Mandarin as the common mother-tongue, the link language for future generations of Chinese Singaporeans will be English only." [. . .]

3   "we"/"us" = Singaporeans? Chinese Community?
E.g.: "The question is whether with the greater use of English, we may lose some aspects of our identity." [. . .]

4   "we" = Chinese Community? Government? Singaporeans? Teachers?
E.g.: "I believe we should make learning the language lively and enjoyable. We should put fun and humor to soften the serious task of teaching Chinese."

5   "we" = Government? Ministry of Information and the Arts?
E.g.: "We want all the ethnic communities to preserve their language, culture and values. We aim to be a harmonious multi-racial nation."

[. . .] The ambiguity in Goh's text can be understood at at least two levels. Firstly, the specific reference of the pronouns can be seen as irrelevant to the general aura and effect of the speech. It does not demand intense scrutiny. If anything, and secondly, the ambiguity enhances the overall effect of community. The ambiguity attempts to diffuse any sense of boundary, and to maintain a discourse of multi-racialism within the "Asianizing of Singapore."

However, this blurring is precisely what has made the juxtaposition of community and nation within the genre of a national campaign problematic. It is precisely because it is not always clear *who* the campaign speeches are directed at, and who is being drawn into the "we" that the non-Chinese communities have reacted against the campaign. They fear an increase in Chinese chauvinism, and worry that there may be a consequent reduction in the status of their languages and cultures, and that the government might weaken its commitment to multi-racialism (*ST*, 16 May 1978). The recent focus on Mandarin-versus-English made these questions even more pertinent. English is not confined to just the Chinese community (unlike dialects), and so the lines between community and nation became increasingly vague. The fault-line broke open during the 1990 *SMC*. The theme that year was about speaking Mandarin at work—clearly not a community-specific domain. *The Straits Times* was flooded with letters from both the Chinese and non-Chinese communities condemning the campaign as chauvinistic and exclusionary. As former Senior Minister Rajaratnam noted, people were questioning the government's commitment to multiracialism, and whether the leaders were "doing all this in favor of a Singaporean Singapore" (*ST*, 29 October 1990). They were questioning the boundary between nation and (Chinese) ethnic community.

Because of such resistance, the leaders must repeatedly qualify the *SMC*'s objectives. First there is the frequent guarantee that the campaign is not about replacing English with Mandarin as the official working language. [. . .] Second, the leaders assert that the promotion of Mandarin is not to diminish the status of the other official ethnic languages. [. . .] Third, the discourse of multi-racialism is frequently brought in to reassure the non-Chinese communities that the campaign is not for them, and not to make Singaporean society more Chinese at the expense of the other communities. [. . .] In his 1991 *SMC* speech, Goh Chok Tong similarly reminded the non-Chinese communities of the government's efforts to promote their languages and cultures. "We want all the ethnic languages to preserve their language, culture and values," he said. "We aim to be a harmonious, multiracial society." Equilibrium is thus restored through the discourse of the "Asianizing of Singapore" and through the reinstatement of the "a race = a language = a culture" equation.

4.3.2   PUBLIC GENRE FOR PRIVATE DOMAIN?[e]

Most national campaigns in Singapore are concerned with issues relating to public behavior. On the surface, the *SMC* also appears to be about behavior in the public domain. Lee Kuan Yew stated unequivocally in 1979 that he would not interfere with the home: "I want to be quite clear, we cannot control what is done at home; that we have to leave to the good sense of the parents and the grandparents." He went on to say, "Because administrative action cannot reach the home where dialects, already entrenched, will prevail," the government will focus on "dramatically" altering the pattern of language usage outside the home, in government offices,

---

e The public–private distinction is also discussed in this volume, in different ways, by Honeyford, Hill, Gumperz and Hernández-Chavez, and Urla.

public transit, hawker stalls and restaurants, shopping centres and so on (*Campaign Speeches* 1989). [. . .] The demarcations between private and public were thus made very explicit.

However, it also is clear that the main objective of the campaign has been to make Mandarin a mother-tongue, the language of the private domain of the home. Quoting again from Lee Kuan Yew, "The ultimate test" of the success of the campaign "is whether Mandarin is spoken at home between parents and their children. That is the meaning of mother tongue" (*ST*, 26 October 1981). Shortly after the campaign began, Goh Chok Tong announced that the 1980 census would for the first time include a survey on what languages Singaporeans speak at home. The same question would be asked in the 1990 census "to monitor the success" of the *SMC* (*ST*, 19 November 1979).

However, the focus on the home (private), voiced according to the conventions of a national campaign (public), has created an explosive contradiction in the campaign. As with the blurred distinction between nation and community, this contradiction has formed a fault-line along which voices of resistance have emerged. This became particularly problematic in 1980 when, in the view of many, the government's efforts moved too far into the private sphere. In 1980, the Director of Education, Chan Kai Yau, announced that, in a "move to take the *Speak Mandarin* drive one step further" (*ST*, 20 November 1980), all students were to be registered in their Hanyu Pinyin names, rather than the dialect names given at birth. His rationale was that pinyinization was necessary to reduce dialect-based identity and to unite the Chinese community. Hanyu Pinyin is a romanized system of transcribing Chinese characters based on Mandarin pronunciation. Most Chinese in Singapore go by the dialect pronunciation of their Chinese names, not Mandarin. The same Chinese character will have different dialect pronunciations, such that, for example, the same name will be Tan in Hokkien, Chan in Cantonese, Sin in Hainanese, and Chen in Mandarin. Thus, by enforcing Hanyu Pinyin, students were required to assume a name different from the one given them by their parents, and different from their father's. Parents were also urged to begin giving their children Mandarin names at birth. Lee Kuan Yew made compliance with this recommendation a measure of one's identification with the Chinese community. [. . .]

However, names are intensely personal and reflect personal, family, and group identity. A *Straits Times* survey conducted shortly after the policy was announced (21 November 1980) revealed a polarized reaction between the English-educated and the Chinese-educated. Reactions from the English-educated "ranged from mild support to an angry denouncement of it as an 'infringement of the individual's right'." [. . .] The Chinese-educated considered the move as "logically in step" with the *SMC*, while dialect speakers, who "believe firmly that whatever the government decides is always for their good, said they have no complaint if that is what the government wants" (21 November 1980). [. . .]

But perhaps the strongest voice of resistance was the "silent" one that spoke against registering children's birth names in dialect. After a full decade, it was clear that most Chinese Singaporeans resisted giving their children full pinyin names. According to *The Straits Times* editor, people simply "have not bought" the government's argument for pinyinizing names (23 December 1991). In 1987, Lee Kuan Yew noted that only 12 percent of all Chinese babies born in January to June 1987 were registered with full pinyinized names, compared to 22 percent in 1983. The number of children who had dialect surnames with Hanyu Pinyin personal names increased. The editor saw this pattern as a reflection of "acts of identity": "After all, most parents would want their surnames and their offspring's to be instantly recognizable as one and the same, as an outward mark of their blood bond . . . There is also the desire to preserve symbolic links with their dialect groups and the provinces and villages of their forefathers in China" (23 December 1991). Parents clearly drew the line: while complying by giving pinyin personal names, they resisted by keeping their dialect surnames. In the 1991 elections, they also demonstrated their resistance by voting in a member of the Workers Party, Low Thia Khiang in Hougang, who used dialects in his campaigning (*ST*, 14 December 1991). The government responded to the parents' voice of resistance by announcing that students would once again be allowed to register in their dialect names.

5   Conclusion

Before 1991, when it was re-designed and re-issued, each person's identity card included information about one's race and dialect. Since 1991, "dialect" no longer appears. In the prescriptive manner that has characterized the *SMC* all along, it is now assumed that if you are Chinese, your mother-tongue is Mandarin. The linguistic diversity characterizing the Chinese community has thus been homogenized. In this chapter, I have charted some of the key features in this prescription of mother-tongue meanings in the imagining of Singapore. The *Speak Mandarin Campaign* has been the catalyst of this journey, capturing the debates within and over language meanings in the imagining of Singapore. It has been the framework of policy interpretation and implementation, and of resistance to these interpretations and implementations. And it is the framework within which it is possible to go beyond a story of ideology production and re-production by a very domineering government, to one that tells of the tensions, negotiations, paradoxes and resistances by different groups. The story thus becomes one of identifying what has been normalized, how that process has occurred, and of how resistance contributed to the direction and nature of these normalized norms.

The tension between homogenization of communities and the pluralization of the nation, which lies at the heart of the *SMC*, certainly deserves deeper exploration as well as comparison to other cases.[f] In many respects, Lee Kuan Yew's idea of a "multicultural" nation does not seem to differ much from dominant ideas of "monocultural" nations, such as those articulated in many types of modern nationalisms (see e.g. Wilmsen and McAllister (eds.) 1996). In the Singaporean project, as much essentializing of (imagined) community characteristics is going on as in monocultural national projects, and a fair amount of reducing of intra-group differences has also been noted. Only, what is elsewhere perceived as a "nation" (i.e. a "people" with its own language, culture and history) is given the status of "community" in Singapore; the Singaporean nation, by consequence, is a patchwork of internally homogenized communities. Homogenization and essentialization is

---

f   Compare Hewitt's notion of 'polyculture', this volume.

shifted down one step from "nation" to "community", so as to safeguard the status of "nation" for Singapore and keep it out of reach for the Chinese and other "ethnic" communities. Not surprisingly, [. . .] an important role is given to language in such homogenizing and essentializing projects. Lee Kuan Yew's statements stand out by the massive amount of theorizing he produces on language in relation to culture, ethnicity, history and society. They prove, among other things, how easily certain linguistic ideologies can be transformed or absorbed into political ideologies, and how easily a rhetoric on language, culture, history and identity can become an instrument of societal streamlining and disciplining.

Notes

1   This denial of mother-tongue status for English has been challenged in recent years, mostly by those English-educated Chinese who felt threatened when the focus of the campaign turned to them. Their voices appeared in some of the headlines in the *Straits Times*, the main English-language newspaper: "Why Mandarin is not my mother-tongue" (*ST*, 23 February 1992), "English a mother-tongue too?" and "English: A Singaporean mother-tongue?" (*ST*, 14 June 1994). The answer to these questions has been the continued reiteration of the merits of Mandarin over English with its inherent embodiment of culture and its link to history. [. . .]

References

Anderson, Benedict 1991 *Imagined Communities: Reflections of the Origins and Spread of Nationalism*. London: Verso.

Bokhorst-Heng, Wendy D. 1998 *Language and Imagining the Nation in Singapore*. PhD dissertation, University of Toronto.

Chua Beng Huat 1995 *Communitarian Ideology and Democracy in Singapore*. London and New York: Routledge.

Chua, S. C. 1962 *State of Singapore: Report on the Census of Population, 1957*. Singapore, Department of Statistics: Government Printing Office.

Harrison, Godfrey 1980 Mandarin and the Mandarins: Language policy and the media in Singapore. *Journal of Multilingual and Multicultural Development* 1: 175–180.

Kachru, Braj B. 1983 *The Other Tongue: English Across Cultures*. Oxford: Pergamon Press.

Kuo, Eddie C. Y. and Björn Jernudd 1994 Balancing macro- and micro-sociolinguistic perspectives in language management: The case of Singapore. In: Gopinathan, S. A. Pakir, Ho Wah Kam and V. Saravanan (eds), *Language, Society and Education in Singapore: Issues and Trends*. Singapore: Times Academic Press, 25–46.

Kuo, Eddie C. Y. and Peter S. J. Chen 1983 *Communication Policy and Planning in Singapore*. London: Kegan Paul International.

Lee Kuan Yew 1972 Traditional values and national identity. Speech presented at the Singapore Teachers Union's 26th Anniversary Dinner, Shangri-La Hotel, 5 November 1972. *The Mirror*, 20 November 1972, Vol.8, No.47.

Lee Kuan Yew 1991 Confucianist values should not be lightly abandoned. Excerpts of Interview by Nihon K. Shimbun. 8 January 1988. In: Loy Teck Juan, Seng Han Tong and Pong Cheng Lian (eds), *Lee Kuan Yew on the Chinese Community in Singapore*. Singapore: Singapore Chinese Chamber of Commerce and Industry and the Singapore Federation of Chinese Clan Associations, 119.

Pendley, Charles 1983 Language policy and social transformation in contemporary Singapore. *Southeast Asian Journal of Social Science* 11(2), 46–58.

Puru Shotam 1987 *The Social Negotiation of language in the Singaporean Everyday Life World*. PhD dissertation, National University of Singapore.

Singapore Ministry of Communications and Information 1989 *Speak Mandarin Campaign Launching Speeches (1979–1989)*. Singapore: Ministry of Communications and Information.

Parliamentary Debates. Republic of Singapore. Official Report [various years], Singapore.

The Straits Times (ST) [various numbers].

Stroud, Christopher 1999 Portuguese as ideology and politics in Mozambique: Semiotic (re)constructions of a postcolony. In: Jan Blommaert (ed.), *Language Ideological Debates*. Berlin: Mouton de Gruyter, 343–380.

Tan Su Hwi 1996 A critical review of sociolinguistic engineering in Singapore. In: Blommaert, Jan (ed.), *The Politics of Multilingualism and Language Planning*. Antwerp: UIA-GER (Antwerp Papers in Linguistics 87), 107–142.

Tham Kok Wing 1983 National campaigns in Singapore politics. Bachelor of Social Science Honours Academic Exercise, Department of Political Science, National University of Singapore.

Tham Seong Chee 1996 *Multi-lingualism in Singapore: Two Decades of Development*. Census of Population, 1990, Monograph No. 6. Singapore: Department of Statistics, Ministry of Trade and Industry.

Wilmsen, Edwin and Patrick McAllister (eds.) 1996 *The Politics of Difference: Ethnic Premises in a World of Power*. Chicago: University of Chicago Press

Wilson, H. E. 1978 *Social Engineering in Singapore: Educational Policies and Social Change, 1819–1972*. Singapore: Singapore University Press.

After a period as Lecturer at the National University of Singapore, Wendy Bokhorst-Heng works at the American University Career Center in Washington DC.

Chapter 14

Roger Hewitt

1992

LANGUAGE, YOUTH AND THE DESTABILISATION OF ETHNICITY[a]

IN THE U.K., as elsewhere, the notion of 'ethnic cultures' that dominated race relations academic production, and to some extent community expression, from the 1950s until very recently, was of community-based, internally coherent cultural systems of mutually supporting religious, linguistic, culinary, aesthetic etc. codes and practices, transmitted through networks of kinship and association. The image of white working-class, inner-city communities in the U.K. is basically that of the medieval English village, perhaps with a pub where the May pole once stood. So it has also gone for minority groups: each coherent 'community' re-expressing its essential 'folk' identity. On this basis political battles have been fought concerning religious or linguistic rights within the larger national plurality. A means of expression becomes a symbol of collective identity.

This notion of minority communities is the classically stable one derived from many sources but certainly from the anthropological monographs on apparently unchanging distant peoples of Africa, the Pacific, etc. (Boon, 1982). It has also informed the discourses of nationalism amongst oppressed peoples, as well as within large modern states (Gellner, 1983). These are discourses, as I have indicated elsewhere (Hewitt, 1990a), going back to Herder through those like the 19th century revolutionary Slav and Italian groups influenced by his ideas on cultural oppression and the nature of the authoritarian state.

But, as we all thought we knew, the high tide of this holistic, organic notion of culture, certainly as an academic construct, has passed – or rather, we recognise that it is a far more complicated matter than that. Despite the overturn of the east European communist order and the unleashing of a thousand nationalisms, it is not difficult to see that 'ethnicity' is not what it was. Cultural forms have been

---

a In C. Palmgren, K. Lovgren and G. Bolin (eds) (1992) *Ethnicity in Youth Culture*. Stockholm: Youth Culture at Stockholm University pp. 27–41.

seen to change or disappear to be replaced with new and unfamiliar insignia; hybrid mixtures of cultures have developed and culture in the old sense may now, perhaps, be practiced only by 'consenting adults in private'. In some respects, it was probably always so, because our ways of talking about culture have themselves undergone a revolution, and it may be that that has more than done its bit to change the world we see.

The messy fragments of 'cultural' production that somehow no longer yield their 'deep grammars' (although in truth they characteristically yielded them convincingly only ever to a few individual anthropologists gifted with a kind of structural second-sight) sprawl before our eyes and how are we now to talk about them?

Both Ulf Hannerz and Frederick Barth have used the expression 'creolisation' to describe the mixing of cultural perspectives (Hannerz, 1989; Barth, 1989). The linguistic metaphor presents a mirror of my own social imaging in a study of London Jamaican Creole language forms and their use by white youth in south London (Hewitt, 1986). One of the difficulties I found in describing the close relationship between some Afro-Caribbean and white working-class youth was how to theorise the fact that good, close friendships exist between black and white youth and many blacks and whites speak of the racial harmony in their locality, while at the same time racism in various forms also exists, sometimes very visibly within the same locality and even, paradoxically, within the same white individuals who, under different conditions, interact amicably with black friends. There is a move here between cultural and social mixing on the one hand and social and cultural closure on the other. A linguistic metaphor that once seemed appropriate to me was that of 'code switching' and I talked in terms of 'ideological code-switching' (Hewitt, 1990b). Just as black and white speakers of Jamaican Creole switched from the code of Creole to the code of English, depending on various contextual and interactional circumstances, so local and immediate conditions might affect the ideological switch between what Les Back (Back, 1990) has called 'harmony discourse' ("We are all friends round here") and different degrees of racist expression.[b] So, I suppose, 'cultures' may be seen as extending this metaphor into what Bourdieu has called a 'linguistic market place' of many discrete ideological codes that may be moved between.

The trouble with the metaphor is that it isn't really how we experience being in a complex culture of this kind. It sounds like a vast railway junction of sweeping lines where one might hop from one train to another. In reality it never looks even as tidy as that. Neither does it capture the fragmentary nature of cultural experience – a few words of Punjabi spoken by a white girl are not the tip of the ice-berg, they are an ice-berg of sorts, and multi-ethnic societies generate a great many fragments of this kind.[c]

---

b In this volume, see Gumperz and Hernández-Chavez on linguistic codeswitching, and Cutler for a case-study of shifting ideological alignments.

c See also Back, this volume. For a succinct account of the use of Punjabi by white and black adolescents, see B. Rampton (1996) 'Language crossing, new ethnicities and school'. *English in Education* 30 (2): 14–26. For book-length treatments of similar processes, see Hewitt 1986 (in references) and B. Rampton (1995) *Crossing: Language and Ethnicity among Adolescents*. London: Longman.

Polyculture

Our experience of living in multi-ethnic cultures reminds me more forcefully of those spaces drawn upon by palaeolithic peoples where figures of animals in outline, antelope, bison, mammoths, bears etc. and even narrative hunting scenes, are piled up by successive artists on the same parietal space – a rock shelter, cave wall and so on. Explanations differ concerning why, when there were other spaces available, palaeolithic painters 30,000 years ago in southern France and more recently in southern Africa did not mind the confusion of superimposed images intersecting, overlapping or obliterating the outline beneath. The effect on the eye, at least for the modern viewer, is both chaotic and suggestive. The experience of seeing even a few simple lines distinguish themselves as formed by human design rather than natural processes is exciting enough – as those lines suddenly make sense as a foreleg, antler or bison's underbelly, and meaning, as it were, emerges from the rock in a moment of recognition when the whole creature suddenly leaps into life.

The craggy surfaces and mineral traces of the cave or shelter which 'host' this confusing parade of meaningful marks are often also not merely the passive recipient of these images but the occasional node in the rock may become incorporated as a creature's eye, or a hair-line crack will be treated as a back-line and a neck or mane be extended from it by the clever artist. For the viewer, however, sifting one image from another, seeing what was original to a certain layer and what marks, animals and bits of animals belong together is taxing, often completely baffling.

It is exactly this fluid chaos that we find in the multiplicity of urban ethnicities where apparently coherent cultural scenes are also superimposed, one upon another, and no single, holistic shape is discernable and all we can say is that they seem to occupy, somehow, 'the same' space. Furthermore, while the palaeolithic artist may have made use of natural features embodied in the surface upon which he or she worked but only rarely made use of the marks of other artists, in multi-ethnic societies a dialogue exists between the cultural fragments, so that totally new forms become established from old, lines become re-interpreted and often the notion of seeking back to find the earlier layers where unified, simple portraits of community life once existed, becomes impossible and pointless.[d] [. . .]

What we have here is not a 'multiculture' as it is represented in multiculturalism, not a pluralist order of discrete patches of culture, all, somehow, 'equally valid' within the polity,[e] but – to form a Greek/Roman creole – a *polyculture*, or at any rate a collection of cultural entities that are not (a) discrete and complete in themselves; (b) that are not in any sense 'intrinsically' 'equal'; and (c) are active together and hence bound up with change.

The graffiti on our inner city walls display these polycultural features clearly. The marks clamour for superiority, rhetorically grapple with power and the social pecking order, display both mixture and imaginary insulation and closure from the Other. Furthermore, they exist in perpetual *dialogue*; the signs talk to one another, refer to one another, redefine and modify each other – a dynamic babble of voices. Just when they seem most confident and certain of their identity – the stark images

---

d Compare Back and Urla, this volume.
e On this kind of 'multiculture', see e.g. Bokhorst-Heng, this volume.

of 'them' and 'us' — another stroke uncouples them from that stability, qualifies them, does battle, destabilises. The discourses of fixity and exclusion themselves grind away producing synthesis and change. 'Half-caste power' daubed on the tenement landing invokes its own inter-textuality. 'Half-caste power fight the black man' says one voice; 'and the white man' appends another. The definition and redefinition are endless.

What is happening to 'ethnicity'?

Away from this parietal Bakhtinian order,[f] what is happening to 'ethnicity'? What can we see, now that our languages of description are themselves more 'creolised'? It seems to me that there are at least three engines of change and 'destabilisation' with respect to the older concept of ethnicity. Firstly, there are the changes that take place *within* groups of people when they move from one place to another or simply have others join them. This happens on at least two planes: (a) the variously productive plane of engagement with other configurations of economic interest, other cultural focussings, other notions of identity and concepts of the person. It means doing and making new things because of existing in a new environment. This engagement will be realised in different ways depending on political power, on majority/minority status, but for any group it can be productive, energetic, transformative. The other plane, (b), is a kind of cultural hermeneutic: a re-reading of old texts in new ways and a consequent generation of new meanings within the recognisable culture of the group. Here flexibility and adaptation facilitate not the *abandonment* of a cultural mode but its transformation into newly active culture: the mosque, gurdwara or temple opened up for new political and social purposes; the school turned from narrow pedagogy into a community resource; kinship networks turned into offensive weapons against racism in the employment or housing markets. Such re-interpretations of traditional cultural processes and institutions continually redefine both majority and minority groups, defying fixity and definitional stability.

The second engine of change for 'ethnicity' is the proliferation of global systems. While it has been argued that these themselves stimulate the *elaboration* of ethnicities, it is also true, whatever the value of that claim, that the globalization of certain ideologies of communication does become encoded in educational systems, particularly, and we find the clear emergence of an ideal of supra-cultural communication in open conflict with, and commonly more powerful than, liberal-pluralist linguistic ideologies seeking to underwrite notions of the place in education of 'community languages'.[g] Indeed, as I have argued elsewhere, there is even evidence that the latter may itself be strategically instrumental in the furtherance of the former [. . .] in some instances — a further sign of the hegemony of the supra-cultural ideal. The linguistic rights of minorities as a political issue may thus become

---

f For a succinct introduction to the work of Mikhail Bakhtin, see e.g. T. Todorov (1984) *Mikhail Bakhtin: The Dialogical Principle*. Manchester: Manchester University Press.
g See Heller, Mazrui and Quirk, this volume.

incorporated into these educational discourses and neutralised (Hewitt, 1989). This is, of course, only one aspect of the globalization/ethnicity issue but it is especially relevant where our concern is predominantly with youth.

The globalization of alternative musical cultures associated with the black diaspora of course, works in a quite different direction, but even here the intersection of the international entertainment industry and resistive diaspora cultures may mirror the hegemonic relationships to be observed in the educational sphere, although the mediation of the state and state interests may be more or less absent, or at least of a different order.

The third engine of change is that perpetual erosion of clear boundaries, definitions and identities at the local level that I referred to at the outset. What is especially interesting here is that not only are new, unholy mixtures of cultural elements compounded – dress, language, music are the most obvious but a much broader spectrum of cultural behaviours is actually encompassed – but, paradoxically, even the strategic stressing of some clearly defined ethnic culture for political purposes contributes to this process. The reason for this is that the very process of selecting out cultural elements to carry a specialised, symbolic load for instrumental reasons within a contested political sphere, simultaneously has the effect of transforming the bases of selection into a second order. The residue of cultural practices not selected for any role in the symbolic economy become even more susceptible to change and destabilisation. While ears are attending to the contours of pronunciation, the very words spoken may be carrying new and alien messages. This is true for both minority and majority cultures in contact.

At the same time, of course, even the clearest beacons of exclusive identity may be appropriated by other groups: "It seems they are stealing our language", one young Afro-Caribbean said to me about whites who use London Jamaican Creole (Hewitt, 1986:161). We have, therefore, at least two modalities of ethnicity generated: one stressed and ultimately political, symbolic, and agonistic;[h] the other unstressed, politically interstitial, having almost the status of an unnoticed medium through which the daily business of getting by is conducted. The former, in being most visible, is especially open to appropriation and sudden transformation; the latter susceptible to continual, non-dramatic but persistent change.

A local multi-ethnic vernacular

For me the play between this politico-cultural condition and the cultural/linguistic condition is most clear. There is a perfect model of it in the situation in the U.K., where we find both a strongly pronounced Caribbean Creole of some kind which is strategically used for certain interactive purposes which categorically include political, anti-racist uses, and, on the other hand, an everyday, vernacular language form which incorporates words from Creole, or even in some areas, Turkish or Punjabi into a basically English stock. This is what is sometimes called 'Black Cockney'. I have called it a 'local multi-ethnic vernacular' and also a 'community

---

h See McDermott and Gospodinoff, this volume, for a case study.

English'. The point about it is that it is the primary medium of communication in the adolescent peer group in multi-ethnic areas [in London]. It is the language of white as well as minority youth and it is the language which is switched from and back into when its users choose to move into Creole or Punjabi or whatever other minority language, yet it is itself an 'impure', mixed form. Nevertheless, there is no evidence of it having any symbolic status on its own territory. Its transparency is what actually allows its permeability by diverse communicative (i.e. including but not restricted to purely linguistic) features. Thus in being unselfconsciously the language of the streets between adolescents of all ethnicities, it strips its contributory ethnic components of any capacity for symbolic stress whilst reassembling these diverse elements, on an ad hoc day to day basis, into a truly mixed, truly 'impure' form. [. . .]

Youth, ethnicity and identity

The notions of both 'youth' and 'ethnicity' attract that of 'identity' like almost no others, but in the case of youth it is certainly ambiguous, embracing both the *interiorised* sense of self and belonging, and the external blazonry of group affiliation, membership — what I would call social registration. There is, of course, traffic between these inner and outer forms of 'identity' but they are not the same. Two cases that came to my notice in the course of ethnographic fieldwork dramatise for me the distinction. One was a teenage boy of West African parents. By report the boy spoke an African language at home. He also spoke good English in school, and when he was out with his friends — who were all from Afro-Caribbean homes — he used quite a lot of 'London Jamaican Creole'. He also identified strongly with black youth culture, followed reggae music and grew dread locks like several of his friends, claiming to be a rastafarian. At a literal level he had no need, personally, to trace his African roots. They were clear and immediately to hand. 'Back to Africa' was, in terms of biography and the inner landscape of identity, of little meaning. But his rastafarian identity was what he sought to socially register and for him this was about black youth cultures at the time, about cultural strategies against racism, and about his peer relationships. Its actual content, though historically located, was arbitrary compared with its interactive, cultural force which was primary. It was essentially instrumental and alongside the political message of rastafari, it shared some of the impermanence of any youth cultural phenomena including that of adoption of black cultural identities by white youth.

The other case was that of a young white man I interviewed over a period of years. He was, surprisingly, always a better Creole speaker than most of the black youngsters who lived in his neighbourhood, having been brought up for a while by a black family, and lived in another area which had an established Afro-Caribbean population. He totally identified as black. He walked, moved, spoke like a young black Jamaican. Black informants listening to recordings of his speech could not distinguish him from black Caribbean-born speakers. Interviewing him was one of the strangest field experiences I have had. On the face of it it was one white man talking to another, but experientially it felt to me as though I was talking to a black person. The whole battery of cultural signals that came my way were Afro-Caribbean yet this was contradicted by a skin the same colour as my own. It had an immanent ambiguity to it which might correspond in some ways with how it might be for me to interview a transvestite. I interviewed and saw him over a period of about five years in all. By the end of that time he had settled down with a black woman and they had a child together. He was totally integrated into her family and, socially, moved exclusively in black company. Certainly at times, especially at first, he proclaimed himself to be a follower of rastafari but not, as had the young African, as part of the youth cultural scene. This young man approached it as a religion. He read the bible, followed the eating observances of rastafari and attended nyabingi – the rasta church. He was not primarily concerned with youth culture but with black culture far more widely, and the identity-work that was going on was far more within the interior landscaping of the self through culture and association than it was to do with social registration *per se*. Of course it had consequences for his social registration – this is partly what I had experienced – but that was not the important part of his identity work. The resolution of inner contradictions through cultural languages is clearly different from the manipulation of cultural materials for social, political and/or aesthetic motives – but these may not be distinguishable at times and the resonance of certain cultural texts may be actually derived from an oscillation between the two.

Both of these cases represent a kind of strangeness, a cultural strangeness, an interactively awry state of affairs that, if not exclusive to youth, is especially privileged in the liminality adolescence often assumes. Some of the most power-ful cultural expressions grow out of strangeness of this kind, derived from attempts – sometimes collective, sometimes individual – to resolve a chord either at the outer or the inner level, or even between the two. This is why the creativity within youth culture is often especially evident at points of cultural intersection, where the inner and outer aspects of identity may converge through some hospitable medium.

Social plurality

The 1984 hit record by Smiley Culture, 'Cockney Translation', is a case in point, and, appropriately, it came from the same social soil as did the informants des-cribed here – Deptford in south London. Smiley Culture was a black DJ with the Deptford-based sound system Saxon, and his record humorously plays with two outsider-resistant codes: Cockney rhyming slang and London Jamaican Creole, providing a loose translation from one to the other and simultaneously excavating much of the ambiguous ground trodden by blacks and whites described in my book *White Talk Black Talk* (Hewitt, 1986). As Paul Gilroy has written:

> The implicit joke beneath the surface of the record was that though many of London's working-class blacks were Cockney by birth and experience (technical Cockneys) their 'race' denied them access to the social category established by the language which real (i.e. white)

Cockneys spoke. 'Cockney Translation' transcended the 'schizophrenic' elements which composed the contradictory unity that provided the basic framework for a potential black Britishness. The record suggested that these elements could be reconciled without jeopardising affiliation to the history of the black diaspora.

(Gilroy, 1987:194–195)

An active consciousness of the black diaspora is seen by Gilroy as a means of rescue both from the kind of disturbed psychological contradiction, described in extreme form by Franz Fanon, and from a limiting and exclusive nationalism and/or ethnicism. Indeed he sees in the black diaspora a global movement of fundamental political as well as cultural importance (Gilroy, 1987:153–222).

The Asian diaspora is, of course, also a substantial political and cultural resource to Asian youth and in Britain throughout the 1980s there was a veritable explosion of cultural production amongst the Asian youth communities, much of which washed back to India and the Asian east-African communities. Despite some points of exchange and cross-over that I have discussed elsewhere (Hewitt, 1990:a), however, there has seemed to be no obvious porous edge where Asian linguistic, musical and dress codes could combine at the popular level with the mainstream, often commercially amplified, youth culture.

A very recent and in some ways revolutionary exception to this has, however, emerged this year in the form of a recording entitled 'Move Over India' made by a young Asian DJ who runs his own sound system in Birmingham. He calls himself 'Apache Indian' and he toasts in impeccable Creole. His family came originally from the Punjab but he was born in Birmingham. He works as a sheet metal worker in a factory but since his mid-teens has been closely involved in the Afro-Caribbean music scene in the [English] Midlands and has for a while hovered in the area of semi-professionalism. At the same time he is also very much part of the local Asian community. Les Back recently interviewed him and kindly allowed me to hear the recording of the interview in which 'Apache Indian' explains how the record had never been produced for commercial consumption but was originally made 'just for fun'.[i] It is chanted half in Creole and half in Punjabi. Indeed it achieves something similar to 'Cockney Translation', although it proclaims itself at the outset to be "For all the Indian ragamuffin' posses". It matches Creole and Punjabi phrase for phrase, starting off talking about an air flight to India, and alluding to Indian film-making, religious sites etc. then providing a kind of Creole glossary of Punjabi words for various items of food and numerous kinship terms etc. The record transcended cultural barriers to the extent of riding to number one in both the local Birmingham reggae and bangra charts, being equally popular with Asian and Afro-Caribbean youth alike.

From the interview it is clear that the social and cultural mix of the singer's own life – a sibling living with an Afro-Caribbean partner, and broad inter-ethnic friendship networks – and the very immediacy with which he felt the proximity of both Afro-Caribbean and Asian cultures induced in him the desire to express it in musical form purely for its own sake. It becomes quite evident from the interview

---

i See Back, this volume.

that he did not for a minute believe in or even consider the possible commercial market for the record. As soon as it was played on the local radio stations, however, the nerve that it struck, the chord that it resolved for local youth was immediately obvious. The inner issues of identity could be at play with the outer forms of ethnicity, and *language*, as ever, and the very notion of 'translation', assumes a more than pre-eminently symbolic significance. In contexts like this language is somehow both Heidegger's 'home of Being' and Wittgenstein's 'way of life'.

It is precisely this double aspect to language, this capacity for fusing the inner and outer, for doing the one through the other, for translating the world of *social plurality* and contradiction into the interiority and sculpture of being, that ethnographers are frequently overwhelmed with in 'interviewing' 'subjects'. This peculiar moment of intersubjectivity has somehow to be rendered into data, yet our understanding of language, of the hovering, hesitant, stepped moments of insight which the people we talk to convey, constantly seem far stronger, more charged with fullness and the immanence of language than our puny attempts to get them on the page.

Sociolinguistics

It is, I feel, an indictment of the scope of sociolinguistics that so few studies reach to either of these aspects. The exceptions – Shirley Brice-Heath's *Ways With Words* (1983) for example – tend to be those that capture something of the life-worlds of communities, but I can think of none that approach the issues of language and self that are glimpsed at work behind the kind of cultural production I have mentioned here, which address not simply the external, social registration of identity, but inner, contoured experience in intersection with the external. It seems to me there is a real challenge here for youth and ethnicity studies. That language and identity are frequently linked is commonly acknowledged but the depth and breadth of this linkage has hardly been recognised or tapped. Partly the problem has been the way in which the domain of social language studies has been overshadowed by linguistics which is itself suffused with a narrowing positivism. This seems to vitiate and limit even the most socially reflexive areas that are derived from linguistics – like discourse analysis. It seems to me that methodologically some of the most suggestive work on language in society is some of the oldest, coming out of the folkloristic end of the 'ethnography of communication' continuum.[j] It seems in retrospect more genuinely exploratory and sensitively speculative than much of the more sociolinguistically respectable work [like, for example, Labov's]. [. . .]

It seems to me that there is an opportunity, in fact a crying need, for a fresh start as far as language and youth is concerned. Especially in multi-ethnic situations where language is constantly appearing as interactively salient and symbolically foregrounded, we have the opportunity for some 'thick' and reflexive ethnography of language use. The linguistic phenomena we have observed in London and elsewhere

---

j   As the name implies, the 'ethnography of communication' uses ethnographic methods to study communicative practices. It covers a wide range of different studies, and in one way or another, it could be said to include most of the papers that come after this one in the volume.

amongst youth in multi-ethnic areas have been essentially three-fold: firstly the use of home languages by minority youth in strategic switches from the local dialect of the national language. So what is important here is not just the fact of fluency or otherwise in two or more languages but the social and interactive circumstances under which they are used in combination. Here most notably the home language, or some generational version of it, takes on a specialised weight that may symbolically create or enact an 'ethnicity' – i.e. a specific construction of cultural identity – for immediate interactive (including political) purposes. Secondly we have observed the growth of the local mixed code – the version of the national language, in this case English – that gets developed by minority youth together and in conjunction with majority youth. So it may contain lexical items or formations drawn from several languages. This is what I called the 'local multi-ethnic vernacular' and it is different in different localities. And thirdly there is the phenomenon of ethnolinguistic cross-over, i.e. members of one group choosing to use the language of another – whites or Afro-Caribbeans using a smattering of Punjabi, Asians or whites using Creole. There is a lot of evidence that all three occur throughout the world in some form or another wherever we find mixed communities, and especially amongst the youth of those communities.

Now these phenomena can be approached, and have been, in purely descriptive, even quantitative terms. However, I believe there is far more insight and interest to be derived from tying these phenomena to the biographical processes of their generation i.e. to the life-histories of the individuals involved in these language processes, through the recording of spontaneous speech, reflexive and retrospective interviews, group conversations about language use and so on. The aim here is to locate biography in language and language in biography, producing a form of social hermeneutic of living speech. Furthermore, what also needs recovering is the folklorist's nose for expressive forms – oral narratives, jokes, sayings, chants etc. – without the folklorist's prejudices against the technological: an approach that melds a sensitivity to creativity in language, with popular cultural analysis, a sense of the contemporary, a sense of agency, within an apprehension of culture not as 'tradition' but rather, as the bricoleur's bag, and meaning as created as much as 'given'.

There is a kind of stubborn core to the question of language and identity that generates mystery for academics and expressivity for those caught up in it. 'Half-caste power' inscribed on the dark recesses of an urban tenement landing seems to perfectly capture in its bold ambiguity a meaning that is ultimately more for 'the black man and the white' than it is 'against' them. The role of the ethnographer of communication may be to bring this 'message' out into the light; to promote a wider knowledge of the benefits of ethnic 'instability' and its impure language.

References

Abrahams, R. 1970. *Deep Down in the Jungle: Negro Narrative Folklore from the Streets of Philadelphia*, New York: Aldine.

Back, L. 1990. *Which Way is Home? Race, Nationalism and Identity within two Contrasting Adolescent Communities in South London*. Paper given at the Open Seminar Series, Centre for Research in Ethnic Relations, University of Warwick, 30 January.

Back, L. 1993. Race, identity and nation within an adolescent community in South London, *New Community*, 19 (2): 217–233.

Barth, F. 1989. The Analysis of Culture in Complex Societies, *Ethnos*, vol. 54, iii–iv, pp. 120–142.

Boon, J. 1982. *Other Tribes, Other Scribes*, Cambridge: Cambridge University Press.

Bourdieu, P. 1991. *Language and Symbolic Power*. Cambridge: Polity Press.

Brice-Heath, S. 1983. *Ways With Words*, Cambridge: Cambridge University Press.

Ehn, B. 1990. *Youth Experiences of Cultural Differences in Multi-Ethnic Sweden*. Paper presented at SIEF's 4th Congress, Bergen, 19–23 June.

Gellner, E. 1983. *Nations and Nationalism*, Oxford: Basil Blackwell.

Gilroy, P. 1987. *There Ain't No Black in the Union Jack*, London: Hutchinson.

Hannerz, U. 1989. Culture Between Centre and Periphery: Towards a Macroanthropology, *Ethnos*, vol. 54, iii – iv, pp. 200–216.

Hewitt, R. 1986. *White Talk Black Talk: Inter-racial Friendship and Communication Amongst Adolescents*, Cambridge: Cambridge University Press.

Hewitt, R. 1989. Creole in the Classroom: Political Grammars and Educational Vocabularies, in R. Grillo (ed.) *Social Anthropology and the Politics of Language*, London: Sociological Review Monographs no.36, Routledge.

Hewitt, R. 1990a. A Sociolinguistic View of Urban Adolescent Relations, in F. Røgilds (ed.) *Every Cloud has a Silver Lining: Lectures on Everyday Life, Cultural Production and Race*, København: Akademisk Forlag.

Hewitt, R. 1990b. 'Language, Youth and Race: Deconstructing Ethnicity?', in L. Chisholm, P. Buchner, H-H. Kruger, P. Brown (eds) *Childhood, Youth and Social Change*, London: Falmer.

Labov, W. 1973. *Language in the Inner City*, Oxford: Blackwell.

Rushdie, S. 1990. 'In Good Faith', *Sunday Independent* 4 February.

Roger Hewitt is Senior Researcher at the Centre for Urban and Community Research at Goldsmith's College, University of London.

Chapter 15

Jane H. Hill

1995

MOCK SPANISH, COVERT RACISM AND THE (LEAKY) BOUNDARY BETWEEN PUBLIC AND PRIVATE SPHERES[a]

[. . .]

THE CONCEPT OF "public sphere" exposes a new arena for our attention, distinct from the interactional field of the market or the kin group, where people who live in states speak "as citizens," with reference to public affairs, yet not as agents of the state. Habermas ([1962] 1991) argued that the bourgeois public sphere flourished only ephemerally before it was captured by the culture industry with its capacity to manufacture inauthentic "public opinion" [, and he] has been much criticized for his nostalgic commitment to the freedom and rationality of the bourgeois public sphere, as well as his neglect of the way in which it functioned as much to exclude as to include (cf. papers in Calhoun (ed.) 1992; and Robbins (ed.) 1993). The concept of "public" is, however, productive precisely because it sketches in the broad outlines of an important arena for the reproduction of exclusions in contemporary societies.[b]

I do not use the term "public" here, however, as a category of sociohistorical theory in the way that Habermas attempts. Instead, I take "public" and "private" to designate "folk categories," or, perhaps better, "ideologies," for certain speakers of American English. [. . .] The English words are polysemous, referring to contexts ("publicity," "public figure," "in public," "go public"), and to social entities (broad ones, as in "public opinion," or more narrowly defined groups, such as "the public" of an actor or singer). This paper aims to suggest that what is most important about the public/private distinction in the United States today is not the zones of life clearly included within each category, but the play of meaning along the ambiguous

---

a From *Pragmatics* 5(2): 197–212.
b The public–private divide is explicitly discussed in the extracts by Urla and Bokhorst-Heng in this collection, and variations on this are also significant in the analysis of codeswitching in the Clark and Gumperz and Hernández-Chavez articles.

boundary between them, especially between kinds of talk defined as "public" and those defined as "private." [. . .] I will be concerned here with how a particular ideology about appropriate styles for "public" talk facilitates the persistence in this sphere of "elite racist discourse" (van Dijk 1993), and thereby constructs the publics for such discourse as "white," excluding people of color as audiences and participants. I discuss the case of what I call "Mock Spanish", a way that Anglos in the United States can use light talk and joking to reproduce the subordinate identity of Mexican-Americans. Mock Spanish, and elite racist discourse in general, seems to oscillate along the boundary between "public" and "private" talk, making the public reproduction of racism possible even where racist discourse is supposedly excluded from public discussion. Mock Spanish is, of course, only one of a whole complex of discourses that have been recognized as covertly "coded" as racist (for instance, talk by white politicians about "teenage welfare mothers" or "gang-bangers" does not conjure up an image of misbehaving white children, in spite of the fact that whites constitute a high percentage of such groups).[c] Mock Spanish is, however, relatively easy to identify and "decode," facilitating our exploration of the leaky boundary between racist joking construed as "private" and "serious public discussion."

Two dimensions of language ideology[d] facilitate this persistence of a racist discourse in public talk. The first is a set of tensions about interest, between a "presumption of innocence" for public discourse – that talk offered up as serious public discussion will be presumed to be addressed to the general good in an un-biased way – and a "presumption of interest" – that such talk will be biased and interested in favor of speakers or those they represent. The second is a set of tensions about style that dates back to the earliest period of the American republic. Cmiel (1990) has traced the history in the United States of what he calls the "middling style": The idea that a speaker in a democracy will eschew the high language of gentility appropriate to monarchies and strike a more popular tone, that admits the possibility of plain speaking including slang and colloquialisms. The preference for the middling style blurs the boundary between serious public discussion and light private talk, such that elements of the latter, in this case Mock Spanish slang, may leak into public usage. [. . .] At the same time, this light talk is protected by conventions of privacy, especially those of solidarity among inter-locutors and the idea that private talk should not be taken too seriously. These two ideological complexes protect racist (and sexist) discourse, and make possible its continued reproduction, even where convention proscribes it. By examining the ways in which the racist register of Mock Spanish can leak across the public-private boundary, we may perhaps make progress in understanding how this reproduction occurs, and thereby develop strategies for intervention. [. . .]

For many Americans the contest about innocence and interest is relevant only when talk is "public": When a person speaks "in public" (as in a letter to the editor or in a public meeting), or when a person speaks as a "citizen" about topics held to be appropriate to "public opinion," even if the talk is conducted within the domestic or intimate sphere. For instance, a speaker telling a racist joke at a family

---

c On the 'covert coding' of nationalism, see Billig in this collection.

d 'Language ideology' is also explicitly discussed in the papers by Bokhorst-Heng, Heller and Urla.

gathering might be judged by her relatives to have poor judgement, or bad character, but she would not be thought of as "advancing an interest," of saying something that might "count" in the formation of opinion.[1] Here, however, we enter a slippery realm of the boundary between "spheres," where the social spaces in which speech occurs, topics and themes for discussion, kinds of persons who are speaking, and styles and genres interact in complex ways.

Consider an interesting case of the ambiguity of a social space, the classroom. On the one hand, it is argued that students and their teachers must be free to voice frank opinions, in the interests of seeking the truth. While many teachers try to move students toward a preference for "objective" grounds for opinions (thereby inculcating the conventions of "public speech"), personal experience is also admitted (as part of a general privileging of individuality that is beyond the scope of the present discussion), thereby eroding the proscription against private bias. This suggests that classroom discussion is not precisely "public." On the other hand, it is argued (probably out of precisely the same ideology that privileges personal experience), that students as individuals have the right to be protected against epithets that may threaten their pride and identity. This drive toward protection against the damage of conflict suggests that the classroom is somehow "public," that what is said there "counts" in a way that a slur shouted across a street would not. Some sites are less seriously contested. Especially in the worlds of business and commerce, there are occasions defined as "off the record" or "backstage" when sexist and racist talk are actually highly conventionalized. Thus a business leader or politician may be known to possess a large repertoire of grossly racist and sexist jokes, deployed when socializing among cronies in the appropriate interstices of business discussion, yet be celebrated for progressive views on diversity advanced in talk framed as "public." These "backstage" zones are increasingly entering the contested boundary realm, as the courts carve out the rights of employees to an environment that is not threatening or demeaning on grounds of race[2] or gender, but there is, of course, substantial backlash against this enlargement of what is "public." Many people continue to recognize a "backstage," an uncontested private zone. When interlocutors are speaking within this zone, it is not considered appropriate to censure their talk, even when it is possible to construe it as racist and sexist, even as grossly so. To censure breaks a contract of intimacy and solidarity, and exposes the censurer as in turn censurable, as a pettifogging killjoy.

Topic and theme also influences judgements as to whether speech is somehow aimed at the formation of opinion. For instance, Nancy Fraser (1990) pointed out an interesting case of a more-or-less successful struggle to move a topic into the public sphere. Feminist discourse extracted what is now called "domestic" violence from the realms of non-momentous gossip and boasting into a zone of "serious public discussion." This [. . .] required the creation of a public that accepted that a woman at the domestic site was not just Joe's long-suffering wife, but a "citizen" whose treatment could be considered within the zone of legal "rights." It required the widespread recognition that interactions within the family were not always and everywhere "personal", but could constitute a site where larger political structures, specifically those of a gender hierarchy that compromised an ideal of individual rights, were produced and reproduced. However, domestic violence remains ambiguous; neighbors who would not hesitate to call the police if they saw a stranger breaking into Joe's house may still feel that they are "poking their noses into other people's business" if they make a call when they overhear the sounds of Joe smacking his wife around, and in many communities police are still reluctant to make arrests in such cases.

Persona or reputation of the speaker is an important factor along the public/private boundary. Certain persons are defined as "public figures" (a formal category in libel law); the term "role model" is also gaining currency, implying that certain people are influential and accountable simply by virtue of reputation. Talk by such a personage may become the object of censure as an accountable "public" utterance even if it is uttered backstage. Exemplary are the recent cases of backstage remarks involving Marge Schott, owner of the Cincinnati Reds baseball team, and Jesse Jackson, a prominent African-American politician.[3] In contrast, there exist other kinds of persons who are judged as absolutely without influence, who can utter racist statements without censure in a context that is unambiguously "public." For example, in a feature on "Sixty Minutes" during the 1992 presidential campaign, Mike Wallace interviewed an elderly, obviously working-class, white man in a bar, asking him his opinion on what the most important issues were facing the country. The man, obviously conscious of constraints on public discourse, said something like, "Well, I probably shouldn't say what I really think." Wallace reassured him that his opinions were valuable. The old man then said, "Well, I think the biggest problem is that the colored people are just trying to get too much." Wallace's facial expression made it clear (at least to some viewers) that he was not pleased with this remark, but he thanked the man politely for participating. The interview was aired nationally with absolutely no public reaction. The notion that a person who is an obvious nonentity should hold such views, even in his role as a citizen asked for his opinion on national television, was unsurprising and undiscussed. This case is disturbing not only because there was no challenge to this obvious racism, but precisely because the old man was not "taken seriously." The incident makes clear the difficulty of making any vernacular opinion into "public" opinion.

A fourth very important zone of ambivalence at the boundary between "public" and "private" talk involves style. The contest over innocence and interest in the "public" zone requires that stylistic choices here index rationality over emotional commitment, the latter being taken as intrinsically more "interested" (Kochman 1984).[e] Cmiel (1990) has traced major changes in the relationship between public talk and stylistic choice. "Neoclassical notions of discourse," writes Cmiel, "assumed that the *homo rhetor* was a gentleman, that his ethos, or character, would guide his every act and word. His refined taste, his avoidance of vulgar speech, was essentially tied to his sense of self, that *humanitas* presumed to commit him to the public good" (Cmiel 1990: 14). Several trends worked during the 19th century to undermine this association. First, technical and professional languages achieved equal footing with the refined literary language of gentility. Second, within the democracy basic skills of "civil speech" spread widely, and ideas of "refinement" and "vulgarity" came to refer to styles, and not to social groups. Finally, the democratic masses supplanted the small "rational elite" as the most important audience

---

e In this collection, Clark discusses a different way in which 'objective', rationalist, style can be racialized.

for public discourse, requiring the incorporation of popular styles of discourse. The resulting triumph of what Cmiel calls the "middling style," defined by informality (including regional and colloquial language and slang), calculated bluntness (including both "plain speaking" and deliberate insult), and inflated speech (including bombast, jargon, and euphemism) is obvious in American public speech today. Among the dominant classes of American English speakers, it is appropriate to inject a light note even into the most serious expression of public opinion. Jokes are a highly institutionalized component of public speaking, and even written opinion, as by newspaper columnists, may be punctuated by light elements including slang, with only a few expressions still widely considered off-limits in the mass media. [. . .] Public figures thought to be of patrician origin are especially constrained to salt their discourse with vernacular jests; George Bush [Senior]'s efforts to achieve a rhetorical "common touch" during his years as vice president and president became something of a national joke. [. . .]

To the degree that a particular stretch of talk is keyed as "light," I believe that it may be relatively resistant to proscription. [. . .] Light talk and joking are prototypically private, associated with the spaces of intimacy, and they are prototypically vernacular, associated with persons of a type whose talk would be unlikely to have public significance. Thus their use "in public" constitutes a sort of metaphorical code switch,[f] permitting "privacy" to be evoked within a larger public context. In "private" spheres the contest of innocence and interest is not in play, or at least it is less likely to be in play than in the "public" sphere. Indeed, the assumption of a key of "lightness" constructs a context of intimacy, and to reject the content of such talk is thereby to reject the intimacy itself. Censurers of offensive talk in the prototypical light style/private space/intimate relationship context must attack, not interest, but character or judgement, a much "heavier" threat to the face of the speaker. They run the risk of being accused of violating the contracts of intimacy that hold "in private," of being overly precious and correct, of "not having a sense of humor." A censurer will be accused of "Political Correctness": A position that is held to deprive speakers of their legitimate right to use light talk and humor. When light talk appears as a code switch "in public," this complex of rights seems to come with it. Those who censure the content of public light talk, who accuse it of unfair "interest," as in accusations of racism and sexism, are vulnerable not only to the above accusations, but to additional ones: They may be accused of elitism, of undemocratically rejecting plain everyday language and, in turn, the "common sense" that has been held to reside in it since the days of Thomas Paine.

I devote the remainder of this paper to the use within the public sphere of a "light" register of American English that I have called "Mock Spanish." [. . .] Spanish loan elements in this register are consistently pejorated and pejorating, which can be shown to derive [. . .] from a racist view of Spanish speakers (and to continually reproduce that opinion). There are two lines of evidence for racism in Mock Spanish. One is that in order to "get the joke" of Mock Spanish expressions, one must have access to negative stereotypes of "Mexicans." The second is the fact that Mock Spanish is often accompanied by racist visual imagery of stereotypical

---

f   The notion of 'metaphorical codeswitching' was developed by Gumperz – see Gumperz and Hernández-Chavez, this volume.

"Mexicans" (Hill 1993a, 1993b). For instance, a farewell card with the caption "Adios" may be accompanied by a picture of a "Mexican" asleep under an enormous sombrero (the equivalent, in the representation of Mexican-Americans, of a picture of a black man with an ear-to-ear grin, rolling eyes, and a huge slice of watermelon). I have collected many greeting cards and other paraphernalia with this sort of imagery, which would invite lawsuits if it were to appear on, say, a corporate logo or in a political cartoon in a newspaper. The position that I am trying to develop here suggests that images of this type on greeting cards, for instance, are acceptable because they are "private," a matter between intimates. Yet the language of Mock Spanish, separated from these kinds of racist images, is permissible and even welcome in public discourse, and in fact is used by people who are universally credited with "progressive" opinions on racism and sexism.

I will briefly summarize what Mock Spanish is (and what it is not).[4] Mock Spanish is a set of strategies for incorporating Spanish loan words into English in order to produce a jocular or pejorative key. Three major strategies govern this borrowing. The first is the semantic pejoration of Spanish expressions, by which they are stripped of elevated, serious, or even neutral meanings in the source language, retaining only the "lower" end of their range of connotations (and perhaps even adding new lowering). For instance, the polite and neutral Spanish farewell, "Adios," has meanings in Mock Spanish ranging from a marking of laid-back, easy-going, Southwestern warmth to the strong suggestion that the target is being insulted, "kissed off." An excellent example (which also exemplifies Chicano awareness of these usages) is a cartoon in the series *La Cucaracha* by Lalo Alcarez, published in the *Tucson Comic News* (December 1994; cited in García 1994) shortly after the passage of Proposition 187[, a law passed overwhelmingly in California in November 1994 which denies access to public education to illegal immigrants and to their children (even where these children are U.S. citizens), and also denies them access to many other social benefits that are normally universally available, including non-emergency medical care].[5] The cartoon showed an Anglo man holding a 187 flag and calling, "Hooray, we saved our state." Next to him is an Anglo woman jumping up and down in hysterical post-election exuberance, shouting "Adios, Pedro!" (The joke is that the supposedly solid ground on which the two are standing turns out to be a mighty fist labelled "Latino Activism"). The second strategy involves the recruitment of Spanish morphological[g] material in order to make English words humorous or pejorating. For instance, in a Joe Bob Briggs movie review (1987), we find the expression "mistake-o numero uno." The third strategy produces ludicrous and exaggerated mispronunciations of Spanish loan material. For instance, a greeting card shows the rear ends of a row of undulating Hawaiian dancers dressed in grass skirts. Opened, the card reads, "Grassy-ass." All of these strategies directly index that the utterance in which they are found should be taken to be humorous, and that the person who produced them has that valued quality, "a sense of humor."[6] However, in order to achieve their humorous effect, it is clear that a second, indirect indexicality [– or connotation –] is required, which reproduces an image of Spanish, and, in turn, of its speakers, as objects of derision. Most

---

g 'Morphology' involves the study of word-structure, and here refers to e.g. the formation of mock Spanish words through the addition of *-o* and *-ista*.

Spanish speakers with whom I have discussed these issues concur, and in fact report that they are acutely aware of Mock Spanish and find it irritating and offensive.

Mock Spanish is very widely used "in public" (on television programs, in films, and in magazines and newspapers). Because of the ambiguities of "social space" discussed above, I give here only examples of the use of Mock Spanish in what is, very explicitly, "public discussion": The realm of political talk intended to help form public opinion. One notable history involves the use of the phrase "Hasta la vista, baby." This tag exemplifies the strategy of pejoration. In Spanish, "Hasta la vista" is a rather formal mode of leave-taking, that expresses a sincere hope to meet again. The pejorated line, taken from Mock Spanish by an alert team of screenwriters, was placed on the lips of Arnold Schwarzenegger in his role as the Terminator in the film *Terminator II: Judgement Day*. It was then exported into public political talk by Schwarzenegger in another role, as a Republican celebrity who appeared alongside George Bush [Senior] in his second campaign for the presidency. From the New Hampshire primary on, Schwarzenegger appeared regularly as a Bush supporter, and his most crowd-pleasing line, uttered at the end of an attack on the current leading Bush opponent, was, of course, "Hasta la vista, baby." The line next appeared in the Texas senatorial campaign held during the winter of 1992–93 to fill the seat left vacant by the appointment of Lloyd Benson as Secretary of the Treasury. While both candidates used Schwarzenegger's tag, the Democratic aspirant, Robert Krueger, made an especially memorable picture, appearing in television ads dressed in a sort of Zorro suit, with black cape and hat, uttering the famous line. It was very important for Krueger to suggest that he had a "common touch," because it was well-known that he was in everyday life a college professor of English, specializing in Shakespeare, and, thereby, a snob and a sissy until proven otherwise. Interestingly, the line backfired; Krueger was apparently considered too much of a wimp to dare to use this famous "tough guy" tag. Increasingly, he became a figure of fun (the commercials were even held up to ridicule on national television), and lost the election by a substantial margin to Kay Bailey Hutchinson. We must also consider the possibility that the large Hispanic population in Texas, a key component of the Democratic electorate there, was offended by these commercials and declined to support Krueger.

A second example that exemplifies the strategy of pejoration was reported in the *Tucson Weekly* (December 8, 1994; cited in García 1994: 11). The organizer of an incipient effort to develop Proposition 187-style legislation in Arizona reported to the *Weekly* that he had had buttons and t-shirts printed up for sale to support his campaign. These items bore the legend, "If you're an illegal, head south, Amigo." This usage obviously invokes the lower reaches of a semiotic range for "amigo" in Mock Spanish that extends from mere jocularity to this case, where "amigo" obviously means anything but "friend." The legend attempts to differentiate "illegals" who should "head south" from legal immigrants and citizens of Latin American background. This distinction is, however, completely undone by the fact that in order to "get" the humor of the legend, audiences must have access to a general negative image of Spanish and its speakers that includes no such subtle discriminations.

Mock Spanish constructions using Spanish [. . .] elements such as -*o*, *el* . . . -*o*, and -*ista* frequently appear in public discourse. In an example heard on the McNeill-Lehrer News Hour in April 1993, a spokesman for President Clinton stated that the then-current draft of the administration's health-care reform plan was "not an el cheapo." This usage, of course, requires access to an image of extreme trashy cheapness associated with Spanish. David Fitzsimmons, the political cartoonist for the *Arizona Daily Star* (who is regularly attacked by conservatives as biased toward the left), produced a cartoon attacking Ross Perot, showing him holding a sign that said, in part, that he was running for "el presidente." The image of Perot thus constructed was, of course, one of a tinhorn dictator, dripping with undeserved gilt medals, an image derived from pejorative stereotypes of Latin American public officials. The liberal newspaper columnist Molly Ivins is a frequent user of Mock Spanish elements, which are a part of the construction of her persona as a Texan. All the cases below are from Ivins columns printed in the *Arizona Daily Star* during 1993. In a column on the Canadian elections, Ivins said, "The chief difference between Campbell and Chretien is that Campbell thinks the Numero Uno priority is to reduce the deficit, while Chretien wants to reduce the deficit without cutting the hell out of the national safety net." In a column on health care, Ivins wrote, ". . . one way to cut a little closer to the heart of the matter is to raise two pertinent questions. One is: What should we be allowed to die of these days? And numero two-o: What is actually going to affect the behavior of individual patients and individual doctors in consultation?" In a column on Kansas senator Bob Dole, Ivins opened as follows, "With the Clintonistas on a peppy schedule of at least two foreign policy crises a week . . ."

A third type of selection from a Mock Spanish repertoire was used by CBS anchorman Dan Rather, on election night, November 1992. Discussing the tight race in Texas, Rather elucidated for his listeners what was at stake as follows: "Texas is the Big Taco . . . If Bush doesn't take [certain Texas counties] there is No Way José he can make it." Here, the expression "big taco," which endows Rather's speech with "involvement" and authenticity, comes from a family of borrowings of Spanish food terms like "the big enchilada," and "the whole enchilada" that constitute exaggeration and emphasis by substituting for English elements like "thing" or "one." By adding the Spanish name José to "No way," this everyday English negative is endowed with special vernacular pungency. Here, the indirect indexicality that is prominent is of course that Spanish is a particularly "vernacular" language appropriate to a slangy style.

Readers might object that English speakers can use other languages in exactly these ways. This is, of course, partly true. For instance, Japanese *Sayonara* can be used in a sense that is almost exactly like Spanish *adios*. However, other European languages cannot easily be substituted in these kinds of expressions. I invite the reader to try out an English epithet like "sucker" in combination with leave-taking expressions from familiar languages. German, like Japanese the language of a former enemy power, almost works: "*Auf wiedersehen*, sucker." Taking up more recent international emnities, I can imagine the hero of a colorful spy novel dispatching a member of the KGB with the wise-crack "*Do svidaniya*, sucker," although I don't think this expression is popularly available in the way that "*Adios*, sucker" is. French and Italian really do not work, in spite of the familiarity of the expressions — "*Ciao*, sucker," "*Au revoir*, sucker" (well, perhaps in some future thriller constructed around the recent Haitian intervention, a villainous attaché might be knocked off to this sound effect by a heroic American agent). In summary, such usages seem to require access to contempt or emnity which is not traceable, in the case of Spanish, to any political threat, real or perceived, since 1898! Similar experiments can be conducted with lexical equivalents of the other expressions cited above, and I predict even less success.

All these are cases where Mock Spanish is part of a code switch into a light register, in which the speaker is represented as a person with a sense of humor and the common touch, a truly egalitarian American who doesn't have fancy pretensions. This characteristic conceit of the "middling style" requires a metaphorical code switch into the "private" social space, where people are thought to be at their most "authentic." Thus Mock Spanish can inject authenticity and "common sense" into public discourse, which might otherwise be "too serious." Such talk blurs the boundaries between public and private discourse. It is fairly easy analytically to show that Mock Spanish is driven by a racist [meaning], and that it functions to reproduce negative views of Spanish-speaking people.[h] Yet Mock Spanish is not racist in an obvious way: There are no epithets here. If the examples above were uttered in private, most people would consider it ridiculous to censure them. This resistance to censure leaks into the public space by way of the metaphorical code switch, so it is extremely difficult to attack these usages even though they are obviously public and contestable along the interest-innocence continuum. Further, such an attack would require that the "interest" involved be characterized: It is, of course, the interest of "whiteness," a quality that is largely invisible and not conventionally defined as an "interest." Furthermore, to characterize such talk as "racist" requires that one familiarize one's audience with the complexities of modern thought on racism, which is again remote from the understanding of a public that thinks of itself as "anti-racist." Thus, such usages of Mock Spanish are generally defined as "innocent."

At the same time that Mock Spanish functions at the blurred boundaries between public and private talk, it also illustrates the permeable boundaries of language itself. Mock Spanish has moved into public discourse in the last decade, at the very same time that heightened concern about language boundaries, in the form of the "Official English" campaign,[i] has grown in American life. Why, then, is there no objection to Mock Spanish by language purists? I believe that no objection occurs because Mock Spanish in fact strongly supports the essence of the purist campaign: That foreign languages, while they may be permitted in the home, should not be allowed in public discourse. As is well-known (Woolard 1989), "Official English" objections to foreign languages have been aimed especially at bilingual ballots and other forms of the public use of Spanish. The use of Mock Spanish constructs a particular place for the Spanish language in American public discourse: It can function only in light talk, in the "code-switching" that protects an American speaking in public from being seen as too pompous and domineering. This function seems to be well

---

h Compare this case (and analysis) with the accounts of language hybridisation and 'crossing' in the extracts by Back, Cutler, Hewitt and Urla in this collection.

i Official English initiatives seek to affirm the dominance of English in the US, and are opposed to bilingual education and the use of languages other than English in the workplace. For further discussion, see e.g. S. L. McKay (1997) 'Multilingualism in the United States' *Annual Review of Applied Linguistics* 17: 242–62, as well as the extracts by Rickford, Gumperz and Hernández-Chavez, and also Honeyford, in this volume.

established, and will make it increasingly difficult for any public uses of Spanish to be heard as "serious." It will, by definition, always be "private," and thus will have in the public sphere no more than a poetic function. For this reason, Mock Spanish in fact advances the purposes of the Official-English movement. Furthermore, to the degree that it is covertly racist, this will presumably be sensed with approval by those with racist agendas.

Finally, the use of Mock Spanish (as well as other subtly and not-so-subtly coded forms of racist discourse) in public talk functions importantly in "constructing the public." If an appreciation of the humor in Mock Spanish requires unreflective access to negative stereotypes of Latinos, then these sallies are clearly shaped for the appreciation of people who define themselves as "not Latino." (I use this phrase rather than "define themselves as 'White' " because the public thus defined almost certainly includes African-Americans, although this fraction of the U.S. population is of course the object of an unending repertoire of other exclusionary discursive strategies). Mock Spanish thus is one of many devices through which the sphere of 'public discussion' in the most widely-diffused media in the United States becomes profoundly, invisibly, exclusionary against people of color.

In closing, I wish to turn to a point raised recently by David Palumbo Liu (1994). Palumbo Liu suggests, in an analysis of the media characterization of racist alignments in the recent Los Angeles riots, that Hispanics in some contexts can stand in as a surrogate for more dangerous and problematic African Americans. Palumbo Liu points out, for instance, that Latino participation in the riots was hardly mentioned in the mass media, which emphasized the polarization of the Black and Asian communities. However, after the riots Hispanics were apparently arrested and deported in great numbers. Palumbo Liu suggests that the deportations projected onto Hispanics desires that were in fact aimed at African Americans – who cannot, of course, be deported because they are all, without doubt, recognized as citizens of the United States. It is interesting to consider a similar complementary distribution between Mock Spanish and African-American materials in the English of Anglos.[j] African-American slang expressions of course move rapidly into the slang of White Americans. Often, this slang is reshaped into virtual unrecognizability, so that those who use it are unaware of its Black English origins. However, a register that might be called "Mock Black English" is an important component of the gross jokes that are told in the zones of privacy mentioned above, in light talk especially among men. Graphically offensive jokes are often told using reported speech in a broad "Sambo" or "Aunt Jemima" dialect. However, as far as I know, no whisper of this practice ever leaks into the public discourse. In fact, as long ago as the 1950's a cabinet officer (Eisenhower's Secretary of Agriculture, Earl Butts), was fired after reporters overheard him telling a grossly offensive "Sambo" joke. To produce obvious parodies of African-American speech of the type that are apparent in Mock Spanish is simply too dangerous. However, Mock Spanish is apparently considered to be entirely harmless. We must consider the possibility that it is a safe substitute for this more dangerous possibility for covert racist discourse, for the voice of Amos 'n Andy, of Minstrelsy. [. . .]

---

j See Cutler (and also Urla) in this collection.

"Mock Spanish" is a very useful tool for exploring the ambiguities and problems of the boundaries between the public and the private. It is easy to spot it: Its obvious morphology and lexicon[k] function like a sort of radioactive tracer, which can be identified immediately when it shows up at a new site. What I think we learn from looking at these materials as they move back and forth across the public/private boundary is that the idea of the "public" and of "public discourse" continues today as an ideology that mystifies and confounds what is going on in the way of race, sex, and class-based oppression in American life, just as it did in the Revolutionary era. The imbrication of "light talk," "plain talk," "humor," and "common sense" have created an impenetrable tangle under which a great deal of racist and sexist talk, both public and private, can be produced, and a shield by which critique of these practices can be very effectively deflected. Through these practices of language the structures of "citizenship" by which people are licensed to participate in public life are produced — and also raced, and gendered.

Notes

1   Scholars, of course, recognize such "private" talk as a very important site for the reproduction of racism.

2   Lest there be any confusion here, my position is that "race" is not a biological category, but is a category available for the purposes of social exclusion that is essentially empty, available to be filled with whatever semiotic elements are most appropriate to a particular epoch (Goldberg 1993).

3   Schott apparently used rough racist language like "nigger" with great frequency. Jackson's problems involved his reference to New York City as "Hymietown." In these cases, the colorful and slangy language was of course provocative, but as the following example shows, the "public" nature of these persons was probably the main reason the language was censurable.

4   What it is NOT is "Spanglish" or "Caló" or "Border Spanish." I take "Spanglish" to be a practice where the target language is Spanish, but a Spanish that is wide open to English loans, often treated in a jocular way. However, from what I know about "Spanglish," it is a much richer and more wide-open set of practices than Mock Spanish, which is, when all is said and done, a narrow, constipated little register of insults that doesn't really offer much potential for play or originality. This is in sharp contrast to the extravagant anglicisms of Cholos, or the rich play with the two languages found in Chicano authors or performers like Guillermo Gómez Peña.

5   Most analysts of the rhetoric in support of the proposition find that it is clearly racist, including nearly all the well-known tropes of elite racist discourse directed at a vision of an "illegal immigrant" who is a person of color, Asian or Latin American. Furthermore, a good deal of the money backing 187 and similar legislation now being proposed in other states comes from organizations with well-known racist agendas.

6   Astonishingly, many Anglos believe that they can produce expressions of this type because they have been exposed to the Spanish language (this is true even of some quite sophisticated informants). Thus, in addition to directly indexing a speaker's sense of humor, such utterances may index that a speaker has some education and cosmopolitanism (but carries it lightly).

---

k 'Lexicon' = vocabulary.

References

Briggs, Joe Bob (1987) *Joe Bob Briggs goes to the drive-in*. New York: Delacorte Press.

Calhoun, Craig (ed.) (1992) *Habermas and the public sphere*. Cambridge, MA: MIT Press.

Cmiel, Kenneth (1990) *Democratic eloquence*. New York: William Morrow.

Fraser, Nancy (1990) Rethinking the public sphere: A contribution to the critique of actually existing democracy. *Social Text* 2:56–80.

García, Rogelio (1994) "Well I've reason to believe, we all have been deceived": California's Proposition 187 and racist discourse. University of Arizona ms.

Goldberg, David Theo (1993) *Racist culture*. Oxford: Blackwell's.

Habermas, Jürgen ([1962] 1991) *The structural transformation of the public sphere*. trans. Thomas Burger. Cambridge, MA: MIT Press.

Hill, Jane H. (1993a) Hasta la vista, baby: Anglo Spanish in the American Southwest. *Critique of Anthropology* 13:145–176.

Hill, Jane H. (1993b) Is it really "No problemo"? In Robin Queen and Rusty Barrett (eds), *SALSA I: Proceedings of the first annual symposium society – Austin. Texas linguistic forum* 33:1–12.

Kochman, Thomas (1984) The politics of politeness: Social warrants in mainstream American public etiquette. In Deborah Schiffrin (ed.), *Meaning, form, and use in context: Georgetown University Round Table '84*. Washington, D.C.: Georgetown University Press, 200–209.

Palumbo Liu, David (1994) L. A., Asians, and perverse ventriloquisms: On the functions of Asian America in the recent American imaginary. *Public Culture* 6:2.365–381.

Robbins, Bruce (ed.) (1993) *The phantom public sphere*. Minneapolis: University of Minnesota Press.

van Dijk, Teun A. (1993) *Elite discourse and racism*. Newbury Park: Sage Publications.

Woolard, Kathryn (1989) Sentences in the language prison: The rhetorical structuring of an American language policy debate. *American Ethnologist* 16:268–278.

Jane H. Hill is Professor in the Department of Anthropology, University of Arizona, US. She is co-author (with K. Hill) of *Speaking Mexicano: The Dynamics of Syncretic Language in Central Mexico* (Tucson: University of Arizona Press, 1986), and is editor of *Language and Society*, one of the founding journals in sociolinguistics and linguistic anthropology.

Chapter 16

Jacqueline Urla

1995

OUTLAW LANGUAGE

Creating alternative public spheres in Basque free radio[a]

R ECENT RETHINKING of Habermas' *Structural Transformation of the Public Sphere* by Negt and Kluge (1993), and feminist and social historians Nancy Fraser (1993), Joan Landes (1988), and Geoff Eley (1992) [. . .] has argued persuasively that the bourgeois public sphere has, from its inception, been built upon powerful mechanisms of exclusion. The idealized image of a democratic theatre of free and equal participation in debate, they claim, has always been a fiction predicated on the mandatory silencing of entire social groups, vital social issues, and indeed, "of any difference that cannot be assimilated, rationalized, and subsumed" (Hansen 1993b: 198). This is especially clear in the case of those citizens who do not or will not speak the language of civil society. The linguistic terrorism performed with a vengeance during the French Revolution and reenacted in Official English initiatives in the United States more recently,[b] reveal to us how deeply monolingualism has been ingrained in liberal conceptions of Liberté, Égalité, and Fraternité. But perhaps silencing may not be the best way to describe the fate of linguistic minorities or other marginalized groups. For, as Miriam Hansen (1993b) notes, what the more recent work on public spheres suggests is that "the" public sphere has never been as uniform or as totalizing as it represents itself to be. Proliferating in the interstices of the bourgeois public – in salons, coffeehouses, book clubs, working class and subaltern forms of popular culture – are numerous counterpublics that give the lie to the presumed homogeneity of the imaginary public. Spurred in part by ethnic nationalist movements of the nineteenth and twentieth centuries, speakers and writers of "barbarous" tongues and "illegitimate patois"

---

a From *Pragmatics* 5 (2): 245–61.

b Official English initiatives seek to affirm the dominance of English in the US, and are generally opposed to bilingual education. For further discussion, see e.g. S. L. McKay (1997) 'Multilingualism in the United States' *Annual Review of Applied Linguistics* 17: 242–62, as well as the extracts by Hill, Rickford and Gumperz and Hernández-Chavez in this collection.

can be seen as one among the counterpublics who avail themselves of any number of "media" – from novels to oral poetry, from song and regional presses to, more recently, various forms of electronic media – to give expression to other kinds of social experience and perspectives on who the public is, what its interests might be, and what its voice sounds like.[c]

This article examines the contemporary formation of one such counterpublic in the small towns and cities of the southern Basque country. Here, in the years since Franco's death, one finds among Basque radical nationalist youth a self conscious attempt to make use of intentionally marginal or "outlaw" publicity – street graffiti, zines, low-power free radio – as well as a lively rock music scene, to give voice to their minoritized language and their not-so-polite critiques of the state, consumer capitalism, police repression, and a host of other social concerns.[d] The alternative media and expressive culture of radical youth can be seen as creating a public sphere [. . .] within which social experience is articulated, negotiated, and contested (Hansen 1993a). However, as I hope to show, the sphere they have created differs significantly from the kind of public typically imagined within minority language revitalization and/or ethnic nationalist movements.[e] The latter typically are bourgeois and universalistic in nature; the nation or linguistic community is imagined in the singular and envisioned primarily as a reading and writing public. Furthermore, in the Basque nationalist movement, as in many other linguistic minority movements, language politics tend to be oriented towards normalization, expanding literacy, and gaining legitimacy within the terms of state hegemonic language hierarchies. The past century has seen ethnic minority intellectuals form their own language academies, literary and scientific societies, and mobilize the tools of linguistic analysis, orthographic reform, mapping, and even the census in order to document the "truth" of their language and to reform the language according to notions of what constitutes a "modern" or "rational" language (Urla 1993). The kind of practical exigencies and urgency minority linguists and planners feel to transform their language into what Bourdieu (1991) calls a "*langue autorisé*", to demonstrate its equivalence to other "world" languages, leads them to a concern with boundary drawing, purifying, and standardizing more commonly associated with the language ideology[f] of the dominant public sphere.

Scholars have tended to focus upon these normalizing processes, yet if we look to other arenas like the marginalized publicity of radical youth, we find a very different picture. What follows is an exploration of the public sphere of radical free radio, its distinctive ideology of radical democratic communication, and how these are reflected in a variety of linguistic strategies. [. . .] Looking beyond formal

---

c In different ways, the relation between public and private spheres is also discussed in the extracts by Hill and Bokhorst-Heng.

d See also Back, this volume.

e See also Heller, this volume.

f 'Language ideologies are shared bodies of commonsense notions about the nature of language in the world' [. . . They] include "cultural conceptions [. . .] of language and language variation, [. . .] of the nature and purpose of communication, and of communicative behaviour as an enactment of the collective order" (K. Woolard (1992) 'Language Ideology: Issues and Approaches' *Pragmatics* 2(3): 235–49). In this collection, 'language ideology' is also an explicit topic in the papers by Bokhorst-Heng, Heller and Hill.

language politics, beyond the academies and literacy programs, to the particular modes of address and other linguistic forms used in these kinds of experiments in local media, I suggest, reveals a more heterogeneous conception of publics and language than our studies of minority language movements might otherwise convey.

The mini fm boom

In a particularly poignant passage from *A Dying Colonialism*, Frantz Fanon paints a vivid portrait of the radio as an instrument of revolutionary consciousness. Crowded together in front of the radio dial, straining to hear through the static [that] the French army used to jam the transmissions, peasants, not-yet-Algerians, heard more than fragmentary accounts of battles, writes Fanon; tuning in to the Voice of Algeria they were witness to and participants in the rebirth of themselves as citizens of the new nation of Algerians.

Besides fueling anti-colonialist sentiment in France, Fanon's text established a link between radio and insurgency that was to inspire many of the originators of the free radio movement that emerged a decade later in Western Europe. Sometimes called illegal, rebel, or pirate radio, free radio began in Italy as an underground movement of the autonomous left in the wake of May '68 and spread quickly among a variety of oppositional groups, young people, and ethnic and linguistic minorities.[1] [. . .] Free radio came somewhat late to the Basque provinces of northern Spain. The first ones appeared in the early eighties and by 1987–88, at the height of the movement, there were about 50 or so stations in operation. [In 1988 . . . ,] new telecommunication legislation [led to the] tightening of controls over the airwaves, [and this] has been a major contributing factor in the closing of many stations. But they are by no means all defunct. [. . .] While it is undeniable that the movement has waned significantly, new radios continue to be created while other stations are renovating their studios and have managed to become permanent fixtures in town life.

The appearance of free radios is related directly to the radical youth movement of the eighties. In the expansive years after the statute of autonomy was passed in 1979,[2] youth, disenchanted with party politics, began to form youth assemblies, *gazte asanbladak*, in many towns across the southern Basque provinces. Drawing on the political philosophy of the autonomous left movement of Italy and France, youth assemblies meld a radical democratic assembly structure with an eclectic blend of nationalist, anarchist, left, and green politics. Anti-authoritarian and bound to no party discipline, their activities call attention to the problems of youth: Problems of unemployment (hovering between 50–60% among people under 25), alienation, lack of housing, compulsory military service, drugs, and repressive Catholic morality. In concert with youth elsewhere in Europe, Basque youth assemblies have been very active in the *okupa*, or squatter's, movement. They have occupied abandoned buildings demanding the right to have a youth center, or *gaztetxe*, where they could have meetings, socialize, listen to music, and organize concerts or other kinds of events outside the framework of political parties. In some cases, depending upon the political climate of the town hall, youth houses were established easily, and in others, as in the case of the *gaztetxe* of Bilbo, the squatters were engaged in a long, drawn out, and violent battle with the police and conservative town council that was ultimately unsuccessful. Youth assemblies and youth houses in many ways draw upon and gain strength from social institutions already well established in Basque social life. Local bars, for example, have long been critical public spaces facilitating a healthy tradition of Basque associational culture (cf. Kasmir 1993). Typically, radical youth will have one or two bars that they frequent on a daily basis. Most often run by individuals sympathetic to the nationalist left, these bars, not unlike gay bars in the United States, function as gathering places and community bulletin boards. The walls are plastered with pictures of political prisoners, posters announcing upcoming demonstrations, sign-up sheets for various activities. Here the owners will play the kind of music youth like to hear and generally tolerate them sitting for hours playing cards, hanging out without ordering much. [. . .] But the idea behind the *gaztetxe* movement was that something more than a hang-out was needed. As one woman explained to me, she felt young people like herself needed an alternative to the bar, someplace where individuals could come to read, organize talks, and do something other than drink alcohol without having music blaring in your ear. Bars were good for meeting your friends and organizing concerts, she felt, but they ultimately were in the business of making money by selling drinks. They could not provide the kind of environment for some of the things she was interested in like film screenings, talks on sexuality, holistic medicine, or creative writing. [. . .]

Free radios, like the media experiments of autonomous collectives elsewhere in Europe, need to be understood as part of this larger effort by youth to create spaces for alternative modes of communication and cultural life (Kogawa 1985). Many radios in fact were begun by youth assemblies and operated out of the youth houses. And there is considerable overlap in the ethos and individuals who work and frequent the radios, *gaztetxes*, squatter's communities, and radical bars. Free radios, for example, place the schedule of programs on the bulletin boards of the bars youth go to, they sell buttons and tee shirts there, and will typically have a *kutxa*, or collection box for donations for the radio on the counter. Free radios perform an interesting role vis-à-vis these alternative spaces. For the radios are themselves sites of cultural production and a technology which makes it possible to take the ideals, communicative practices, aesthetic forms, and cultural values of radical youth, and broadcast them beyond the spatial limits of any specific site.

In contrast to large well-financed regional Basque radio stations that have emerged since autonomy, free radios are unlicensed, low-cost, low-tech initiatives with a broadcast range of no more than a few miles. Being low-tech is not just a function of inadequate money; low-tech is a part of free radio's political commitment to democratizing access to media, making it as cheap and easy as possible to set up and sustain. Similarly, having a narrow broadcasting range corresponds to free radio's attempt to use radio to create an egalitarian communicative sphere. As Kogawa, an activist in the Japanese free radio movement explains, "the service area should be relatively small, because free radio does not *broadcast* (scatter) information but *communicates* (co-unites) messages to a concrete audience" (Kogawa 1985: 117). Because they are local creations and locally controlled, each one bears the imprint and reflects the interests of those who create and run the station. Those, and only those people who participate in the radio manage the station's daily affairs, finances, and determine what will go on the air. Programmers have virtually complete control over the content of their shows. All policy decisions regarding content or language are made by the general assembly. For example, the use of sexist language in some of the programs came up often as a problem in my discussions with women radio programmers. But instead of writing a language code or policy, it was their feeling that the best way to address this problem was to raise the issue at general assembly and to raise awareness among members about the way in which this kind of language use reinforced gender hierarchies. What unites free radios is a fierce commitment to freedom of expression, economic independence, and democratic control by assembly. In this respect, free radios are quite different in practice and in their ideology from the British offshore pirate radio stations that were so important to the development of Afro-Caribbean music and cultural styles (Barbrook 1987; Gilroy 1987). In contrast to the pirates, which were largely commercial music stations, free radios are vehemently non-commercial and refuse advertising of any sort. [. . .]

Free from state regulation on the one hand, or the tyranny of the top forty on the other, Basque free radios take on the identity of unruly "provocateurs" (*zirikatzaile*). This is reflected in the names radios adopt, which range from the incendiary to the irreverent: For example, one station calls itself "Molotoff Radio", after the favored weapon of urban guerrilla warfare; another calls itself "Zirika", or Pesky Thorn, while others have chosen more nonsensical or humorous names like "Monkey Radio" or "Kaka Flash." In the words of Jakoba Rekondo, one of the newscasters in the free radio of Usurbil, "we didn't want to make just another normal radio with lots of music and so on. For that, you can listen to a commercial station and get better quality anyway. We saw our radio as a way of contributing to the movement, *la movida*."

Being part of the movement for free radios means first and foremost, in their words, "giving voice to those without voice" and to provide what they call, "counter-information." In practical terms this entails opening the airwaves to all the *herriko taldeak*, that is, local cultural and grass roots organizations – feminists, ecologists, amnesty groups for Basque political prisoners, Basque language schools, mountaineering clubs, and literary groups – to take part in the radio. Currently, for example, free radios are, together with political comic-zines like *Napartheid*, an important forum for one of the largest youth movements today, the *insumisos*, that is, youth who are refusing to comply with the mandatory military service requirement. Free radios see their function in large part as one of community bulletin boards, providing a public forum for otherwise marginalized political and cultural perspectives which previously have had to rely on demonstrations, graffiti, and posters in the street as their primary media of public expression.

Sustained by and firmly rooted in an array of oppositional social movements, sympathetic to, but independent of, the Basque nationalist left political parties, free radios constitute an alternative public sphere that challenges the exclusions of the liberal bourgeois media, both Spanish and Basque. Curiously enough, tension surrounding these exclusions is becoming more, not less, heightened in the autonomous Basque provinces. [. . .] The [. . .] slogan, "We, too, are the People," is a particularly clear indication of the ongoing contestation in the Basque Country over who will get to speak as a public citizen, and whose concerns or interests come to be regarded as matters of the commonweal. Free radios, together with other grass roots organizations, Basque language and cultural revitalization groups, understand themselves to be serving the cultural interests of "the people," the *herria*. *Herria* is a semantically dense and highly resonant term in Basque nationalist discourse, which, as a noun, can mean, "the town," "the people," or "the nation," and, when used as an adjective, as in *herriko*, or *herrikoia*, may mean "popular," "public" and even "patriotic" (Aulestia 1989). Free radios claim to be the voice of "the People," the *herria*, that has been left outside the imagined community of the middle class Basque media. And what is left out, in their view, is not only the perspectives of oppositional groups, but also the perspective and participation of local communities in defining public knowledge.

At stake for free radios and other experiments in local or community based Basque language media is something more than *access* to the public sphere. Especially important in the eyes of free radio activists is not just finding a public space to express themselves, but getting members of the community, especially teenagers, to become *producers* rather than simply *consumers* of public knowledge. If, under consumer capitalism, mass mediated forms of publicity construct the public as viewers or spectators (Lee 1993; Kogawa 1985), free radio imagines the public as *participant*. In interviews I had with programmers, they would often describe the radio as trying to be an open mike, where anyone "from the street," as they say, could come and express their opinion. The ideology of communication in free radios, according to Guattari, is to maintain a system of direct feedback between the station and the community [(1981: 233–4)]. This can happen in a number of ways; radios encourage people to participate in creating the news by phoning in a piece of information and, in some cases, they will broadcast directly on the air. Listener call-ins are encouraged during many programs and especially when there are demonstrations or confrontations with the police, the radio will try to get reports from participants who are on location. In contrast to the mainstream media, individuals can speak publicly on free radio, but they do so not as designated representatives, experts, journalists, or official spokespersons. There is a kind of counter-authority attached to free radio's defiant non-professionalism. People who speak the reality of the street, who speak as the common man or common woman, appear to be valorized and endowed with an authority that comes precisely from their marginality to any institutional authority. Such individuals are seen as possessing more authentic knowledge based on lived experience, and to contribute new perspectives and fresh truths via their direct plain speech. [. . .] More than just an alternative news outlet, free radios imagine themselves almost like a Habermasian ideal sphere of open communication: A communal space where local residents and especially youth can speak *as citizens* and engage in defining public knowledge and public culture.

Irreverent speech

This brings us directly to the question of language ideology and practice. How are these ideological commitments expressed in the linguistic practices of free radio? The political ideology and organizational structure of free radios seems to be fairly consistent from one station to the next. However, the variation in sociolinguistic make-up of communities across the southern Basque Country makes generalization about language use impossible. Some stations based in predominantly Castilian speaking towns – *Hala Bedi* in Gazteiz (Alava), *Eguzki* in Iruna (Navarre), or *Zintzilik* in Renteria (Gipuzkoa) – operate almost entirely in Castilian, while others based in areas with high numbers of Basque speaking youth use much more Basque in their programming. The analysis which follows is based on observations of two radio stations in the province of Gipuzkoa: "Molotoff" located in the town of Hernani, (population 20,000) and "Paotxa" located in Usurbil, 7 kilometers away (population 5000). Paotxa operated entirely in Basque, while Molotoff had approximately 80% of its programming in Basque, the other programs were identified as "bilingual" or Castilian.

Language policy is probably one of the most controversial issues among Basque free radios. During my research at Molotoff in the spring of 1994, the radio's general assembly had reached an impasse over whether the station should adopt a Basque-only language policy. Some members closely connected to the language activist organization, Basque in the Basqueland, had proposed this, arguing that the radio had a moral responsibility to assist in the struggle to normalize the usage of Basque in public life and that without such a policy, Basque would continue in its minoritized status within the station and in Hernani as a whole. For others, this policy went against the ideology of the station which is to be open to all youth, regardless of their mother tongue. Furthermore, it was argued that a formal language policy went against the station's commitment to freedom of expression and autonomy from any kind of political doctrines, including that of language revivalists. Few stations, in fact, have opted for a Basque-only broadcasting policy, and those that do operate in Basque tend to be in towns where Basque speakers are in the vast majority. Nevertheless, there is a clear solidarity between free radios in the Basque Country and the language revival movement. This is signaled by the fact that virtually all the free radios adopt Basque language names (*Txantxangorri*, *Tximua*, *Eguzki*), even if many of their programs are in Spanish or bilingual. This kind of emblematic or titular Basque identity is actually one of the distinguishing features of membership in many grass roots organizations in the radical or *abertzale* left. Basque functions as a sign of alterity and oppositionality to the Spanish state and its institutions. At Molotoff, for example, there are several programs in Castilian whose programmers do not know Basque. Yet a conscious decision has been made to have all *kuñas* or program call signs, and station identifications like, "You're listening to the voice of Molotoff Irratia," be in Basque, *Euskera*. Commonly used in mainstream radio broadcasting, the introduction of these devices domesticates the anarchic pleasure Guattari celebrated in free radio's uncontrolled free-form broadcasting aesthetic by giving a sense of order and pacing within and between programs. It is significant that while the station could not agree to a language policy for all the programs, the code choice of call signs and station identifications did become a subject of explicit debate in the general assembly of Molotoff. While individuals are believed to be entitled to complete freedom within the context of their programs, call signs occupy a special status as the voice of the radio as a whole. Interjected into programs, the use of Basque call signs, together with station identifications, work as framing devices for the ensuing talk, establishing for the radio and its audience symbolic membership in a Basque speaking *euskaldun*, public, even if later, Castilian could be used inside the program and certainly was frequently used in joking and other off-the-record comments.

In keeping with their anti-institutional and oppositional politics, free radio broadcasters interject a great deal of slang and colloquialisms, that mark themselves as closer to what they see as "the language of the street." One of the more interesting places to look for this is, again, in the pre-recorded opening and closing of programs. At Usurbil's Paotxa radio, for example, in the opening to the community news program, announcers use Basque informal modes of address, *aizak, hi!* (for males) and *aizan, hi!* (for women), roughly translatable as "Hey You!", to address each other and by extension, the listening audience. In Gipuzkoa, this informal [pronoun] system is found most frequently among native speakers in rural areas where it is most commonly used among siblings, same sex peer groups, and for addressing animals on the farm. The use of *hitanoa*, as it is called, ind[icates] familiarity associated with intimate friends of equal status. Opposite sex siblings will use *hika* with one another, but men and women, especially married couples, generally maintain the more formal, respectful *zuka* pronouns with one another.[3] *Hika* may also index lesser status; children, for example, may be addressed frequently as "*Hi*" by adults, but the reverse would elicit a reprimand, especially if the adult is not a member of the family. These forms have been lost in many, especially urban areas, and are not generally known by non-native Basque speakers. However, recently, *hitanoa* has enjoyed somewhat of a renewed interest among some politicized *euskaldun* (Basque speaking) writers, intellectuals, and youth interested in maintaining this distinctive aspect of spoken Basque. My observations of speech patterns in Usurbil indicate that radical *euskaldun* youth in this community, particularly males, make a point of using *hitanoa* in most of their everyday interactions with each other and with women in their *cuadrilla* or friendship circle. They will also occasionally use *hika* with store keepers, teachers, the mayor, the priest, or other individuals who would normally be addressed more formally. Strategic use of *hika* pronouns in these circumstances, I would argue, is one among several ways that some radical *euskaldun* youth express their rejection of the traditional status hierarchies that have dominated Basque society including much of nationalist political culture. When Paotxa newscasters use these salutations, *aizak* and *aizan*, to introduce the local news, they construct the communicative sphere as an imagined community of "horizontal comradeship" that is in keeping with free radio's vision of radical democracy. This is accentuated by the fact that, at Paotxa, like most free radios, announcers almost never identified themselves by name: There was none of the cult of personality of named dee jays found on commercial and some pirate stations. Everyone is nameless and in some sense equivalent in status. Extending the sphere of intimacy to the town as a whole, of course, might just as easily be perceived not as an expression of solidarity, but as a kind of rude speech. Such a reading probably wouldn't bother most radio programmers since they often deliberately pepper their broadcasts with humorous, rude, sometimes scatological expressions. Either way, it sets free radio apart from mainstream broadcast etiquette and differentiates it markedly from the language movement's emphasis on creating a formal standard Basque – on making the Basque a language of science, technology, and high culture.[4]

As part of their commitment to the language revival, most free radio stations will broadcast Basque language classes. But the overall goal of the station's language use is not didactic. Language play seems to be more valued than imparting normative or standard Basque. Parody and humor are valued traits in both programming and in language use. Here again, we see some of the best examples of this in the introductions and titles of programs. For example, a program on Molotoff radio ironically called "Spanish Only?" is put on by the local Basque language activist group, Basque in the Basqueland, and generally features debates, interviews, and announcements of various Basque language cultural events. The program, however, begins with a short little dialogue that parodies non-Basque speakers:

[Sounds of lightning and thunder crashing in the background]

Woman:	*Pues, chico, yo ya hago algo; le he puesto a la tienda el nombre de Garazi.*
	Hey, guy, I'm at least doing my part; I named my store *Garazi*.
Young man:	*Yo al perro ya le digo etorri, y al niño ixo.*
	Now I say *etorri* (come) to my dog, and *ixo* (hush) to my baby.
Male, "grunge" voice:	*Ba, yo paso del euskera.*
	Bah, I'm through with Basque.
Young man:	*Pero, si esa lengua ya no tiene futuro, no?*
	But, that language doesn't have a future, does it?
All together:	*Erderaz eta Kitto EZZZZZZ!*
	Spanish Only? Nooooooo!

Especially interesting is the way it pokes fun at people who consider themselves to be Basque patriots, the *abertzale*, doing their part for the language struggle, by sprinkling a few Basque words into their Spanish. Such ridicule of the *abertzale* is uncommon in the public discourse of the language movement which has generally tended to use a strategy of welcoming and encouraging people to use Basque in whatever form they can. By juxtaposing the well-meaning but Spanish-speaking patriot with the *pasota*, those who reject Basque altogether, the programmers of this show bring what activists often complain about in private into the public domain. From their perspective, this way of "speaking Basque" is really no better than no Basque at all. Indeed, it might be worse, for the way in which using a few Basque words to speak to children or to call a dog trivializes the goal activists have of creating a living Basque language and Basque speaking culture.

One final example involves the parodic spellings of Spanish words. The most common forms this takes is the use of Basque letters, K and TX, in otherwise Castilian words. Both of these forms are found in Basque orthography, but not in Castilian. They appear in Spanish phrases like *ke txorrada* for *que chorrada* (what a foolish or stupid thing) or *la martxa* for *la marcha* (the rhythm, the movement). I also found them appearing often in the titles of punk music programs like: *El Moko Ke Kamina (The Travelling Boogar)* and another called *Koktel de Mokos* (boogar cocktail).[g] These kinds of orthographic mixings and the kind of Beavis and Butthead humor they engender are found throughout radical Basque youth culture: My examples appear in free radio program schedules, but they also occur in comics, graffiti, and in the lyrics and album covers of Basque music groups associated with Basque Radical Rock movement (*rok radikal basko*), all of which are self-identified as oppositional. In the case of one program title, called *Mierkoles Merkatu* (Wednesday Market), the use of the letter "k" makes it ambiguous as to whether we should classify this phrase as colloquial Basque or local Spanish. Such usages play on mis-recognition, blurred language boundaries, and a feigned illiteracy in Spanish.

These examples of "bad Spanish" are very much in keeping with free radio activists' rude language ideology. In their deliberate "misspelling" of Spanish words, radical youth are turning what was once a source of stigma for many native rural Basques – that is the inability to read and write standard Castilian – into a way of mocking Castilian. Recent work on "mock Spanish" by Jane Hill (1993) offers an elegant analysis of how joking imitations do their symbolic work. Expanding on the work of Bakhtin and Spitzer, Hill argues that absurd or parodic imitations perform a dual function of both distancing the speaker from the voice they are imitating, and denigrating the source of that voice, making the source, whether it be women, Hispanics, or working class people, appear ridiculous or contemptible.[h] Hill takes as her case the joking imitations of minority group speech forms by majority language speakers to show that linguistic play can have very serious metalinguistic messages. The linguistic practices of radical Basque youth give us an example of this same semiotic principle in reverse. The impossible spellings of Spanish by radical youth perform a kind of ironic reversal in which it is the language of the dominant group, Castilian, that is pragmatically lowered.[5] My sense is that within radical youth culture, these parodic hybrid spellings create a kind of symbolic allegiance with Basque oppositionality which allows youth to simultaneously use Spanish while distancing themselves from any associations it has with state hegemony.

Alternative public spheres

In short, Basque free radios create an alternative form of public culture that differs significantly in its language ideology and modes of resistance from the institutionalized sectors of the Basque language movement. Free radios may see part of their mission as that of "exporting" Basque to the wider community, transgressing the existing geography of the language, but they care little for norms and diplomas. In contrast to the conservative codifying concerns of the academicians and planners who dominate the language movement or the bureaucrats of the Ministry of Culture and Tourism, free radio tolerates and at times embraces a mongrel and hybridized "Basque" language and culture. Subversive humor, parody, rude speech, and occasional inventive code mixing are valued skills and markers of participation in this alternative public sphere. It is important not to exaggerate here: Basque free radios are not as linguistically anarchic as Guattari [1981] might have liked them to be.

---

g 'Boogar' = nose mucus.
h See Hill, this volume.

Radical Basque youth have not gone the way, for example, of Latino performance artists, rappers, and radio programmers in the U.S. who deliberately seek to blur the boundaries with their artful uses of Spanglish (Fusco and Gomez-Peña 1994). Unlike diasporic minorities, it appears that Basque youth have more of an investment in retaining the boundary between Basque and Spanish even in their irreverent speech.

The fact that youth have turned to radio as a medium of oppositional cultural expression speaks to an awareness of the centrality of media in shaping cultural life. Free radio, like other forms of alternative media, operate on the philosophy that one must take what is dominant in a culture to change it quickly. One of the changes youth are attempting is to put their language and ideas into motion. In doing so, free radio uses the media not to disperse information to people – the consumer model of mainstream broadcast media – but to draw them in to local communicative networks. To borrow from Guattari, free radio's motion is centripetal, hoping to foster in those who listen a sense of involvement in local events and local culture (Guattari in Kogawa 1985). This is quite different from the strategy of language standardization, which offers up a single translocal language with which to communicate across towns. As a form of activism, the logic of free radio is bottom-up rather than top-down. It works by poaching on the airwaves, rather than by direct confrontation. For Guattari, free radios were to be extensions of the conversations people have in the street, in the cafe, around the dinner table. This is especially clear in the news reports called *infonnatiboa* or *albisteak*. At Paotxa radio, for example, programmers attempted to give priority to topics that they believed interested residents. In this way free radio news broke with the formulaic categories of news as found in mainstream media: Local, national, international, sports, and weather.[i] Even when radio announcers were repeating news reported in the papers, they were encouraged to annotate the reports with their own opinions and perspectives. They also introduced into their news reports a section on town gossip and rumors – who was getting married when, what they were going to wear, whether they were going to have it videotaped, and so on. This was done very tongue in cheek of course, but programmers claim that of all the shows, the gossip section was the most popular. They also announced on the radio the recent deaths of town residents. One of Paotxa's programmers explained this to me in the following way:

> the first thing our mothers do when they get the paper is read the death notices. They used to be posted on the wall of the church. We are just taking that custom and putting it on the radio. We are taking what people actually talk about in town, in the street, and making that our definition of news.

The public sphere of free radio is thus framed as emphatically local. But we have to ask, what does local mean in this context? If we look at the programming as a whole, these "local" expressions of Basque radical youth culture draw upon and are enriched by a wide array of extra-national cultural images, narratives, and modes of representation. In the past couple of years, African American culture and

---

i Compare Billig, this volume, on British newspapers.

politics were everywhere to be found in the form of rap music, Public Enemy clothing, Malcolm X insignia, and "Fight the Power" slogans which were written on the program tapes members of Molotoff radio gave to me. Radical youth appropriate these images and slogans into symbols of Basque oppositionality, inserting them into local narratives, debates, and modes of representation.[6] A quick scan of public cultures today shows us that such complex cultural brews are increasingly common in the urban neighborhoods of London, Paris, and Berlin, forcing us to rethink and redefine not only "the spatial, territorial, and geopolitical parameters of the public sphere," but also the counterpublics, like free radio, that emerge in its orbit (Hansen 1993b). As Miriam Hansen has pointed out:

> The restructuring and expansion of the communications industries on a transnational, global scale more than ever highlights the quotation marks around the terms of national culture and national identity. Indeed, the accelerated process of transnationalization makes it difficult to ground a concept of the public in any territorial entity, be it local, regional, or national.
>
> (1993b: 183)

This is *not* to say, of course that free radios are not tied to specific places and specific times. They are. Radios are linked to identifiable social networks of radical youth in urban and semi-urban areas; they come out of particular social settings, bars and youth houses, and are linked to contestations for particular public spaces. In this sense, the alternative public sphere they create does have a location that we need to address in attempting to make sense of their linguistic strategies. It *is* to say, however, that these "local" expressions of Basque radical youth culture are constituted through a kind of cultural bricolage that is facilitated by transnational flows of media, commodities, images, and people. This is nowhere more apparent than in the musical programming which juxtaposes folk with thrash, funkadelic with *txalaparta* (a wooden percussive instrument), tex mex with Basque accordion music. Through these juxtapositions, radical youth affirm connections to resistance struggles and marginalized groups elsewhere in ways that challenge the bounded and unified representation of Basque language and identity found in nationalist treatises or the census map.

Precisely because they have a history of marginalization, minority language groups have had the burden of establishing their difference from and equivalence to dominant languages. As a result, in certain domains activists have shunned hybrid cultural and linguistic forms as threatening to the integrity of their language (Jaffe 1993). This is not the prevailing attitude for all spheres of minority language production. Free radio works by a different logic creating a space that is simultaneously syncretic, local, and transnational. Free radios open up new spaces at the same time that they address the spatiality of linguistic domination which relegates the minority language to the sphere of private talk. They aim to take the Basque language out of the private domain and into the street, and to take, as they say, the reality of the street into the public domain. [. . .] Radio is conceptualized [. . .] as an instrument of back talk/talking back (hooks 1990). In many ways, the imaginary space of free radios is heterogeneous in contrast to the unitary space of nationalism.

It is also profoundly urban in the sense that Salman Rushdie gives to this term in his *Satanic Verses*. For Rushdie, what distinguishes the urban experience is not skyscrapers or concrete streets, but the simultaneous co-presence of multiple realities. Free radios are urban not because they exist only in cities – in some cases like Usurbil, the town has no more than 5000 inhabitants. These low powered, ephemeral stations, with their radical philosophy of democratic communication, are urban in the sense that they try, in however imperfect ways, to place the heterogeneity of Basque society on the airwaves. These representations too, deserve our attention as part of the ongoing construction of minority languages.

Notes

1   For general overviews of the alternative radio movement in Western Europe and how it compares to pirate and community radio projects see e.g. Barbrook (1987), Lewis (1984), and McCain (1990).
2   [This created t]he Basque Autonomous Community, *Comunidad Autónoma Vasca*, [as] an administrative unit within the Spanish state [. . .]
3   *Zuka* was also described to me as being sweeter (*goxoa*) than *hika*. It is the preferred form to use with infants, for example, while *hika* may be used when the child gets older.
4   It should be emphasized that use of *hitanoa* varies widely from community to community. Very little *hitanoa*, for example, was used at Molotoff radio only 7 kilometers from Paotxa. Besides considering how this form constructs the listening public, we might also think about how free radio changes the way speakers view *hitanoa*. It is possible that using *hitanoa* in oppositional radio, making it a part of the hip transnational music and culture of radical youth, may also have an effect on the connotations of *hitanoa*, shaking loose its associations with rural life and giving this form of speech a new urban feel.
5   Keith Basso's study of joking imitations of "the Whiteman" by Apache speakers (1979) is another good example of how subaltern groups may use parody to construct, at least temporarily, a symbolic order in which they are culturally superior to and different from dominant groups.
6   The appropriation of African American rap music and cultural style by European ethnic and linguistic minorities is not uncommon. For a fascinating parallel case among Franco-Magribi youth see Gross, McMurray, and Swedenburg (1992). (*Editors:* See also the papers by Back, Hewitt and Cutler.)

References

Aulestia, Gorka (1989) *Basque-English dictionary*. Reno, NV: University of Nevada Press.
Barbrook, Richard (1987) A new way of talking: Community radio in 1980s Britain. *Science as culture* 1:1.81–129.
Basso, Keith (1979) *Portraits of the Whiteman: Linguistic play and cultural symbols among the western Apache*. Cambridge: Cambridge University Press.
Bourdieu, P. 1991 *Language and Symbolic Power*. Cambridge, MA: Harvard University Press.
Brecht, Bertolt (1964) The radio as an apparatus of communication. In John Willett (ed.), *Brecht on theatre*. New York: Hill and Wang.
Cheval, Jean-Jacques (1992) Local radio and regional languages in southwestern France. In H. Stephen Riggins (ed.), *Ethnic minority media: An international perspective*. London: Sage, 165–197.

Eley, Geoff (1992) Nations, publics, and political cultures: Placing Habermas in the nineteenth century. In Craig Calhoun (ed.), *Habermas and the public sphere*. Cambridge, MA: MIT Press.

Fraser, Nancy (1993) Rethinking the public sphere: A contribution to the critique of actually existing democracy. In Bruce Robbins (ed.), *The phantom public sphere*. Minneapolis, MN: University of Minnesota Press, 1–32.

Fusco, Coco and Guillermo Gómez-Peña (1994) New world radio. In Daina Augaitis and Dan Lander (eds.), *Radio rethink: Art, sound and transmission*. Banff, Canada: Walter Phillips Gallery, 223–244.

Gilroy, Paul (1987) *There ain't no black in the Union Jack: The cultural politics of race and nation*. Chicago: University of Chicago Press.

Gross, Joan, David McMurray and Ted Swedenburg (1992) Rai, rap and ramadan nights: Franco-Maghribi cultural identities. *Middle East Reports* (September–October) 22:5.11–16.

Guattari, Félix (1981) Las radios libres populares. In Lluís Bassets (ed.), *De las ondas rojas a las radios libres*. Barcelona, Spain: Editorial Gustavo Gili, 231–236.

Hansen, Miriam (1993a) Early cinema, late cinema: Permutations of the public sphere. *Screen* 34:3.197–210.

Hansen, Miriam (1993b) Unstable mixtures, dilated spheres: Negt and Kluge's *The public sphere and experience*, twenty years later. *Public Culture* 5:2.179–212.

Hill, Jane (1993) Hasta la vista, baby: Anglo-Spanish in the american southwest. *Critique of Anthropology* 13:2.145–176.

hooks, bell (1990) Talking back. In R. Ferguson, M. Gever, T. Minh-ha, C. West (eds), *Out there: Marginalization and contemporary cultures*. Cambridge, MA: MIT Press.

Jaffe, Alexandra (1993) Obligation, error, and authenticity: Competing cultural principles in the teaching of Corsican. *Journal of Linguistic Anthropology* 3:1.99–114.

Kasmir, Sharryn (1993) The myth of Mondragón: Cooperatives, politics, and working class life in a Basque town. Unpublished PhD. dissertation. Graduate Program in Anthropology, City University of New York.

Kogawa, Tetsuo (1985) Free radio in Japan. In Douglas Kahn and Diane Neumaier (eds), *Cultures in contention*. Seattle, WA: The Real Comet Press, 116–121.

Landes, Joan (1988) *Women and the public sphere in the age of the French revolution*. Ithaca: Cornell Unversity Press.

Lee, Benjamin (1993) Going public. *Public culture* 5:2.165–178.

Lewis, Peter (1984) Community radio: The Montreal conference and after. *Media, Culture, and Society* 6:137–150.

McCain, Thomas and G. Ferrel Lowe (1990) Localism in western european radio broadcasting: Untangling the wireless. *Journal of Communication* (Winter) 40:1.86–101.

Negt, Oskar and Alexander Kluge (1993) *The public sphere and experience*. Trans. Peter Labanyi, Jamie Daniel and Assenka Oksiloff. Minneapolis: University of Minnesota Press.

Ormazabal, Sabino (n.d.) El movimiento juvenil vasca. Unpublished manuscript.

Urla, Jacqueline (1993) Cultural politics in an age of statistics: Numbers, nations and the making of Basque identity. *American Ethnologist* 20:4.818–843.

Jacqueline Urla is Professor in the Department of Anthropology at the University of Massachusetts in the US.

Chapter 17

Monica Heller

1999

ALTERNATIVE IDEOLOGIES OF *LA FRANCOPHONIE*[a]

[. . .]

1 Introduction

THE PURPOSE OF THIS PAPER is to explore the ways in which ideologies of language and national identity are changing as part of current processes of globalization. One of the central characteristics of this current period of high modernity (Giddens 1990) is the breakdown of modern ideologies of language and nation-state. In their stead, what we see developing are the following phenomena:

1   the commodification of language;
2   pressures towards standardization for international communication; and
3   the opposite, the valuing of local characteristics in order to legitimate local control over local markets, and in order to attach a value of distinction to linguistic commodities in world markets of culture and tourism. [. . .]

The first part of th[e] paper will set up the problem of globalization and language ideologies, especially as this is reflected in French Canada. The second part will show how modern and high modern perspectives confront each other in one particular French-language minority high school in Ontario. [. . .]

2 Modernity, high modernity and linguistic ideologies

As we well know, one of the major components of nationalist ideologies is language (Hobsbawm 1990; Blommaert 1999).[b] From the nineteenth century, we have

---

a From *Journal of Sociolinguistics* 3(3): 336–59.
b See also Fishman, this volume.

inherited a strong association of monolingualism and language standardization with the legitimization of nation-states and their entry into international economic and political networks. This cluster of phenomena is one of the hallmarks of modernity; to enter the modern world, a people (generally fictively imagined by its bourgeoisie in order to create national markets and accompanying state structures over which they exert control and which benefit their interests; Anderson 1983; Bochmann et al. 1993) must demonstrate itself to be unified, by possessing a common language and a state. Alternatively, the creation of a state requires the creation of its authenticating people (cf. Balibar 1985; Handler 1988). The legitimacy of the particular arrangements which are the goal of such social change is usually vested in symbolic terrains, notably in linguistic ideologies. These ideologies focus on authenticity and integrity: the language is the inherent, essential property of the people, and the guarantee of its peoplehood. Properties of the language (its correctness, its beauty, and so on) make it uniquely valuable and important as the symbol and vehicle of public life.

However, the more modern nation-states expand their capitalist networks, the more, we are finding, they are subsumed under international ('globalized') networks, control over which escapes any given state.[c] High modernity (Giddens 1990) is a state of tension between monolingual nation-states and supra-national structures and processes. Beyond the nation-state, two opposing tendencies seem to emerge: one is a tendency toward uniformization (what some call the McDonaldization of the world, reflected in a global orientation towards a unified consumer market, and the spread of English). This tendency is, of course, not without its opponents, and not without its struggles. Notably, there is competition among former and emerging imperial powers for privileged access to at least a piece of the action. France and the French-speaking world are an important example of this (but see also China, and the Spanish-speaking world). At the same time, globalization creates new opportunities at local levels for access to the global market which bypass the nation-state, opening up of local (and non English-speaking markets) to world trade, and the valuing on the global market of signs and goods which reflect the opposite of the uniformization of globalization. Tourism and culture in particular are places where local identities and languages are valued, although they are valued principally as commodities and less as legitimating symbols of nation-states (or proto-nation-states). Language skills of varying kinds are also of increasing value in internationalized service and information sectors. The question is: who gets to decide what counts as the legitimate language of international communication, and what counts as local languages which are valued as commodities? How much room is there for local control, and what kinds of people emerge locally as the new elite?

These questions are particularly important for Western linguistic minorities. For the last thirty years or so, members of these minorities (think of Wales, Brittany, Corsica, Catalonia, Québec) have engaged in a quintessentially modern discourse. They have argued that they are authentic peoples, and they should therefore have a state. The only real point of contention between linguistic minority movements and the states whose power they contest, is which state is the authentic, legitimate

---

c See Mazrui, this volume, on English within a globalized capitalist economy.

representative of the people (Canada or Québec? France or Brittany?). Or conversely, which people is the real, authentic one, the one constituted by the minority, or the one constituted by the state of which they are a part (are we/you Breton or French? Welsh or British?).

Linguistic minorities have been somewhat successful in playing the nation-state game.[d] Their emerging middle classes have staked out control over local markets, and have established legitimate institutions on the basis of their modernist claims to autonomy. In the new economies of high modernity several things have happened. For most linguistic minorities, local characteristics have acquired new value in tourism and cultural industries. World music, for example, is a popular and lucrative domain in which new practitioners of old musical forms are able to participate (although frequently the point is not to completely reproduce authentic forms, but rather to introduce old forms of music into new global musical trends, with care to legitimize the old forms through a historicized account of their origins). Linguistic and cultural capital is quite literally commodified. At the same time, minorities like those of francophone Canada have a basis from which to participate in world markets, as long as they can use their vernacular forms as a basis for acquiring competence in standardized ones, and as long as they can turn their vernacular competencies into valued locally distinctive goods. Francophones in Canada have access to both French and English, and this can be turned to their advantage in new job sectors.

The transition from modernity to high modernity thus provokes a reworking of ideas over the value of multilingualism, the nature of whatever multilingualism might be valued, and over what count as legitimate forms of language varieties and language practices. In the following section I will discuss some of the specificities of these dilemmas as they are played out in francophone Canada.

3   *La francophonie* [. . .]

[. . .] The French-speaking world, as the major inheritor of ideologies of language and nation which crystallized during the French Revolution, has a specific version of ideologies of monolingual nation-states which I discussed above, both in terms of beliefs about monolingualism and in terms of beliefs about language. We still believe that the best way to ensure equal access to the benefits of the Revolution (liberty, equality, fraternity, of course) is to make sure, through the intervention of the State, that everyone speaks the same language (Balibar 1985). We understand the normal state of our social world to be monolingual (indeed, the word 'normal' appears consistently in the discourse of Québec nationalism; by way of parallel, it is also a key figure in Catalan sociolinguistic discourse, cf. Vallverdu 1981). It is possible to be bilingual, but this entails being, in effect, monolingual twice over. In order to accomplish this, monolingual spaces must be created. In addition, we have to work at creating a unified language.

Furthermore, the form of the language which we are all supposed to share equally, that is French, embodies important principles which are related to social

---

d See also Urla, this volume.

and political values. Historically, these have been linked to the Enlightenment and its impact on the Revolution, and have focussed on virtue, clarity and reason (Outram 1987; Swiggers 1990). Speaking well thus has a moral dimension (Crowley 1991; Cameron 1995). We see traces of these orientations today, in the way grammar is taught in schools, in debates over orthography, in world-wide *dictées*, and other activities, in which much of the francophone world either participates directly or reproduces at a regional or local level. The unilingualism of public space and the 'quality' of language, both guaranteed by the State and its institutions, are the two central tenets of this historically-based ideological orientation.

At the same time, the weakening of the old, classic nation-states creates stress fractures within the world once dominated by the former imperialist powers. We have all heard about the Empire striking back in Britain (that is, the ways in which former colonies are appropriating English and English identity),[e] and something along those lines is happening within *la francophonie*. This can be seen in discussions over what constitutes French; everyone agrees that such a thing exists, the problem is who gets to define it. Here the question is principally whether the source of such definition is (still) France, or whether it is possible to develop regional standards. It is not surprising, for example, that as France's international influence wanes, sociolinguists should begin to talk about French as a polycentric language (cf. de Robillard and Beniamo 1993, 1996).[f]

But what happens within regions reveals the persistence of the same ideological orientation that gave us the *Académie française*, an ideological orientation which supposes that someone is going to get to define regional norms along some lines which are considered to be credible and legitimate in terms of what constitutes the underlying legitimacy of the states in question. A clear example of this process can be found in the current, and rather vicious, debates in Québec over whether or not such a thing as Québec French exists, and if so, what it might look like (cf. Cajolet-Laganière and Martel 1995; Dor 1996; Laforest et al. 1997; Heller 1999b). There are those who argue for a universal French, others for a French which reflects local, Québec characteristics. Among the latter, there are those who want to embrace all local forms as guarantors of authenticity, while others wish to retain only those features which embody a new, modern image of Québec (an example of this is a preference for *tu* over *vous* as the second person singular pronoun, as a reflection of egalitarian and solidarity-building values).[g] What is at stake is nothing less than the legitimacy of the State (in this instance, Québec), and the definition of the values it embodies.

However, the fragmentation of big empires, or of big states into little states, is not the only process going on at the moment. The expansion of corporate capitalism through globalization, and the growing importance of service and information as economic activities, are connected to a process of disintegration of state nationalist ideologies and the emergence of a second ideological orientation towards language and identity. In this perspective, it matters more what resources are

---

e In this volume, on Britain see Hewitt, Back and Honeyford, and Quirk internationally.

f For comparable debates around English, see Quirk and Rampton, this volume.

g Traditionally, *tu* is regarded as the familiar form for 'you', while *vous* is considered the formal/polite one.

accessed through the private sector than what can be gained through the State. The basis of the legitimacy of the private sector is principally economic; language is thus commodified. At the same time, language does have great value as a commodity, since it is central to the functioning of the new service- and information-based economies. Here, *la francophonie* is principally of interest as a market and as a source of commodifiable linguistic resources. As a result, the question of norms is subject to different, and sometimes countervailing, tendencies:

1   a desire to develop communicative norms that permit efficient, that is to say, common, modes of functioning across regions and across social divisions within regions;
2   a value accorded to local, that is, vernacular, products which are commodifiable, especially in tourism and culture; and
3   a prevailing ideology of customer service, which entails speaking the various languages or linguistic varieties of the clientèle.

What is produced is a multiple set of tensions. One set pits the modernist orientation against its fragmentation by high modernity. The other concerns the tensions within high modern processes themselves. In both cases, part of these tensions has to do with who gets to define norms, and for whom. In what follows, I will provide some examples of these tensions as they play themselves out in francophone Ontario, a site where the sociohistorical conditions underlying the ideological orientations I have just outlined intersect. On the one hand, it is a region subject to the strong influence of France's colonizing (and post-colonizing) practices as well as to the effect of post-1960s linguistic nationalism (Heller 1994). On the other, it is a typically *fin-de-siècle* place, a centre of global capitalism and a pole of attraction for international immigration. Who is a Franco-Ontarian, what is French, and who gets to decide, are all key questions at the moment.

4   Linguistic nationalism in French Ontario

The ideology of the nation-state has a specific manifestation in French Ontario. Unlike Québec (or Corsica, or Brittany, or Wales), francophone Ontario cannot lay claim to any homogeneous territory (however fictively constructed). The unilingual spaces it has sought to create have therefore been institutional. This is most clearly seen in a long struggle for unilingual and autonomously-controlled French-language schools, but there have also been struggles for other such institutional, collective spaces (in the areas of culture, media, health and social services especially), and also struggles on an individual basis for the construction of unilingual zones in one's life (for example, for francophones married to anglophones, who seek friends with whom or activities in which they can speak just French for a while; Heller and Lévy 1994). Within these spaces, there is constant debate over the nature of the space, that is, over what kinds of people get to participate, and over what the conventions of linguistic practice should be.

One dimension of these debates is directly connected to the difficulty, in a minority setting, of creating unilingual zones; they have to do, that is, with constructing the boundary between French and English. In practical and concrete terms, this means establishing the extent to which speakers of languages other than French should be allowed to participate, and what degree and kind of influence from English might be allowed into participants' linguistic practices in these ostensibly unilingual zones. This is especially difficult due to the fact that, while the school wants to set itself up as a French monolingual zone, it does so in order to facilitate the construction of a specific type of French-English bilingualism, a bilingualism which is essentially two unilingualisms, one French and the other English, stuck together (as opposed to a code-switched or mixed variety). Nobody, in other words, disputes the importance of knowing English; what is at issue is where you learn it and how you use it.

A second dimension has to do with the tension between the two major legit-imating ideologies of these institutions. On the one hand, these institutions are supposed to represent the authentic members of a homogeneous francophone nation. On the other hand, they are supposed to be both democratic (that is, not practice exclusion on the grounds of essential characteristics, like race or gender) and oriented to facilitating francophone entry into the modern, increasingly globalized world on the basis of the use of French (and, if necessary, other languages, but not other languages instead of French). What this produces is an orientation towards an integrally French, monolingual-type standard language, accompanied by (more or less successful) strategies for at once appropriating and containing the vernaculars which are the simultaneous source of stigmatization and authenticity, and for containing the leakage of English into this space. What is lacking, however, is the means to cope with other regional varieties of French or with the other languages whose presence is increasing.

Let us take a look at some of the ways these dimensions play themselves out in one example of such an institution, a French-language high school in which I conducted ethnographic work for four years in the early 1990s (see Heller 1999a). Schools, like other public institutions, are interesting for my purposes because they are examples of state agencies which are directly linked to a modernist orientation towards language and identity. Minority schools are in a particularly interesting position, since the minority tries to use them as though they were the majority, but in fact these schools are subject to the control of the English-speaking majority of Ontario (autonomy, it turns out, only goes so far). At the same time, schools are particularly revealing sites because they are at the intersection between public and private sectors (they are public sector institutions which train students for the job market), and so are especially vulnerable to the effects of high modernity. Neo-liberal ideologies of education, with their emphasis on education as work-related training, reinforce this position.

The specific school in which I worked is well-located to illustrate my argu-ments. It exists as the product of political mobilization in the 1960s, a kind of indirect result of Québécois nationalism. Québec's redefinition of French Canada had the effect of fragmenting the older, pan-Canadian francophone nation (Martel 1997); in its wake, local province-based institutional nationalisms were created. At the same time, provinces like Ontario, with the strong backing of the Canadian federal government, attempted to counter the Québec nationalist argument that a state would be the only way to preserve French in Canada by setting out to prove that it was possible to live in French elsewhere. The 1960s and 1970s saw as a result the founding of numerous francophone schools (albeit not without major struggles against reluctant anglophone élites). The school discussed here, L'École Champlain,[1] was the first French language high school established in its region, and still stands today as a symbol of Franco-Ontarian struggles for their rights.

As a result, the school's historical orientation is modernist. It exists in order to provide a monolingual French space, and to contribute to the advancement of Franco-Ontarians, seen as a homogeneous and authentic people. Its main struggles were originally seen as being to establish French as a monolingual variety, and to privilege linguistic forms that were standard enough to fulfill the goals of social, economic and political advancement and local enough to be authenticating.

The school's conditions of existence, however, are resolutely high modern. All participants in school life experience at least two languages in the course of every single day, just by virtue of the combination of who they are and where they live, work or study. High modernity has brought with it the dissolution of the former processes of social and cultural reproduction, and so even 'old-style' Franco-Ontarians are likely to be extremely bilingual, and may even be married to non-francophones. The same processes (notably with respect to the growth of globalized service and information economies) have placed a value on French, which becomes a resource to which others want to gain access, drawing even anglophones to schools such as Champlain. And high modernity has also been accompanied by immigration, so that the schools are filled with students from places where French has historically been a language of prestige, or anyway instruction, but may not be a family's first language. High modernity has brought with it a calling into question of the value of authenticating local forms and of the homogeneity of the 'people' the school is meant to serve. At the same time, it places the school in the crucial position of being the only institution of social and cultural reproduction which might guarantee privileged access to the opportunities of high modernity to those who can claim special rights to it; the school is the only institution which can provide the kind of credentialized form of linguistic competence which is necessary for the recognition of that competence in the new job markets; and the school simultaneously must act according to prevailing ideologies of democracy and meritocracy. As we will see below, the school's linguistic ideologies, in its representations and its practices, reveal traces of all these tensions.

The first set of examples (1–5) shows how the school constructs itself as a monolingual zone, and copes with challenges to that attempt which stem from the very real presence of English and of a wide variety of kinds of French in the lives of both staff and students. These examples show the force of the nation-state ideological orientation, but also some ways in which the heterogeneity of real life challenges and ends up fragmenting the normativity and fictive homogeneity which underlies the existence and legitimacy of the school as a minority institution. (The second set of examples (examples 6–9) will show how middle-class bilingual and immigrant-origin students make common cause to push the school towards a globalizing, pluralist and commodifying vision of French in ways which systematically marginalize vernacular speakers.)

The following is taken from a resource document and course guide distributed to all students. The text is a concise representation of the school, as it tries to define its image for incoming and current students and their parents. However, one has to ask why it seems necessary to be so insistent on French monolingualism; clearly, the reality of student life at school is that it bears traces of the contact with English which a modernist orientation requires be kept at bay.

Example 1   From École Champlain course listing (*Répertoire des cours*), 1992–1993, p. 3

1   Usage du français: L'École
2   Champlain est une école de langue
3   française. Toutes les activités,
4   qu'elles soient purement scolaires ou
5   qu'elles soient culturelles ou
6   récréatives se déroulent en français.
7   On attend également de vous que
8   vous vous adressiez en français à vos
9   enseignant-e-s et à vos condisciples;
10   en classe et pendant toutes les
11   activités scolaires et parascolaires.
12   La loi sur l'éducation précise que
13   dans l'école de langue française la
14   langue d'administration et de
15   communication est le français. Une
16   école de langue française, en plus
17   d'être une maison d'enseignement
18   est aussi un foyer de rayonnement de
19   cette langue et de la culture qu'elle
20   véhicule. Aucun être humain ne peut
21   se développer harmonieusement, se
22   réaliser pleinement s'il ne maîtrise
23   pas parfaitement cet outil de pensée
24   et de communication. Chaque
25   enseignant-e et chaque secteur
26   auront une politique visant à vous
27   encourager à n'utiliser que le
28   français à l'école et dans les salles
29   de classe.

Use of French: Champlain School is a French-language school. All activities, whether strictly academic, cultural or recreational take place in French. We also expect of you that you speak in French to your teachers and fellow students; in class and during all school and extra-curricular activities. The Law on Education stipulates that in a French-language school the language of administration and communication is French. A French-language school, in addition to being a teaching institution is also a source of extension of this language and of the culture it transmits. No human being can develop in harmony, can develop his or her full potential if he or she does not master perfectly this tool of thought and of communication. Each teacher and each department will have a policy aimed at encouraging you to use only French in school and in the classroom.

Evidence of similar struggles can be found in daily life at school, where teachers find themselves constantly reminding students '*parlez français!*', and correcting both the students' (Examples 2 and 3 [. . .]) and their own *anglicismes* (Example 4) [. . .].

Example 2 is from an 11th grade Accounting class. Julien, the student, is giving a presentation about the financial difficulties of his favourite hockey team, the Québec Nordiques. [. . .] The teacher, Thérèse, provides feedback not on content, but on form, seizing the pedagogical opportunity to make a point to the entire class (*beaucoup d'élèves*) about the influence of English on their French.

Example 2   11th grade *Comptabilité*, 1994

1	*Julien:*	Ça veut dire que, lui s'embarquer	*That means that for him to get*
2		là-dedans c'est vraiment un	*involved in that, it's really a*
3		risque pour lui. Perdre son poste	*risk for him. To lose his job*
4		puis trouver une somme d'argent	*and find such a large sum of*
5		aussi énorme, ça ça sera le euh très	*money, it it will the uh very*
6		le c'est comme un peu irréalistique	*the it's a bit unrealistic for the*
7		pour la ville de Québec	*city of Québec*
8	*Thérèse:*	(. . .) Les mots en -ic hein?	*(. . .) Words ending in -ic eh?*
9		c'est des mots souvent anglais,	*they are often English words,*
10		*realistic*, (xx) il y a plusieurs qui	*realistic (xx) there are many*
11		l'utilisent comme ça. C'est	*who use it like that. It's*
12		réaliste, euh réaliste, idéaliste,	*réaliste uh réaliste, idéaliste,*
13		et cetera, mais il y a beaucoup	*et cetera, but there are many*
14		d'élèves qui utilisent ces mots-là	*students who use those words*
15		avec la la terminaison *-ic*, ça	*with the the ending -ic, it*
16		n'existe pas en français, ça c'est	*doesn't exist in French, that*
17		de l'anglais (. . .)	*is English (. . .)*
18			

Example 3 is from a 10th grade French class. Martine, the teacher, is setting up a reading activity by initiating a discussion about reading. Again, her comment on Michel's answer is about form, not content, and specifically about the influence of English on students' French.

Example 3   10th grade *Français avancé*, 1991

1	*Martine:*	pourquoi lit-on?	*why do we read?*
2	*Michel:*	pour relaxer	*to relax*
3	*Martine:*	pour se détendre, "relaxer"	*to "se détendre" [relax], 'relaxer'*
4		c'est anglais	*is English*

The following example, (4), shows a [. . .] teacher self-monitoring. Lise catches herself mid-stream having used the word *timé* ('timed') and not only self-corrects, but admonishes herself.

Example 4   10th grade *Français général*, 1991

1	*Lise:*	(. . .) alors ce qu'on va faire	*(. . .) so what we're going to do*
2		aujourd'hui, on va sortir les	*today, we're going to take out*
3		textes que vous avez eus hier sur	*the texts which you got yesterday*
4		le futur dépasse souvent la	*on the future often overtakes*
5		technologie [. . .] ça va être uh	*technology [. . .] it will be uh*
6		*timé*, moi je pense c'est vraiment	**timed**, *I think it's really the*
7		le le (pause) chronométré	*the (pause) "chronométré"*
8		je devrais dire, mot anglais, okay	*I should say, English word, okay*
		t'as ton texte . . .	*you have your text . . .*

Now, we can see how the nationalist ideology of the school runs into trouble when it meets the real world, but we have also seen how representatives of the school find strategies to cope with contradictions between the ideological unilingualism of the school and the real contact with English which forms part of its conditions of existence, as well as between pressures towards the production of standard 'international' French versus the legitimizing authenticity of the local vernacular. Their discursive strategies create a distinction between front and backstage (in Goffman's sense), which allows them to construct a public image which conforms to ideological pressures (the production of a monolingual, standardizing and yet somehow also locally authentic French face), and at the same time to relegate to the backstage practices which would otherwise bring out into the open the contradictions and tensions which would threaten the successful reproduction of dominant discourses.

It is more difficult to cope with the second set of contradictions, that stemming from the authentic nationalist legitimacy of the institution, and its vocation to provide access to the modern world. We can see this clearly in struggles school representatives have with defining what is meant to count as good French (beyond French which is not influenced by English). We can also see it in the ways in which students collaborate with or contest the school's efforts to construct a norm.

The following example, 5, [. . . shows how a school representative (Liliane, an elected school trustee) positions herself] with respect to the problem of constructing a norm which democratically includes not only the French spoken in Ontario, but that which is spoken by the regionally and ethnoculturally diverse student body. [. . .] Liliane tries to resolve the contradiction between her sense of a unified, correct French, and the value she places on tolerating linguistic variability not the least of which is the authenticating value of otherwise stigmatized vernaculars. She does so by positing a kind of supra-French which is universal, and which allows within itself a certain amount of variation (although how much and what kind are not specified).

Example 5 Interview with Liliane, 1991

1	*Monica:*	en Français t'as mentionné	*in French you mentioned the*
2		l'importance d'avoir euh la	*importance of having uh the*
3		représentation de différents (xx)	*representation of different (xx)*
4		est-ce qu'il y a d'autres éléments	*are there other elements uh*
5		euh directives générales?	*general directives?*
6	*Liliane:*	oui euh une des choses qui nous	*yes uh one of the things which*
7		est aussi importante c'est	*is also important to us is*
8		l'utilisation du français euh dans	*the use of French uh in uh its*
9		euh son euh dans sa forme écrite	*uh in its written and spoken*
10		et parlée (. . .) qu'on soit sûr	*form (. . .) that we be sure*
11		que la qualité soit là et euh	*that the quality is there and uh*
12		avec l'aisance que l'on veut qu'ils	*with the facility that we want*
13		obtiennent en même temps	*them to get at the same time*
14	*Monica:*	par qualité qu'est-ce que tu	*by quality what do you*
15		entends?	*understand?*

16	*Liliane:*	qualité du français euh je pense	*quality of French uh I think*
17		que ça c'est dans notre volonté	*that it is part of our desire for*
18		d'avoir une éducation excellente	*excellent education uh that*
19		euh qu'ils s'experiment mais	*they express themselves but that*
20		qu'ils s'expriment en français	*they express themselves in*
21		puis là je vais utiliser quelque	*French and here I will use*
22		chose qui qui va être peut-être	*something which which will be*
23		interpreté comme racisme	*perhaps interpreted as racism*
24		comme on disait	*as we used to say in the old*
25		autrefois en chinois il faut que ça	*days "(not) in Chinese" it has*
26		soit un français normal il faut que	*to be a normal French it has*
27		ça soit un français point	*to be a French period*
28	*Monica:*	est-ce que	*is*
29	*Liliane:*	ce qui ne veut pas dire un français	*which does not mean a French*
30		sans accent euh y a y a le français	*with no accent uh there there is*
31		correct qui est le français normal	*correct French which is normal*
32		mais qui peut être utilisé	*French but which can be used*
33		avec x nombre d'accents ou	*with x number of accents or*
34		même x nombre de variations	*even x number of variations*
35		entre un vocabulaire qui est	*between a vocabulary which is*
36		aussi riche et aussi important	*as rich and as important*

In cases [like this], we can see the traces of the tension between retaining some notion of 'French' (notably as opposed to English), and the fragmentation of that notion caused by the very success of French Canada's efforts to enter the modern world. The efforts have been so successful that they have had an unexpected consequence: the modern world is now in French Canada's own classrooms. Indeed, we can see clearly here how modernity leads to high modernity. By participating as a homogeneous group in the modern world, francophone Canada contributes to the revaluing of French as a resource on the global market, and thereby attracts others to its institutions, thereby undermining the (already fictive) homogeneity of those institutions. It brings itself into closer contact with other linguistic resources (English, of course, but also a variety of forms of French, and of other languages of *la francophonie internationale*), the relationship with which must be carefully managed. Finally, it finds itself struggling over privileged access to and control over the definition of the linguistic resources it produces, distributes and credentializes.

5   Towards globalization

Students sense these tensions, although of course they are in a different position from the representatives of the school. [. . .] Very briefly, what emerges is a conflict between the 'authentic' French-Canadian speaking clientèle (see Example 6) and two other groups of students: one of which I have characterized as bilingual, and which is principally oriented towards the commodified dimension of French as linguistic capital; and one with origins outside Canada which is oriented towards a globalized notion of *la francophonie* (see Example 7). Despite initial friction over the propensity of bilingual students to speak English outside of class, a practice which effectively excluded all newcomers who did not already speak that language, these latter two groups developed converging interests. They both felt that the value of French as linguistic capital is increased by a global francophone market, and sensed that the global francophone community is increasingly tied together as a market in which language is commodified.

The first group, made up mainly of working-class French Canadians, feels and acts marginalized at school. Some of them react through absence or various forms of silence: they cut classes, they hang out in the smoking area behind the school, they sit in class with portable tape- or CD-player earphones in their ears, they refuse to take part in public displays of language skills (or find ways to get around them, like singing instead of talking). When they do talk in class, they tend to codeswitch a lot between French and English. A few express their dismay, as in the following example (6), which is from a discussion in a restaurant among an English-speaking research assistant, Mark, and three students, Diane, Simone and Claudia. All three are from francophone backgrounds in one way or another (Diane is a recently-arrived student from Québec, of French Canadian background; Simone's family is also from Québec, although they have been in Ontario for a number of years; Claudia has one francophone parent, and grew up in Québec, although she was only in elementary school when her family moved to Ontario). All are in [lower,] general-level classes [at the school].

Example 6   Interview, Mark, Diane, Simone and Claudia, June 1994

1	*Mark:*	what happens when you use French in the classroom? do you get
2		respect for your type of French or do they
3	*All three:*	nooooo, no
4	*Claudia:*	The French they're teaching us, is instead of saying *toi* I'll say *toé,*
5		*moi-moé* okay, and that's Québec French, that's how we were
6		taught that French and now they're trying to change it to be
7		French from France, *un vélo, une bicyclette* (laughter, xx) okay
8		they're changing it. It's like she did this, where you put a lemon
9		in your mouth and you're talking (xx)
10	*Mark:*	so they don't respect your type of French?
11	*Simone:*	no, they say that that's not real French
12	*Diane:*	yeah, like in French we gotta say *oui* and us Québécois say like
13		*ouais ouais ouais,* you know you're not on their couch, you're not
14		at their house, in your house and you say *oui* at school
15	*Mark:*	okay, let me ask you whether you agree with this or don't agree
16		with this or would like to change something. Look, the school
17		doesn't respect the type of French that you speak, so what you
18		do often is that you'll use English, that's kind of a way of saying
19		"to hell with you"
20	*Claudia and Simone:*	no no no
21	*Claudia:*	because even if they tell me not to talk my French, I'll do it.
22		'Cause it's my language. The English we're talking right now,
23		it's not the proper English, the real English is from England.

24		The proper French for them is from France. So we're like the
25		English ones right now (xx simultaneous talk) Because most of
26		the black people (xx) they're always transferred in France, and
27		then they come here. So of course they have a better French,
28		like, okay I have this problem with Isaak (xx) he was in my class,
29		but my teacher was Monsieur Dumont at that time and he was
30		from Québec and everything, and then we started talking about
31		the French language. I go (xx) I'm sorry you're not going to tell
32		me what's the right French (xx simultaneous talk)
33	*Simone:*	and also last time it was Madame Martin, it was in geography
34		class, and I started speaking French, and then she goes, "you
35		know, you really have a bad French". I'm like "excuse me
36		Madame, my Mom taught me how to speak that way". You're
37		not gonna start dissin' my mother, because she kind of dissed
38		my mother, because my Mom taught me how to speak that way,
39		and I'm proud to be bilingual
40	*Claudia:*	(xx) it's not an insult for you (xx) it's an insult for your parents
41		'cause that's how they raised you. They think they did good.
42		Screw the French we're talking about
43	*Mark:*	okay would you ever sometimes use your type of French in a
44		classroom just to drive home the point?
45	*Simone:*	I'm not gonna change my French for anybody
46	*Claudia:*	we'll write a composition in French, we write it in our French,
47		and then you get it back and you see all these red circles
48		(. . .)
49		Look, I left Québec when I was in Grade 3, when I just learned
50		out how to write like tied together, you know? But when I
51		moved to Ontario, I went to a French school, okay, French
52		elementary school. But they would tell me I'm not allowed to
53		write compositions with your Québec words, so I would get
54		angry, and I would write it anyway, you know. So I'm not gonna
55		change my French, I understand some of it don't make sense,
56		and I'll let them correct it right, but I don't agree with it
57		sometimes, just change the mistakes, or tell me this would sound
58		better, but you can't change my composition, because it won't
59		be called my composition, it would be called hers (xx). Me,
60		English and French, I write it the way I speak. Instead of writing
61		"*toi*" t-o-i, I'll write "*toé*" t-o-e and the accent, with the accent,
62		and that's the way I'll write, I'll write like I speak, and like for
63		me that's the way (xx) that's the way that I speak and then they
64		go and change it on you. I'm like listen, that's the way I speak

Clearly, all three girls feel that the linguistic resources they possess are devalued by the school. They may try to resist, but they know they will not convince the school to change its practices. Nonetheless, they continue to value these practices, as marks of their identity; one can read their stance as one of resistance against the dominant discourse of the school.

Not only do such students feel marginalized by the school, other students marginalize them. The 'bilinguals' mock their accent in public skits on the school stage. The students from outside Canada complain that they cannot understand this local French, and claim that it is 'bad' French, or 'not real' French. [. . . E]xample (7) is from an interview with a student from Africa[, . . . and we can see how such] students construct themselves as speakers of good, or normal, or real (*vrai*), or pure, or standard French, as opposed to the varieties of French they encounter in Canada, and which they consider at best hard to understand:

Example 7   Interview, Monica and Aïcha, 1992

1	Aïcha:	(. . .) ici, tu vois, les langues	(. . .) here, you see, the Québécois
2		québécoises sont plus faibles	languages are weaker than the
3		que les langues françaises	French languages
4	Monica:	dans quel sens?	in what sense?
5	Aïcha:	si on voit la qualité, et puis les	if you look at the quality, and
6		Français ils parlent le pur	the French they speak pure
7		français, et ici ils sont mélangés,	French, and here they're mixed,
8		comme si, c'est mélangé, j'ai	as if, it's mixed, I understood
9		compris du "là, là, là", mais on	"là, là, là," but they don't want
10		veut pas de répétitions en	any repetitions in France.
11		France. Le français, il faut pas	In French, there should be no
12		qu'il y ait de répétitions, oui,	repetitions, yes, but here,
13		mais ici alors là!	honestly!
14	Monica:	est-ce que tu trouves que c'est	do you find it difficult to
15		difficile à comprendre, le	understand the French
16		français d'ici?	here?
17	Aïcha:	oui, ah moi, j'avais du mal à	yes, oh I had difficulty under-
18		comprendre, parce qu'il y	standing, because there were
19		avait beaucoup de "là",	many "là"s, I understood
20		je comprenais rien	nothing

In the event, what happened at Champlain was the emergence of a new way of thinking about the school. A global image of diversity incorporating the authentic symbols of French Ontario is taking over; the conflict is being resolved through incorporation. This is seen in the success of a slate of students running on this precise platform in the student council elections of 1993. It is also evident in the physical construction of symbols, such as a Canadian flag drawn by one art class in 1996 which is a collage of flags of students' countries of origin, including the Franco-Ontarian flag; or the lobby display of a statue of the French explorer who gave his name to the school surrounded by banners with cultural symbols from around the world, and with a plaque with the following text:

Example 8   Plaque in front of the statue of Samuel de Champlain

| 1 | L'École Champlain en 1969, fut | *L'École Champlain was, in 1969, the* |
| 2 | le pionnier des établissements scolaires | *pioneer of the educational establish-* |

3 du Grand Toronto. Elle marque la	*ments of Metropolitan Toronto. She*
4 célébration de son vingt-cinquième	*marks the celebration of her twenty-*
5 anniversaire, le 19 mai 1994,	*fifth anniversary, the 19th of May*
6 en inaugurant cette statue. Ainsi,	*1994, by inaugurating this statue.*
7 les élèves, leurs parents et le personnel	*In this way, the students, parents and*
8 entier de l'école entendent renouveler	*entire staff of the school intend to*
9 leur engagement au respect et à la	*renew their commitment to the respect*
10 promotion de l'idéal commun dont	*and the encouragement of the common*
11 on apu dégager l'exemple dans la vie	*ideal the example of which we have*
12 de notre patronyme, celui de	*been able to find in the life of our*
13 "l'Unité dans la diversité"	*patronym, that of "Unity in diversity"*

This plaque signals a long tradition of dealing with unity and diversity, and anchors the school both in the authenticating local past and in the diversified present. This new image of diversity is even more evident in the triumph of a hip-hop culture in the school, symbolized by the following rap, written and performed by Frantz, a Haitian student, with the support of two friends, one born in Israel, the other in Colombia.

Example 9   Frantz's rap, June 1994

1 on parle d'aujourd'hui, on parle de	*we talk about today, we talk about*
2 demain c'est pour ça qu'on dit qu'il	*tomorrow that's why we say we*
3 faut se donner les mains	*have to give each other our hands*
4 quand je parle comme ça c'est pour	*when I talk like that it's for us*
5 nous qu'il faut nous parler	*we need to talk to each other,*
6 c'est pour ça que je suis en train de	*that's why I'm singing*
7 chanter je chante en partant en	*I sing from the beginning, thinking of*
8 pensant de toi de toi à moi	*you of you of me (for me)*
9 et tout est fait en chocolat	*and everything is made of chocolate*
10 je suis comme moi et tu es comme ça	*I am like me and you are like that*
11 et c'est pour ça qu'il faut pas être	*and that's why we should not be*
12 séparé toujours être ensemble	*separated always be together*

6   What *francophonie* and for whom?

For many francophones, and would-be francophones, the fragmentation of norms, the attempts to make connections around the world and the ability of the school to distribute a form of linguistic capital which seems to be increasingly valuable in the new economies, all constitute a useful development. Based on a nationalist, modernizing ideology, francophone Canada has built institutions which now serve as a launching pad for participation in the expansion of corporate capital across the world, and from a privileged position, at least as long as *la francophonie* constitutes itself as an important market, access to which is controlled through the use of French.

High modernity has placed schools like Champlain in a difficult position. The success of their modernizing mission has led them to abandon the very group whose existence legitimizes the schools' existence. At the same time, that group also provides the material of distinction which can be of value in world markets, and which is the source of an internal struggle over who gets to wield whatever local control there remains to wield. In addition, the school must now try to tread a path which recognizes the value of 'international' French within a multilingual repertoire along with the importance of pluralism.

What goes on at schools like this is of course connected to what goes on elsewhere. The view from Champlain also gives us a glimpse of the situation of linguistic minorities elsewhere, and of *la francophonie* in general. The empirical linkages lie beyond the scope of this paper, but they might take various forms. With respect to Western linguistic minorities, we can see how the modernist nationalist ideologies which have served local bourgeoisies so well are now called into question by high modernity.[h] Where local languages are not global ones, there may be fiercer struggles over local authenticity and distinctiveness. With respect to *la francophonie*, we can see how crucial the ability to maintain a market alternative to that dominated by English is to the position of new elites, and how difficult it is likely to be for France to maintain its control over the definition of that market. Areas like francophone Ontario may ironically be better placed to define and profit from the competition between French- and English-speaking worlds.

Certainly we can see how important it has become to balance the paradoxes of high modernity, that is, to work both sides of the tension between fragmentation and uniformization. This tension seems to open up opportunities for local elites, as long as they are well-connected to globalized economic activities. We have also seen how important it is to produce linguistic competencies that have value in the new economic order, which means not only defining and mastering 'international' standards, but also the local capital of distinction. Finally, these competencies have to take forms which are recognizable, and this increasingly means that they must be measured and credentialized.

Three questions emerge. One has to do with what is going to count as French. The tensions between globalizing efficiency and local autonomy are far from resolved, although if the sympathies of many students and staff members at Champlain are anything to go by, it appears that we are in the throes of inventing some kind of new core standard, which allows for a certain amount of variation but not much. (Tolerable variation may be limited principally to spoken, rather than written French, and even in spoken French perhaps principally to [pronunciation].) The second has to do with who profits and who does not from current developments. There seems to be less and less room for the working class speakers of the French Canadian vernacular, or any other local variety which is too far from the standard. Groups like this might legitimize certain forms of local control, but are unlikely, I think, to have much access to that local power themselves. The final question has to do with the legitimacy of institutions like the schools. Their existence is predicated on the very ideology they are busily undoing. How will they re-invent themselves?

La francophonie is in flux. Ideologies of language and nation are confronted with new ideologies of language as commodity, and the role of the State is in question.

---

h See Urla, this volume.

There is a tension between standardized forms of some version of French (which might be just the old France-based standard, renamed, or which might be something at least somewhat different) and regional (or even class-based) varieties; there is tension between valuing monolingual and multilingual markets, repertoires and practices. There are many places in which these tensions play themselves out, many sites in which to track their development. Nonetheless, it is principally through the language practices of francophones that we can get a sense of which way the wind is blowing.

Note

1   All names have been changed. I have tried to make the transcriptions as readable, and therefore text-like, as possible. This has meant using punctuation to indicate, for example, falling intonation and pausing at clause boundaries. The use of (. . .) indicates that a section has been omitted; (xx) indicates that a few syllables are unintelligible.

References

Anderson, Benedict. 1983. *Imagined Communities*. London: Verso.

Balibar, R. 1985. *L'Institution du Francais. Essai sur le Colinguisme des Carolingienns à la République*. Paris: Presses Universitaires de France.

Blommaert, Jan (ed.). 1999. *Language Ideological Debates*. Berlin: Mouton de Gruyter.

Bochmann, Klaus, Jenny Brumme, Louis Guespin and the Leipziger Forschungsgruppe Soziolinguistik. 1993. *Sprachpolitik in der Romania. Zur Geschichte sprachpolitischen Denkens und Handelns von der Französischen Revolution bis zur Gegenwart*. Berlin: Walter de Gruyter.

Cajolet-Langanière, Hélène and Pierre Martel. 1995. *La qualité de la langue au Québec*. Québec: Institut québécois de recherche sur la culture.

Cameron, Deborah. 1995. *Verbal Hygiene*. London: Routledge.

Crowley, Tony. 1991. *Proper English? Readings in Language, History and Cultural Identity*. London: Routledge.

de Robillard, Didier and Michel Beniamo (eds). 1993. *Le français dans l'espace francophone* (Tome 1). Paris: Honoré Champion.

de Robillard, Didier and Michel Beniamo (eds). 1996. *Le français dans l'espace francophone* (Tome 2). Paris: Honoré Champion.

Dor, Georges. 1996. *Anna braillé ène shot (Elle a beaucoup pleuré). Essai sur le langage parlé des Québécois*. Montréal: Lanctôt Éditeur.

Giddens, Anthony. 1990. *The Consequences of Modernity*. Cambridge: Polity Press.

Handler, Richard. 1988. *Nationalism and the Politics of Culture in Québec*. Madison, Wisconsin: University of Wisconsin Press.

Heller, Monica. 1994. *Crosswords: Language, Education and Ethnicity in French Ontario*. Berlin: Mouton de Gruyter.

Heller, Monica. 1999a. *Linguistic Minorities and Modernity: A Sociolinguistic Ethnography*. London: Longman.

Heller, Monica. 1999b. Heated language in a cold climate. In Jan Blommaert (ed.) *Language Ideological Debates*. Berlin: Mouton de Gruyter, pp. 143–70.

Heller, Monica and Laurette Lévy. 1994. Mariages linguistiquement mixtes: les stratégies des femmes franco-ontariennes. *Langage et société* 67: 53–88.

Hobsbawm, Eric. 1990. *Nations and Nationalism since 1780*. London: Verso.

Laforest, Marty et al. 1997. *États d'âme, états de langue*. Québec: Nuit blanche.

Martel, Marcel. 1997. *Le deuil d'un pays imaginé*. Ottawa: University of Ottawa Press.

Outram, Dorinda. 1987. *Le language mâle de la vertu*: Women and the discourse of the French Revolution. In P. Burke and R. Porter (eds) *The Social History of Language*. Cambridge: Cambridge University Press. 120–135.

Swiggers, Pierre. 1990. Ideology and the 'clarity' of French. In John E. Joseph and Talbot J. Taylor (eds.) *Ideologies of Language*. London: Routledge. 112–130.

Vallverdu, Francesc. 1981. *El conflicto linguistico en Cataluña: historia y presente*. Barcelona: Ed. Peninsula.

Monica Heller is Professor in the Department of Sociology and Equity Studies and the Centre de recherches en éducation franco-ontarienne at the Ontario Institute for Studies in Education/University of Toronto, Canada.

SECTION THREE

Language, Discourse and Ethnic Style

Introduction

FOR THE MOST PART, the extracts in this Section examine the role played by language, ethnicity and difference in ordinary people's everyday life.

In the first three extracts, ethno-linguistic identity is taken to be a matter of communicative *disposition*, a matter of the habits of thinking, understanding and/or talking laid down during early socialisation in particular networks or communities. Whorf argues that the grammatical distinctiveness of Hopi, an American Indian language, is intimately linked to a vision of the world that is radically different from that of Anglo or European people, and shifting the focus from grammatical structure to the uses of language in social interaction, Philips argues that Native American students don't do well in education because schools don't properly adjust to the ways of talking and acting they have learnt at home. Gumperz extends this line of analysis to the experience of immigrants in urban work and service settings, but this logic is then challenged by McDermott and Gospodinoff, who argue that rather than ethnicity causing inequality, it's inequality that leads people to emphasise ethnic identity.

Following McDermott and Gospodinoff, the last four extracts see language and ethnicity being bound together in the dynamics of communicative *performance* and *activity*. Rather than being an obdurate burden, ethnicity here seems to be more of a flexible resource that speakers can draw on in the flow of talk, and also it now seems less determinate, more ambiguous, harder to differentiate from the range of other meanings with which, on any given occasion, it's often intermingled (e.g. humour, personal stance, social class). Focusing on strips of interaction involving bilingual speakers, Gumperz and Hernández-Chavez show how the selection of one language rather than another generates a feeling of co-membership, while Clark shows shifts of language creating a sense of otherness. The extracts by Cutler and

Back focus on cultures of popular music performance, and include biographical accounts of the conflicts and achievements experienced by two very different individuals as they use language and music to mix, cross and blur traditional ethnicities.

The studies in this Section focus on the US and the UK, though their relevance is more general. To give a little more detail on each paper:

- In 'An American Indian model of the universe' (c.1936), Benjamin Lee Whorf argues that a European's intuitive sense of time moving from past to future finds no counterpart among the Hopi Native Americans. This is due to fundamental differences in language structure, and drawing on very careful grammatical analysis, Whorf proposes that instead of 'time' and 'space', the Hopi see manifest-ness as central to the organisation of the universe, a conception, he stresses, that works just as well.

- In 'Participant structures and communicative competence: Warm Springs children in community and classroom' (1972), Susan U. Philips focuses on educational underachievement among Native American students in the US, and drawing on extensive ethnographic observation, her descriptions of communication in school, at home and in the community suggest that classroom expectations are ill-matched to the ways these youngsters learn and interact outside.

- John Gumperz's 1979 interview on 'Cross-cultural communication' with John Twitchin focuses on the interaction between Anglo monolinguals and first generation migrants to the UK from India and the Caribbean. Questioning a strict separation of language and culture, Gumperz looks beyond grammar and vocabulary to differences in styles of talking, and argues that because they aren't adequately recognised, ethnic discourse differences often generate serious misunderstandings in 'gatekeeping' events like interviews. Gumperz suggests that these misunderstandings ultimately contribute to racism and inequalities of opportunity, and he considers ways of avoiding them.

- R. P. McDermott and Kenneth Gospodinoff's extract, 'Social contexts for ethnic borders and school failure' (1979), disputes the claim that ethnic differences in communicative style result in educational failure in the US. After reviewing situations which undermine the mismatch explanation, they use the detailed analysis of one classroom incident to argue that what initially looks like 'miscommunication' can be strategically adaptive, and that far from causing the problem, a sense of ethnicity is itself produced by difficulties in the working environment – ethnicity is something that participants under stress resort to in order to account for what's gone wrong.

- In 'Bilingual codeswitching' (1972), John Gumperz and Eduardo Hernández-Chavez show that rather than just being chaotic or linguistically incompetent, language switching and mixing are often rhetorically expressive. But in their analysis of bilingual Mexican-American discourse, they argue that neither the patterns nor the meanings of language switching can be predicted of the basis of objective factors like ethnicity, gender, setting, topic etc. Speakers draw on the associations of each language creatively from one moment to the next, actively choosing which language to use to emphasise a point, to generate feelings of solidarity, etc. In other words, rather than existing independently, culture and ethnicity are an integral part of everyday talk.

- John Taggart Clark's paper, 'Abstract inquiry and the patrolling of black/white borders through linguistic stylization' (2003), looks at the fine detail of how people make shifts in accent to articulate their position on what's being said. He describes some African American students in a US high school using typically white and elite pronunciations to parody their black teacher and to distance themselves humorously from the abstract discourse that they are faced with in the class and that they see as a dominant white style.

- In 'Yorkville crossing: White teens, hip hop and African American English' (1999), Cecilia Cutler describes a white middle class teenager's appropriation of black speech forms over several years. She situates this within his fluctuating affiliation to hip hop culture, documents some of the tensions it gives rise to, and points to some complex personal dynamics of which language forms only a part.

- Les Back's paper, 'X amount of Sat Siri Akal!: Apache Indian, reggae music and intermezzo culture' (1995), focuses on the fusions of Caribbean, south Asian and urban English musics and language articulated by the UK rap artist, Apache Indian. Back describes the intersection of reggae and bhangra dance cultures, the development of Apache's career, and the local and global uptake of his music. These explorations lead Back to ask what kinds of conceptualisation of ethnicity and culture can do justice to a case like Apache's, and what kinds of cultural politics it might point to.

Chapter 18

Benjamin Lee Whorf

*c.*1936

AN AMERICAN INDIAN MODEL
OF THE UNIVERSE[a]

I FIND IT GRATUITOUS to assume that a Hopi who knows only the Hopi language and the cultural ideas of his own society[b] has the same notions, often supposed to be intuitions, of time and space that we have, and that are generally assumed to be universal.[c] In particular, he has no general notion or intuition of TIME as a smooth flowing continuum in which everything in the universe proceeds at an equal rate, out of a future, through a present, into a past; or, in which, to reverse the picture, the observer is being carried in the stream of duration continuously away from a past and into a future.

After long and careful study and analysis, the Hopi language is seen to contain no words, grammatical forms, constructions or expressions that refer directly to what we call 'time,' or to past, present, or future, or to enduring or lasting, [. . .] or that even refer to space in such a way as to exclude that element of extension or existence that we call 'time,' and so by implication leave a residue that could be referred to as "time." Hence, the Hopi language contains no reference to 'time,' either explicit or implicit.

At the same time, the Hopi language is capable of accounting for and describing correctly, in a pragmatic or operational sense, all observable phenomena of the

a From J. B. Carroll (ed.) (1956) *Language, Thought and Reality: Selected Writings of Benjamin Lee Whorf.* Massachusetts: MIT Press pp. 57–64.

b Hopi is an American Indian language based in Arizona, but Whorf actually began to work on it with a Hopi speaker resident in New York City in 1932, and he didn't go to the Hopi reservation until 1938 (see S. O. Murray (1998) *American Sociolinguistics.* Amsterdam: John Benjamins pp. 19). So the point of departure here, the notion of 'a Hopi who knows only the Hopi language and the cultural ideas of his own society' was something of an idealisation, not based on any real living individuals known to Whorf personally.

c Here Whorf expounds the theory of 'linguistic relativity', also often known as the 'Sapir-Whorf' hypothesis. There has been much dispute about this, and a succinct but authoritative contemporary overview of research can be found in J. Lucy (1996) 'The scope of linguistic relativity: An analysis and review of empirical research', in J. Gumperz and S. Levinson (eds) *Rethinking Linguistic Relativity.* Cambridge: Cambridge University Press pp. 37–69.

universe. Hence, I find it gratuitous to assume that Hopi thinking contains any such notion as the supposed intuitively felt flowing of "time," or that the intuition of a Hopi gives him this as one of its data. Just as it is possible to have any number of geometries other than the Euclidean which give an equally perfect account of space configurations, so it is possible to have descriptions of the universe, all equally valid,[d] that do not contain our familiar contrasts of time and space.[e] The relativity viewpoint of modern physics is one such view, conceived in mathematical terms, and the Hopi Weltanschauung is another and quite different one, nonmathematical and linguistic.

Thus, the Hopi language and culture conceals a METAPHYSICS, such as our so-called naïve view of space and time does, or as the relativity theory does; yet it is a different metaphysics from either. In order to describe the structure of the universe according to the Hopi, it is necessary to attempt—insofar as it is possible—to make explicit this metaphysics, properly describable only in the Hopi language, by means of an approximation expressed in our own language, somewhat inadequately it is true, yet by availing ourselves of such concepts as we have worked up into relative consonance with the system underlying the Hopi view of the universe.

In this Hopi view, time disappears and space is altered, so that it is no longer the homogeneous and instantaneous timeless space of our supposed intuition or of classical Newtonian mechanics. At the same time, new concepts and abstractions flow into the picture, taking up the task of describing the universe without reference to such time or space—abstractions for which our language lacks adequate terms. These abstractions, by approximations of which we attempt to reconstruct for ourselves the metaphysics of the Hopi, will undoubtedly appear to us as psychological or even mystical in character. They are ideas which we are accustomed to consider as part and parcel either of so-called animistic or vitalistic beliefs, or of those transcendental unifications of experience and intuitions of things unseen that are felt by the consciousness of the mystic, or which are given out in mystical and (or) so-called occult systems of thought. These abstractions are definitely given either explicitly in words—psychological or metaphysical terms—in the Hopi language, or, even more, are implicit in the very structure and grammar of that language, as well as being observable in Hopi culture and behavior.[f] They are not, so far as I can consciously avoid it, projections of other systems upon the Hopi language and culture made by me in my attempt at an objective analysis. Yet, if

---

d Contrast Jespersen, this volume. For discussions around the vexed issue 'linguistic equality', see e.g. Honeyford and Rickford, this volume.

e As Whorf wrote elsewhere: "We dissect nature along lines laid down by our native languages. The categories and types that we isolate from the world of phenomena we do not find there because they stare every observer in the face: on the contrary, the world is presented in a kaleidoscopic flux of impressions which has to be organised by our minds – and this means largely by the linguistic systems in our minds. We cut nature up, organise it into concepts, and ascribe significances as we do, largely because we are parties to an agreement that holds throughout our speech community and is codified in the patterns of our language" (Carroll (ed.) 1956: 213). On 'race' as a category of perception shaped by language, see Ashcroft, this volume.

f Compare Whorf's emphasis on how cultural outlook is encoded in grammatical structure with Gumperz's and Philips' account of cultural differences in how language actually gets used (this volume). On the ways in which patterns in the use of language can covertly articulate political ideologies, see Billig.

MYSTICAL be perchance a term of abuse in the eyes of a modern Western scientist, it must be emphasized that these underlying abstractions and postulates of the Hopian metaphysics are, from a detached viewpoint, equally (or to the Hopi, more) justified pragmatically and experientially, as compared to the flowing time and static space of our own metaphysics, which are *au fond* equally mystical. The Hopi postulates equally account for all phenomena and their interrelations, and lend themselves even better to the integration of Hopi culture in all its phases.

The metaphysics underlying our own language, thinking, and modern culture (I speak not of the recent and quite different relativity metaphysics of modern science) imposes upon the universe two grand COSMIC FORMS, space and time; static three-dimensional infinite space, and kinetic one-dimensional uniformly and perpetually flowing time—two utterly separate and unconnected aspects of reality (according to this familiar way of thinking). The flowing realm of time is, in turn, the subject of a threefold division: past, present, and future.

The Hopi metaphysics also has its cosmic forms comparable to these in scale and scope. What are they? It imposes upon the universe two grand cosmic forms, which as a first approximation in terminology we may call MANIFESTED and MANIFESTING (or, UNMANIFEST) or, again, OBJECTIVE and SUBJECTIVE. The objective or manifested comprises all that is or has been accessible to the senses, the historical physical universe, in fact, with no attempt to distinguish between present and past, but excluding everything that we call future. The subjective or manifesting comprises all that we call future, BUT NOT MERELY THIS; it includes equally and indistinguishably all that we call mental—everything that appears or exists in the mind, or, as the Hopi would prefer to say, in the HEART, not only the heart of man, but the heart of animals, plants, and things, and behind and within all the forms and appearances of nature in the heart of nature, and by an implication and extension which has been felt by more than one anthropologist, yet would hardly ever be spoken of by a Hopi himself, so charged is the idea with religious and magical awesomeness, in the very heart of the Cosmos, itself.[1] The subjective realm (subjective from our viewpoint, but intensely real and quivering with life, power, and potency to the Hopi) embraces not only our FUTURE, much of which the Hopi regards as more or less predestined in essence if not in exact form, but also all mentality, intellection, and emotion, the essence and typical form of which is the striving of purposeful desire, intelligent in character, toward manifestation—a manifestation which is much resisted and delayed, but in some form or other is inevitable. It is the realm of expectancy, of desire and purpose, of vitalizing life, of efficient causes, of thought thinking itself out from an inner realm (the Hopian HEART) into manifestation. It is in a dynamic state, yet not a state of motion—it is not advancing toward us out of a future, but ALREADY WITH US in vital and mental form, and its dynamism is at work in the field of eventuating or manifesting, i.e. evolving without motion from the subjective by degrees to a result which is the objective. In translating into English, the Hopi will say that these entities in process of causation 'will come' or that they—the Hopi—'will come to' them, but, in their own language, there are no verbs corresponding to our 'come' and 'go' that mean simple and abstract motion, our purely kinematic concept. The words in this case translated 'come' refer to the process of eventuating without calling it motion—they are 'eventuates to here' (*pew'i*) or 'eventuates from it' (*angqö*) or 'arrived' (*pitu*, pl. *öki*) which refers only to the terminal manifestation, the actual arrival at a given point, not to any motion preceding it.

This realm of the subjective or of the process of manifestation, as distinguished from the objective, the result of this universal process, includes also—on its border but still pertaining to its own realm—an aspect of existence that we include in our present time. It is that which is beginning to emerge into manifestation; that is, something which is beginning to be done, like going to sleep or starting to write, but is not yet in full operation. This can be and usually is referred to by the same verb form (the EXPECTIVE form in my terminology of Hopi grammar) that refers to our future, or to wishing, wanting, intending, etc. Thus, this nearer edge of the subjective cuts across and includes a part of our present time, viz. the moment of inception, but most of our present belongs in the Hopi scheme to the objective realm and so is indistinguishable from our past. [. . .]

If we were to approximate our metaphysical terminology more closely to Hopian terms, we should probably speak of the subjective realm as the realm of HOPE or HOPING. Every language contains terms that have come to attain cosmic scope of reference, that crystallize in themselves the basic postulates of an unformulated philosophy, in which is couched the thought of a people, a culture, a civilization, even of an era. Such are our words 'reality, substance, matter, cause,' and as we have seen 'space, time, past, present, future.' Such a term in Hopi is the word most often translated 'hope'—*tunátya*—'it is in the action of hoping, it hopes, it is hoped for, it thinks or is thought of with hope,' etc. Most metaphysical words in Hopi are verbs, not nouns as in European languages. The verb *tunátya* contains in its idea of hope something of our words 'thought,' 'desire,' and 'cause,' which sometimes must be used to translate it. The word is really a term which crystallizes the Hopi philosophy of the universe in respect to its grand dualism of objective and subjective; it is the Hopi term for SUBJECTIVE. It refers to the state of the subjective, unmanifest, vital and causal aspect of the Cosmos, and the fermenting activity toward fruition and manifestation with which it seethes—an action of HOPING; i.e. mental-causal activity, which is forever pressing upon and into the manifested realm. As anyone acquainted with Hopi society knows, the Hopi see this burgeoning activity in the growing of plants, the forming of clouds and their condensation in rain, the careful planning out of the communal activities of agriculture and architecture, and in all human hoping, wishing, striving, and taking thought; and as most especially concentrated in prayer, the constant hopeful praying of the Hopi community, assisted by their exoteric communal ceremonies and their secret, esoteric rituals in the underground kivas—prayer which conducts the pressure of the collective Hopi thought and will out of the subjective into the objective. The inceptive form[g] of *tunátya*, which is *tunátyava*, does not mean 'begins to hope,' but rather 'comes true, being hoped for.' Why it must logically have this meaning will be clear from what has already been said. The inceptive denotes the first appearance of the objective, but the basic meaning of *tunátya* is subjective activity or force; the inceptive is then the terminus of such activity. It might then

---

g Whereas the 'expective' verb form refers to a process at the border of the subjective that is beginning to emerge into the manifest/objective, the 'inceptive' verb form refers to a process that belongs at the edge of the manifest/objective, emerging from the subjective.

be said that *tunátya* 'coming true' is the Hopi term for objective, as contrasted with subjective, the two terms being simply two different inflectional[h] nuances of the same verbal root, as the two cosmic forms are the two aspects of one reality.

As far as space is concerned, the subjective is a mental realm, a realm of no space in the objective sense, but it seems to be symbolically related to the vertical dimension and its poles the zenith and the underground, as well as to the 'heart' of things, which corresponds to our word 'inner' in the metaphorical sense. Corresponding to each point in the objective world is such a vertical and vitally INNER axis which is what we call the wellspring of the future. But to the Hopi there is no temporal future; there is nothing in the subjective state corresponding to the sequences and successions conjoined with distances and changing physical configurations that we find in the objective state. From each subjective axis, which may be thought of as more or less vertical and like the growth-axis of a plant, extends the objective realm in every physical direction, though these directions are typified more especially by the horizontal plane and its four cardinal points. The objective is the great cosmic form of extension; it takes in all the strictly extensional aspects of existence, and it includes all intervals and distances, all seriations and number. Its DISTANCE includes what we call time in the sense of the temporal relation between events which have already happened. The Hopi conceive time and motion in the objective realm in a purely operational sense—a matter of the complexity and magnitude of operations connecting events—so that the element of time is not separated from whatever element of space enters into the operations. Two events in the past occurred a long 'time' apart (the Hopi language has no word quite equivalent to our 'time') when many periodic physical motions have occurred between them in such a way as to traverse much distance or accumulate magnitude of physical display in other ways. The Hopi metaphysics does not raise the question whether the things in a distant village exist at the same present moment as those in one's own village, for it is frankly pragmatic on this score and says that any 'events' in the distant village can be compared to any events in one's own village only by an interval of magnitude that has both time and space forms in it. Events at a distance from the observer can only be known objectively when they are 'past' (i.e. posited in the objective) and the more distant, the more 'past' (the more worked upon from the subjective side). Hopi, with its preference for verbs, as contrasted to our own liking for nouns, perpetually turns our propositions about things into propositions about events. What happens at a distant village, if actual (objective) and not a conjecture (subjective) can be known 'here' only later. If it does not happen 'at this place,' it does not happen 'at this time'; it happens at 'that' place and at 'that' time. Both the 'here' happening and the 'there' happening are in the objective, corresponding in general to our past, but the 'there' happening is the more objectively distant, meaning, from our standpoint, that it is further away in the past just as it is further away from us in space than the 'here' happening.

---

h 'Inflection' is a grammatical term that refers to the way in which word forms change to express different meanings – in English, for example, words 'inflect' for meanings such as past tense ('walk' → 'walked'), plural ('chair' → 'chairs') etc.

As the objective realm displaying its characteristic attribute of extension stretches away from the observer toward that unfathomable remoteness which is both far away in space and long past in time, there comes a point where extension in detail ceases to be knowable and is lost in the vast distance, and where the subjective, creeping behind the scenes as it were, merges into the objective, so that at this inconceivable distance from the observer—from all observers—there is an all-encircling end and beginning of things where it might be said that existence, itself, swallows up the objective and the subjective. The borderland of this realm is as much subjective as objective. It is the abysm of antiquity, the time and place told about in the myths, which is known only subjectively or mentally—the Hopi realize and even express in their grammar that the things told in myths or stories do not have the same kind of reality or validity as things of the present day, the things of practical concern. As for the far distances of the sky and stars, what is known and said about them is supposititious, inferential—hence, in a way subjective—reached more through the inner vertical axis and the pole of the zenith than through the objective distances and the objective processes of vision and locomotion. So the dim past of myths is that corresponding distance on earth (rather than in the heavens) which is reached subjectively as myth through the vertical axis of reality via the pole of the nadir—hence it is placed BELOW the present surface of the earth, though this does not mean that the nadir-land of the origin myths is a hole or cavern as we should understand it. It is *Palátkwapi* 'At the Red Mountains,' a land like our present earth, but to which our earth bears the relation of a distant sky—and similarly the sky of our earth is penetrated by the heroes of tales, who find another earthlike realm above it.

It may now be seen how the Hopi do not need to use terms that refer to space or time as such. Such terms in our language are recast into [Hopi] expressions of extension, operation, and cyclic process provided they refer to the solid objective realm. They are recast into expressions of subjectivity if they refer to the subjective realm—the future, the psychic-mental, the mythical period, and the invisibly distant and conjectural generally. Thus, the Hopi language gets along perfectly without tenses for its verbs.

Note

1   This idea is sometimes alluded to as the 'spirit of the Breath' (*hikwsu*) and as the 'Mighty Something' (*ʔaʔne himu*), although these terms may have lower and less cosmic though always awesome connotations.

Benjamin Lee Whorf (1897–1941) is one of the greatest figures in US anthropological linguistics, but although he was offered academic positions, he never held a full-time university post. Instead he worked as a fire prevention engineer for an insurance company from 1919 to 1941.

Chapter 19

Susan U. Philips

1972

PARTICIPANT STRUCTURES AND COMMUNICATIVE COMPETENCE

Warm Springs children in community and classroom[a]

Introduction

RECENT STUDIES OF NORTH American Indian education problems have indicated that in many ways Indian children are not culturally oriented to the ways in which classroom learning is conducted. The Wax-Dumont study (Wax *et al.*, 1964) of the Pine Ridge Sioux discusses the lack of interest children show in what goes on in school and Wolcott's (1967) description of a Kwakiutl school tells of the Indian children's organized resistance to his ways of structuring classroom learning. Cazden and John (1968) suggest that the "styles of learning" through which Indian children are enculturated at home differ markedly from those to which they are introduced in the classroom. And Hymes (1967) has pointed out that this may lead to sociolinguistic interference when teacher and student do not recognize these differences in their efforts to communicate with one another.[b]

On the Warm Springs Indian Reservation in central Oregon, where I have been carrying out research in patterns of speech usage, teachers have pointed to similar phenomena [. . .]. To help account for the reluctance of the Indian children of Warm Springs (and elsewhere as well) to participate in classroom verbal interactions, I am going to demonstrate how some of the social conditions governing or determining when it is appropriate for a student to speak in the classroom differ

a From C. Cazden, V. John and D. Hymes (eds) (1972) *Functions of Language in the Classroom*. New York: Teachers College Press pp. 370–94.
b Gumperz (this volume) puts differences in communicative style in a wider context, and S. B. Heath's (1983) *Ways with Words: Language, Life and Work in Communities and Classrooms* Cambridge: Cambridge University Press is a classic study of differences in home and school language use, focusing on black and white, working class and middle class communities (see also S. Heath (1982) 'What no bedtime stories means' *Language in Society* 11: 49–76). For an alternative interpretation of ethnicity and educational achievement, see McDermott and Gospodinoff, this volume).

from those that govern verbal participation and other types of communicative performances in the Warm Springs Indian community's social interactions.

The data on which discussion of these differences will be based are drawn, first of all, from comparative observations in all-Indian classes in the reservation [elementary] school and non-Indian or white classes in another [elementary] school at the first and sixth-grade levels.[c] [. . . D]iscussion will [then] shift to consideration of the social conditions in Indian cultural contexts that define when speaking is appropriate, attending to children's learning experiences both at home and in the community-wide social activities in which they participate.

The end goal of this discussion will be to demonstrate that the social conditions that define when a person uses speech in Indian social situations are present in classroom situations in which Indian students use speech a great deal, and absent in the more prevalent classroom situations in which they fail to participate verbally. [. . .]

Cultural and educational background of the Warm Springs Indians

Before embarking on the main task of the discussion outlined above, some background information on the setting of the research, the Warm Springs Indian Reservation [. . .].

Today the reservation of 564,209 acres is populated by some 1,500 descendants of the "bands" of Warm Springs Sahaptin, Wasco Chinook, and Paiute Indians who gradually settled there after the reservation was established in 1855. The Warm Springs Indians have always been the largest group numerically, followed by the Wasco, with the Paiutes so small in number that their influence in the culture of the reservation has been of relatively small significance. Although they spoke different languages, the Warm Springs and Wasco groups were geographically quite close to one another before the reservation was established and were culturally similar in many respects. Thus, after over a hundred years together on the reservation, they presently share approximately the same cultural background.

The "tribe," as the Indians of Warm Springs now refer to themselves collectively, today comprises a single closely integrated community with strong tribal leadership, which receives the full backing of the people. Until after World War II the Indians here experienced considerable poverty and hardship. Since that time, however, tribal income from the sale of reservation timber has considerably improved the economic situation, as has tribal purchase of a sawmill and a small resort, which provide jobs for tribal members.

With the income from these enterprises, and drawing as well on various forms of federal aid available to them, the tribe has developed social programs to help members of the tribe in a number of ways. Chief among their concerns is the improvement of the education of their children, whom they recognize to be less successful in school than their fellow non-Indian students. Tribal leaders have taken

---

c US first-graders tend to be about six years old, while sixth-grade is normally for 11 and 12 year olds.

numerous important steps to increase the educational opportunities of their young people, including the establishment of a scholarship program for college students and a tribal education office with half a dozen full-time employees supervising the tribally sponsored kindergarten, study halls, and community center courses as well as the federally sponsored programs such as VISTA, Head Start, and Neighborhood Youth Corps. The education office employees also act as liaisons between parents of children with problems in school and the administrators and teachers of the public schools the children attend. In sum, the tribe is doing a great deal to provide the Warm Springs children with the best education possible.

Despite their efforts, and those of the public school officials, [. . .] the Indians continue to do poorly in school when compared to the non-Indian students in the same school system.

One of the most important things to know about the schools the Indian children attend is the "ethnic" composition of their classes. For the first six grades, Warm Springs children attend a public school that is located on the reservation. Here their classmates are almost all Indians and their teachers are all non-Indians or whites. After the first six grades, they are bused into the town of Madras, a distance of fifteen to thirty miles, depending on where they live on the reservation. Here, encountering their fellow white students for the first time, the Indian students are outnumbered by a ratio of five to one. From the point of view of tribal leaders, it is only when they reach the high school, or ninth grade, that the Indian students' "problems" really become serious, for it is at this point that hostility between Indian and non-Indian is expressed openly, and the Indian students' failure to participate in classroom discussions and school activities is recognized by everyone.

There is, however, abundant evidence that Indian students' learning difficulties begin long before they reach the high school. The statistics that are available on their educational achievements and problems are very similar to those which have been reported for Indians in other parts of the country (Berry, 1969). On national achievement tests the Warm Springs Indian children consistently score lower than the national average in skills tested. Their lowest scores are in areas involving verbal competencies, and the gap between their level of performance on such tests and the national averages widens as they continue into the higher grade levels (Zentner, 1960).

Although many people on the reservation still speak an Indian language, today all of the Warm Springs children in school are monolingual speakers of English. The dialect of English they speak, however, is not the Standard English of their teachers, but one that is distinctive to the local Indian community, and that in some aspects of grammar and [pronunciation] shows influence from the Indian languages spoken on the reservation.

In addition, there is some evidence that many children are exposed to talk in the Indian languages that may affect their acquisition of English. [Many] older people [. . .] make a concerted effort to teach young children an Indian language, particularly the Warm Springs Sahaptin [, . . . and e]very Indian child still knows some Indian words [. . . M]any informants report that while their children refuse to speak the Warm Springs Sahaptin—particularly after they start school—they understand much of what is said to them in it. [. . .]

Conditions for speech use in school classrooms

When the children first enter school, the most immediate concern of the teachers is to teach them the basic rules for classroom behavior upon which the maintenance of continuous and ordered activity depends. One of the most important of these is the distinction between the roles of teacher and student. In this there is the explicit and implicit assumption that the teacher controls all of the activity taking place in the classroom and the students accept and are obedient to her authority. She determines the sociospatial arrangements of all interactions; she decrees when and where movement takes place within the classroom. And most important for our present concern with communication, she determines who will talk and when they will talk.

While some class activities are designed to create the sense of a class of students as an organized group with class officers, or student monitors carrying out various responsibilities contributing to the group, actual spontaneous organization within the student group that has not been officially designated by the teacher is not encouraged. It interferes with the scheduling of activities as the teacher has organized them. The classroom situation is one in which the teacher relates to the students as an undifferentiated mass, much as a performer in front of an audience. Or she relates to each student on a one-to-one basis, often with the rest of the class as the still undifferentiated audience for the performance of the individual child.

In comparing the Indian and non-Indian learning of these basic classroom distinctions which define the conditions in which communication will take place, differences are immediately apparent. Indian first-graders are consistently slower to begin acting in accordance with these basic arrangements. They do not remember to raise their hands and wait to be called on before speaking, they wander to parts of the room other than the one in which the teacher is conducting a session, and they talk to other students while the teacher is talking, much further into the school year than do students in non-Indian classes. And the Indian children continue to fail to conform to classroom procedure much more frequently *through* the school year.

In contrast to the non-Indian students, the Indian students consistently show a great deal more interest in what their fellow students are doing than in what the teacher is doing. While non-Indian students constantly make bids for the attention of their teachers, through initiating dialogue with them as well as through other acts, Indian students do very little of this. Instead they make bids for the attention of their fellow students through talk. At the first-grade level, and more noticeably (with new teachers only) at the sixth-grade level, Indian students often act in deliberate organized opposition to the teacher's directions. Thus, at the first-grade level, if one student is told not to put his feet on his chair, another will immediately put his feet on his chair, and he will be imitated by other students who see him do this. In non-Indian classrooms, such behavior was observed only at the sixth-grade level in interaction with a substitute teacher.

In other words, there is, on the part of Indian students, relatively less interest, desire, and/or ability to internalize and act in accordance with some of the basic rules underlying classroom maintenance of orderly interaction. Most notably, Indian students are less willing than non-Indian students to accept the teacher as director and controller of all classroom activities. [. . .]

Within the basic framework of teacher-controlled interaction, there are several possible variations in structural arrangements of interaction, which will be referred to from here on as "participant structures." Teachers use different participant structures, or ways of arranging verbal interaction with students, for communicating different types of educational material, and for providing variation in the presentation of the same material to hold children's interest. [. . .]

In the first type of participant structure the teacher interacts with all of the students. She may address all of them, or a single student in the presence of the rest of the students. The students may respond as a group or chorus in unison, or individually in the presence of their peers. And finally, student verbal participation may be either voluntary, as when the teacher asks who knows the answer to her question, or compulsory, as when the teacher asks a particular student to answer, whether his hand is raised or not. And always it is the teacher who determines whether she talks to one or to all, receives responses individually or in chorus, and voluntarily or without choice.

In a second type of participant structure, the teacher interacts with only some of the students in the class at once, as in reading groups. In such contexts participation is usually mandatory rather than voluntary, individual rather than chorus, and each student is expected to participate or perform verbally, for the main purpose of such smaller groups is to provide the teacher with the opportunity to assess the knowledge acquired by each individual student. During such sessions, the remaining students who are not interacting with the teacher are usually working alone or independently at their desks on reading or writing assignments.

A third participant structure consists of all students working independently at their desks, but with the teacher explicitly available for student-initiated verbal interaction, in which the child indicates he wants to communicate with the teacher by raising his hand, or by approaching the teacher at her desk. In either case, the interaction between student and teacher is not witnessed by the other students in that they do not hear what is said.

A fourth participant structure, and one that occurs infrequently in the upper primary grades, and rarely, if ever, in the lower grades, consists of the students' being divided into small groups that they run themselves, though always with the more distant supervision of the teacher, and usually for the purpose of so-called "group projects." As a rule such groups have official "chairmen," who assume what is in other contexts the teacher's authority in regulating who will talk when.

In observing and comparing Indian and non-Indian participation or communicative performances in these four different structural variations of contexts in which communication takes place, differences between the two groups again emerge very clearly.

In the first two participant structures where students must speak out individually in front of the other students, Indian children show considerable reluctance to participate, particularly when compared to non-Indian students. When the teacher is in front of the whole class, they volunteer to speak relatively rarely, and teachers at the Warm Springs [elementary] school generally hold that this reluctance to volunteer to speak out in front of other students increases as the children get older.

When the teacher is with a small group, and each individual must give some kind of communicative verbal performance in turn, Indian children much more frequently refuse, or fail to utter a word when called upon, and much less frequently, if ever, urge the teacher to call on them than the non-Indians do. When the Indian children do speak, they speak very softly, often in tones inaudible to a person more than a few feet away, and in utterances typically shorter or briefer than those of their non-Indian counterparts.

In situations where the teacher makes herself available for student-initiated communication during sessions in which students are working independently on assignments that do not involve verbal communication, students at the first-grade level in the Indian classes at first rarely initiate contact with the teachers. After a few weeks in a classroom they do so as frequently as the non-Indian students. And at the sixth-grade level Indian students initiate such relatively private encounters with teachers much more frequently than non-Indian students do.

When students control and direct the interaction in small group projects, as described for the fourth type of participant structure, there is again a marked contrast between the behavior of Indian and non-Indian students. It is in such contexts that Indian students become most fully involved in what they are doing, concentrating completely on their work until it is completed, talking a great deal to one another within the group, and competing, with explicit remarks to that effect, with the other groups. Non-Indian students take more time in "getting organized," disagree and argue more regarding how to go about a task, rely more heavily on appointed chairmen for arbitration and decision-making, and show less interest, at least explicitly, in competing with other groups from their class.

Observations of the behavior of both Indian and non-Indian children outside the classroom during recess periods and teacher-organized physical education periods provide further evidence that the differences in readiness to participate in interaction are related to the way in which the interaction is organized and controlled.

When such outside-class activity is organized by the teachers, it is for the purpose of teaching children games through which they develop certain physical and social skills. If the games involve a role distinction between leader and followers in which the leader must tell the others what to do—as in Simon Says, Follow the Leader, Green Light Red Light, and even Farmer in the Dell—Indian children show a great deal of reluctance to assume the leadership role. This is particularly true when the child is appointed leader by the teacher and must be repeatedly urged to act in telling the others what to do before doing so. Non-Indian children, in contrast, vie eagerly for such positions, calling upon the teacher and/or other students to select them.

If such playground activity is unsupervised, and the children are left to their own devices, Indian children become involved in games of team competition much more frequently than non-Indian children. And they sustain such game activities for longer periods of time and at younger ages than non-Indian children. While non-Indian children tend more to play in groups of two and three, and in the upper primary grades to form "friendships" with one or two persons from their own class in school, Indian children interact with a greater number of children consistently, and maintain friendships and teams with children from classes in school other than their own.

In reviewing the comparison of Indian and non-Indian students' verbal participation under different social conditions, two features of the Warm Springs children's behavior stand out. First of all, they show relatively less willingness to perform or participate verbally when they must speak alone in front of other students. Second, they are relatively less eager to speak when the point at which speech occurs is dictated by the teacher, as it is during sessions when the teacher is working with the whole class or a small group. They also show considerable reluctance to be placed in the "leadership" play roles that require them to assume the same type of dictation of the acts of their peers.

Parallel to these negative responses are the positive ones of a relatively greater willingness to participate in group activities that do not create a distinction between individual performer and audience, and a relatively greater use of opportunities in which the point at which the student speaks or acts is determined by himself, rather than by the teacher or a "leader." [. . .]

The consequences of the Indians' reluctance to participate in the [particular speech situations identified above] are several. First of all, the teacher loses the primary means she has of receiving feedback on the children's acquisition of knowledge, and is thus less able to establish at what point she must begin again to instruct them, particularly in skills requiring a developmental sequencing, as in reading.

A second consequence of this reluctance to participate in speech situations requiring mandatory individual performances is that the teachers in the Warm Springs [elementary] school modify their teaching approach whenever possible to accommodate, in a somewhat ad hoc fashion, what they refer to as the Indian students' "shyness." [. . .]

[Although it is not easy early on] to make very many modifications because of what teachers perceive as a close relationship between the material being taught and the methods used to teach it[, . . .] at the first-grade level there are already some changes made to accommodate the Indian children that are notable. When comparing the Indian first-grade classes with the non-Indian first-grade classes, one finds very few word games being used that involve students' giving directions to one another. And even more conspicuous in Indian classes is the absence of the ubiquitous "show and tell" or "sharing," through which students learn to get up in front of the class, standing where the teacher stands, and presenting, as the teacher might, a monologue relating an experience or describing a treasured object that is supposed to be of interest to the rest of the class. When asked whether this activity was used in the classroom, one teacher explained that she had previously used it, but so few children ever volunteered to "share" that she finally discontinued it.

By the time the students reach the sixth grade, the range of modes and settings for communication has increased a great deal, and the opportunity for elimination of some participant structures in preference to others is used by the teachers. As one sixth-grade teacher put it, "I spend as little time in front of the class as possible." In comparison with non-Indian classes, Indian classes have a relatively greater number of group "projects." Thus, while non-Indian students are learning about South American history through reading texts and answering the teacher's questions, Indian students are doing group-planned and -executed murals depicting a particular stage in Latin American history; while non-Indian students are reading science texts and answering questions about how electricity is generated, Indian students are doing group-run experiments with batteries and motors.

The teachers who make these adjustments, and not all do, are sensitive to the inclinations of their students and want to teach them through means to which they most readily adapt. However, by doing so they are avoiding teaching the Indian children how to communicate in precisely the contexts in which they are least able but most need to learn if they are to "do well in school." [. . .] And it is not at all clear that students do acquire the same information through one form of communication as they do through another. Thus these manipulations of communication settings and participant structures, which are intended to transmit knowledge to the students creatively through the means to which they are most adjusted, may actually be causing the students to miss completely types of information their later high school teachers will assume they picked up in [elementary] school.

The consequences of this partial adaptation to Indian modes of communication become apparent when the Indian students join the non-Indian students at the junior and senior high school levels. Here, where the Indian students are outnumbered five to one, there is no manipulation and selection of communication settings to suit the inclinations of the Indians. Here the teachers complain that the Indian students never talk in class, and never ask questions, and everyone wonders why.

Conditions for speech use in the Warm Springs Indian community

To understand why the Warm Springs Indian children speak out readily under some social conditions but fail to do so under others, it is necessary to examine the socio-linguistic assumptions determining the conditions for communicative performances, particularly those involving explicit demonstrations of knowledge or skill, in the Indian community. It will be possible here to deal with only some of the many aspects of communication involved. Attention will focus first on the social structuring of learning situations or contexts in which knowledge and skills are communicated to children in Indian homes. Then some consideration will be given to the underlying rules or conditions for participation in the community-wide social events that preschool children, as well as older children, learn through attending such events with their families.

The Indian child's preschool and outside-school enculturation at home differs from that of many non-Indian or white middle-class children's in that a good deal of the responsibility for the care and training of children is assumed by persons other than the parents of the children. In many homes the oldest children, particularly if they are girls, assume these responsibilities when the parents are at home, as well as when they are not. Frequently, also, grandparents, uncles, and aunts assume the full-time responsibility for care and instruction of children. Children thus become accustomed to interacting with and following the instructions and orders of a greater number of people than is the case with non-Indian children. Equally important is the fact that all of the people with whom Indian children form such reciprocal nurturing and learning relationships are kinsmen. Indian children are rarely, if ever, taken care of by "baby-sitters" from outside the family. Most of their playmates before beginning school are their siblings and cousins, and these peer relationships typically continue to be the strongest bonds of friendship through school and adult life, later providing a basis for reciprocal aid in times of need, and companionship in many social activities.

Indian children are deliberately taught skills around the home (for girls) and in the outdoors (for boys) at an earlier age than many middle-class non-Indian children. Girls, for example, learn to cook some foods before they are eight, and by this age may be fully competent in cleaning a house without any aid or supervision from adults.

There are other areas of competence in which Indian children are expected to be proficient at earlier ages than non-Indian children, for which the means of enculturation or socialization are less visible and clear-cut. While still in [elementary] school, at the age of ten or eleven, some children are considered capable of spending afternoons and evenings in the company of only other children, without the necessity of accounting for their whereabouts or asking permission to do whatever specific activity is involved. At this same age many are also considered capable of deciding where they want to live, and for what reasons one residence is preferable to another. They may spend weeks or months at a time living with one relative or another, until it is no longer possible to say that they live in any particular household.

In general, then, Warm Springs Indian children become accustomed to self-determination of action, accompanied by very little disciplinary control from older relatives, at much younger ages than middle-class white children do.

In the context of the household, learning takes place through several sorts of somewhat different processes. First of all, [. . .] there are many adult conversations to which children pay a great deal of silent, patient attention. This contrasts sharply with the behavior of non-Indian children, who show little patience in similar circumstances, desiring either to become a full participant through verbal interaction, or to become completely involved in some other activity.

There is some evidence that this silent listening and watching was, in the Warm Springs culture, traditionally the first step in learning skills of a fairly complex nature. For example, older women reminisce about being required to watch their elder relatives tan hides when they were very young, rather than being allowed to play. And certainly the winter evening events of myth-telling, which provided Indian children with their first explicitly taught moral lessons, involved them as listening participants rather than as speakers.

A second type of learning involves the segmentation of a task by an older relative, and the partial carrying out of the task or one of its segments by the child. In household tasks, for example, a child is given a very simple portion of a job (e.g., in cleaning a room the child may begin by helping move the furniture) and works in cooperation with and under the supervision of an older relative. Such activities involve a small amount of verbal instruction or direction from the older relative, and allow for questions on the part of the child. Gradually the child comes to learn all of the skills involved in a particular process, consistently under the supervision of an older relative who works along with him.

[. . . T]his type of instruction among the Warm Springs Indians differs from that of non-Indians i[n] the absence of "testing" of the child's skill by the instructing kinsman before the child exercises the skill unsupervised. Although it is not yet clear how this works in a diversity of situations, it appears that in many areas of skill, the child takes it upon himself to test the skill unsupervised and alone, without other people around. In this way, if he is unsuccessful his failure is not seen by others. If he is successful, he can show the results of his success to those by whom he has been taught, whether it be in the form of a deer that has been shot, a hide tanned, a piece of beadwork completed, or a dinner on the table when the adults come home from work.

Again there is some evidence that this type of private individual's testing of competency, followed by public demonstration only when competency is fully developed and certain, has been traditional in the Warm Springs Indian culture. [. . .] In the vision quests through which adolescents, or children of even younger ages, acquired spirit power, individuals spent long periods in isolated mountain areas from which they were expected to emerge with skills they had not previously demonstrated. While some of these abilities were not fully revealed until later in life, the child was expected to be able to relate some experience of a supernatural nature that would prove that he had, in fact, been visited by a spirit. Along the same lines, individuals until very recently received and learned, through dreams and visions, ritual songs that they would sing for the first time in full and completed form in the presence of others.

The contexts described here in which learning takes place can be perceived as an idealized sequence of three steps: (1) observation, which of course includes listening; (2) supervised participation; and (3) private, self-initiated self-testing. [. . .] The use of speech in the process is notably minimal. Verbal directions or instructions are few, being confined to corrections and question-answering. Nor does the final demonstration of skill particularly involve verbal performance, since the validation of skill so often involves display of some material evidence or non-verbal physical expression.

This process of Indian acquisition of competence may help to explain, in part, Indian children's reluctance to speak in front of their classmates. In the classroom, the processes of *acquisition* of knowledge and *demonstration* of knowledge are collapsed into the single act of answering questions or reciting when called upon to do so by the teacher, particularly in the lower grades. Here the assumption is that one will learn, and learn more effectively, through making mistakes in front of others. The Indian children have no opportunity to observe others performing successfully before they attempt it, except for their fellow classmates who precede them and are themselves uninitiated. They have no opportunity to "practise," and to decide for themselves when they know enough to demonstrate their knowledge; rather, their performances are determined by the teacher. And finally, their only channel for communicating competency is verbal, rather than non-verbal.

Turning now from learning processes in the home to learning experiences outside the home, in social and ritual activities involving community members other than kinsmen, there is again considerable evidence that Indian children's understanding of when and how one participates and performs individually, [. . .] differs considerably from what is expected of them in the classroom.

Children of all ages are brought to every sort of communitywide social event sponsored by Indians (as distinct from those sponsored by non-Indians). There is rarely, if ever, such a thing as an Indian community event that is attended by adults only. [. . .] Sociospatially and behaviorally, children must always participate minimally, as do all others, in sitting quietly and attentively alongside their elders.

One of the social features that characterizes social events that are not explicitly kin group affairs, including activities like political general councils, social dinners, and worship dances, is that they are open to participation by all members of the Warm Springs Indian community. [. . .]

A second feature of such activities is that there is usually no one person directing the activity verbally, or signaling changes from one phase to another. Instead the structure is determined either by a set procedure or ritual, or there is a group of people who in various complementary ways provide such cuing and direction. Nor are there any participant roles that can be filled or are filled by only one person. In dancing, singing, and drumming there are no soloists, and where there are performers who begin a sequence, and are then joined by others, more than one performer takes a turn at such initiations. The speaking roles are handled similarly. In contexts where speeches are appropriate, it is made clear that anyone who wants to may "say a few words." [. . .] In all situations thus allowing for anyone who wants to to speak, no time limit is set, so that the talking continues until everyone who wants to has had the opportunity to do so.

This does not mean that there are never any "leaders" in Indian social activities, but rather that leadership takes quite a different form from that in many non-Indian cultural contexts. Among the people of Warm Springs, a person is not a leader by virtue of holding a particular position, even in the case of members of the tribal council and administration. Rather, he is a leader because he has demonstrated ability in some sphere and activity, and many individuals choose to follow his suggestions because they have independently each decided they are good ones. If, for example, an individual plans and announces an activity, but few people offer to help him carry it out or attend it, then that is an indication that the organizer is not a respected leader in the community at the present time. And the likelihood that he will repeat his efforts in the near future is reduced considerably.

A final feature of Indian social activities [. . . is that there is no sharp] distinction made between participants or performers and audience. At many Indian gatherings, particularly those attended by older people, this aspect of the situation is reflected in its sociospatial arrangement: People are seated in such a way that all present are facing one another, usually in an approximation of a square, and the focus of activity is either along one side of the square, or in its center, or a combination of the two.

And each individual chooses the degree of his participation. No one, other than, perhaps, those who set up the event, is committed to being present beforehand, and all participating roles beyond those of sitting and observing are determined by the individual at the point at which he decides to participate, rather than being prescheduled.

In summary, the Indian social activities to which children are early exposed outside the home generally have the following properties: (1) they are community-wide, in the sense that they are open to all Warm Springs Indians; (2) there is no single individual directing and controlling all activity, and, to the extent that there are "leaders," their leadership is based on the choice to follow made by each person; (3) participation in some form is accessible to everyone who attends. [. . .]

If one now compares the social conditions for verbal participation in the classroom with the conditions underlying many Indian events in which children participate, a number of differences emerge.

First of all, classroom activities are not community-wide, and, more importantly, the participants in the activity are not drawn just from the Indian community. The teacher, as a non-Indian, is an outsider and a stranger to these events. In addition, by virtue of her role as teacher, she structurally separates herself from the rest of the participants, her students. She places herself outside the interaction and activity of the students. This encourages their cultural perceptions of themselves as the relevant community, in opposition to the teacher, perhaps much as they see themselves in opposition to other communities, and on a smaller scale, as one team is in opposition to another. In other words, on the basis of the Indians' social experiences, one is either a part of a group or outside it. The notion of a single individual being structurally set apart from all others, in anything other than an observer role, and yet still a part of the group organization, is one that children probably encounter for the first time in school, and continue to experience only in non-Indian-derived activities (e.g., in bureaucratic, hierarchically structured occupations). This helps to explain why Indian students show so little interest in initiating interaction with the teacher in activities involving other students.

Second, in contrast to Indian activities where many people are involved in determining the development and structure of an event, there is only one single authority directing everything in the classroom, namely the teacher. And the teacher is not the controller or leader by virtue of the individual students' choices to follow her, as is the case in Indian social activities, but rather by virtue of her occupation of the role of teacher. This difference helps to account for the Indian children's frequent indifference to the directions, orders, and requests for compliance with classroom social rules that the teacher issues.

Third, it is not the case in the classroom that all students may participate in any given activity, as in Indian community activities. Nor are they given the opportunity to choose the degree of their participation, which, on the basis of evidence discussed earlier, would in Indian contexts be based on the individual's having already ascertained in private that he was capable of successful verbal communication of competence. Again these choices belong to the teacher.

Conclusion

In summary, Indian children fail to participate verbally in classroom interaction because the social conditions for participation to which they have become accustomed in the Indian community are lacking. The absence of these appropriate social conditions for communicative performances affects the most common and everyday speech acts that occur in the classroom. If the Indian child fails to follow an order or answer a question, it may not be because he doesn't understand the linguistic structure of the imperative and the interrogative, but rather because he does not share the non-Indian's assumption in such contexts that use of these syntactic forms by definition implies an automatic and immediate response from the person to whom they were addressed. For these assumptions are sociolinguistic assumptions that are not shared by the Indians.

Educators cannot assume that because Indian children (or any children from cultural backgrounds other than those that are implicit in American classrooms) speak English, or are taught it in the schools, that they have also assimilated all of the sociolinguistic rules underlying interaction in classrooms and other non-Indian social situations where English is spoken.[d] To the extent that existing cultural variation in sociolinguistic patterning that is not recognized by the schools results in learning difficulties and feelings of inferiority for some children, changes in the structuring of classroom learning situations are needed. Ultimately the nature of the changes to be made should be determined by the educational goals of the particular communities where this type of problem exists.

If, as may be the case on the Warm Springs Indian Reservation, the people's main concern is to enable Indian children to compete successfully with non-Indians, and to have the *choice* of access to the modes of interaction and life styles of non-Indians, then there should be a conscious effort made in the schools to teach the children the modes for appropriate verbal participation that prevail in non-Indian classrooms. Thus, rather than shifting away from situations in which children perform individually in front of their peers only with great reluctance, conscious emphasis on and encouragement of participation in such situations should be carried out in the early grades.

If, on the other hand, as also may be the case in Warm Springs (there are strong differences of opinion here on this issue that complicate the teachers' actions), there is strong feeling in the community that its culturally distinctive modes of communication should be maintained and encouraged to flourish rather than be eliminated through our educational system's apparent pursuit of cultural uniformity throughout the country, then quite a different shift in the orientation of classroom modes of instruction would be called for. Here an effort to adapt the community's conditions for appropriate speech usage to the classroom should be made, not in an ad hoc and partial fashion as at Warm Springs, but consistently and systematically. And where the classroom situation is one in which children of more than one cultural background come together, efforts should be made to allow for a complementary diversity in the modes of communication through which learning and measurement of "success" take place.

Bibliography

Berry, Brewton. *The education of American Indians: a survey of the literature.* Prepared for the Special Subcommittee on Indian Education of the Committee on Labor and Public Welfare, United States Senate. Washington, DC: Government Printing Office, 1969.

Cazden, Courtney B.; and John, Vera P. "Learning in American Indian children." In *Styles of learning among American Indians: An Outline for Research.* Washington, DC: Center for Applied Linguistics, 1968.

d Compare Gumperz and McDermott and Gospodinoff on this.

Hymes, Dell. "On communicative competence." [In J. Pride and J. Holmes (eds) *Sociolinguistics*. Harmondsworth: Penguin, pp. 269–293.]

Wax, Murray; Wax, Rosalie; and Dumont, Robert V., Jr. *Formal Education in an American Indian Community*. Social Problems Monograph No. 1. Kalamazoo, Mich.: Society for the Study of Social Problems, 1964.

Wolcott, Harry. *A Kwakiutl Village and School*. New York: Holt, Rinehart and Winston, 1967.

Zentner, Henry. *Oregon State College Warm Springs Research Project*. Vol. II: Education. Corvallis: Oregon State College, 1960.

Susan U. Philips is Professor of Anthropology at the University of Arizona, USA. She is the author of *The Invisible Culture: Communication in Classroom and Community on the Warm Springs Indian Reservation* (New York: Longman, 1983).

Chapter 20

John Gumperz

1979

CROSS-CULTURAL
COMMUNICATION[a]

WHILE IN LONDON during the making of the [cross-cultural communication training] film *Crosstalk*, John Gumperz was interviewed by John Twitchin, the BBC producer of the film. This was an informal interview, and more academic and detailed accounts of John Gumperz's research [can] be found in his published papers[b] [. . .]

T is producer, John Twitchin
G is John Gumperz

T: Can you start by explaining a few of the basic ideas behind your research into the use of English by different ethnic groups?

G: Our research has been into the use of English by Asian and West Indian groups in Britain[c] and by various other minority groups in the United States. We're interested in the different conventions of using English which these different ethnic groups have. The way these groups use English really affects the way they get along. We're interested in finding out whether and how and in what ways people are disadvantaged by the way they use English in what they want to do and can achieve in their everyday life.

---

a Originally published in J. Gumperz, T. Jupp and C. Roberts (1979) *Crosstalk* London: BBC. Republished in J. Twitchin (1990) *Crosstalk: An introduction to cross-cultural communication* London: BBC pp. 46–55.
b See for example, J. Gumperz (1982) *Discourse Strategies*. Cambridge: Cambridge University Press. For accessible work that has been influenced by Gumperz and is also oriented to intercultural communication training, see C. Roberts, E. Davies and T. Jupp (1992) *Language and Discrimination*. London: Longman. Also R. Scollon and S. Scollon (1995) *Intercultural Communication*. Oxford: Blackwell. In this volume, Philips articulates a broadly comparable view of cross-cultural communication differences.
c Compare the account here with the papers by Hewitt and Back in this volume, which focus on generations coming after the speakers that Gumperz has principally in mind.

We've not been looking at people who don't speak English very well. Amongst Asians, for example, we are interested in fluent speakers of English who know enough English to get along in everyday situations. [. . .] But there are certain special situations where difficulties of communication arise between people from different groups and the majority English group, and these are particularly formal and informal interviews. The kind of situation that one is in when one has to talk to somebody else *intensively*. We really have to do this a great deal in our lives. We have to talk in order to establish our rights and to get the benefits that we are entitled to. We have to go through employment interviews to get jobs, and when we're at work we need to talk to people to get things done. The need for skill in this type of intensive interview talk is much greater than it used to be; for example, with the growth of unionisation, and with the development of services that go right into the community, it's necessary to be able to communicate with the people who staff these services. Now, if people have different conventions in using English, there are potentially problems in these types of interactions for both sides.

T: What do you mean by different conventions in using English? Can you give me examples?

G: What we are talking about are the ways of signalling in speech our attitudes, our assumptions and our expectations about what we are saying, about what the other person is saying, and about our relationship with the other person. These ways of signalling turn out to be very important in longer discussions.

Let me be specific. Everything that we say is said in a tone of voice: for example, we use pitch, and the power of our voice (loudness) to indicate degrees of emphasis. We have ways of signalling whether we expect somebody to know what we're talking about or whether we're saying something new to them. Now these signals of tone of voice are automatic; they're something we use without thinking. But they're also conventional because they're shared by people of the same group and they're different for people of different backgrounds. So one thing that we're talking about is *tone of voice*.

Here's another important point. Conversation is not simply talk, it involves *turn-taking* and we have to know when it's our turn to talk and when we have to give somebody else a chance. There are conventional ways of recognising whether somebody has finished or whether there is something more to be said. To interrupt somebody inappropriately is to be impolite, and not to give them a chance to say what they want to. As a matter of fact, what we manage to say is really a function of what we're allowed to say by the others to whom we are talking; very often we get cut off.

Another important convention is the way we constantly signal to each other in conversations how we think the other person is coming across. We say things like 'yes', 'no', 'OK', 'that's right'. We give out these little *back-channelled signals*, as a communication specialist calls them, to tell others how we're getting along. These back-channelled signals are very important because they enable us to plan our argument.

T: And if people use different kinds of signals to communicate about these things what's the result?

G: Well, they may end up talking past each other, or they may find that they're saying something quite differently from the way they intended to say it. In a longer discussion or meeting, people just may never get down to make their point; they may feel that they've never really discussed a point, they've never really dealt with it. Instead, people just keep talking alongside each other; they go along 'in parallel', as some of the people that we've worked with describe this experience.

T: But isn't this just a minor irritation? Or are you saying that it is has results more important than that?

G: I think it's a lot more important than that. If attitudes are conveyed through speech, and if attitudes include stereotypes, then miscommunication at the level of conversation tends to perpetuate attitudes and stereotypes. In a society such as ours where racial and ethnic stereotyping exists, where prejudice exists, prejudice therefore tends to be reinforced rather than destroyed or alleviated by communication. As a matter of fact, I think social psychologists have long said that intensity of communication does not necessarily lead to the disappearance of mutual suspicion, and that prejudice is often increased with intensity of communication. I think it's these different uses of conventional ways of speaking that often lead to that intensification of prejudice as a result of contact.

T: Now what are the groups in Britain which use different conventions in the way they speak English?

G: We're talking about conventions that are a function of somebody living in what the anthropologists would call a 'culture area'.[d] Continents such as Europe, and Africa are examples of different culture areas. Although people speak many different languages in Europe, for example, we nevertheless share many of the same kind of cultural conventions in using them. We say 'please' and the French say 's'il vous plait', but we use these politeness forms in much the same ways. Now in other areas of the world, such as Asia, there are completely different conventions for using politeness forms. For purposes of our analysis in Britain, we make a distinction between people of Asian origin, people of Afro-Caribbean origin, and English Europeans.

T: Well, with reference to the first group, can you outline some of the conventions that the Asian groups have in using English, even after they've been long settled in Britain?[e]

G: Well, I've already explained that there are very important differences in the way tone of voice is used by Asian groups. Asians do not use tone of voice in the same way as English people to indicate emphasis, agreement or disagreement, or to indicate new information as opposed to information that everybody is assumed to know. They have different ways of signalling when they've finished speaking, and that affects turn-taking as I said earlier.

---

d Compare this with Sapir (this volume) (though in the Sapir extract, the notion of language is both more structural/formal, and more sharply separated from culture – see also footnote f).

e For another perspective on conventions from one language carrying over into another, see Alleyne in this volume.

Another very important difference is the way Asians signal the relationship between various parts of an argument: the transition from an introduction to the main part of an argument to a conclusion. Again they signal differently the speaker's relationship to the message: whether he or she is quoting somebody else, or whether he or she is indirectly attributing a statement to somebody else. All these things are done by different locutions and different kinds of uses of intonation, of stress, and of loudness.

At another level, the *rhetorical level*, Asians have radically *different ways of structuring their answers* to a question. It's not considered polite, for example, to go directly into one's answer; one has to set the background for what one says by giving some less relevant facts. English people very often expect a direct answer, especially in employment interviews. We expect a direct and to the point answer to a question, but that is impolite in Asian society; it's putting oneself forward too much. But this different way of answering tends to create confusion for an English interviewer when an Asian uses it.

Finally, there is the whole use of politeness formulae. The 'thank yous', and the 'please's', that we constantly use, are not as frequent in Asian languages. These forms are used for different purposes. They indicate pleading rather than politeness, and they are not used in talking with people of equal status. So Asians tend to see English politeness formulae in ways that to us seem either too much or not enough.

T: So those are some characteristic conventions in the way Asian Britons use the language. Now what about the other groups? What about West Indians and Africans living in Britain? What particular differences of convention in the use of English do they have?

G: Well, again, I think the most important differences are at the level of tone of voice, at the level of stress, and the level of use of loudness. Afro-Caribbeans tend to use loudness to indicate emphasis, while we tend to use loudness to associate loudness with excitement. Or they tend to use loudness to indicate they want to stress a point of information, while we tend to associate loudness with emotion. So we tend to mis-read each other and to think that somebody's being excited when they are simply making an important point. There are other important differences. Ways of quoting another person are different. There are ways of indicating progression of an argument which differ. Information is structured slightly differently, although Afro-Caribbeans don't have the difference of directness and indirectness that Asians have. So there are differences at all levels. And, of course, Africans and Asians are not alike; their conventions are also very different.

T: So this may be why so many English people in dialogue with West Indians or African people in Britain often come up with the stereotype that they are being a bit aggressive, and often assume that they've got some sort of chip on their shoulder. Are you saying that this happens simply because of different mannerisms in using the language, rather than objective fact?

G: It's because of the way they use language to get the ordinary tasks of conversation done. These uses of English have got nothing to do with intending or feeling anger, or intending to express marked emotion in any way whatsoever. Yes, we (Europeans) tend to think that Afro-Caribbeans are overloud and over-aggressive, and we tend to think that Asians are quiet, unemotional or over-submissive sometimes. These stereotypes are in part reinforced by the way people speak. [. . .]

T: What about the effect of English people's conventions in using language on West Indians and Asians? What are the conventions we have, that they find confusing or even irritating?

G: Well, there may well be difficulty in interpreting English people's use of tone of voice for all the purposes which I have already referred to. [. . . W]hat is so difficult is that the cause of all this is largely unrecognised on both sides. At the *conscious* level of irritation and stereotyping, Asian and West Indians may react to what seem to them an over-extensive use of 'thank you' and 'please'. This is often interpreted as hypocritical because they know we don't mean it, and they wonder why we say it. Other examples are lack of directness in making requests, and our over-use of greetings before we state what we want. That's the sort of thing that irritates people, and leads them to think that we're not 'straight'.

T: What scope is there for us to do something about all this? Are you implying that West Indians and Asians have somehow got to learn these English speech conventions if they're to communicate effectively with the majority of English people?

G: I think that's putting it too simply because these conventions are things that we learn from the time we grow up and that we practise with our friends and our families, and that stand us in good stead when we're talking to people who know us, people in our own group. Besides, these conventions are used subconsciously, in other words they're very hard to change; in fact they're much more difficult to change than one's grammar and one's lexicon.[f] We tend to keep these conventions even when we learn a different language. So Asians tend to use their Asian tone of voice when speaking English. As long as Asians, and Afro-Caribbeans, and others continue to live largely in their own communities, they will use these conventions when talking English to their friends and relatives, and that's fine. These conventions only really fail them when they're faced with communicating with someone from another group, particularly if it's for official purposes. But these relatively formal situations are very important for people because that's the way you get things done in life. One of the problems is that these conventions of speech are learned in everyday life, they are automatic. You would need re-training to give them up, but few of us get enough training or practice in the kind of situations and interviews where you may need other conventions for it to be any good.

So the problem is not simply teaching or learning these conventions, because one can't teach them as such. But what one can do is become aware

---

f Compare Gumperz's view of cultural differences in the *way that language is used* with Whorf's view (this volume) of cultural differences in *grammatical structure*. For a recent collection of scholarly papers related to this, see J. Gumperz and S. Levinson (eds) 1996 *Rethinking Linguistic Relativity* Cambridge: Cambridge University Press.

of the differences. And this is a matter not only for Asians and Africans to do something about, it is equally a matter for English people, especially those who have to deal with ethnic minorities in their daily work and life. There are many English people whose jobs include assisting members of ethnic minorities—people such as careers officers, housing officers, teachers in contact with parents, job centre staff. These people say they want to help, but frequently think that they're not getting co-operation from ethnic minority people. These people need to become much more aware of these conventions and realise that their problem is often the way they communicate with ethnic minority people.

T: It seems from what you're saying that the only long-term solution to this set of problems is that somehow Asian and West Indian people in Britain should spend less time with their friends, less time with their families, and more time mixing socially and at work with white people, and of course, vice versa?

G: No, I don't think that's the solution at all. We all need the support of our family, and a sense of social cohesion. The quality of life depends on the existence of small groups and on a human environment in which we are able to interact with people like ourselves. But this is what creates the dilemma, and what I'm saying is that we need to maintain our differences to some extent, but we also need to be aware of causes of miscommunication and learn how to overcome it.

T: Now all these points you've made about the details of the way language is used are very interesting, but in terms of race relations and achieving a successful multi-racial society, isn't it all an extremely marginal consideration? I mean, isn't this matter of language really unimportant, compared with the fundamental problems of racial discrimination and the social and economic disadvantages of black and other ethnic minorities in Britain?

G: Certainly, there's no denying that politics and economic conditions are extremely important in race relations, and that ultimately redressing the balance of discrimination is a matter of power. But communication *is* power. Our social position depends on our ability to communicate, we get things in life by communicating. If we want to get a flat, we need to go to the housing authorities. To get a position in employment, we have to go through job interviews. We are tested in school at every turn, at every transition, and how we do in these tests determines how we do in later life. In all these cases, communication can make the difference. We need to communicate even to keep what we have. So communication is power—that I think is the point.

T: But even accepting that, isn't it really cultural differences which explain the way people don't get on, rather than these linguistic points?

G: It's true that we are not talking about language in the very narrow sense. What we're talking about really is an area of conventionality which is partly linguistic and partly cultural. This area of conventionality is automatic; it's something that we do without thinking and without reflection. We don't think about *how* we're going to say things. We think about *what* we're going to say and then we automatically select our style of speaking. What is involved is this automatic process by which we select our style of speaking, and whether you call it cultural or whether you call it linguistic isn't really that important. The point is that it's something a person does automatically, but that affects our judgement of each other in ways that we are rarely aware of. [. . .]

T: A lot of people would feel that [. . .] white people face problems of miscommunication as well when they seek jobs and advice, particularly when there is a marked class difference or regional difference between the people involved. Similar problems happen to white people as well, don't they?

G: Yes, in a sense you are right because miscommunication occurs everywhere. But despite differences of class attitudes, accents, or social traditions, English people will still share similar linguistic conventions. And so they at least have the *means* with which to correct what's gone wrong, and sort out any miscommunication. They don't get involved in talking past each other to the same degree. When people do not share these linguistic conventions, the kind of minor misunderstanding which would hardly bother people with similar conventions becomes dangerous because the very means that you use to repair a misunderstanding or error are themselves misunderstood. So you may be wanting to repair a situation and you're really making it worse.

You see, it's this cumulative effect in an inter-ethnic conversation which is so difficult and damaging. The misunderstanding may arise for reasons of different cultural assumptions, or rhetorical style or different use of linguistic conventions such as tone of voice. But since so much about attitude and meaning is automatically interpreted in terms of your own conventions, once things start to go wrong and the interaction becomes stressful, you have less and less chance of overcoming your misunderstanding because your strategies of repair are subject to the same process of misinterpretation. [. . .]

Very serious miscommunication can occur between English people in these same situations and this is more likely to happen when there are class and regional differences. But this miscommunication does not happen for the same reasons [. . .] and seldom happens with the same intensity.

T: Since, as you say, these linguistic conventions are so in-built, aren't you asking for an impossible change? Aren't you asking for a degree of insight into other people's conventions of use of language which it's completely unrealistic to expect non-specialists to be able to adopt?

G: It's true that the initial analysis of these conventions requires a great deal of special knowledge, but once this analysis has been done, we find that the basic signalling mechanisms that are involved are relatively simple to understand. So once the basic facts have been made clear by the experts it then becomes relatively easy for other people to become aware of them. What we need to work for really is not so much learning each other's conventions, and understanding technical details, but simply (1) an awareness that the problem exists, (2) a willingness to perceive differences in communication, and then (3) a willingness to seek ways of alleviating the difficulties [. . .]. We don't need to alleviate these problems by trying to become exactly like the other person; but we do need to understand the other person. [. . .] If we listen to an Asian speaker of English in the right way, and if we familiarise ourselves with the linguistic conventions of Asian English in Britain, we are more likely

to understand an Asian person and be able to deal with these important situations. So those people in key positions such as personnel officers, shop
stewards, social workers, teachers, government officials—anyone in a public
position—need to receive some special training that deals not so much with
the broader aspects of culture perhaps, but with these everyday matters of
miscommunication.[g] We need to pay attention to culture with a little 'c'
rather than constantly thinking of culture with a big 'C' in terms of gross
cultural differences.

T: If I was a social worker going into work at an advice centre tomorrow morning
      and I had a list of clients who were West Indian or Asian, and I had not had
      this training, are there any practical points that I should bear in mind to help
      me to become better at my job in dealing with my clients?

G: Well, to begin, as I've said, I think what's needed is awareness, and I think
      the point is to learn and to practise awareness immediately. Perhaps the best
      thing to do is to listen to how others react, to watch for what they say volun-
      tarily rather than simply trying to get one's own point of view across. Try
      to spot volunteered information, look for the way people rephrase what you
      say and see if there's any pattern, any consistency. Observe whether there
      are some ways in which *you* talk that consistently get the wrong kind of
      responses in terms of the kind of information that people volunteer. I think
      watching things in this way, one can do quite a bit. But ultimately there's no
      doubt that what's needed is some kind of linguistic awareness training; some
      kind of systematic discussion of the areas where communication can occur,
      and perhaps analysis of them [. . .]. Another very useful thing that can be
      done is tape recording, and role play. In fact that's the most effective method
      of analysis. There's no need for real technical analysis, but I think a great deal
      can be done just simply by being aware of these problems and examining how
      people behave.

      What we need to do is a sort of action replay like our T.V. newscasters
      do when they use a slow-down mechanism to show us the detail of a partic-
      ular piece of play in football. We need to use a tape recorder in just the same
      way, and to use it to analyse our communication strategies. If we analyse and
      emphasise exactly what happens in communication, I think we may begin to
      overcome some of the attitudinal problems. [. . .]

T: Finally, what about the defensive attitudes of many English people who may
      resent the suggestion that they need to modify their practice in relation to
      some aspects of their job?

G: Well, I think that's difficult because I think people tend to feel threatened
      when they find that their judgement is not as good as they thought and that it
      therefore may be influenced by prejudice and stereotypes. This may be espe-
      cially upsetting for those who have very liberal views, those who think of them-
      selves as being very tolerant, when they find that there are hidden ways in
      which they discriminate. People who think of our system as being fair will
      find that our system has all kinds of hidden mechanisms for perpetuating exactly

g Contrast the analysis of problematic communication in an institutional setting provided by McDermott
and Gospodinoff (this volume).

the kind of prejudice, the kind of stereotyping that we're all interested in destroying. Now I think that's often frightening, and it may threaten some people, but the dangers in ignoring these mechanisms are greater than the risks in shaking some people up.

John Gumperz was Professor of Anthropology at the University of California, Berkeley, for many years. He has been a major pioneer in the study of codeswitching, intercultural communication, interactional discourse, and the relations between language, interaction and ethnicity more generally.

Chapter 21

R. P. McDermott and Kenneth Gospodinoff

1979

SOCIAL CONTEXTS FOR ETHNIC BORDERS AND SCHOOL FAILURE[a]

I   Introduction

THIS PAPER CONSIDERS the recently popular claim that many minority children fail in school because there is a mismatch between their procedures or codes for making sense with each other and the codes used by their teachers who generally come from a socially more powerful group.[b] In most claims, the emphasis is on the fact that the minority and majority group members have different languages, dialects, gestural systems, or interactional rhythms, etc., that they accordingly produce much miscommunication with each other, and that in the classroom such miscommunication leads to alienation and failure. This paper is different in that, while we do not deny that communicative code differences exist, we emphasize that they are secondary to the political relations between members of the different groups both in the classroom and in the larger community. [. . .]

Primarily, we offer an analysis of only a few moments of some minority children miscommunicating with their teacher and failing in school. But we offer these moments as a systematic part of the contexts in which the teacher and the children are immersed. The most immediate context is that of the children and the teacher trying to understand each other while face-to-face during their reading lessons. At this level, everyone appears to make sense in that they simultaneously act upon and respond to each other's behavior in systematic ways. In terms of the organization of a given piece of face-to-face behavior, what appears to be a miscommunication may be a carefully arranged and sensible way for all the participants to proceed, given the

---

a From Aaron Wolfgang (ed.) *Non-verbal Behaviour: Application and Cultural Implications*. New York: Academic Press; and H. Trueba, G. Guthrie and G. Au (eds) (1981) *Culture and the Bilingual Classroom*. Rowley, Mass: Newbury House pp. 212–30.
b See Philips and Gumperz in this volume.

interactional and pedagogical problems confronted by members of the classroom. We present an analysis of such a case in Section III [of this chapter].

By itself, the detailed analysis of the good sense of a miscommunication will leave the reader confused. What is needed is an account of how the classroom came to be organized in such a way that the development of codes for miscommunicating came to be a sensible adaptation. The usual account of miscommunication and school failure simply in terms of communicative code differences does not deal with this difficult task. Instead, it usually is assumed that people from different groups are naturally different and that their differences can be in the long run irremedial; with such an assumption in hand, it is not necessary to show how people develop vested interests in being different from one another. Our point is that without such vested interests being created from one moment to the next, people usually develop metacommunicative procedures for altering their communicative codes in order to make sense of each other. When communicative differences become irremedial, it is because there are sound political or economic reasons for their being so. [. . .]

The setting for our analysis is a first-grade classroom in a comparatively successful school in a suburb not far beyond the New York City limits. School failure by minority group children was quite visible in this classroom. Shortly after the start of the school year, most children were ranked into one of three groups on the basis of the teacher's analysis of their reading abilities. The top group consisted of white children, primarily Italian and Jewish. The bottom, or least literate, group consisted of three Puerto Rican, one black and finally two white children, one of whom was considered the group's best reader and destined to move into a higher group, the other of whom was considered brain damaged. There was one other Puerto Rican boy who was originally assigned to the bottom group, but who had been put out for being too disruptive. Thereafter, the boy had no reading group, and he wandered around the classroom causing trouble. The one other minority child in the class belonged to the middle reading group.

So five of six minority children are in the bottom group or in no group at all, despite the efforts of a teacher who was considered excellent by her peers, and incidentally, by us. The teacher of this class gets the most difficult first graders into her room each year and is often successful in teaching them the basics of classroom behavior and reading. However, in the year under analysis, not all the children emerged with such survival skills, and by the end of the second year in school, two Puerto Rican children and one white boy, all from the bottom group, had been reassigned to special schools for various functional handicaps, namely, for being "slow," "emotionally disturbed," and "brain damaged." Essentially, the children were sent to special schools because their teacher found them impossible to work with in the classroom. The other children in the group were not doing too much better in that they were not learning to read up to grade level, a *sine qua non* of institutional success, but at least they had escaped placement (for the moment) in a slowed down program.

The process just described is in no way unusual. [. . . In the following section, we will] direct our attention to the argument that minority children fail in school because they communicate differently and are accordingly unappreciated and misunderstood.

II   Ethnic differences do not cause irremediable miscommunication

According to [. . .] the communicative code account, members of minority groups do less well than others in school because the schools generally are staffed by majority group members who do not understand minority group children [. . .]. This argument is most appealing when we consider large differences such as those that exist between a teacher who speaks only one language and students who speak only another. The case for the smaller systems of differences, i.e., systems of touching, spacing, gesturing, speaking rights, etc., can be argued along the same lines. People with different communicative codes may want the same things and work equally hard at achieving their goals, but, to the extent that they do not share codes for making sense with members of the dominant groups, they will mis-interpret each other's behavior and eventually create unpleasant environments for each other. It is in such unpleasant environments that minority children begin to "act up" and become alienated from the teacher and the learning enterprise.

This stand is attractive. For one thing, it holds out great hope for the children; it assumes they can all do well in school if we could only build more sensitivity for communicative code differences into our teachers. It also has the advantage of not off-handedly condemning the teachers as incompetents or racists. [. . .]

As attractive as this stand is, we have been forced to conclude that it is much too simple. Certainly, when the communicative resources of two groups are different, the people will generate much miscommunication. But the question is why this keeps generating problems. Why do the people not repair the miscom-munication? This line of thought leads to an even more difficult question, namely, why are there [different] communicative codes at all? [. . .] Our communicative codes, as persuasive and entrapping as they are, do not turn us into communica-tive robots incapable of coming to grips with other people simply because they communicate differently. The social world is subject to negotiation. If [separate] codes exist, it is because we all help create them in the very process of communi-cating. [. . . If there are] communication problems between members of different groups, [they need to be understood] as the accomplishments of people trying to get the most out of the political and economic contexts for their being brought together.

Before proceeding with [our argument against the communicative code account . . .], we want to point out that our position rests on some assumptions about the nature of ethnic groups and that these assumptions have proved helpful in explaining interethnic relations around the world. The case we are making for class-rooms is manifested in many diverse situations in which groups of people find themselves at odds. In most cases, it has become clear that the differences between people are only incidentally a problem; the differences between people are as much a resource for mutual exploration and celebration as they are a resource for conflict (J. McDermott, 1976; R. McDermott, 1976). Our problem is not ethnicity, but ethnic borders. Our problem is not that people are different, but that the differ-ences are made to make more of a difference than they must, that the differences are politicized into borders that define different kinds of people as antagonists in various realms of everyday life [. . .].

Barth (1969 [. . .]) has articulated this view and shown how we must understand the ethnic identities of many people in terms of how these identities are related to the maximization of physical and economic security and/or identity enhancement in contrast to other available alternatives. Moerman (1965 [. . .]) has made the same point for groups in Northern Thailand. His point of departure was to try to answer the question, "Who are the Lue?" with a description of the behavior and attitudes of the Lue people. His job proved so difficult that he had to rephrase his question to when, where, why, and how are the Lue. The complexities of having a Lue identity could not be understood without a specification of the circumstances under which it made sense for the Lue to emphasize their Lue identity over the various alternative identities available to them. [. . .]

[With these assumptions clarified, we would now like to consider three types of situation which present considerable difficulties for the communicative code explanation of ethnic minority failure at school . . .]

1   [We can most easily tell that communicative codes do not determine behaviour from . . .] the records of millions of immigrants who move to other lands and pick up new and diverse languages and customs in only a few years. Here the political circumstances for learning the ways of the people who control the resources of the new land are obvious. Sometimes, it is even necessary for immigrants to learn two languages, one of the poorer working-class people who surround them upon their entrance to the country, the other the language of the politically more dominant group. For example, the Italians who immigrated to the bilingual city of Montreal work with, live near, and intermarry with the French. But the majority of Italian parents send their children to schools to learn English, which the parents feel is the language of the successful, a feeling they apparently share with both French and English speakers of Montreal ([. . .]; Lambert, 1967). In New York City, Puerto Ricans are exposed mostly to Black neighbors and co-workers, and the children first become competent in Black language (Wolfram, 1973). Although Black English is useful in the most immediate politics of everyday life, in the long run the children are forced to learn a more standardized English in order to get by in the larger urban scene. The result in both these cases are populations with three different codes for their participation in the three different communities. People who do not become trilingual can suffer exclusion from certain institutions. [. . .]

Even without the extreme example of immigration, the social science literature is filled with accounts of people overcoming structurally complex communicative code differences in order to make sense of each other on certain occasions. The fascinating records of whole groups together generating pidgin and creole languages come from all parts of the world.[c] [. . . Most often,] pidgins develop among different groups of people who have much interaction with each other in the market place of a third and more powerful group and, under such conditions, it is good to have a way of communicating with each other without becoming part of the dominating market society (DeCamp, 1971). Similar processes have been demonstrated on the

---

c See Alleyne and Rickford, this volume.

kinesic[d] level by Erickson (1975 [. . .]), who has shown that members of different ethnic group alter their communicative styles to fit "panethnic" groupings made up of various ethnic groups aligned according to the dictates of local politics; for example, Blacks and Puerto Ricans in Chicago would fall together against Irish, Poles, and Italians on one hand, and WASPs on the other.

2   The case of people's refusing to repair minor communicative code boundaries also makes the point that the divergence of communicative patterns into mutually exclusive codes must be understood in terms of their function in interaction and not simply in terms of structural differences. The differences between the vernacular English of many American Blacks or the creole English of many West Indians are minute compared to the differences between mutually unintelligible languages. Yet these smaller barriers to mutual intelligibility appear to be much more difficult to overcome in schools and other institutional settings (Cazden, et al., 1972; Craig, 1971). What makes a difference is the politicization of language and dialect differences in the schools in which the children are asked to learn.

In fact, some research efforts are beginning to show that dialect use by Black children in American schools actually increases as children proceed through school ([. . .] Labov, 1972; Piestrup, 1973). Given the correlation between dialect use and success in school in numerous minority-dominant group settings, this is an important finding that can give us a rough sense for the social processes underlining the emergence of communicative code boundaries together with failing school records. Labov and Robins (1969) have shown, for example, that the use of dialect increases as peer-group participation increases and school performances decline. This result is further illustrated by Piestrup (1973) who found that in the first grades she analyzed, the Black children's use of dialect either stayed the same or soared in direct proportion to how much the children were hassled for their use of dialect. The more their speech was corrected, the more they used dialect, and in such classrooms, reading scores were low. In classrooms in which the children were allowed to express themselves and read orally in dialect, the use of dialect did not increase and their reading scores were higher, with many children above the norms.

The presence or absence of dialect in the children's speech is not the crucial determinant of successful communication in school. Rather, dialect appears to function as a focus for the relational work of the children and the teacher. If the teacher and the children are alienated from each other, their dialects will take center stage and the teacher and the children will battle each other about the proper way to speak. In this sense, the emergence of a dialect in each new generation of different minorities represents more than a passing on of a set of speaking skills. It also represents an active adaptation to conditions in classrooms across the country. And the conscious claiming of a dialect, or any other aspect of a communicative code, from a clenched fist to a particular kind of walk, represents a political activity, a statement of one's identity as a member of a particular community.

---

d Kinesics involves the study of facial expression and bodily gesture.

3   The point that communicative codes are not determinants of people's relations with each other, that they are in fact adaptations to the various relations between the people who use the codes, is most clearly made by cases in which a group invents a communicative code in order to build cohesion into the home community and to block out the surrounding communities (Halliday, 1976 [. . .]). The Pennsylvania Dutch (Amish) are a good example of people who work at keeping themselves different, and they specify these differences not only at the level of general values against modern life, but at the level of the minutiae of everyday communication, at the level of language and dress, right down to the kinds of hooks used to fasten their clothing together. Such communicative strategies can have an effect on classrooms. The code differences do not in and of themselves enhance or detract from the children's learning. But the work that the Amish do to make themselves different apparently does interfere with the children's performance in public schools, where they do not do well academically. But this same work apparently creates a communal learning environment in their own schools in which Amish children do well, even by the standards of state tests (Hostetler and Huntington, 1971). These differential school results can only be understood in terms of the mutually distrustful relations between the Amish and the surrounding communities, on the one hand, and the positive relational environments generated by Amish teachers and children, on the other (McDermott, 1977). [. . .]

The three [types of situation . . .] we have just cited should demonstrate that an account of minority group problems in school in terms of communicative code differences is too simple. [. . .] Our [own] notion is that when ethnically specific patterns are used and appear to cause trouble, the cause of that trouble will not be with the communicative code disparity but with the function of the disparity in the relations between the students and the teacher in the classroom. The relations between the teacher and the children will be the key to the members' interpretations and evaluations of the importance of ethnic borders and school learning in their lives with each other (McDermott, 1977). With this in mind, we will present an account of a teacher and a child having trouble with each other in ways that could be understood in terms of a communicative code conflict, but which upon analysis appears to be a function of much mutual understanding of their circumstances by the child and the teacher.

III   A context analysis of the function of a miscommunication

In the classroom we introduced above, there was a Puerto Rican boy who was assigned to the bottom group for most of the year. There Juan (as we shall call him), made life miserable for all, and much of his time was spent being put out of the group or chastised while in the group. Although we never tracked this boy's activities alone, there were times when he would show up in our notes more than ten times an hour as the focus of a disruptive incident in classroom routines. Later in the year, the teacher became concerned enough to have the school officials discuss his case as a candidate for a special school for disturbed children. And this is where he is today. By the time the films were taken, this child was no longer a part of the bottom reading group. He was in no group at all, and he either busied himself with little projects the teacher gave him or he wandered around the classroom interacting with the other children, interactions that often led to disagreements. When the bottom group was at the reading table, he appeared to monitor their actions carefully, and any disturbance usually was followed by his showing up at the table anxious to participate.

We should mention how we came by our observations; one of us was in the classroom throughout the year observing behavior and recording it in a notebook, on Super-8 film mounted in one corner of the room and on videotape often centered on the reading groups. [. . . W]e [then] carefully analyzed tapes of the top and bottom reading groups at work and identified how the participants struggled to understand and organize their own behavior. The result was a complex structural analysis, only a diluted example of which will be presented in this section. By virtue of the extended observation in the classroom and a more detailed interactional analysis, as in R. P. McDermott (1976), we feel our statements about Juan and ethnic borders are warranted.

On one occasion, Juan came to the teacher complaining that another child was bothering him and that her intervention was necessary. It came at a time that the teacher was working with the bottom group in a reading lesson. She was standing in front of the group writing a word on the board. All were quite involved. At this point, the young boy started across the classroom shouting the teacher's name, "Hey, S ——, you better tell him to stop!" The teacher ignored the boy until he reached her and made contact by touching her on the buttocks. Thus, the boy violated two apparent rules of mainstream culture. He skipped the teacher's title and used only her last name in trying to get her attention.

He got her attention by contacting a prohibited area. The teacher immediately responded to the boy's touch and gave witness to the violation status of his attention-getting techniques. She turned quickly and left the bottom group without instruction as to what they should do next. She took the boy by the arm to a corner near her desk where she had a brief conversation with him before they broke contact.

The discovery of this behavior was easy. The boy violated not only the teacher's rules for contact, but our rules also, and we attended to his violation almost immediately. With a little more looking at the videotape it became probable that the teacher was not pleased with the boy, for throughout the year, when the teacher was annoyed, the same arm raising procedure was used. The procedure consisted of the teacher raising the child's arm to a height that made the child dependent on guidance for a means of transport.

So we have some behavior that can be used as an anecdote relating ethnicity to miscommunication. The child wanted the teacher's attention, went about it in the wrong way, and got nothing but trouble for his efforts. The teacher in turn has the trouble of being hassled and having to hassle the child. No one is getting what the institution has defined as desirable. At first, we thought that the problem was simple. People from different cultures have different systems for doing touch. The teacher is a rather classic Northern and Eastern (non-Jewish) European in this regard, and she has little tactile involvement with other people in public. This should be difficult on the Mediterranean and Caribbean children who come from more tactile cultures and who could suffer relational mishaps with the teacher because of their different ways of making sense (Efron 1941; Hall, 1966; Scheflen, 1974). [Perhaps t]his little anecdote supports this notion. Numerous other examples can be found in the literature on cross-cultural communication in educational settings ([. . . e.g.] Erickson, 1975; Philips, 1972).

With this supporting literature, it is easy to jump from the anecdote to conclusions. One is that the boy is working with a different communicative code than the teacher and unwittingly causes some trouble for himself by not learning her code. The second response is that the teacher should be aware that the child has a different way of proceeding and should be more adaptable in order to give the boy the most satisfying relational environment in which to learn and adapt to mainstream culture. In this way, it might be possible to minimize miscommunication and restrict the possibility that the boy might eventually work at achieving school failure, rather than school success.

But two other questions have forced themselves on us. One, given the adaptability children display in many of their activities, why is it that this boy is not using the mainstream code to get the teacher's attention? Why is it that after nine months in school, he still has not figured out the teacher's rules for addressing and touching? Is it possible that there are other contexts for this behavior than is obvious in the anecdote? Two, might there be more reasons for the teacher being annoyed than is obvious in the anecdote? The teacher generally displays tremendous patience with the children. Is there something else going on than simply a touch deemed inappropriate in the teacher's native culture? Is it possible the boy is breaking more rules than those of the culture at large? Is it possible the boy is breaking rules that govern the relational work between the children of the classroom and the teacher? And is it possible the teacher's annoyance is only a part of more inclusive contexts for the sequencing of their behavior? The anecdotal description we offered cannot be used to address these questions. Instead, we need a description of the people's contexts for their behavior as they are defining those contexts and using them in the organization of concerted behavior. Fortunately, both the theory and the method of context analysis has been well worked out (Bateson, 1955; Birdwhistell, 1970; McQuown, Bateson, Birdwhistell, Brosin, and Hockett, 1971 [. . .]).

Perhaps the most immediate context or environment for people's behavior is the answer they might collectively give to the question "What is it that is going on here?" or "What's happening?" ([. . .] Goffman, 1974). Many have shown that it is possible to locate people's answers to this question, because people must constantly inform each other of what is going on in order to continue producing concerted behavior with each other. So much of the behavior of members when face to face is related to this task that it would seem to be the *sine qua non* of any interaction (Birdwhistell, 1970). [. . .] Kinesically, they do this by moving and positioning their bodies in relation to each other in particular ways at particular times. Thus, what it is that people are doing together can be seen in the positions or postural configurations they work out for each other ([. . .] McDermott, et al., 1978).

In the bottom group, the children and the teacher move in and out of three different major activity types [. . .]. These are the most immediate contexts for their answers to the question that they constantly put to each other and to themselves, namely, "What's going on?" As these were located primarily by an analysis of postural shifts performed by the members, we will call them positionings (see Figures 21.1–21.3).

For our present purpose, it is only important to know that each of these positionings is marked by a different kind of work at the outer boundaries of the group. That is, depending upon which of the three positionings the children and the teacher assume, outsiders to the group appear to have different degrees of license to enter the group. This is not an unusual phenomenon, and an outsider's rights to enter a group have been clearly documented as subject to the postural work of the people already in the group [. . .] For example, in the bottom group, when the teacher is out of the group and the children are waiting for her return (positioning III), outsiders are invited in to visit. When the children are struggling to get a turn to read from the teacher (positioning II), the children carefully monitor the teacher's activities; accordingly, no one is invited in, but if outsiders have business with the teacher, they will usually make an entrance. However, when the children are actively engaged in reading with the teacher no outsider enters the group. Interestingly, the top reading group assumes this organization throughout its reading lesson and is never disturbed by outsiders.

Now we must reconsider the boy's attention-getting behaviors in terms of the immediate contexts in which they occur. The behaviors occur at a special time and must be understood as they function at that time. With such a reconsideration, for example, the teacher does not have to be such a cultural imperialist to respond in the way she does. No one except this boy enters the reading table while the group is reading (positioning I). The top group is never disturbed, and when a member of the bottom group even went near the top group while the members were reading (positioning I), the teacher, three top group members and one member of the bottom group at the other end of the room conspired to prevent a possible disturbance by chasing the boy back to his part of the room. On the other hand, children from the top group often disturb the children of the bottom group while they are at the reading table, but never enter the table while the bottom group is reading (positioning I). This avoidance is no accident, for there are examples of a top group child entering the periphery of reading activity (positioning I), waiting until it is complete, and finally moving in to address the teacher at the start of the children calling for a turn (positioning II). The only case of a child violating a reading positioning comes when Juan enters and contacts the teacher's buttocks. Suddenly, this episode does not look like a simple case of culture conflict. The conflict at hand is not between the patterning of behavior of Caribbean Spanish versus that of Northern and Eastern European. It is far more localized than that. Given the particular ways of doing the order of the classroom, as that order is negotiated, formulated and done by the teacher and the students for their moment-to-moment life in school, the important question here asks how it is that this particular boy becomes involved in conflicts of scheduling as well as conflicts of naming and touching. Whatever the reasons, the teacher's reactions appear to be quite sensible.

More context must be considered for the boy's behavior. Recall that the boy was formerly a member of the bottom group and has since been put out. However, the boy still monitors the group's activities quite carefully. For example, every time there is a disturbance while the teacher is away from the reading table

Figure 21.1   Positioning I: Looking at the book.

Figure 21.2   Positioning II: Getting-a-turn to read.

Figure 21.3   Positioning III: Waiting for the teacher.

and the children struggle, squirm, and fight, this boy shows up on the scene. During one such episode, a child takes a pencil belonging to another child and throws it to the floor at the other end of the reading table. The pencil has barely hit the ground as the boy in question runs across the room and picks the pencil up. Later, when two children square off in an argument, the prodigal child again appears on camera examining the scene. The boy monitors the group carefully and gives evidence of knowing the difference between the three positionings. More examples are possible, and each of them would contrast the boy's entering behavior in the buttocks scene to the boy's usual behavior during a reading positioning, in which he moves past the table the same as everyone else, without any disturbance whatsoever. So there is some reason to think that the boy moves to the table misaddressing and mistouching the teacher at a time that he *understands* as inappropriate.

Can we still talk about the teacher and the child miscommunicating? The child appears to have mastered the basic rules of the classroom and simply uses them for a different purpose. What could be the function of his behavior? Remember that the teacher takes the child to a corner and chastises him (unfortunately out of the range of the microphone). What happens next is interesting. The teacher then goes off camera to the back of the room where she is picked up by another camera. There she chastises the boy that Juan was complaining about. On her way, she is followed by Juan, in no way crushed, clapping his hands and delighting in the fact that his adversary is also getting into trouble. The plot thickens. In short, he received from the interaction what he might have wanted all along, namely, to get the other child in trouble, no mean feat in a classroom in which the teacher discourages snitching, particularly while she is busy working with a group. So the small anecdote locating a miscommunication, if properly contextualized, shows the miscommunication not only to be sensible, but quite functional as well.

It is not as easy to locate the teacher's behavior as functional. By placing her behavior in its larger context, we have located that her annoyance was based on more than a misunderstanding of cross-cultural norms for touching. Rather, her behavior appears to be based as well on a "knowledge" of the interactional norms governing her particular classroom. The boy breaks the rules and the teacher chastises him for it. Up to this point, her behavior makes sense, but then she crowns his efforts by attending to the matter he brought before her in the way he might have hoped. She breaks the first rule of classroom management by rewarding a person for breaking the rules and norms she otherwise enforces. Meanwhile, the bottom reading group is wasting its time on the other side of the room; a fight has started and reading has stopped. A good portion of the class is also disrupted by this episode. There is little reason for him not to proceed in the same way at another time. How then can we say that the teacher's behavior makes sense? The answer to this question is in no way complete, but consider the following pattern.

Often, as the bottom group gets into a positioning II in which they are struggling for a turn to read or a positioning I in which they are engaged in reading or some other lesson activity with the teacher, they are disrupted by the teacher yelling at the rest of the class or actually leaving the group to attend to outsiders. The teacher's attending to the boy's behavior in both a negative and positive way at a particular time may have to be understood in terms of this larger pattern of the teacher exiting from the bottom group at key points, when the group is highly focused around a particular task. By way of inference, it can be claimed that the teacher is uncomfortable with the bottom group once it is settled and ready for instruction. In terms of the readiness of some of the children to engage in reading activities, the teacher's response to the bottom group is quite understandable. It is easier to teach children how to read when they already know how to read. The top group does not present the problems the bottom group does. If this is the case, then the teacher's positive response to the boy's request appears to be a self-serving activity in that it is a way of getting out of the group for a little while. In the long run, everyone pays heavily for this escape, but in the short run it is to everyone's advantage; the boy gets someone in trouble and the teacher and the children in the bottom group get a brief rest from their intense organizational negotiations. [. . .]

Juan and the teacher seem to have agreed unknowingly on how to miscommunicate with each other. [. . .] How then can we talk of communicative code differences causing misbehavior and failure in school? Their choices are adaptive given their circumstances. We will now [move to consider the wider circumstances and . . .] the longterm consequences of their behavior.

IV The circumstances and consequences of miscommunication in school

[. . . H]ow is it that things are set up so that many children, particularly minority children have the kinds of problems just detailed? [. . .] Most often, it is not the case that the schools are staffed with teachers consciously trying to keep minority children from succeeding in school. Nor is it generally the case that there is something wrong with the children as they enter school. Although these two explanations are the most popular accounts of minority school failure, we suspect that cases to which they actually apply are rare, and we will not deal with them as such. Our problem is neither racist teachers nor dumb kids. Our problem is that our school systems are set up to have conscientious teachers function as racists and bright little children function as dopes even when they are all trying to do otherwise.

More specifically, our claim is that poor and minority children start school knowing less about how to read and write than do the children of the enfranchised groups that survive in the modern nations via literacy skills. This is in no way a deprivation argument. We are not suggesting that the children of the minorities do not have the skills for immediately learning how to read; we have only suggested that many have not learned how to read before they come to school. From everything we know about the proper age for starting to learn how to read around the world, being more or less prepared at age six should have no effect on the eventual acquisition of literacy by the children (Wanat, 1976). Yet, given the nature of the classrooms in which the children are asked to catch up, learning to read at school becomes an organizational impossibility.

In the early grades, schools are best set up for reinforcing and practicing what children have already learned at home. When minority children show up in school not knowing how to read, they are placed in special groups like the one described in this paper. The teacher's job is not only to teach them how to read, but to make sure that they achieve a certain competence and demonstrate it on a standardized test by a certain date. In other words, the teacher is trained, paid, and held accountable for producing certain kinds of reading children by a certain date. Children in the bottom group create difficult organizational and pedagogical problems for the teacher. Many of the communication problems that exist between teachers and minority children can be understood as mutual adaptations to these organizational problems. For example, in the classroom we analyzed, the teacher handled the top and bottom groups quite differently. With the top group, the teacher likes to have the children take turns reading, one after the other, from left to right, around the table. This is not possible with the bottom group, because there are children who cannot be expected to read any page that comes along. So the teacher spares them some embarrassment and picks a special reader for each page. This means that she cannot divert her attention from this group for more than a minute without their needing her direction in picking a new reader. Concentrated attention with the bottom reading group is hardly possible while the teacher has two other groups and some stragglers busy (and not so busy) in other parts of the room. Accordingly, the members of the bottom group are often left without direction about how to proceed in their reading lesson, and they spend more than half their time waiting for the teacher or trying to get the teacher's attention to their pleas for a turn to read.

Recall the three positions that the members of the bottom group achieve with each other; two of them, getting-a-turn and waiting for the teacher (positionings II and III respectively) pit the children and the teacher in a struggle for each other's attention. The top group shares only the first positioning with the bottom group, [Position I] in which all the members focus on reading. Now recall that these three positionings are different in that they allow different visiting rights for outsiders. The fact that the top group stays in the reading positioning (even when they are not actually reading) means that no outsiders enter the group during its lesson. However, by adapting to the teacher's procedures for calling on special children for special pages, the children in the bottom group arrange themselves into positionings II and III, and suffer constant interruptions from the children in the top group entering to ask the teacher questions during the bottom group's time at the reading table. Each of these interruptions further necessitates the elaborate procedures the children in the bottom group develop to get the teacher's attention in order to get a turn to read. Juan became so good at getting the teacher's attention in unorthodox, but situationally adaptive ways that he was put out of the bottom group. As we have seen, he still exercises his communicative skills by entering the group in the way that he does. Other children in the bottom group are developing similar skills. [. . .]

We have suggested that the children in the bottom group come into the first grade not knowing how to read. They start off behind. Then they are put into the bottom group where they suffer the organizational problems we have described. The significant fact is that although they spend the same amount of time at the reading table as the children in the other groups, due to all the interruptions, two-thirds of them initiated by the other groups, they get only one-third the amount of time as the children in the top group get in a reading positioning. The rest of their time is spent in attentional struggles with the teacher. The net effect of this is that the children in the bottom group fall further behind the children in the top group for every day they spend in the classroom. [. . .]

Without learning how to read, there are few other paths for upward mobility for minority children in modern nations. Thus the children achieve the same adaptational skills of their parents, and a new generation of the so-called disadvantaged takes its place in the world. If we wanted a mechanism for sorting each new generation of citizens into the advantaged and the disadvantaged, into the achieving and the underachieving, we could have done no better than to have invented the school system we have. Not only is it efficient in assigning many generations of the same people to the top and bottom slots, but, and this is one of the ironies of contemporary life, it does so in ways that make sense to the hard working, caring, and talented people who are trying to help break the cycle of the disadvantaged becoming more disadvantaged and the advantaged becoming more advantaged.

Lastly, we want to note that the ethnic border conflicts that mark all the nation states and plague most modern cities are reinforced in the classroom. People need a way to explain the persistent failure of minority children in schools. Rather than taking a look at how this is done, as we have tried to do here in only a limited way, most of us have ethnic labels available for talking about and explaining the failure of the different kinds of children. Ethnic group membership does not cause school failure or success, but after different kinds of children differentially succeed and fail, ethnicity becomes salient in negative ways. In the classroom we have just analyzed, at the beginning of the year, the white, Black, and Puerto Rican children divided their time with each other without regard to ethnicity. By the end of the year, the two Black children, the four Puerto Rican children and the eighteen white children began to form isolates. By late May, the terms "nigger" and "spic" began to show up, and border fights between members of the different groups became a daily occurrence. How this happened is worth another paper. We are pointing to this phenomenon now because we believe that it flows rather directly from the experiences we have described for the children in this classroom. For it is the minority children who engage in the bulk of the miscommunication with the teacher. Under these conditions, ethnic solidarity becomes a refuge from the negative relationships offered to the children in the classrooms. [. . .] The problem in this classroom was not ethnicity, but a set of contexts in terms of which ethnic differences were turned into ethnic borders. [. . .]

References

Barth, F. 1969. Introduction. In F. Barth (ed.) *Ethnic Groups and Boundaries*. Boston: Little, Brown and Company.

Bateson, G. 1955. The message 'This is play'. In B. Schaffner (ed.) *Group Processes*. New York: Josiah Macy Jr Foundation.

Birdwhistell, R. 1970. *Kinesics and Context*. Philadelphia: Pennsylvania University Press.

Cazden, C., V. John and D. Hymes (eds) 1972. *Functions of Language in the Classroom*. New York: Teachers College Press.

Craig, D. 1971. Education and Creole English in the West Indies. In D. Hymes (ed.) *Pidginisation and Creolisation of Languages*. Cambridge: Cambridge University Press.

DeCamp, D. 1971. Introduction. In D. Hymes (ed) *Pidginisation and Creolisation of Languages*. Cambridge: Cambridge University Press.

Efron, D. 1941. *Gesture and the Environment*. New York: King's Crown Press.

Erickson, F. 1975. Gatekeeping and the melting pot: Interaction in counseling interviews. *Harvard Educational Review* 45 (1): 44–70.

Goffman, E. 1974. *Frame Analysis*. New York: Harper Colophon Books.

Hall, E. T. 1966. *The Hidden Dimension*. New York: Doubleday.

Halliday, M. 1976. Antilanguages. *American Anthropologist* 78: 570–578.

Hostetler, J. and G. Huntington 1971. *Children in Amish Society*. New York: Holt, Rinehart & Winston.

Labov, W. 1972. *Language in the Inner City*. Philadelphia: University of Pennsylvania Press.

Labov W. and C. Robins 1969. A note on the relation of reading failure to peer group status in urban ghettos. *Florida FL Reporter* 7: 54–57, 167.

Lambert, W. 1967. A social psychology of bilingualism. *Journal of Social Issues*. 73: 91–109.

McDermott, J. 1976. *The Culture of Experience*. New York: New York University Press.

McDermott, R. P. 1976. *Kids Make Sense: An Ethnographic Account of the Interactional Management of Success and Failure in One First Grade Classroom*. PhD dissertation, Stanford University.

McDermott, R. P. 1977. School relations as contexts for learning in school. *Harvard Educational Review* 47: 298–313.

McDermott, R. P. et al. 1978. Criteria for an ethnographically adequate description of concerted activities and their contexts. *Semiotica* 24 (3/4): 245–275.

McQuown, N. et al. 1971. *The Natural History of an Interview*. University of Chicago Library Microfilm Collection of Manuscripts in Cultural Anthropology Series 15, no. 95–98.

Moerman, M. 1965. Ethnic identification in a complex civilisation: Who are the Lue? *American Anthropologist* 67: 1215–1226.

Philips, S. U. 1972. Participant structures and communicative competence: Warm Springs children in community and classroom. In C. Cazden, V. John and D. Hymes (eds) *Functions of Language in the Classroom*. New York: Teachers College Press.

Piestrup, A. 1973. *Black Dialect Interference and Accommodation of Reading Instruction in First Grade*. Berkeley: Monographs of the Language-Behaviour Research Laboratory.

Scheflen, A. E. 1974. *How Behaviour Means*. New York: Anchor Press.

Wanat, S. 1976. Reading and readiness. *Visible Language* 10: 101–127.

Wolfram, W. 1973. Objective and subjective parameters of language among second generation Puerto Ricans in East Harlem. In R. Shuy and R. Fasold (eds) *Language Attitudes*. Washington, DC: Georgetown University Press.

Ray McDermott is Professor of Education and Anthropology at Stanford University, US, and is co-author (with H. Varenne) of *Successful Failure: The School America Builds* (Boulder: Westview Press, 1998). Kenneth Gospodinoff was a Research Assistant at the Albert Einstein School of Medicine in the Bronx (1973–76) and The Rockefeller University in Manhattan, US (1976–77).

Chapter 22

John Gumperz and Eduardo Hernández-Chavez

1972

BILINGUAL CODE-SWITCHING[a]

R ECENT SYSTEMATIC RESEARCH in the inner city has successfully disproved the notions of those who characterize the language of low-income populations as degenerate and structurally underdeveloped. There is overwhelming evidence to show that when both middle-class and nonmiddle-class children, no matter what their native language, dialect, or ethnic background, come to school at the age of five or six, they have control of a fully formed grammatical system. The mere fact that their system is distinct from that of their teacher does not mean that their speech is not rule governed. Speech features that strike the teacher as different do not indicate failure to adjust to some universally accepted English norm; rather, they are the output of dialect or language-specific syntactic rules every bit as complex as those of Standard English (Labov, 1969).[b]

It is clear furthermore that the above linguistic differences also reflect far-reaching and systematic cultural differences. Like the plural societies of Asia and Africa, American urban society is characterized by the coexistence of a variety of distinct cultures. Each major ethnic group has its own heritage, its own body of traditions, values, and views about what is right and proper. These traditions are passed on from generation to generation as part of the informal family or peer-group socialization process and are encoded in folk art and literature, oral or written [. . .]

[But m]inority groups in urbanized societies are never completely isolated from the dominant majority. To study their life ways without reference to surrounding populations is to distort the realities of their everyday lives. All residents of modern industrial cities are subject to the same laws and are exposed to the same system

a These extracts are taken from J. Gumperz and E. Hernández-Chavez (1972) 'Bilingualism, bidialect-alism, and classroom interaction', in C. Cazden, V. John and D. Hymes (eds) *Functions of Language in the Classroom* New York: Teachers College Press pp. 84—108.
b See Rickford, this volume.

of public education and mass communication. Minority group members, in fact, spend much of their day in settings where dominant norms prevail. Although there are significant individual differences in the degree of assimilation, almost all minority group members, even those whose behavior on the surface may seem quite deviant, have at least a passive knowledge of the dominant culture. What sets them off from others is not simply the fact that they are distinct, but the juxtaposition of their own private language and life styles with those of the public at large.[c]

This juxtaposition, which is symbolized by constant alternation between in-group and out-group modes of acting and expression, has a pervasive effect on everyday behavior. Successful political leaders, such as Bobby Seale and the late Martin Luther King, rely on it for much of their rhetorical effect. C. Mitchell-Kernan, in her recent ethnographic study of verbal communication in an Afro-American community (1969), reports that her informants' everyday conversation reveals an overriding concern—be it positive or negative—with majority culture.

Majority group members who have not experienced a similar disjuncture between private and public behavior frequently fail to appreciate its effect.[d] They tend merely to perceive minority group members as different, without realizing the effect that this difference may have on everyday communication. This ignorance of minority styles of behavior seems to have contributed to the often discussed notion of "linguistic deprivation." No one familiar with the writings of Afro-American novelists of the last decade and with the recent writings on black folklore can maintain that low-income blacks are nonverbal. An exceptionally rich and varied terminological system, including such folk concepts as *sounding, signifying, rapping, running it down, chucking, jiving, marking*, etc., all referring to verbal strategies (i.e., different modes of achieving particular communicative ends), testifies to the importance Afro-American culture assigns to verbal art (Kochman, 1969; Mitchell-Kernan, 1969). Yet, inner-city black children are often described as nonverbal, simply because they fail to respond to the school situation. It is true that lower-class children frequently show difficulty in performing adequately in formal interviews and psychological tests. But these tests are frequently administered under conditions that seem unfamiliar and, at times, threatening to minority-group children. When elicitation conditions are changed, there is often a radical improvement in response (Labov, 1969; Mehan, 1970).

[Bilingual code-switching][e]

The fact that bilingualism and biculturalism have come to be accepted as major goals in inner-city schools is an important advance. But if we are to achieve this goal we require at least some understanding of the nature of code alternation and

---

c Compare the account here with Hewitt's notion of 'polyculture' (this volume).

d For other discussions in this volume of race, ethnicity and the relationship between public and private spheres, see Hill, Bokhorst-Heng and Honeyford.

e For an introductory view of code-switching, see e.g. Chapter 2 of J. Holmes (2001) *Introduction to Sociolinguistics: 2nd Edition*. London: Pearson Education. For a relatively recent collection of research papers, see e.g. P. Auer (ed.) (1998) *Code-Switching in Conversation*. London: Routledge.

its meaning in everyday interaction. Bilingualism is, after all, primarily a linguistic term, referring to the fact that linguists have discovered significant alternations in [pronunciation, word structure and grammar] in studying the verbal behavior of a particular population. Although bilingual phenomena have certain linguistic features in common, these features may have quite different social significance.

Furthermore, to the extent that social conditions affect verbal behavior, findings based on research in one type of bilingual situation may not necessarily be applicable to another socially different one.

Sociolinguistic studies of bilingualism for the most part focus on the linguistic aspects of the problem. [. . .] [and t]he assumption is that the presence or absence of particular linguistic alternates directly reflects significant information about such matters as group membership, values, relative prestige, power relationships, etc.

There is no doubt that such one-to-one relationships between language and social phenomena do exist in most societies. Where speakers control and regularly employ two or more speech varieties and continue to do so over long periods of time, it is most likely that each of the two varieties will be associated with certain activities or social characteristics of speakers. This is especially the case in formal or ceremonial situations, such as religious or magical rites, court proceedings, stereotyped introductions, greetings, or leave-takings. Here language, as well as gestures and other aspects of demeanor, may be so rigidly specified as to form part of the defining characteristics of the setting—so much so that a change in language may change the setting.

There are, however, many other cases where such correlations break down. Consider the following sentences [. . .] from a recently recorded discussion between two educated Mexican-Americans.

Excerpt 1

Woman:	Well, I'm glad that I met you. Okay?
M:	Andale, pues and do come again, mmm?
Translation:	*Okay, swell*

Excerpt 2

M: Con ellos dos. With each other. La señora trabaja en la canería orita,
with the two of them   *The mother works in the cannery right now*

you know? She was . . . con Francine jugaba . . . with my little girl.
she used to play with Francine . . .

Excerpt 3

M: There's no children in the neighborhood. Well . . . sí hay criaturas
there are children.

Excerpt 4

M: . . . those friends are friends from Mexico que tienen chamaquitos
who have little children.

Excerpt 5

    M: . . . that has nothing to do con que le hagan esta . . .
                                with their doing this.

Excerpt 6

    M: But the person . . . de . . . de grande is gotta have something in his
                               as an adult
    mouth.

Excerpt 7

    M: An' my uncle Sam es el mas agabachado
                        is the most Americanized.

It would be futile to predict the occurrence of either English or Spanish in the above utterances by attempting to isolate social variables that correlate with linguistic form. Topic, speaker, setting are common in each. Yet the code changes sometimes in the middle of a sentence.

Language mixing of this type is by no means a rarity. Linguists specializing in bilingualism cite it to provide examples of extreme instances of interference.[f] Some native speakers in ethnically diverse communities are reluctant to admit its existence. It forms the subject of many humorous treatises, and in Texas it tends to be referred to by pejorative terms, such as Tex-Mex.[g] Yet in spite of the fact that such extreme code-switching is held in disrepute, it is very persistent wherever minority language groups come in close contact with majority language groups under conditions of rapid social change.

One might, by way of an explanation, simply state that both codes are equally admissible in some contexts and that code-switching is merely a matter of the individual's momentary inclination. Yet the alternation does carry meaning. Let us compare the following passage from a recent analysis of [the use of pronouns in Russian] with an excerpt from a conversation.

Excerpt 8

> An arrogant aristocratic lieutenant and a grizzled, older captain find themselves thrust together as the only officers on an isolated outpost in the Caucasus. Reciprocal formality at first seems appropriate to both. But while the latter is sitting on the young lieutenant's bed and discussing a confidential matter he switches to *ty* (tu). When the lieutenant appears to suggest insubordination, however, the captain reverts to *vy* (vous) as he issues a peremptory demand. [. . .]
>
>   [Friedrich, 1966, p. 240]

[Compare this with Excerpt 9, from a bilingual conversation between a linguist, E, and his colleague, M:]

---

f See Alleyne, this volume.
g Compare Hill, this volume.

Excerpt 9

> M: I don't think I ever have any conversations in my dreams. I just dream.
> Ha. I don't hear people talking: I jus' see pictures.
>
> E: Oh. They're old-fashioned, then. They're not talkies yet, huh?
>
> M: They're old-fashioned. No. They're not talkies, yet. No. I'm trying to
> think. Yeah, there too have been talkies. Different. In Spanish and
> English both. An' I wouldn't be too surprised if I even had some in
> Chinese. *(Laughter).* Yeah, E. Deveras. (M *offers* E *a cigarette, which is*
>   *Really*
> *refused.)* Tú no fumas, ¿verdad? Yo tampoco. Dejé de fumar.
>   *You really don't smoke? Me neither. I gave up smoking*

The two societies, the social context, and the topics discussed differ, yet the shift from English to Spanish [in 9] has connotations similar to the alternation between the formal (second person pronoun) *vy* (vous) and the informal *ty* (tu) [in 8]. Both signal a change in interpersonal relationship in the direction of greater informality or personal warmth. Although the linguistic signs differ, they reflect similar social strategies. What the linguist identifies as code switching may convey important social information [. . .]

[Some further data analysis]

The conversation cited in Excerpts [1—7 and 9] was recorded in an institution specializing in English instruction for small Mexican immigrant children. The staff, ranging in age from recent high school graduates to persons in their middle fifties, includes a large number of people of Mexican or Mexican-American descent as well as some English-speaking Americans. Of the latter group, several speak Spanish well. The recording was made by [. . .] E, a native American of Mexican ancestry who is employed as an adviser for the program. [M, his interlocutor,] is a community counselor employed in the program. She is a woman without higher education who has been trained to assist the staff in dealing with the local community. She has had some experience in public affairs. In spite of the difference in education and salary, both participants regard each other as colleagues within the context of the program. When speaking Spanish they address each other by the reciprocal *tú*. The program director or a Spanish-speaking outsider visitor would receive the respectful *usted*. Conversations within the office are normally carried on in English, although [. . .] there are marked stylistic differences that distinguish interaction among Mexican-Americans from interaction across ethnic boundaries.

For analysis the taped transcript was roughly divided into episodes, each centering around a single main topic. Episodes were then subdivided into "turns of speaking" (i.e., one or more sentences reflecting a speaker's response to another's comment). The author and the interviewer cooperated in the analysis of social meaning.

Two types of information were utilized. Turns containing a code-switch were first examined as to their place within the structure of the total conversation in terms of such questions as, What were the relevant antecedents of the turn and what followed? or, What was the turn in response to, either in the same or preceding episodes? The purpose here was to get as detailed as possible an estimation of the speaker's intent. In the second stage a phrase from the other language would be substituted for the switched phrase [. . . — b]y this method it was possible to get an idea of what the code switch contributed to the meaning of the whole passage.

Before discussing the social aspects of code-switching, some discussion of what it is that is being switched is necessary. Not all instances of Spanish words in the text are necessarily instances of code switching. Expressions like *ándale pues* (Excerpt 1) or *dice* (he says) are normally part of the bilingual's style of English. Speakers use such expressions when speaking to others of the same ethnic background in somewhat the same way that Yiddish expressions like *nebbish, oi gewalt*, or interjections like *du hoerst* characterize the in-group English style of some American Jews. They serve as stylistic ethnic identity markers and are frequently used by speakers who no longer have effective control of both languages. The function of such forms as an ethnic identity marker becomes particularly clear in the following sequence, already cited in Excerpt 1, between M and a woman visitor in her office.

Excerpt 10

> WOMAN: Well, I'm glad that I met you. Okay?
> M: Andale, pues and do come again, mmm?
>   *Okay, swell*

The speakers, both Mexican-Americans, are strangers who have met for the first time. The *ándale pues* is given in response to the woman's *okay*, as if to say, "Although we are strangers we have the same background and should get to know each other better." [. . .]

There are [. . .] also some examples of change within single sentences [. . .] [In Excerpt 4, the switch is in the relative clause and in Excerpt 5, it occurs in] the verb complement. [. . . But] aside from single loan words, entire sentences are most easily borrowed. [. . .]

When asked why they use Spanish in an English sentence or vice versa, speakers frequently come up with explanations like the following taken from our conversation:

Excerpt 11

> If there's a word that I can't find, it keeps comin' out in Spanish.

Excerpt 12

> I know what word I want and finally when I . . . well, bring it out in
> Spanish, I know the person understands me.

Difficulty in finding the right word clearly seems to account for examples like [13]

Excerpt 13

> M: ¿Será que quiero la tetera? para pacify myself?
> *It must be that I want the baby bottle to . . .*

[. . .] In other instances, some items of experience, some referents or topics are more readily recalled in one language than in another, as in:

Excerpt 14

> M: I got to thinking vacilando el punto este
> *mulling over this point.*

Excerpt 15

> M: They only use English when they have to . . . like for cuando van
> *when they go*
>
> de compras
> *shopping.*

Linguistically motivated switches into English occur when the discussion calls for psychological terminology or expressions, e.g., *pacify, relax, I am a biter.* Such expressions or modes of talking seem rarely used in typically Mexican-American settings [. . .]

In many other instances, however, there seems to be no linguistic reason for the switch. *Sí hay criaturas* (Excerpt 3) is directly translated without hesitation pause in the following sentence. Many other Spanish expressions have English equivalents elsewhere in the text. Furthermore, there are several pages of more general, abstract discussion that contain no Spanish at all.

One might hypothesize that [the participants follow each other in their selection of a code, but t]his clearly not the case. Several questions asked in English elicit Spanish responses and vice versa.

In discussing the social aspects of switching, it is important to note that while the overt topic discussed is the use of English and Spanish, much of the conversation is dominated by a concern with Mexican versus non-Mexican, i.e., common middle-class values or group membership. Spanish occurs most in episodes dealing with typically Mexican-American experiences. In several places fears are expressed that Mexican-American children are losing their language and thus, by implication, denying their proper cultural heritage. To some extent the juxtaposition of English and Spanish symbolizes the duality of value systems evidenced in the discussion.

At the start of the conversation several exchanges dealing with the mechanics of tape-recorder operation are entirely in English. Code shifts begin with a sequence where M asks E why he is recording their talk and E responds:

Excerpt 16

> E: I want to use it as a . . . as an example of how Chicanos can shift
> back and forth from one language to another.
> M: Ooo. Como andábamos platicando
> *Oh. Like we were saying.*

M's switch to Spanish here is a direct response to his, E's, use of the word *Chicanos*. Her statement refers to previous conversations they have had on related subjects and suggests that she is willing to treat the present talk as a friendly chat among fellow Chicanos rather than as a formal interview. [. . .]

On the whole, one has the impression that, except for a few episodes dealing with recollections of family affairs, the entire conversation is basically in English. English serves to introduce most new information, while Spanish provides stylistic embroidering to amplify the speaker's intent. Spanish sentences frequently take the form of precoded, stereotyped, or idiomatic phrases.

While ethnic identity is important as the underlying theme, the actual contextual meanings of code alternation are more complex.

Turning to a more detailed analysis, many of the Spanish passages reflect direct quotes or reports of what M has said in Spanish or of what other Mexican-Americans have told her, for example:

Excerpt 17

> Because I was speakin' to my baby . . . my ex-baby-sitter, and we were talkin' about the kids you know, an' I was tellin' her . . . uh, "Pero, como, you know . . . uh . . . la Estela y la Sandi . . .
> *"But, how, you know . . . uh . . . Estella and Sandi are*
>
> relistas en el telefón. Ya hablan mucho inglés." Dice,
> *very precocious on the telephone. They already speak a lot of English." She says,*
>
> "Pos . . . sí. Mira tú," dice, "Pos . . . el . . . las palabras del televisión.
> *"Well, yes. Just imagine," she says, "well the words on television*
>
> Ya que me dice . . . ya me pide dinero pa'l ayscrín y . . ." You know?
> *And she already asks me for money for ice cream and . . .*
>
> "Ya lue . . . y eso no es nada, espérate los chicharrones, you know, when
> *"And then . . . and that isn't anything, wait for the kids*
>
> they start school" . . .

Throughout the conversation Spanish is used in quoting statements by individuals whose Chicano identity is emphasized [, . . . b]ut the pattern of quoting Chicanos in Spanish and talking about them in English is reversed in the following passage, in which M reports on the way she talks to her children:

Excerpt 18

> Yeah. Uh-huh. She'll get . . . "Linda, you don'do that, mija . . . La vas . . .
> *daughter you are going to . . .*
>
> you're going to get her . . . give her . . . a bad habit." Le pone el dedo
> *he gives her her finger,*
>
> pa'que se lo muerda you know, "Iiya, she'll bite the heck out of you." "Ow!"
> *to bite,*
>
> La otra grita So, una es sadist y la otra es masochist (*Laughter.*)
> *The other one yells. one is a sadist and the other is a masochist.*

Further enquiry again reveals that in M's family children are ordinarily addressed in English.[h] [. . .]

In the next group of examples the switch to Spanish signals the relative confidentiality or privateness of the message. The first example, cited in Excerpt 2 above, is a case in point:

Excerpt 19

> With each other. La señora trabaja en la canería orita,   you know?
> *The mother works in the cannery right now*

Here M's voice is lowered, the loudness decreasing in somewhat the same way that confidentiality is signaled in English monolingual speech. Next, consider the following:

Excerpt 20

> E: An'how . . . about how about now?
> M: Estos . . . me los hallé . . . estos Pall Malls me los hallaron
>   *These . . . I found . . .   these Pall Malls they were found for me . . .*
>
>   No, I mean . . .

M has been talking about the fact that she smokes very little, and E discovers some cigarettes on her desk. Her Spanish, punctuated by an unusually large number of hesitation pauses, lends to the statement an air of private confession. She is obviously slightly embarrassed.

Note the almost regular alternation between Spanish and English in the next passage:

Excerpt 21

> Mm-huh. Yeah. An' . . . an' they tell me, "How did you quit, Mary?" I di'n'
> quit. I . . . I just stopped. I mean it wasn' an effort I made que voy a dejar
>   *that I'm going to stop*
> de fumar porque me hace daño o
> *smoking because it's harmful to me, or . . .*
>
> this or that, uh-uh. It just . . . that . . . eh . . . I used to pull butts out of
> the . . . the . . . the wastepaper basket. Yeah. *(Laughter)*. I used to go
> look in the *(unclear)* se me acababan los cigarros
>   *my cigarettes would run out*
>
> en la noche I'd get desperate, y ahi voy al basurero a buscar, a sacar, you
> *at night*   *and there I go to the wastebasket to look for some, to get some.*
>
> know? *(Laughter)*.

The juxtaposition of the two codes here is used to great stylistic effect in depicting the speaker's attitudes. The Spanish phrases, partly by being associated

---

h More generally, though, when reporting someone else's speech, bilingual speakers often use a language that's different from the language that was originally used in the utterance reported.

with content like "it is harmful to me" or with references to events like "cigarettes running out at night" and through intonational [. . .] clues, convey a sense of personal feeling. The English phrases are more neutral by contrast.[i] The resulting effect of alternate personal involvement and clinical detachment vividly reflects M's ambiguity about her smoking [. . .]

[Meaning in code-choice]

It seems clear that, in all these cases, what the linguist sees merely as alternation between two systems serves definite and clearly understandable communicative ends. The speakers do not merely switch from one variety to another, but they build on the coexistence of alternate forms to convey information.

It can be argued that language choice reflects the speaker's minority status within the English-speaking majority, and that selection of forms in particular cases is related to such factors as ethnic identity, age, sex, degree of solidarity or confidentiality, etc. But the relationship of such social factors to speech form is quite different from what the sociologist means by correlation among variables. One could not take a rating of, for instance, ethnicity or degree of solidarity, as measured by the usual questionnaire techniques or other scaling devices, and expect this rating to predict the occurrence of Spanish or black dialect and Standard English in a text. Such ratings may determine the likelihood of a switch, but they do not tell *when a switch will occur, nor do they predict its meaning*. What seems to be involved here, rather, is a symbolic process akin to that by which words convey semantic information. Codeswitching, in other words, is meaningful in much the same way that [vocabulary] choice is meaningful.

How and by what devices does the speaker's selection of alternate forms communicate information? The process is a metaphoric process somewhat similar to what linguists interested in literary style have called *foregrounding* (Garvin, 1964). Foregrounding, in the most general sense of the term, relies on the fact that words are more than just names for things. Words also carry a host of culturally specific associations, attitudes, and values. These cultural values derive from the context in which words are usually used and from the activities with which they are associated. When a word is used in other than normal context, these associations become highlighted or foregrounded. Thus, to take an example made famous by Leonard Bloomfield (1936), the word *fox* when it refers to a man, as in "He is a fox," communicates the notions of slyness and craftiness that our culture associates with the activities of foxes.

We assume that what holds true for individual words also holds true for alternates [in pronunciation and grammar]. Whenever a speech variety is associated with a particular social category of speakers or with certain activities, this variety comes to symbolize the cultural values associated with these features of the non-linguistic environment. In other words, speech varieties, like words, are potentially

---

i Compare Hill and Clark (this volume) on involvement vs neutrality in switches between vernaculars and (standard) English.

meaningful, and in both cases this is brought out by reinterpreting meanings in relation to context. As long as the variety in question is used in its normal environment, only its basic referential sense is communicated. But when it is used in a new context, it becomes socially marked, and the values associated with the original context are mapped onto the new message.

In any particular instance of code-switching, speakers deduce what is meant by an information-processing procedure that takes account of the speaker, the addressee, the social categories to which they can be assigned in the context, the topic, etc. (Blom and Gumperz, 1970). Depending on the nature of the above factors, a wide variety of contextual meanings derives from the basic meaning inclusion (we) versus exclusion (they). This underlying meaning is then reinterpreted in the light of the co-occurring contextual factors to indicate such things as degree of involvement [. . .], anger, emphasis [. . .], change in focus [. . .], etc. [. . .]

The ability to interpret a message is a direct function of the listener's home background, his peer group experiences, and his education. Differences in background can lead to misinterpretation of messages. The sentence "He is a Sikh" has little or no meaning for an American audience, but to anyone familiar with speech behavior in northern India it conveys a whole host of meanings, since Sikhs are stereotypically known as bumblers. Similarly, the statement "He is a fox," cited above, which conveys slyness to middle-class whites, may be interpreted as a synonym for "He is handsome" by blacks. Communication thus requires both shared grammar and shared rules of language usage. Two speakers may speak closely related and, on the surface, mutually intelligible varieties of the same language, but they may nevertheless misunderstand each other because of differences in usage rules resulting from differences in background.[j] We must know the speakers' normal usage pattern, i.e., which styles are associated as unmarked forms with which activities and relationships, as well as what alternates are possible in what context, and what cultural associations these carry.

Note that the view of culture that emerges from this type of analysis is quite different from the conventional one. Linguists attempting to incorporate cultural information into their descriptions tend to regard culture as a set of beliefs and attitudes that can be measured apart from communication [. . .] Our own material suggests that culture plays a [more complex] role in communication [. . .] A person may have every intention of avoiding cultural bias, yet, by subconsciously superimposing his own interpretation on the verbal performance of others, he may nevertheless bias his judgment of their general ability, efficiency, etc. [. . .]

Bibliography

Blom, Jan Petter; and Gumperz, John J. "Social Meaning in Linguistic Structures." In John J. Gumperz and Dell Hymes (eds), *Directions in Sociolinguistics*. New York: Holt, Rinehart and Winston, 1970.

Bloomfield, Leonard. *Language*. New York: Holt, Rinehart, 1936.

j See the extracts in this volume by Philips and Gumperz (on intercultural communication).

Friedrich, Paul. "Structural Implications of Russian Pronominal Usage." In William Bright (ed.), *Sociolinguistics*. The Hague: Mouton and Co., 1967.

Garvin, Paul (ed.). *A Prague School Reader*, Washington, DC: Georgetown University Press, 1964.

Kochman, Thomas. "Rapping in the Black Ghetto." *Transaction*, February 1969: 26–34.

Labov, William. "The Logic of Non-Standard Negro English." In James E. Alatis (ed.), *Linguistics and the Teaching of Standard English*. Monograph Series on Languages and Linguistics, No. 22. Washington, DC: Georgetown University Press, 1969.

Mehan, B. Unpublished lecture on testing and bilingualism in the Chicano community, delivered to the Kroeber Anthropological Society Meetings, April 25, 1970.

Mitchell-Kernan, Claudia. "Language Behavior in a Black Urban Community." Doctoral dissertation (Working Paper No. 23, Language Behavior Research Laboratory), University of California at Berkeley, 1969.

John Gumperz was Professor of Anthropology at the University of California, Berkeley, for many years. He is a major pioneer in the study of code-switching, intercultural communication, interactional discourse, and the relations between language, interaction and ethnicity more generally. (See e.g. J. Gumperz 1982 *Discourse Strategies* Cambridge: Cambridge University Press.) Eduardo Hernández-Chavez is Director of the Chicana/o Studies Program at the University of New Mexico, US.

Chapter 23

John Taggart Clark

2003

ABSTRACT INQUIRY AND THE PATROLLING OF BLACK/WHITE BORDERS THROUGH LINGUISTIC STYLIZATION[a]

UNTIL RECENTLY, the anthropological "gaze of surveillance" within the racialized white/black binary fell almost exclusively upon African Americans (Fine 1997:64). Even if this gaze was motivated by liberal goodwill or radical praxis, its effects contributed rather disturbingly to the larger historical discursive process of making whites and whiteness natural, normal, central and unmarked.[b] Nowhere has this tendency been stronger than among linguists who continue to highlight the systematicity and richness of African American Vernacular English grammar in countering those who seek to legitimate the oppression of diasporic Africans based on linguistic differences. This same enlightening and liberating effort, however, has had the effect of fetishizing African-American interactional products (Morgan 1994; Smitherman-Donaldson 1988; Walters 1995), as well as promoting the ideology that Englishes thought to be opposite of African American and vernacular (white and elite) are somehow more standard, normal, and central.[c]

Recently the anthropological gaze has been redirected toward investigating whiteness, and how its unmarked status is re/produced and masked so as to attribute to it a timeless and natural centered status (Fine, et al. 1997; Frankenberg 1993). With some exceptions, however, these studies have tended to describe the discursive production of whiteness through large-scale social practices over longer

---

a This paper draws on J. T. Clark (1998) *Can anyone say what is reasonable?: Promoting, accommodating to, and resisting elite rhetorical inquiry in a high school classroom*, PhD dissertation, Linguistics Department, Graduate School of Arts and Sciences, Georgetown University, USA. An earlier version appeared as Patrolling class and ethnic borders through linguistic stylization, in: Goss, Nisha Merchant, Amanda R. Doran, and Anastasia Coles (eds) *Proceedings of the Seventh Annual Symposium About Language and Society* Austin, TX: University of Texas Department of Linguistics, Volume 43, Texas Linguistic Forum.

b See also Billig, this volume.

c On AAVE grammar, see Rickford (this volume); on its fetishization, see Cutler and also Urla. On standard English counterposed to AAVE, see Quirk (and also Honeyford).

stretches of time and place. Few of them focus on how whiteness is re/produced in face-to-face interaction through the most fleeting and easily overlooked linguistic details. Accordingly, this paper will show how several high school students identify a kind of rhetorical style, which I call "abstract/speculative inquiry," as white and elite through the parody of their teacher's speech. They do so by performing parodies of this inquiry with exaggerated pronunciations of [speech sounds] that in turn [evoke or "index"] white linguistic stereotypes among their interlocutors.[d]

The primary data are transcripts based on audio- and videotaped classroom interaction during a year of fieldwork in a Washington D.C. high school class (entitled "Street Law") intended to educate the (predominantly African American) students about citizen rights, law and legal procedure. The original study focussed on African American teenagers' accommodation and resistance to "Standard English." The most interesting aspects of language variation in [this class were not to be found] among the well-described and understood [grammatical] variables that linguists have used to differentiate "Standard" and "Vernacular" Englishes, but rather among discourse-level features. Indeed the teacher, himself an African American student fulfilling a community service requirement at his law school, was promoting a kind of style "regarded as more persuasive and worthy of being taken seriously (. . .) in [the] boardrooms of major corporations, or in the seminar rooms of major universities" (Erickson 1984:83). This inquiry style privileges the exchange of abstract, speculative, and vicarious information in which speakers assume an "objective" stance in discussing situations where concrete people are either absent or abstracted. The teacher's efforts to promote abstract/speculative inquiry were often challenged by Street Law students who sought to conduct inquiry based on "real-world," concrete, empirically demonstrated, and personally experienced instances of human behavior related, preferably, in anecdotal form or "concrete/empirical style" (Erickson 1969; Clark 1998). Here I investigate some of these student challenges to the Street Law teacher's language promotion project. I argue that to the extent that the Street Law students invoke white, elite, and *un*black linguistic stereotypes at the same moment that they are resisting abstract/speculative inquiry, they identify abstract/speculative inquiry as a white (and elite, and unblack) way of talking.

Abstract speculative and concrete/empirical inquiry

Users of abstract/speculative inquiry appear to pass themselves off as spokespersons for the "objective truth." They present themselves as reliable, honest brokers for their ideas by presenting a proposition as if it were independent of them, and therefore not besmirched by their subjectivity. They achieve this godlike objectivity or "deity mode" (Kiesling 1996) by typically leaving their personal selves out of the arguments they are presenting. In addition to removing themselves from their inquiry, abstract/speculative users extract other humans from their

---

d See Hill and Gumperz and Hernández-Chavez (this volume) on both neutral vs personalized style, and on processes of symbolic evocation.

argumentation through such well-known linguistic processes as passivization and nominalization (Schatzman and Strauss 1966; Fowler and Kress 1979).[e] Together these linguistic processes work to give interlocutors the impression that the ideas have "an objective life, existing independent of any person expressing them" (Kochman 1981:21).

The Street Law teacher, Len, models such objectivity for the students during a class discussion of obscenity in raunchy music videos and First Amendment protection of the freedom of speech (Example 1).

Example 1[1]

39   Len: So Juan is they—are they obscene, should they be taken off, or
             are they not obscene and they should stay on, or—
40   Juan: Well, they doin' their *thing*. (*laughter*) They alright.
41   Aisha: They, they do anything they gotta do to sell their lives.

In initiating inquiry on whether raunchy rap videos should be considered protected speech under the U.S. Constitution, Len does not elicit the students' opinions on this or on the dancers' motives. Rather, he asks the class whether the videos partake of abstract, nominalized "obscenity." The processes of passivization (*be taken off*) and the lack of a human semantic experiencer for the predicate *obscene* (obscene to *whom?*) further drain Len's inquiry of human reference. Len's de-populated rhetoric contrasts with the students' response in lines 40 and 41, which eschews abstraction and focuses on relatively concrete human actors and their motivations.

My description of these two inquiry styles recalls, but is distinct from, Bernstein's (1971) distinction between (middle-class) elaborated code and (working-class) restricted code, which, read in the most [. . .] overdeterministically Whorfian way,[f] attributes elaborated and restricted *cognitive* capacities to the speakers of each code, respectively. It is important to note that the Street Law students are able to "do" both inquiry styles. Indeed, I will show that the students' ability to parody the abstract/speculative style entails a sufficient degree of competence to know which features to parody. Nevertheless, the Street Law students cannot "do" abstract/speculative inquiry as well as their law student teacher can. There is, in other words, a learning gap. The students, in turn, politicize this learning gap as a site of class and ethnic struggle.[g]

Marking white

Mitchell-Kernan uses the term *marking* to describe the African-American speech event of a speaker's parodistic representation of another person's speech. Marking

---

e Changing 'They lost the money' into 'The money was lost' is an example of passivisation. Changing 'The men fought each other' into 'There was a fight' is an instance of nominalisation, the verb ('fight/fought') being turned into a noun ('a fight').

f See Whorf, this volume.

g See McDermott and Gospodinoff, this volume.

functions to attribute outgroup status to the person whose speech is so marked and, by extension, to the speech itself. Following Mitchell-Kernan (1974) and Morgan (1998), I define *marking white* as the parodistic verbal performance of linguistic and paralinguistic features (e.g. gestures) commonly recognized to be stereotypically white.[h] The details of this representation are often as fleeting and subtle as a single, parodied sound, which nonetheless utters volumes of social meaning. In the examples below, I consider how the students exaggerate three such sounds to parody the white/elite style: the diphthong [ai], the vowel [i], post-vocalic [r], and prevocalic [l].[i]

Exaggerated [ai]: Example 2

Example 2 shows how one Street Law student, Chanika, marks the author/ethnographer as white in something as brief as a greeting. I had set up the camera and turned it on, pointing it in Chanika's direction. Then I left the room. During my absence, Chanika scowled at the camera and rudely saluted it with an extended middle finger. Moments later, I reentered the room and greeted her.

Example 2

John: How are you doin'?
Chanika: H[ai]. (*1 second pause*) F[ai]n

Chanika pronounces these vowels quite differently than she usually does[, and evokes a linguistic stereotype of whiteness that we both have access to.] Erickson (1987) and Giroux (1992) have described such moves as "border constructions," that is, the making salient of racial, ethnic, class and gender differences. Thus, Chanika marks me as white through this linguistic performance and through my understanding of its social meaning.

Exaggerated [i]: Example 3

The following example shows an instance of students explicitly attributing white identity to Len, the African American teacher, in their reaction to a phrase he utters. During a discussion of defamation, I bring up an example of how a tabloid magazine claimed that a 97-year-old Arkansas woman was pregnant and ask how that might or might not constitute defamation. Len responds:

Example 3

484 Len: . . . but then she's also gonna have to prove, uh reputation damage too. If everybody thinks it's a joke hee hee ho ho funny, (*Chanika breaks into laughter*)
485 Len: (*chuckling*) [You know nobody could—

---

h Compare Hill (this volume), and for some non-parodic crossing, Cutler and Hewitt.
i [ai] as in the words 'price', 'ripe', 'write'; [i] as in 'fleece', 'creep', 'speak'; post-vocalic [r] as in US 'car', 'card', 'start'; prevocalic [l] – L sounds before a vowel.

486   Lakesha: Oh he [said "hee hee ho ho funny". A little white kid!
487   Chanika: [Hee hee ho ho funny
488   Len: [Nobody could really, you know get— (   )

Upon hearing the phrase *hee hee ho ho funny*, Chanika bursts into laughter. Lakesha then repeats this expression using a exaggeratedly high and tense pronunciation of the [i] sound in *hee* and *funny*. To top it off, Lakesha utters *a little white kid* immediately following her linguistic performance, explicitly steering the performance's interpretation among her interlocutors. Like Chanika in the previous example, Lakesha is marking Len as white. Unlike the previous example, the source of this outburst of linguistic lampoonery seems to have come from Len's use of the phrase *hee hee ho ho funny*. What triggered Chanika's laughter? Was it solely Len's pronunciation of the /i/ tokens in the phrase? Perhaps the students find something humorously incongruous about an adult black man uttering a phrase they deem to be more becoming—as Lakesha points out—to a "little white kid." Attributing childishness and whiteness to Len's utterance may also indicate a kind of gender censure. What is significant is that Lakesha and Chanika grab onto the scant linguistic resource available (the sound [i]) and mark whiteness in it.

Exaggerated [r]: Examples 4a and 4b

The two previous examples have shown Street Law students marking the talk of the ethnographer and the teacher as white. I now turn to instances of students marking abstract/speculative inquiry itself as white. Examples 4a and 4b come from the same class as the previous example, in which the topic was "limitations of free speech." Len asks the class whether raunchy music videos are obscene, and therefore not protected speech. Akeem suggests that they have artistic value.

Example 4a

1   Len: *Do they abide, to li[terary, a**r**tistic political or scientific value*
2   Akeem: [No they dancin' they showin' a**r**t. It's a**r**t
3   Len: You know, so music video-dancin' is an *a**rr**t*.
4   Akeem: It's a *a**r**t*. They showin'
5   *Chanika:*   (   ) **aa**t
6   Aisha: I, I, I didn't know a**r**t supposed to be those—

As in Example 1, Len uses the word *art(istic)* in a packed, abstract context, complete with the formal lexical item *abide* (turn 1). Various pronunciations of the /r/ [sound] emerge in this passage—from [zero—/r/ pronounced as a vowel ('vocalised')—to [r] that is strongly pronounced]. This range of pronunciation is represented here by a three-way distinction:

vocalized (zero) [r] →a**a**t
mildly pronounced [r] →a**r**t
strongly pronounced [r] →a**rr**t.

Chanika's pronunciation of *art* (turn 5) is a vocalized or zero "r" in contrast to Len's moderate or heavy pronunciation of the "r." This is typical of both speakers' pronunciations of the sound in that environment. Later, the word comes up again.

Example 4b

128	Len:	So we got a, what uh, what do those videos express? Do you think they're expressing a valuable information or idea that need to get out there?
129	Manuel:	It's music. It's just music, and it should be allowed to be expressed in any way. It's a[r]t.
130	Len:	Okay. So you see it as a[r]t.
131	Chanika:	A[*rrt^h*]
132	Len:	What about Juan, he said it was fine what do you see it as?
133	Juan:	I see it as [aat].
134	Len:	What kind of a[rr]t?
135	Juan:	Nasty! (dancin' ( ))
136	Lakesha:	I see it as a crazy performance.
137	Len:	Akeem
138	Akeem:	Same thing, it's a[r]t.
139	Chanika:	I don't, I don't know what kind of **aat** it is, it's just something on television.
140	Lakesha:	=Crazy, crazy.
141	Aisha:	It shouldn't even be, considered, a[rr]t

Again, Len echoes an institutional and abstractly worded legal definition of "obscenity" in line 128. In fact, the phrase *valuable information or idea* comes directly from a written definition of obscenity that Len had distributed that day. Presumably, this wording is based on "official" legal texts as well. Manuel, in 129, continues the same stylistic key. Len then positively evaluates Manuel's contribution and his justification. At this point (line 131), Chanika, who is not a ratified interlocutor, at least in classic classroom discourse, utters the word *art* with a heavy, "hyper-rhotic" [r], and a clearly [enunciated] final [t].

However, Chanika's typical pronunciation of the "r" in *art* (in the middle and at the end of words) is zero, and [sounds like [t] aren't generally enunciated so clearly at the end of words]. Chanika's one-word utterance is potentially more than a light-hearted commentary on outgroup pronunciations of a sound. It is also a commentary on the raced and classed abstract/speculative talk that is going on. Regarding the former, Chanika highlights the [r] and [t] among her fellow interlocutors who have access to linguistic stereotypes that contrast [the use of [r] among whites] with vernacular black r-lessness.[j] Regarding the latter, Chanika's pronunciation of the final /t/ in *art* is highly exaggerated for *any* variety of English. [. . .] This overly fussy pronunciation indexes another linguistic stereotype among

---

j See Cutler, this volume.

her interlocutors, which she described for me in a personal interview: that of the "uppity," upwardly striving, speaker who goes to great lengths to "speak correctly." Chanika's marking the word *art* serves to show that the talk that is now going on around her is foreign, alien.

Exaggerated [l]: Example 5

Another example showing the Street Law students marking the abstract/speculative rhetorical style as white and outgroup comes after Len asks the students whether a sportscaster's description of an African American athlete as a "great, fast, wild jungle cat" should be considered an ethnic slur, and therefore an example of speech not protected by the U.S. Constitution.

Example 5

638	Len:	So, so we're sayin', so, does, does does it depend on your interpretation of what "great, fast wild jungle cats" mean?
639	Aisha:	Yeah.
640	Len:	You know, does it, is-are are, is he, is he com—is he comparing the players to animals?=
641	Aisha:	[=He could.
642	Chanika:	[If the man white, it's an ethnic slur
643	Len:	[Or is he sayin', or is he sayin' that you know, what if he's a cat lover?
644	Chanika:	[If he black, it's fighting words
645	Len:	What if he likes lions and tigers? He thinks they're very powerful, very quick.
646	Aisha:	Oh, come on!
647	Len:	What the [thing is what the thing is, we do, we do we do have a tendency]
648	Akeem:	[Here goes the hypothetical questions.
649	Len:	[to relate people to uh=
650	Chanika:	[I don't think so John I mean uh, [Len. I don't think so **Len**.
651	Lakesha:	[Len
652	Juan:	[Let's go with the black fan on the field.

At 650, Chanika mistakenly calls Len "John," the name of the white ethnographer. Chanika catches her slip, and as she begins to repair it, Lakesha conveniently reminds Chanika of the teacher's correct name. Immediately after, Chanika performs the [l] in the word *Len* with a [style of] pronunciation[2] that is understood by her interlocutors (and many other North Americans) as part of a stereotypical white southern accent. In both instances, fleeting as they are, Chanika white-identifies the teacher in addressing him with the name of the white ethnographer as well as pronouncing his name in a stereotypical (southern) white manner. Crucially, this happens in response to Len's posing of speculative inquiry in turn 645, which Akeem, remarkably, names explicitly in 648 (*Here goes the hypothetical questions*). Chanika's slip of the tongue and pronunciation in this context mark Len's abstract/speculative "what if" inquiry as white.

Marking white, marking elite

In Street Law, as elsewhere, issues of race and class (as well as gender) are not easily separated. In fact, several instances of the students' lampooning of abstract/speculative inquiry cannot be called "marking white" without rendering the students' class border constructions invisible and/or reducible to their racial border constructions. Example 6 shows an instance of the Street Law students rather explicitly ridiculing the teacher's highly abstract framing of a discussion of Affirmative Action.

Example 6

614	Len:	So so Jennifer, I'll ask you again, based on that example, you know, do you think that, do you think that Affirmative Action is working?
615	Jennifer:	[Yes
616	Juan:	[( ) question.
617	Len:	Do you think it's a good thing to have?=
618	Lakesha:	=I know! You should be, a a a a law professor.
619	Len:	Who?
620	Lakesha:	[You!
621	Juan:	[uh, heh, heh, heh
622	Len:	Why?
623	Lakesha:	[Cause you ask so much, so much *questions* (*creaky voice*).
624	Juan:	[heh heh heh heh heh uh heh heh heh
625	Lakesha:	And every time!
626	Len:	Well how else are you [gonna work? how else are you gonna learn?
627	Chanika:	["Do you think that should wo[**rrk**ʰ]?" "Do you think this is wo[**rrk**]**ing** now
628	Lakesha:	Every minute!
629	Chanika:	"Do you think this is where it's gonna be?" (*laughs*)
630	Juan:	"How can it be—What can you do to make this possible"
631	Lakesha:	[Creating stories and everything.
632	Akeem:	[( ) backfire
633	Chanika:	["How can it be—"
634	Len:	But but I'm but I'm sayin' let's say this is this this is this is a serious question. We, you know you live in America, you live in this society, you know. Do we, do we think that this is working? Is this, this is, for

many of us this is a serious question. Do you think that
it's working?

This example quite clearly shows the Street Law students commenting on
abstract/speculative inquiry, both through marking, as well as in more explicit
linguistic metacommentary. At 618 and 623 Lakesha expresses pique with Len's
inquiry style as well as explicitly describing and critiquing what he sounds like—
"a law professor," "creating stories and everything." While Lakesha herself does not
mock Len's inquiry in the imitative fashion that I call marking, Chanika (turns
627, 629, 633) does so with send-ups of speculative questions. In addition to
mocking Len's rhetorical inquiry, she accents these parodies with exaggerated
postvocalic [r]s, a [. . . very standard] -ING suffix [. . .], and a [very clearly
enunciated final K in *work*] (wor[k^h]). The marking/mocking continues as Juan
joins Chanika with questions that not only imitate Len's inquiry style, but also
exaggerate it.

Elements of this commentary such as Chanika's exaggerated [r] mark white as
I have described in previous examples. However, other elements of this group
mockery such as [exaggerated] [k], [standard] -ING, and the parodistic recasts do
not index shared cultural knowledge of white stereotypes as much as they mark
Len's talk as outgroup along class lines. Most of the above linguistic elements used
to display a mocking stance are *formal* and *hyperformal* rather than stereotypically
white linguistic variants [. . .]. Crucially, however, these less racially tinged variants appear alongside Chanika's hyper-rhotic white-marking, so as to implicate
whiteness not only with abstract/speculative inquiry but also with formal and
hyperformal language.

Conclusion

I have shown how a class of African American high school students mark the abstract,
speculative rhetorical inquiry promoted by their teacher as white and elite. In doing
so, I have shown how a prestigious, economically valuable way of talk loses its
purported neutrality and becomes white in real-time, face-to-face interaction. With
these parodies the students are drawing a cultural and political border, in effect
saying, "This is not our kind of talk." The consequences of such border construction have been documented elsewhere (Fordham 1996; Delpit 1995; Urciuoli
1996). Namely, the Street Law student who wishes to practice and become fluent
in the kind of inquiry that Len is promoting—and thereby gain a piece of economically valuable cultural capital—does so only at the risk of peer ostracization and
censure, by talking like one of *Them* instead of one of *Us*.

References

Bernstein, Basil 1971 *Class, Codes and Control.* London: Routledge and Kegan Paul.

Clark, John T. 1998 *"Can Anyone Say What Is Reasonable?": Promoting, Accommodating to, and Resisting Elite Rhetorical Inquiry in a High School Classroom.* Unpublished PhD dissertation, Georgetown University.

Delpit, Lisa 1995 *Other People's Children.* New York: New Press.

Erickson, Frederick 1969 *Discussion Behavior in the Black Ghetto and in White Suburbia.* Unpublished PhD dissertation, Northwestern University.

Erickson, Frederick 1984 Coherence Strategies in Black American Conversation. In *Coherence in Spoken and Written Discourse.* Deborah Tannen, ed. Pp. 81–154. Norwood, NJ: Ablex.

Erickson, Frederick 1987 Transformation and School Success: The Politics and Culture of Educational Achievement. *Anthropolgy and Education Quarterly* 18(1):335–356.

Fine, Michelle 1997 Witnessing Whiteness. In *Off White: Readings on Race, Power, and Society.* Michelle Fine *et al.*, eds. pp. 57–65. New York: Routledge.

Fine, Michelle, *et al.*, eds. 1997 *Off White: Readings on Race, Power, and Society.* New York: Routledge.

Fordham, Signithia 1996 *Blacked Out: Dilemmas of Race, Identity and Success at Capitol High.* Chicago: University of Chicago Press.

Fowler, Roger, and Gunther Kress 1979 Rules and Regulations. In *Language and Control.* Roger Fowler *et al.*, eds. pp. 26–45. London: Routledge and Kegan Paul.

Frankenberg, Ruth 1993 *White Women, Race Matters: The Social Construction of Whiteness.* Minneapolis: University of Minnesota Press.

Giroux, Henry 1992 *Border Crossings.* New York: Routledge.

Hartigan, John, Jr 1999 *Racial Situations: Class Predicaments of Whiteness in Detroit.* Princeton, NJ: Princeton University Press.

Kiesling, Scott 1996 *Shifting Constructions of Gender in a Fraternity: A Case Study.* Unpublished PhD dissertation, Georgetown University.

Kochman, Thomas 1981 *Black and White Styles in Conflict.* Chicago: University of Chicago Press.

Mitchell-Kernan, Claudia. 1974 *Language Behavior in a Black Urban Community.* Berkeley: Language Behavior Research Laboratory.

Morgan, Marcyliena 1994 Theories and Politics in African American English. *Annual Review of Anthropology* 23:325–345.

Morgan, Marcyliena 1998 More than a mood or an attitude: Discourse and verbal genres in African-American culture. In *African-American English: Structure, history and use.* Salikoko Mufwene *et al.* pp. 251–281. London and New York: Routledge.

Schatzman, Leonard, and Anselm Strauss 1966 Social Class and Modes of Communication. In *Communication and Culture: Readings in the Codes of Human Interaction.* A.G. Smith, ed. pp. 442–453. New York: Holt, Rinehart, and Winston.

Smitherman-Donaldson, Geneva 1988 Discriminatory Discourse on Afro-American Speech. In *Discourse and Discrimination.* Geneva Smitherman-Donaldson and Teun van Dijk, eds. pp. 144–175. Detroit: Wayne State University Press.

Urciuoli, Bonnie 1996 *Exposing Prejudice: Puerto Rican Experiences of Language, Race, and Class.* Boulder, CO: Westview.

Walters, Keith 1995 Contesting Representations of African American Language. *Proceedings of SALSA III* (Symposium About Language and Society—Austin). pp. 137–161. Austin: University of Texas Department of Linguistics.

Notes

1   Transcription conventions.
[   ] : phonetic transcription (*Editors:* elsewhere, square brackets indicate our own editorial amendments to the authors' texts).
(   ): unintelligible speech.
(*italics*): 'stage directions'.
Italics outside brackets : emphatic speech.
<u>Underlining</u> and **bold**: parts of the utterance focused on in the analysis.
=: latched utterances (i.e., two utterances closely connected without a noticeable overlap).

[
[: overlapping speech

2   Lengthened low, back and velar.

––––––––––––––––––––

John Taggart Clark is Assistant Professor in the English Department at California State University, Sacramento, US.

Chapter 24

Cecilia Cutler

1999

YORKVILLE CROSSING

White teens, hip hop and African American English[a]

1 Introduction

THIS PAPER RETURNS to some of the issues raised in Hatala's (1976) study of Carla, a 13 year-old white girl who was thought to speak African American Vernacular English (AAVE). When Labov reassessed Hatala's work, he argued that Carla was not an authentic speaker of AAVE because she had only acquired a subset of [pronunciation] and [intonation] features (Labov 1980).[b] In my paper, I look at the speech of 'Mike', a white 16 year-old boy who, like Carla, demonstrates the use of many AAVE [pronunciation and vocabulary] features but lacks the tense and aspect system. There were, though, some important social differences between Mike and Carla. Carla grew up in an overwhelmingly African American neighborhood and school environment in Camden, New Jersey, whereas Mike was living on Park Avenue in a neighborhood known as 'Yorkville' (one of the wealthiest in New York City) and attended an exclusive private high school. Carla's friends were mainly African American whereas most of Mike's friends were white. Carla's adoption of AAVE features may have reflected an effort to adapt to her environment, but Mike's linguistic behavior begs another explanation.

According to Tricia Rose, whites are 'fascinated by [black culture's] differences, drawn in by mainstream social constructions [of black culture] . . . as a forbidden narrative, [and] a symbol of rebellion' (1994a: 5). In this line of interpretation, the adoption of African American speech markers is an attempt by young middle class whites like Mike to take part in the complex prestige of African American youth culture, and in the following pages, I shall elaborate on this,

---

a From *Journal of Sociolinguistics* 3(4): 428–43.
b For another case study which questions the essentialism in a lot of sociolinguistic analysis, see J. Sweetland (2002) 'Unexpected but authentic use of an ethnically-marked dialect' *Journal of Sociolinguistics* 6(4): 514–36.

referring to Mike's case in order to discuss the role of hip-hop culture in young whites' motivations to use AAVE features in their speech.

2   The informant: Mike

Mike is the son of a close friend of mine and I have watched him grow up since he was six years old. I have been observing his language practices since 1993 when he was about 13, and I began collecting data in late 1995 when he was 15. At around age 13, he began to identify quite strongly with hip-hop culture.[1] He wore baggy jeans, a reverse baseball cap, designer sneakers, and developed a taste for rap music – a 'wigga' or 'white nigga' according to Smitherman's definition (1994: 168). He became part of a growing cohort of white, well-to-do teenagers referred to as 'prep school gangsters' in the popular press (Sales 1996). At around the same time he began to change the way he spoke, 'crossing' into AAVE (Rampton 1995). His everyday linguistic repertoire was strongly influenced by AAVE [pronunciation . . .][2] and hip-hop slang, and this was commented on negatively by family members who said he 'sounded like a street kid or hoodlum.' One incident in particular marks an early attempt at imitating AAVE. During a phone call with his best friend, Mike demonstrated a quick conversational repair to a typical AAVE form:

1   Mike (age 13): I gotta ask, I mean aks my mom.

In Britain, Hewitt (1986) showed that some white adolescents in primarily white neighborhoods pass through a phase 'in which they display their cultural allegiance with blacks' (1986: 159).[c] When Mike was 13–14 years old, this manifested itself in vocal criticism of groups he viewed as anti-African American (including Jews and Koreans), and he accused his mother of racism when she affectionately referred to one of his African American childhood friends as 'el negrito' (his mother is from Spain). He tried to hide the fact that he lived in an expensive neighborhood in Manhattan by giving out his older brother's Brooklyn phone number to friends and acquaintances, and in fact, this is somewhat in line with research done on hip-hop chat lines on the internet, where it is common for fans (who are primarily middle class) to try to prove their authenticity in hip-hop by claiming a connection with poverty (Rebensdorf 1996).

Mike's self-alignment with hip-hop drew on stereotyped conceptions of gangs and African American urban street culture. Discussing formative sociolinguistic studies of AAVE, Morgan criticizes their simplistic depiction of vernacular or core black culture and language as 'male, adolescent, insular, and trifling' (1994: 328), and indeed a comparable reductionism seems to be at work in the way that many white male teens interpret hip-hop culture. Mike's claims of authenticity took the form of activities he and others associated with urban black and Latino youth: he adopted a 'tag' name which he scrawled on the walls of banks and expensive apartment buildings near his house, he began experimenting with drugs, he joined

---

c See also Hewitt and Back, this volume.

a gang, and he had frequent run-ins with the police. At the end of his first year of high school (when he was 14), a 'friend' (in his words) pushed him through a glass door, cutting through several tendons and a nerve in each wrist. Following surgery and several weeks of recovery, he went out to Central Park against the doctor's orders where some rival gang members – most of them also white – held him down and broke his arms with baseball bats. His mother hoped that these experiences would scare him into changing his behavior but this was not played out immediately. Mike continued to see the same friends and was asked not to return to the private school he had been attending since kindergarten.

The following year, when he was 15, Mike began attending another private school. He seemed happier, got passing grades and began thinking about college. He was now more likely to modify his speech in the direction of standard English forms in the presence of authority figures, but he continued to use AAVE [pronunciation], hip-hop terms and tags such as 'yo' and 'know what I'm sayin' as part of his everyday speech style (and still does now at age 19). Mike is presently in his second year at a conservative private college. He has shed the gangster/ghetto image he projected in his early teens in favor of a more clean cut, 'preppie' look, yet he continues to get involved in violent confrontations. In fact, he is struggling to get out of academic and disciplinary probation at the same time as fighting a multi-million dollar legal case resulting from an altercation he had with a bouncer at a restaurant. Mike's life has of course been influenced by much more than his hip hop affiliations, and among other things, he has had to deal, like a lot of his peers, with the divorce of his parents. Even so, in spite of its origins in mainstream misrepresentations and its waning as he got older, his hip hop self-portrayal has been much more consequential for him than notions like 'adolescent phase' and 'stylistic flirtation' might at first imply.

3   Mike's speech

My long-standing relationship with Mike as a family friend allowed for longitudinal observations over more than 5 years, but for the main part of my account of his language, I will draw on individual interviews, group sessions and participant observation when Mike was 15–16 years old. In 1995–6, I began recording some one-on-one interviews with him. Later on, I was able to tape some group sessions with several of his friends, all of whom were also white (as indeed am I). On his suggestion, I also loaned him a tape recorder so he could record some sessions with his friends, and these sessions are characterized by some self-conscious addressing of the microphone interspersed with animated, interactions between Mike and his friends against a backdrop of 'hip-hop' and 'techno' music. In all, I base my account on approximately six hours of recorded material plus the observations I have made from 1992–1998.

Labov (1972, 1980), Labov and Harris (1983), and Ash and Myhill (1986) have all commented on the relative ease with which outsiders can acquire superficial [accent and vocabulary] features of another dialect as opposed to the grammar, and in line with this, most of the AAVE-like elements in Mike's speech were indeed [related to pronunciation].

In terms of grammar, there were a few cases of copula deletion[d] but it would be hard to make any claims about Mike's command of this feature, partly because there were so few [instances], but also because it occurred in [. . .] an idiomatic expression which many non-African American teens had incorporated into their vocabularies:

2   Mike (age 16; 1996): What up? What up?

He also occasionally used *is* with non-singular third person subjects (compare Wolfram and Fasold 1974: 157):

3   Mike (age 16; 1996): These niggas is got shoes on.

But he didn't display features of the AAVE grammatical system such as third singular -s absence, habitual *be*, or systematic copula deletion.[e]

His orientation to AAVE was much more evident [in his pronunciation of individual sounds – his 'segmental phonology' – and it] was displayed in for example: [the use of a weak vowel, or 'schwa', in '*the*' in front of another word beginning with a vowel;[f] in the omission of R-sounds after a vowel;[g] and in the pronunciation of 'th' as '*d*' or '*t*' ('TH-stopping')].[h] I analyzed these in random samples of his speech, counting tokens of each variable for the duration of one side of tape (approximately 15 minutes for each). Whereas in standard American English [the vowel in] *the* is pronounced [with a weak form] if a consonant follows[i] and with [a strong form] if a vowel follows,[j] many AAVE speakers use the [weak or schwa] pronunciation everywhere (Wolfram and Fasold 1974: 146). Mike used the schwa pronunciation 70 percent (n=10) of [the time . . .], as compared to 30 percent among the whites studied by Ash and Myhill (1986). Extract 4 is an example of this:

4   Mike: Dass the othah side that fucks it up.
      [dæs də ʌdə saːd dæt fʌks ɪɾ ʌp]

With regard to R-lessness, Labov showed that black speakers differed from whites [when there was an opportunity to use an R before a vowel ('linking R')]: even white New Yorkers [who are generally R-less] pronounce an (r) when followed by a vowel as in *four o'clock*, but for many in the AA speech community, '(r) . . .

---

d 'Copula deletion' involves the omission of 'is' and 'are' in phrases like 'She _ happy' and 'they _ talkin'

e 'He walk_' displays 3rd person singular -s absence; 'she be runnin', meaning 'she is usually running' in Standard English, illustrates habitual *be* (see Rickford, this volume). On the complex issue of systematic copula deletion, see Rickford, J. 1999 *African American Vernacular English* Oxford: Blackwell.

f Schwa pronunciation of *the* preceding a vowel – so in a phrase like 'the other', the 'e' in 'the' would sound like the first vowel in '*about*' rather than the vowel in '*tea*'.

g Post-vocalic r-lessness, as in 'sistuh' for 'sister' and 'fouh' for 'four'

h Stop pronunciations of inter-dental fricatives. So '*th*in' would be '*t*in', and '*th*en' would be '*d*en'.

i Written in phonetic script as [ðə]. See note f.

j Written in phonetic script as [ðɪy]

disappears in this position' (1972: 13). Mike wasn't R-less before the age of 13 and neither were any of his family, but at age 16, he was r-less on 61 percent (n=18) of [the occasions when R might have been used at a word boundary before a vowel]. [In this case,] Mike's r-lessness comes closer to Labov's Black Working Class speakers, who average 60–80 percent [r-lessness], than to white New York City vernacular speakers, [averaging] only 5–10 percent [. . .] (Labov 1972: 39). Extract 5 illustrates this feature:

5   Mike: Yo, she still looks he' age.
      [jo ʃi stɪl lʊks hə eɪdʒ]

Lastly, in relation to TH-stopping, Mike's [use of 'd' in the pronunciation of TH at the start of words like *the, this* and *those*] reached 36 percent (n=22), while approximately 50 percent (n=12) of the final TH consonants in the word *with* were pronounced as 't' . . . According to] Labov 1966, levels of ['d' for TH] in casual speech among upper middle class New York City whites (ages 20–39) [were] 5 percent (1966: 365). The only tabulated data he gives on African Americans in New York City comes from out-of-town speakers who average about 44 percent [. . .] (Labov 1966: 645). Extract 6 below is an example from Mike's speech:

6   Mike: nuh . . . yeah, but I had to verify DUH SHIT WIT YOU.
      [nʌ jɛ bʌr aɪ hæd tə vɛrəfaː dʌ ʃɪʔ wɪt tʃu]

Figure 24.1 on p. 319 gives an impression of these patterns, comparing Mike's use of these three variables with the findings of Ash and Myhill (1986) on schwa pronunciations of *the* before a vowel, with Labov['s findings] on pre-vocalic r-less-ness at a word boundary (1972), and Labov['s 1966 findings] on voiced TH-stopping [('d' for TH)]. As we can see, Mike's speech follows that of African Americans more closely than northern whites across these particular variables.

Grammar and segmental phonology do not, of course, provide the only – or even the strongest – indication that Mike was orienting to AAVE in his speech. He also employed [pronunciation] features such as vowel lengthening, syllable contraction and expansion, and stress and rhythm which approximated AAVE. Measuring and quantifying such features is difficult, since as Baugh (1983) points out, they are common to most English dialects. Generally speaking however, informal AAVE shows a tendency to contract the initial syllable and expand the second syllable in polysyllabic words (Baugh 1983: 61). The second syllable variably undergoes vowel lengthening and/or receives greater stress than it would in more formal conversation. Examples of this from Mike's speech are his pronun-ciation of ['suppose' as 's'*pose* ([spoːz]), 'fifteen' as *fifteeen* ([fɪf'tiːːn]), and *confuusion* ([kə̄'fjuːːʒn]).]

Lastly, an alignment with AAVE showed up in the [vocabulary (or 'lexis')] he used. Some of the most common lexical items and expressions from mid-1990s hip-hop culture are reported by an internet hip-hop dictionary.[3] In examples

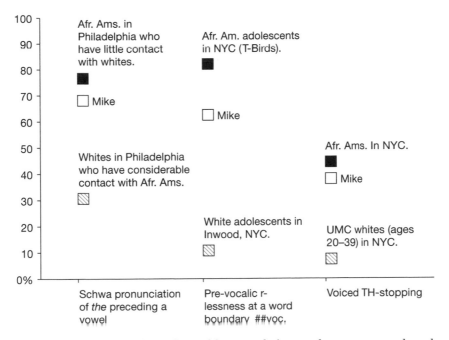

Figure 24.1   Three phonological variables in Mike's speech are compared to those of African Americans and whites. The data on schwa pronunciation of *the* comes from Ash and Myhill (1986: 39). The data on /r/ is from Labov (1972: 39), and on TH stopping from Labov (1966: 365, 645).

7–9 below we see a few of the items Mike used with regularity (in bold face type).

7   Mike (age 16; 1996): You ever hear of Frank Frazetta? Dis is some **phat** shit, yo. **Yo,** when the dude dies, dis book will probably be worth like a thousand dollars. **Yo,** tell me **that shit** is not **phat**!

8   Mike (age 15; 1995): **Yo,** he better know some **bomb bitches** down there!

9   Mike (age 16; 1996): Dis is gonna sound **mad** weird, **yo.** Don't worry, don't worry. I'll put **THE SHIT** OFF! Don't touch it. **Chill,** DON'T TOUCH IT! DON'T TOUCH IT! I got this over here!

4   Sources of access to AAVE

For urban white youth, living in a city like New York provides regular opportunities to observe first hand a variety of linguistic forms in subways, on street corners, in parks, night clubs etc. As a teenager, Mike spent a great deal of time outside, 'hanging out' on the street with his friends where he came into contact with kids from Harlem, the Bronx, and Brooklyn. Some of his regular social activities, 'tagging' (scrawling graffiti), playing pool, drinking beer on the street with friends and going out to clubs on the weekends brought him into contact and sometimes conflict with kids from other neighborhoods and other ethnic or social groups. He also had a particular white friend he had known since childhood who was something of a linguistic role model. This friend lived in a poor area and was in a much better position than Mike to acquire AAVE directly. Hewitt (1986) points out the 'Janus-like' role of such whites whose contacts with black culture make them a beacon for its promotion 'amongst white youth' (1986: 144). In this way words and expressions spread to white adolescents who have little direct contact with black people.

But beyond more and less direct face-to-face encounters, access to AAVE is also electronically mediated. As already mentioned, the internet is one increasingly important source for hip-hop terms and expressions, and young people can turn to a host of on-line dictionaries and chat lines to improve their hip-hop repertoires.[4] For Mike and many others, though, popular music was particularly important. Ever since 'Yo! MTV Raps' went on the air in 1989, sales figures for rap music among middle class white teenagers have sky-rocketed (Rose 1994a). 'Rap music videos have animated hip-hop cultural style and aesthetics and have facilitated cross-neighborhood, cross-country (transnational?) dialogue in a social environment that is highly segregated by class and race' (Rose 1994a: 9). Rap fans can consult lyric sheets in CD cases allowing them to learn the latest expressions coming out of New York City and Los Angeles, and to quite an extent, the words and expressions from these have become incorporated in the speech of teenagers across the entire country. At age 16 Mike's favorite groups included Ice-T, LL Cool J, Two Live Crew, Public Enemy, Snoop Doggie Dog among others, and I often overheard him quoting lyrics to himself from his CD collection. Since then he has gotten interested in 'techno' music which grew out of the DJ dance-hall scene and which also has a lot of cross-over appeal for rap fans.

Thirdly, films on black inner-city life have played a role in the transmission of AAVE to whites. Mike saw all the so-called 'Hood Films' – several times in some cases – which emerged in the early 90s including 'Straight out of Brooklyn' (1991), 'Boyz'n the Hood' (1991), 'Hangin' with the Homeboys' (1991), 'House Party' (1990), 'Menace to Society' (1993), and 'New Jack City' (1991). He also claimed to have seen Spike Lee's 'Do the Right Thing' (1989) at least three or four times. These films have served to transmit views of inner-city ghetto life, in some cases a glamorized version, from which white teenagers can selectively choose to construct their stereotypes about African Americans and hip-hop culture.

5   Mike, AAVE, and the dynamics of identification

At certain points in the account above, I may have seemed equivocal as to whether AAVE was associated with urban African American, Latino or indeed white youth. This ambiguity is in fact part of hip-hop itself, and in this section I shall trace the shifts in Mike's alignment across such groupings.

Mike's early experimentation with AAVE at age 13–14 reflected an active identification with African Americans. But after changing schools at age 15 he began expressing resentment toward his African American peers, complaining that they 'always hang together' and 'separate themselves', and by 16 he seemed to see himself in opposition to the black community. He continued, however to use AAVE [pronunciation and vocabulary], but this was no longer an attempt to construct a black identity. Instead, it laid claim to participation in hip-hop as the dominant consumption-based youth culture.

. Hip-hop is increasingly claimed to be a multi-cultural lifestyle rather than a symbol of ethnic group identity, particularly by white adolescents but also by others. As such, it seems to allow whites access to a commodified, ephemeral black experience at various moments or phases of their lives without requiring overt claims of black ethnicity, and the sociolinguistic meaning of AAVE appears to be adjusted in the process.

Labov argued that 'if a certain group of speakers uses a particular [form] then the social values attributed to that group will be transferred to that linguistic [form]' (1972: 25), and Hewitt (1986) suggests that the history of black oppression has led to lower class forms of black language being associated with toughness and survival (1986: 137). [. . .] For some white teenage boys and girls, the adoption of black speech forms may indeed be a survival strategy (cf. Carla perhaps), and Mike certainly had some harrowing encounters with gang culture. But for Mike, this was largely by choice rather than necessity. His white middle class background provided no routine contact with gang culture, and instead he had to seek it out, inspired no doubt by the proliferation of 'gangsta rap' during the early 1990s – a genre which glamorized inner city life for many young people (Rebensdorf 1996). Broadly speaking, Mike's orientation to AAVE and hip-hop looked increasingly like a commodified life-style choice, and in the process, the political histories behind AAVE's connotations of urban toughness faded from view. Many young whites feel they have the right to appropriate the hip-hop look and language, and that black adolescents who oppose them are racists. As one presumably white youth wrote in to the online Hip Hop Style Page, 'Hey hey hey wut is goin' down with this shit???? Not all of us here are blacc, alright.' [. . .] Like their British counterparts in Hewitt's work, they often 'fail to perceive the social and political aspects of the culture or fail to be sensitive to the issue of group boundaries' (Hewitt 1986: 48).

Some of the complicated cross-currents involved in this process showed up in an interview with Mike (aged 16) and his (white) friends Funny, Joey and Nikki. Mike had heavily bought into elements of African American culture, but he didn't show that he understood or respected any declaration of limits or conditions to his participation. Instead, he and his friends seemed at times to demand the erasure of differences in race and class history and position. At one point, they complained about what they viewed as 'anti-white skits' and overt demonstrations of black pride on black television programs such as 'Def Comedy Jam', and in the process[, they] united relatively 'straight', unperformed uses of AAVE (line 22) with its use in parody and caricature (lines 24–36):

10   Interview with Mike (age 16) and friends (Funny, Joey, and Nikki)[5]

1	Funny:	And I also think that there's a lot of racism from
2		blacks to whites.
3	Mike:	**Yeah, hell yeah, like a lot.**
4	Funny:	Like if you watch 'Def Comedy Jam' or anything
5		they're always making cracks about whites but if a
6		white guy gets up on the stage says a little joke I
7		mean you're gonna have Reggie Jackson knocking at
8		his door or JESSE Jackson you know (.) with the
9		whole rainbow coalition, you know, I'm
10		not racist, but I, I think there's a lot of =
11	Mike:	=And like I hate the way, I hate the way they
12		they completely separate themselves. When you
13		have that, like (.) I'm glad you brought that up.
14		'Def Comedy Jam', I HATE THAT SHOW. Like
15		you see a freekin' (.) like (.) that's what I call a
16		**jigaboo**, a person ((loud laughter)) no, no, no
17		that's what I call a person, when they when they
18		seclude themselves they're they're just as bad, that's
19		that's what I call **boom**, a bastard, because they go
20		up there and they have a '*Black as Hell*' white shirt,
21		white sweat shirt and there up there, "**Yo, man,**
22		**you know I was walkin' down the street the**
23		**other day and I was wit my girl Juanita**"=
24	Funny:	="**wit my fuckin' BITCH!**"
25	Mike:	="**you know! An' wit Juanita, you know, I**
26		**was jus chillin' you know, my BLACK girl,**
27		**my BLACK princess, my BLACK**"=
28	Funny:	="**My BITCH!**"
29	Mike:	="**and I emphasize twenty more times that**
30		**she's black** ((laughter)) **to make sure**
31		**everybody knows that she's black** ((laughter))
32		**because I don't want anyone to think I had**
33		**to do with white!**"
34	Funny:	Yeah, yeah!
35	Mike:	**You know?** That's exactly how they are.

A little later, uneasiness about their own race and class identity showed itself:

11   Interview with Mike, Funny, Joey, and Nikki:

    1 Mike: Yeah, I mean ((tooth sucking)) I have a lot of
    2   friends that are of other races and I don't care but
    3   once I hear somebody say you know, "**Oh, word-**
    4   **up, black pride**" then they like become another
    5   thing for me. Then I see 'em then I see 'em
    6   different, then I see 'em much [different.
    7 Joey: [Or "**White boy!**" I
    8   hate that shit, when they say white boy to me,
    9   there's like if I walk around and like um you know
    10   in a nice outfit, "**Hey white boy**," just cause I'm
    11   in a nice or or because I'm in a private school, this is
    12   my favorite thing, or I, I've gotten into arguments
    13   like you know, it's come close you know? You you
    14   remember "oh, **white boy**" you know "**from a**
    15   **private school**" you know . . .

But desire for the neutralization of all social difference certainly wasn't a steady principle, and elsewhere boundaries of class and race were stressed in mockery of whites who 'want to be black'. During the same group session Mike and his friends mentioned the 'Yorkville crew' in response to a question about 'wannabes'. Yorkville, Mike's neighborhood, encompasses the upper east side of Manhattan and is demographically upwards of 90 percent white, and the Yorkville crew are all white:

12   Interview with Mike, Funny, Joey, and Nikki:

    1 Joey: You see, **nah**, I'm sayin' you see a lot of kids who
    2   live down here ((Yorkville)) who wished they lived
    3   there ((Harlem)) (.) you see a lot of kids running
    4   around here who look like they want to be up from
    5   up there you know (.) like you see like all these like
    6   (.)
    7 Joey: They ((the Yorkville crew)) go around, like these
    8   these these these rich, white kids go around robbin'
    9   kids. I mean it's like so stupid (.) and they only rob
    10   kids when they have like
    11   fifteen or twenty kids in a gang.
    12 Mike: [They like, they like have their own
    13   crew 'n shit, and like every (.) and then every night,
    14   like every other night they all hang out like all two
    15   hundred of 'em by the Metropolitan Museum at night
    16   time.

Funny said that he had friends who actually came from the Bronx, knew of this Yorkville 'crew' and were particularly critical of its members.

13   Interview with Mike, Funny, Joey, and Nikki:

    1 Funny: =They ((white Yorkville crew kids)) wouldn't step a
    2   foot over like (.) you know they wouldn't (.) they're
    3   like, set foot into Harlem but they try
    4   to act like they're from Harlem you know. I, I mean
    5   last year, he gotta go round and like
    6   **"Yo, dis is Yohkville, dis is Yohkville"**=
    7 Joey: =yeah, they're like, **"Get outta Yohkville,**
    8   **muthafucka!"**=
    9 Funny: ((continuing the imitation)) **"Wes' side, eas'**
    10   **side we at woh** ((war)), **we at woh."**

Neither Funny nor Joey employed many AAVE features in their own speech, but they both parodied the Yorkville kids' speech by trying to affect AAVE pronunciation such as the stop pronunciation in *this* (line 6), post-vocalic r-lessness in *Yorkville* (lines 6 to 8) and *war* (line 10), and even copula deletion (line 10). Mike, on the other hand, did employ quite a bit of AAVE [pronunciation and vocabulary] in his everyday speech, and his imitation of the Yorkville crew contrasted with his friends' when they were actually talking about the inauthenticity of the Yorkville crew's AAVE (they had already agreed that the crew didn't 'even like black kids'):

14   Interview with Mike, Funny, Joey, and Nikki:

    1 Funny: Well they have the 'homeboy handbook' so I
    2   guess they just follow (.)
    3 Mike: All right, all right ((with heavily affected white
    4   accent:)) 'When I'm stepping to somebody (.)'
                 [hwɛn aim stɛpɪŋ tə sʌmbəɾi]
    5 Funny: You know they like practice in front of the mirror,
    6   pull their pants down to their knees, I don't know.

When Mike ridiculed the Yorkville crew kids' speech in lines 3 to 5, he used a marked black phrase 'stepping to somebody' (meaning to act aggressively in a way that would lead to a fist fight – see note [3]) in a very exaggerated 'white' accent. He didn't use AAVE pronunciation – to do so could have implied the anomaly of his own speech style.

    In fact, more generally during this discussion, Mike was somewhat hesitant to provide direct information about the 'Yorkville crew' and seemed uncomfortable that the subject had come up at all. When I asked whether any of the boys knew the specific names of other 'crews' in Yorkville, all eyes went toward Mike who exclaimed indignantly, 'Why y'll lookin' at me for?' Later he gave some absurd, fictitious names such as the 'first avenue mob' and 'heavy phat losers' to the great amusement of his friends, and his behavior during the interview suggested he was somewhat ashamed that his friends would associate him with one of these groups or that they would think he himself had been involved with the Yorkville Crew.

At first glance one might conclude that young whites embracing hip-hop represents a cultural rapprochement between blacks and whites and perhaps even the creation of a new multi-ethnic youth culture. But Mike's relationship to African Americans was more complex and more subject to competing pulls. From a position of remoteness from the realities of lower class urban life, he wanted very much to define and participate in an essentialized version of urban black male youth culture, but he was uncomprehending about the restrictions, angered about rejection, and worried about being labeled a 'wannabe' by his peers.

6 Conclusion

White appropriation of black cultural forms is certainly not a new phenomenon, and the language, the music and fashions of black culture have long provided a rich source of inspiration for whites and others in the US and around the world. Indeed, there is little that the case study of a single individual can say about the general development of new trends in this relationship. Labov might be right that there is growing divergence between black and white vernaculars, that this is 'symptomatic of a split between the black and white portions of our society' (1987: 10), and as one factor within this, African Americans may be pulling away from white attempts to imitate them, as in the rhythms of appropriation and divergent innovation suggested by Giles (1979). Even so, a case like Mike's can usefully remind us that in spite of its reductive oversimplification of the sources that it targets, the adolescent construction of 'style' can involve tense negotiations of the relationship between self and other. Styling like Mike's may not match the standards of authenticity laid out in traditional sociolinguistics, and there may be major limits to the political understanding that accompanies it, but both personally and socially, its origins are complex, its consequences can be serious, and although its representativeness can't be stated systematically, it is not an isolated instance.

Notes

1   According to Rose (1994b), 'hip hop culture emerged as a source of alternative identity formation and social status for youth' that started in the South Bronx in the early 1970s (1994b: 74). Its central forms are graffiti, breakdancing and rap music. 'Alternative local identities were formed in fashions and language, street names and most importantly, in establishing neighborhood crews or posses. *The crew*, a local source of identity, group affiliation and support system, appears in virtually all rap lyrics and cassette dedications, music video performances and media interviews with [rap] artists.' (Rose 1994b: 78). (*Editors:* see also Back in this volume.)
2   I adopt Morgan's (1994) definition of AAVE as the language varieties used by people in the US whose major socialization has been with US residents of African descent but I would like to specify that it is a particular variety of AAVE that young whites are targeting: that variety of AAVE used by rap and hip-hop artists.

3   Expressions from on-line rap dictionary: http: //www.sci.kun.nl:80/thalia/rapdict/
     dict_en.html [1998]

ayite	'all right'
bitch	'woman, girl' (pejorative)
bomb	'excellent, great'
boom	pre-sequence emphatic expression or filler
bro'	'brother, friend'
buggin'	'going crazy'
chill	'calm down'
dat shit	'that shit'
dope	'good, great'
frontin'	'trying to seem/appear'
hell yeah	'yes indeed'
ill	'weird, obnoxious'
jigaboo	'black person' (pej.); nigga (pej.)
mad	'very'
nigga	'fellow black brother' or pejoratively
phat	'good, great'
steppin' to	'to be aggressive'
whassup?; what up?	'what's up?'
word up; word	'for real; in fact; indeed'
yo	tag expression
you know?	'do you understand?'
wack	'weak, stupid'

4   Yet the existence of 'rap dictionaries' on the internet is highly contested. Rebensdorf
     (1996) observes that while some on-line discussions argue in favor of dictionaries in
     order to understand rappers' lyrics, others complain that rap dictionaries defeat the
     purpose of using hip-hop slang and that the role of rap is not to teach outsiders, but
     to communicate within their community (Rebensdorf 1996).

5   Conventions used in transcriptions

[	overlapping turns
=	latching (a turn comes very rapidly after the one before)
(.)	pause of less than one second
(1.5)	approximate length of pause in seconds
CAPITALS	loud enunciation
((text))	stage directions
( )	speech inaudible
Bold	instance of crossing of central interest in discussion

References

Ash, Sharon and John Myhill. 1986. Linguistic correlates of inter-ethnic contact. In David
     Sankoff (ed.) *Diversity and Diachrony*. Philadelphia: Benjamins. 33–44.
Baugh, John. 1983. *Black Street Speech: Its History, Structure, and Survival*. Austin: University
     of Texas Press.
Cutler, Cecilia. 1997. Yorkville Crossing: The influence of hip hop on the speech of a white
     middle class teenager in New York City. *University of Pennsylvania Working Papers in
     Linguistics* 4: 371–397.
Giles, Howard. 1979. Ethnicity markers in speech. In Klaus R. Sherer and Howard Giles
     (eds) *Social Markers in Speech*. Cambridge: Cambridge University Press. 251–289.

Hatala, Eileen. 1976. Environmental effects on white students in black schools. Unpublished MA thesis. Philadelphia: University of Pennsylvania.

Hewitt, Roger. 1986. *White Talk Black Talk: Inter-racial Friendship and Communication amongst Adolescents*. Cambridge and New York: Cambridge University Press.

Hill, Jane H. 1993. Is it really 'no problemo'? Junk Spanish and Anglo racism. Paper presented to the first annual Symposium About Language and Society. University of Texas, Austin.

Jacobs-Huey, Lanita. 1996. Is there an authentic African American speech community?: Carla Revisited. *University of Pennsylvania Working Papers in Linguistics* 4: 331–370.

Jones, Simon. 1988. *Black Culture White Youth*. Basingstoke: Macmillan.

Labov, William. 1966. *The Social Stratification of English in New York City*. Washington, DC: Center for Applied Linguistics.

Labov, William. 1972. *Language in the Inner City*. Philadelphia: University of Pennsylvania Press.

Labov, William. 1980. Is there a creole speech community? In Albert Valdman and Arnold Highfield (eds) *Theoretical Orientations in Creole Studies*. New York: Academic Press. 369–388.

Labov, William. 1987. Are black and white vernaculars diverging? *American Speech* 62: 1–80.

Labov, William and Wendell A. Harris. 1983. De facto segregation of black and white vernaculars. In David Sankoff (ed.) *Diversity and Diachrony*. Philadelphia: Benjamins. 1–24.

Mitchell-Kernan, Claudia. 1972. Signifying and marking: Two Afro-American speech acts. In John J. Gumperz and Dell Hymes (eds) *Directions in Sociolinguistics: The Ethnography of Communication*. New York: Holt, Rinehart and Winston. 161–179.

Morgan, Marcyliena. 1994. Theories and politics in African American English. *Annual Review of Anthropology* 23: 325–35.

Rampton, Ben. 1995. *Crossing: Language and Ethnicity among Adolescents*. New York: Longman.

Rebensdorf, Alicia. 1996. Representing the real: Exploring appropriations of hip hop culture in the Internet and Nairobi. Unpublished senior undergraduate thesis. Portland, Oregon: Lewis and Clark University. http://Iclark.edu/~soan/alicia/rebensdorf.express.html

Rose, Tricia 1994a. *Black Noise: Rap Music and Black Culture in Contemporary America*. Hanover, New Hampshire: Wesleyan University Press.

Rose, Tricia. 1994b. A style nobody can deal with. In Andrew Ross and Tricia Rose (eds) *Microphone Fiends: Youth Music and Youth Culture*. New York: Routledge. 71–88.

Sales, Nancy J. 1996. Teenage gangland. *New York Magazine*, December 16: 32–39.

Smitherman, Geneva. 1994. *Black Talk: Words and Phrases from the Hood to the Amen Corner*. Boston: Houghton Mifflin.

Spiegler, Marc. 1996. Marketing street culture: Bringing hip-hop style to the mainstream. *American Demographics* (online), November. http://www.tomco.net/~afrimale/hiphop.htm

Urciuoli, Bonnie. 1991. The political topography of Spanish and English: The view from a New York Puerto Rican community. *American Ethnologist* 18: 295–310.

Wolfram, Walt and Ralph W. Fasold. 1974. *The Study of Social Dialects in American English*. Englewood Cliffs, New Jersey: Prentice Hall.

This paper relates to Cecilia Cutler's Ph.D. research at New York University, which she completed in 2002.

Chapter 25

Les Back

1995

X AMOUNT OF SAT SIRI AKAL!

Apache Indian, reggae music and intermezzo culture[a]

[. . .]

> X amount of sat siri akal
> X amount of salam 'l' acum
> > Fe all the Muslim ragamuffin posse
> X amount of time ca any time we come is excessive
> > Amount of lyrics have fe rhyme
> Ca all the people round the world say the love reggae music fe real
> I want you know say any time we come in a combination style
> > Fe reveal reggae music everyone should a feel
> > > (Apache Indian *Fe real* [1993])

[. . .]

THE TITLE OF THIS CHAPTER is drawn from the lyrics of the Birmingham based musician Apache Indian. The phrase signifies a greeting. Its two components bring together the lexicon of the African Caribbean and south Asia. *X amount* has its origins in the language of the reggae dance hall and it means a quantity beyond calculation: *sat siri akaal* is a Punjabi salutation. Apache himself was raised in the multi-ethnic area Handsworth, Birmingham, born of Hindu Punjabi parents from Jalandhar. He performs and expresses himself through snatches of Jamaican patois, Punjabi and a unique form of English which is being generated by groups of young people who are growing up alongside each other in Birmingham.[b]

Apache's music is a cultural crossroads, a meeting place where the languages and rhythms of four continents intermingle producing a culture that cannot be

---

a From A. Ålund and R. Granqvist (eds) (1995) *Negotiating Identities*. Amsterdam: Rodopi, pp. 139–68.
b See also Hewitt, this volume.

reduced to its component parts. Rather, it needs to be understood in the context of the global passage of linguistic and cultural forms and the localities where they converge: the culture is simultaneously both local and global. In this paper I want to try and explore these processes through a discussion of the cultural crossroads from which Apache Indian's music emerges and the implications this has for conceptualising identity and contemporary culture.

As Paul Gilroy commented, the metaphor of the crossroads might provide an 'appropriate conceptual vehicle for rethinking the dialectical tension between cultural roots and cultural routes' (Gilroy 1992a: 305). Recently the understanding of passage of culture through space has been based on the idea of flows (Hannerz 1989a, 1989b). The challenge is how to keep sight of the histories which propel these cultural flows while remaining open to the new possibilities that emerge at the crossroads where unforeseen things happen. This is perhaps the tension to which Gilroy alludes, i.e. between cultural roots that fix and ossify and *routes* (Chambers 1990) which allow passage, transcendence and lines of flight.

The concept of the crossroads alone cannot provide an adequately detailed theoretical tool to unpick what happens at the conjunction of cultural routes. Here I want to introduce the notion of *rhizome* as elaborated in the writings of Gilles Deleuze and Felix Guattari (1986). For Deleuze and Guattari rhizomes offer an alternative to the vertical root/tree structure of dichotomous arborescent thinking. Through adventurous growths and rhizomes horizontal connections can be developed between things that have no necessary relation with each other.

Cultural rhizomes (see also Mercer 1992) form places where political and cultural connections can take place through the creation of a *throng of dialects, patois, slangs and specialised languages* (Deleuze and Guattari 1986: 7). A rhizome has no beginning or end, it is always in the middle. The usefulness of the notion of rhizome is that it provides a way of describing forms of cultural interbeing. What I want to argue here is that the proximity of the children of African and south Asian diasporas in Birmingham is leading to what I shall refer to later as an *intermezzo culture*. Before going on to do this I want to outline the origins and character of black musical cultures in Britain.

From the reggae blues to *bhangra beat*: the expressive culture of the dance

In the post-war era black people encountered racism most starkly in the housing and labour markets, but comparable divisions also appeared in the institutions of working-class leisure (Sivanandan, 1981/82). As Simon Jones points out:

> The same racism that operated in the job and housing markets also operated to bar black workers from many white working-class leisure institutions, such as pubs, clubs, dance palais and bingo halls.
>
> (Jones 1988: 33)

Faced with a racially debarred urban culture black workers had to find alternative forms of leisure. The emergence of black-owned clubs and religious organisations such as Mosques and Temples provided a context in which black workers could socialize without encountering racism (Hiro 1971, Gutzmore 1978).

Within Afro-Caribbean communities music was central to many of these leisure activities (Hinds 1980). The emergence of a black British reggae sound system scene is linked to the exclusive practices operated in white working-class leisure. Ribs, of Unity Sound system comments:

> So where is there for black people to go on a weekend? Where is there for us? We don't go to the pub, so we go a dance.
>
> (*Echoes* 11th August 1984)

By the beginning of the eighties sound systems operated in all the major regions where black communities lived. A politically engaged form of Rastafari was the dominant ethos within a reformed black working-class culture.[c]

These expressive musical cultures are produced through the interaction between the audience and the performers. In sound system culture the consumption of the music becomes a collective celebratory event where listening is an active process (Gilroy 1985). The call and response, or *antiphonic*, nature of this culture has its roots in a long history of folk art originating from Africa (Oliver 1970, Finnegan 1970). The end result is a democratic process of mechanically reproduced art (Benjamin 1968a) which converges with the participatory elements in lyrical performance: 'Lines between self and other are blurred and special forms of pleasure are created as a result' (Gilroy 1991: 13). The dance provides an alternative public sphere, a unifying context for the sharing and celebration of collective experiences.

During the mid-eighties the sound system and the microphone provided a platform from which black young people could re-write and document their own history (Back 1988). The physical and social reality common to the audience and the performers alike made the music relevant and accessible. The hegemony of politically focused forms of reggae music shifted during the late eighties as new innovations entered the culture. In particular the impact of synthesized rhythms, like Wayne Smith's 'Under Me Sleng Teng' moved the nature of dance-hall culture in a new direction. DJs would come to rely on digitally produced rhythms which were sparse and hard hitting. This would later be called *raga* or *ragamuffin*.

There are direct parallels between the development of sound-system culture and the emergence of new south Asian musical cultures in Britain during the 1980s. In particular, forms derived from *bhangra* served similar functions to those of the reggae dance hall. The dance and song genre bhangra originates in the Punjab and it 'celebrates the robust and energetic punctuated rhythms and lambic meter of the double-sided drums *dhol* and *dholki*, the supple directness of Punjabi language, and the pleasures associated with its main social occasions, the harvest festival *bhaisakhi*' (Baumann 1990: 81). Within the context of Britain bhangra music has been re-invented. Bands like *alaap* in West London's Southall district incorporated

---

c On Rastafari, see also Alleyne, this volume.

sound sampling, drum machines and synthesizers to produce the new form called *bhangra beat*, also known as Southall beat. In the Midlands other influences from hip hop and house music have been incorporated producing *northern rock bhangra* and *house bhangra*.

The development of these robust and rich new forms have been read as a focal point for an incipient British Asian youth culture. Bhangra created an overarching reference point cutting across cleavages of nationality (Indian, Pakistani, Bangladeshi and other), religion (Sikh, Muslim and Hindu) and caste/class. One distinctive feature of this culture was the so called 'daytimer,' a live event which took place during school hours to compensate for the young Asians inability to attend night time clubs. The function of the daytimer is described here by *Mac*, singer with the group *Dhamaka*:

> Daytimers reinforce our culture and values, girls dress in sulwaars (*salwaar-kamiz*, the traditional dress of Punjabi women), boys can come in turbans and get no hassle. The music is our music, and it's their show, not 'goray' [white] gig or a 'kale' [black] show. Do parents want for kids to go out to gora shows? Would they rather have Asian kids disowning and abandoning their culture, to become Sharons and Garys tomorrow.
>
> (quoted in Baumann 1990: 87)

The connection of bhangra with a youthful sense of Asian unity is also expressed in the following quote from Komal one of the lead singers of the east London bhangra group *Cobra*:

> I can remember going to college discos a long time ago, when all you heard was reggae, reggae, reggae. Asians were lost, they weren't accepted by whites, so they drifted into the black culture, dressing like blacks, talking like them, and listening to reggae. But now Bhangra has given them 'their' music and made them feel that they do have an identity. No matter if they are Gujaratis, Punjabis or whatever, — Bhangra is Asian music for Asians.
>
> (quoted in Baumann 1990: 91)

The emergence of Bhangra in the 1980s signalled the development of a self conscious and distinctively British Asian youth culture which expressed the primacy of an Asian identity. The result was the development of an alternative public sphere for young Asians which was comparable to the reggae dance hall.

However, by the early 1990s complex fusions of reggae and bhangra have emerged. This has gone far beyond any crude sense of mimicry alluded to in the quote from Cobra cited above. In particular the popularity of the MC Apache Indian has come to symbolize this innovation. Apache, formerly a sheet metal worker from Handsworth, takes his name from his Indo-Jamaican idol the Wild Apache Supercat. Equally, in London's East End, Bengali youth are operating sound systems and appropriating rap and reggae lyrical styles.[1]

Liminal space and cultural rhizomes

In addition to providing sites for cultural affirmation, the dance-halls and clubs can also be characterised as liminal spaces. What I mean by this can be best illustrated by an example. Towards the end of 1992 Apache Indian and the black South London reggae singer Maxi Priest collaborated on a tune called *Fe Real*. I will come back to the significance of this tune later. Apache Indian and Maxi Priest performed a small number of PAs (i.e. a live vocal performance rendered over a backing track) together. The first show was scheduled to take place in the unlikely setting of a provincial town called Peterborough. Peterborough has a small Afro-Caribbean and south Asian population and it is about 100 miles from Birmingham.

I set off from Birmingham with a friend about 9.30 pm. [. . .] We arrived at the *Las Vistos Nightclub* just before midnight. I recounted later:

> La Vistos is a classic seventies night club with a full complement of glitz and neon. It could have been in any provincial town. The club was complete with revolving light rigs, strobes and a terminal that breathed dry ice over the heads of the people on the dance floor. The multi-coloured lights revolved and the dry ice flowed — it could have been 1976 and John Travolta might feasibly have been preening himself in the toilets. But this was not just a white disco scene. There were probably about 40% of the audience who were black and Asian dance-hall goers. It was almost as if the rituals of the dance-hall and the kitsch disco cultures had seamlessly fused. The fault lines showed but they were not totalising, as if for one brief moment the divisive identities of race and nation were up for grabs. It was a carnival of identity, a place where time and social designation seemed temporarily suspended under the omnipresent groove of the drum and the bass. One could feel things opening up.
>
> Before Apache and Maxi took the stage the DJ proclaimed a dance competition. 'I have a bottle of champagne for the best dance-hall shaker.' He stood on top of a stack of speaker cabs and rode the rhythm, finger outstretched scanning the dance floor for crucial moves. Shabba Ranks offered a rhythm and it was almost physically impossible to stand still. The DJ presided over the swaying mass of people. First up was a black woman in her forties. In the corner a white woman moved to the rhythm in a way that was indistinguishable from her black friends. Her white boyfriend looked on disapprovingly. She turned her back on him and moved with a mass of people of all shades. The DJ recognised the shattered binary and proclaimed her, as the dance-hall massive tore up racial boundaries. 'Yes, yes, nuff respect — come here sister!' The white sister picked up her prize, she took it over to her disapproving boyfriend and put it on the table in front of him.
>
> Three black women had been dancing with their white friend when one of them beckoned an Asian man. The pair moved in unison locked in motion at the hip, yet not touching. Another division was exploded in an expression of Afro-Asian unity. The DJ called them. The black

woman took the bottle, she turned, a path was cleared on the dance-floor and the two partners slowly worked their way towards one another as if the music drew them together.

Last up was a black man in his thirties winning his bottle through sheer commitment rather than style. The DJ passed judgement — 'This man has been dancing his ass off all evening, come here brother.' As I scanned the dancefloor I could see some white men on the periphery trying to find a groove, stiffly jerking their bodies like a car that turns over but will not start. Others stood unimpressed demanding that the DJ 'Get on with it and play the music'. Both for those whites who embraced the rhythm or those who were unable to be possessed by it there was no escape. The Next fashions and the Dorothy Perkins dresses all moved — however awkwardly — to the beat of a different drum.

The lights went down and Apache took the stage. 'This one is dedi-cated to all the Indian ragamuffin posse — X amount of sat siri akal, X amount salaam alakum for all the Muslim posse'. While the microphone failed him, Apache lead the crowd through a tour of his hits. A group of Afro-Caribbean young men looked on unimpressed. One young man wearing a turned around baseball cap with 'X' showing, stood arms folded surveying the scene. His friend moved and swayed with the dance-hall massive composed of Asian, black and white but he stood motionless. Apache paused 'I am going to bring out a friend of mine now'. Maxi Priest strolled on stage. He proceeded to sing snatches from his hits through this awful sound system with such beauty that would have melted the 'whitest heart'. After the vocal overture Maxi addressed the crowd: 'This tune that we have recorded is for the India people. In it I try to sing in Indian'. Fe Real begins Apache proclaims Maxi in Punjabi — 'Maxi Ji'. As the tune draws to an end Maxi sings his Punjabi lines over and over again. The black young man standing on the side of the dancefloor is still unimpressed but as one of his friends grabs him and pulls him onto the floor the group move in unison to a new style. The tune draws to an end to frantic whistling as the crowd shout a chorus of approval 'Bo, bo, bo!' I looked at my watch and it was 2.30 am.

There are a number of things that I want to emphasise with regard to this story. First, it demonstrates the degree to which the dance also offers a place where social divisions can be temporarily suspended. I think that the notion of liminality is useful here (Turner 1969). Liminality refers to a state of separation from the mundane aspects of life usually associated with a rite of passage. As Turner points out, limi-nality is not merely about assigning identity, it can also relate to the inversion and transformation of public roles (Turner 1984: 26).

In this sense I want to argue that the alternative public sphere of the dance can produce liminal ethnicities (Back 1991).[2,d] Equally, I want to argue that what results

---

d Compare Urla, this volume, on free radio as an alternative public sphere.

from this is the opening up of new identifications. These processes are not completely autonomous from external forces and divisions but I am arguing that these dialogues can result in the development of new *intermezzo cultures*. The notion of 'intermezzo' features in the work of Deleuze and Guattari (1986: 25) and draws appropriately on a musical metaphor. Its literal meaning is a short dramatic musical performance serving as a connecting link between the main divisions of a large musical work. Here I am using this as an analogy to refer to a space which links social collectivities producing cultures of interbeing and mutual identification. The prime one I am concerned with here is the fusion of elements of south Asian culture and the rituals of the reggae dance-hall.

Through the call and response between performer and audience these new cultural forms are endorsed. There are two examples from Apache's musical collaborations which demonstrate this process. During the promotion of *Fe Real* Maxi Priest and Apache performed at a celebration held in Leicester of the religious festival Divali. The event drew an audience of 8,000 Hindus. Apache remembering the show comments on its significance:

> It was a nice warm kind of evening. They had 8,000 Asian kids on the streets. We never realised it was going to be that big. When we went on stage Maxi did his Indian [Punjabi] chorus, when they saw him singing that, it meant so much. The Maxi Priest thing was a huge thing it is all to do with us being a very self contained people and thinking that people around us don't want to know what is happening. They see a Black person wanting to use the language, wanting to come aboard what Apache is doing. Then it is like Maxi is an international star singing in Punjabi and then the Asian youth check it as — 'yeah, people do want to know about us'. It was special.

The music in this setting addresses a specific Asian constituency, and was embraced and in turn legitimated. Similar processes occurred when Apache performed at prestigious reggae venues. Notably he was acknowledged during a televised performance at the celebrated black London venue, the 291 Club, winning over many of his detractors. In 1991 he was voted Best New Comer at the British Reggae Industry Awards. In these kinds of contexts the music is being authenticated by a distinctly African Caribbean constituency. Apache comments here on an experience of playing a African-Caribbean venue in Southall where he performed his tune *Arranged Marriage*, in which he takes himself through a marriage, and the dance-floor rouser *Chok There* (which means raise up or lively up):

> I did a show, a reggae show for Daddy Ernie from Choice FM at Tudor Rose, Southall — black crowd, 99% black crowd. Before I did Arranged Marriage I said 'Buoy I am looking for a girl for my arranged marriage who will dress up in a sari and come to Delhi' and all the black girls threw up their hands. When I was singing Chok There I had two thousand black people singing out Chok There.

These constitute powerful moments where social and musical conventions are being played with and transgressed: an African-Caribbean performer singing in Punjabi to a south Asian audience, and an African-Caribbean audience singing Punjabi with an Asian artist.[e] The result is an exciting tangle of rhizomorphous connection, a *sound block* that no longer has a point of origin but forms a conjunction. [. . .]

The Handsworth translation: '*bhangramuffin*', Apache Indian and Afro-Asian dialogue

Apache Indian — aka Steven Kapur — released his first record entitled *Movie Over India* in 1990.[3] By January/February 1991 *Movie Over India* was topping both the reggae and bhangra charts. The new form was dubbed in the media *bhangramuffin* after its raga counterpart. The first point to make about Apache's biography is that his relationship to reggae music cannot be separated from his broader involvement in multi-racial peer groups and the wider black community.

Apache is 27 years old and was born on the same day that Bob Marley was later to die. He grew up in the multi-racial district of Handsworth of Hindu parents from the Punjab. At school his closest friend was a black young man and the sound of reggae music captured his imagination from a very early age:

> I remember this record shop in Handsworth it was called Rough Groove Records, or something, and I always wanted to go into the shop, but there were always so many black people hanging around the shop and I was almost frightened to go in. But I always slowed down as I passed by because I loved the music.

His early preferences were roots reggae including Bob Marley and Burning Spear. Despite early feelings of ambivalence towards going into black record shops he continued to identify with the music and the physical culture which surrounded its performance.

> I was so much into reggae by the time I was fourteen. I remember I cut up one of my wardrobes to try and make it into a speaker box. I had this big wardrobe in those days and I dragged it out into the garden. I cut three holes in it, I didn't even know what size they were. I wanted to fit speakers in the holes. I painted the whole thing black inside and out and that was my speaker box. But you could never use it as a speaker box because the wood was too thin. When my parents came back — Jesus Christ. That was probably me trying to get close to reggae and I wanted to do something. So I just cut up my wardrobe and put three holes in it and the speakers never did fit.

Apache was inducted into sound system culture by a young black man of Caribbean parentage called Sheldon who ran *Siffa* sound system. Sheldon introduced him to important people within Birmingham's reggae scene and later he became his

---

e   For an account of the language and the dynamics of black and white involvement with bhangra, see Part IV of Rampton, B. (1995) *Crossing: Language and Ethnicity among Adolescents.* London: Longman.

brother-in-law. By the time he was sixteen Apache was working with a sound system in the Birmingham area. He invested in his own set calling it *Simeon*, the dread name given to the month of May — the month in which he was born — by Rastafari and the *Twelve Tribes of Israel*. Apache joined forces with Sheldon under the name of *Sunset*. By the age of 18 he had his own amps and speaker boxes and was learning the culture of the dance-hall. The next crucial step was his decision to become a 'van man'. He raised the money to buy a Luton van and ended up driving some of Birmingham's premier sound systems all over the country. At this time he had also followed his male relatives into a job in a local engineering factory where he was employed as a welder.

His involvement with dance-hall culture intensified when he met a prominent Birmingham soundman called Wooligan who ran *Orthodox 38* sound system.

> When I met Woolly I realised that I met someone who was as crazy about the music as me. If you go to his house he eats off speaker boxes. He sleeps in a speaker box. It is in his blood. I was the van man and I just loved to drive to the dance — just to be around the sound. What happened was that one night, it was in Slough, his DJ and the people who were supposed to chat never showed up. So I started chatting on the mike. Somebody said 'Who is that chatting? It's the van man, van man doesn't chat, van man drives the van'.

This marked the end of a long induction into the culture:

> Even down to loading the van. There is an art to loading a van. If you put too much boxes on one side the van will be unbalanced when you drive fast down the motorway. This was also the stage when I started to learn patois. People ask me how did I learn patois? Did you have to sit down and study it? Being in a sound [system] driving hundreds of miles with a bunch of guys falling asleep at 4.00 am in the morning — that was my education, that was my school.

His identification with reggae and black style was taken to serious lengths.

At sixteen he started to grow dreadlocks. Reflecting on this he explains his desire to grow locks as an extension of his love and identification with reggae music and dance-hall culture. His experience of having locks was highly formative with regard to his own sense of politicisation. He describes an incident surrounding a shopping expedition on Handsworth's main street — The Soho Road.

> I remember I walked in [to a shop] and as soon as I walked through the door people started to talk in Punjabi. They saw my locks and they checked me as a black guy. I can't remember exactly what the shop-keeper said but it was something like 'watch out this black guy is going to tief [thieve] something' . . . This made me realise, that opened my eyes to what was happening in the street and what people like Bob Marley were saying about what black people go through and what tribulation meant. What made it worse was that it wasn't white people who were saying these things.

Apache talks about a period where he felt that he was effectively living out a kind of Afro-black identity.[4] This was part and parcel of an identification with a culture but also a wider community. It was also about learning what the culture stood for historically and politically.

> I know it is a serious culture, I know it is a serious thing. I look around and see people playing with it today and I tell them this is a serious, serious thing. It has roots which go back a long way and you have to respect that. It means a lot to black people and I found that out being around black people. Me having locks was nothing cultural, it was me just trying to get closer to the music that I loved. I cut off my locks out of respect but I will always have my *locks in my mind*. (my emphasis)

The significance of this story is in that it shows that Apache's initiation into this culture was part of a long standing dialogue. Similar experiences have been documented elsewhere with regard to black culture and white young people (Hewitt 1986, Jones 1988).

It is no surprise then that Apache's early records dealt with the central theme of translation. The first *Movie Over India*, provided rudimentary lessons in Punjabi and patois. The tune modelled on the classic *Shankai Shek riddim*, might have never been made had Apache not been able to convince his cousin to give him some studio time. The second single, which was not officially released because of problems with bootlegging, continued the theme and was called *Come Follow Me* and featured the Birmingham MC Mikey G.

Apache adopted a style which took everyday phrases from both cultures and used them interchangeably and in elaborate combinations. A good example of this is *O Chok there fut air* which in Punjabi means raise the floor boards or lively up yourself. This idiom would be used along side creole grammar and phrases like *fe real*, *X amount* and *big up* which all have their origins in dance-hall culture. The emerging language, what Apache calls Indian patois, is an urban lingua franca which provides a suture between communities while acknowledging specificities of their African and south Asian origins. This is the 'Handsworth translation' it makes sense in the Birmingham context, but it also resonates with global reference points. Tunes like *Movie Over India* and *Come Follow Me* take the listener on an imaginary journey through diasporas from Jalandhar and Bombay, to Kingston/Jamaica and back again to Handsworth. It is not just a matter of making Punjabi and patois mutually intelligible but it is also about plotting the nodal points of an *inter-diaspora imaginary*.

Identity and racial authenticity

This intermezzo culture is scrutinized both within the African Caribbean and South Asian communities. Sonia Poulton, a journalist for Britain's black music paper *Echoes* and *Kiss-FM* presenter, comments that 'the fascination of Apache Indian's music is his fusion of bhangra and reggae, but that doesn't make him a reggae artist'.[5] Poulton sees Apache's mode of cultural expression as a limited form of impersonation.[f] In the same vein the prominent black British MC Tipper Irie reviewing *Fe Real* in Britain's black music newspaper *Echoes* questioned Apache's suitability to collaborate with Maxi Priest. Equally, during a recent visit to a mainly Asian school in Slough, London he was asked whether he was black or Asian! After a similar visit to a youth club in Stoke-on-Trent an egg was thrown at him by a young person.

Incidents like these immediately beg a whole range of questions relating to the nature of racial/ethnic authenticity. These objections are connected to a version of absolutist identity politics which — for whatever reasons — seek to protect claims over African and Asian modes of cultural production and expression. However, are such moves missing the radical potential of creative intermezzo cultures? Paul Gilroy suggests that 'the most important lesson music still has to teach us is that its inner secrets and its ethnic rules can be taught and learned . . . black music cannot be reduced to a fixed dialogue between a thinking racial self and a stable racial community' (Gilroy 1991: 134). He goes on to suggest that the notion of antiphony — of call and response — needs to be modified.

The point that I would make in extending these suggestive comments is that a variety of social groups can respond to the call of black music. It is important to raise the question of who holds the power in this process of inter-cultural traffic. The crucial dimension here, is the way the antiphonic dialogue between the performers and the audiences provides the arena in which the legitimacy of these forms can be established and their political valency scrutinized.

Signs of these dialogues can be seen with the swelling numbers of Asians following established reggae sound systems such as Jah Shaka.[6] Equally, the Coventry based producer Bally Sagoo is combining bhangra beats, raga and hip hop in his *Wham Bam* collections with richly syncretic results. His work includes swing beat mixes of the Muslim devotional singers Nusrat Fateh Ali Khan and raga versions of classic Punjabi folk songs featuring singers like Rama alongside the white MC Cheshire Cat.[7] A whole wave of Asian musicians are beginning to emerge and include Bradford's *Fun' da' mental*, Leicester's indie rock band *Corner-shop*, the *New Conscious Kaliphs*, *State of Bengal* and *Sasha*, a major contributor to Multitone's bestseller *Ragga for the Masses*.

It is equally important to realise that African Caribbean musicians are answering the call of the musics of the south Asian diaspora. For example, a young band called *XLNC* from Birmingham's neigbouring town of Wolverhampton are developing a unique 'combination style'. At the core of their music is bhangra beat, yet their bass player Derrick is born of Jamaican parents. They cover the reggae classic *Red Red Wine* but in the form of a traditional Punjabi song *Lwt Ke Le Gaye* (meaning 'she swept me away'). Similarly, the Southall based African Caribbean singer *Mixmaster Ji* combines lyrics sung in impeccable Punjabi with dance beats. This antiphonic exchange makes the music a junction box for cross-cultural flows resonant with the sounds of reggae, house, techno, soul and Indian folk.

Apache Indian faces a range of pressures to place himself within a singular definition of 'identity', to reterritorialise himself as either black or Asian, Hindu

---

f Compare Hill, this volume, on the limited impersonation of Spanish by Anglo-Americans.

or Sikh, English or Indian. Yet his music and experience confound such segmenta-
tions. On a recent tour of India he was asked about his religion, echoing Gandhi
he replied 'I am a Hindu, a Sikh, a Muslim, a Jew – anything you want me to be'
(*New Musical Express* 7th August 1993: 47). He reflects:

> That was my way of saying to people if you are going to ask me a stupid
> question then I am going to come back at you like that. When I really
> sit down and think about it I am not Jamaican, I am not fully Indian: I
> am a mixture of everything. I also feel very English. I think that the
> fusion of culture is something that is going to become a normal thing
> and whoever is fighting it is fighting a battle that they are going to lose.
> How can you stop fusion? You can never stop it.

The types of 'fusion' that Apache's music personifies are not arbitrary. What his
music demonstrates is a series of departures, identifications which traverse a number
of continents then return, and pause at Birmingham's cultural crossroads only to
re-depart again. It is to the nature of these global networks that I now turn.

Outernational culture: India and inter-diasporic connections

> When I came back from Jamaica, it was just Jamaica, Kingston . . . and
> nothing else mattered. I just wanted to do pure raga tracks and I wasn't
> so much concerned with the Indian side. I was in a *raga frame of mind*.
> (my emphasis)

In the past three years Apache Indian has travelled extensively, performing and
recording in some of the crucial sites of reggae music production. On June 6th
1992 he performed in Port of Spain, Trinidad with a host of diaspora figures
including *Heavy D & The Boyz, Lisa Lisa*, and his early Indo-Caribbean idol *Apache
Supercat*. He travelled to Bob Marley's *Tuff Gong* studio in Jamaica to record part
of his debut album *No Reservations*, collaborating with such reggae luminaries as
Frankie Paul, Bobby Digital, Robert Livingston and Sly Dunbar. The significance
of this is partly to do with the process of making these fusions legitimate.[8]

This tangle of inter-diaspora connections is also present in the political fragments which underpin Apache Indian's music: Mahatma Gandhi's *Satyagraha*
(literally meaning 'holding on to truth' and the name given by him to the doctrine
of non-violent resistance) is coupled with the dread maxims of Bob Marley. What
is striking within this music is that stylistics and ideological combinations can be
made accessible and comprehended by Caribbean, European and Indian audiences.
In Trinidad and Jamaica people of African origin sang along to Punjabi lyrics while
in India vast crowds in Delhi and Bombay sang Jamaican patois choruses. Here
Apache reflects on his experience of performing the cut *Moving On* in Andheri
Stadium, Bombay.

> There was a problem with understanding what I was trying to say in
> India. So before every song I would do it acapella so that they would

understand what it was all about. I made a big speech before *Moving On* and I said the Hindu, Muslims and Sikhs must stick together and move on as one people. They stood up put their hands in the air and sang *Moving on moving and we na turn back*! An Indian crowd singing this in [Jamaican] patois and it was so powerful almost as if they really wanted to move on. Even [Kid] Milo the security said he wanted to cry. 25,000 people singing *Moving on moving and we na turn back*.

Released in 1993 on the back of the *Chok There* single, *Move On* puts forward a clear position on the issue of inter-communal violence.

On the 6th December in 92
In a India there was curfew
Ca a Mosque get destroyed mon by the Hindu
So the Muslim talk say revenge is due
So them lick down a temple a next one too
People get kill here when me tell you
And you know segregation bound fe follow through
All this have fe stop it cannot continue
. . . Me say an eye for an eye make the whole world blind.

The promotional poster carried a message in Urdu, Punjabi and black English. It also stated unity: 'The Hindu, Muslim, and Sikh brother, live as one and you get further, All of us are bound to prosper, One god, one love and unity, Share the land that god lef fe we.' Here black English becomes the medium for the message — a transcendent, 'one love' human unity.

The visit to India in June 1993 is crucially important in understanding the inter-diasporic significance of this music. Apache's music is extremely popular on the subcontinent largely due to the exposure of his first Indian single *Chok There* on Music Television (MTV) Asia transmitted from Hong Kong.[9] The June visit caused unprecedented media attention. His arrival was front page news in the Bombay *Midday* and the *Afternoon Despatch & Courier* (3rd June) *Indian Express, The Independent* (4th June), *The Metropolis* (June 5th). During the mini tour he performed to a 25,000 strong audience in Bombay's Andheri Stadium and to a similar size crowd at New Delhi's Rabindra Rangshala where he came on stage on a white horse while 5,000 people stood outside unable to get tickets. Apache was invited to meet the Governor of Bombay, Sonia Gandhi and the President of India. This raises some important issues in relation to the cultural politics of diaspora communities.

In a recent essay Ruth Frankenberg and Lata Mani argue that:

Not all places in this transnational circuit are similarly 'postcolonial'. The active, subjective, inescapable, everyday engagement with the legacies of colonialization/decolonization that is part of the British matrix for reggae, bhangra rap . . . are not the terms of the theoretical artistic or political endeavours in India.

(Frankenberg and Mani 1993: 302)

The political terrain and theoretical language of India and the United Kingdom is far from uniform. However, the spectre of 25,000 Delhites singing a message of inter-faith Indian unity in a Birmingham cut of Jamaican patois may signal the potential for the development of a translational matrix for cultural politics in India. The Africanological notion of antiphony is again useful to describe modest forms of 'postcoloniality'. Apache Indian, answering the call of black music, heralds a subcontinent with a *diasporic triple consciousness* that is simultaneously the child of Africa, Asia and Europe. In the language of black vernacular cultures the music has gone *outernational*, simultaneously inside and beyond the nations through which it passes. [. . .]

Conclusions

> Rhizome is alliance, uniquely alliance.
> (Deleuze and Guattari [1986: 25])

Throughout this paper I have tried to explore the ways in which music provides the site for the creation of an intermezzo culture, a culture of interbeing that cannot be confined within unitary definitions of 'the subject' or identity. I have particularly concentrated on the way in which the suggestive writing on cultural routes and crossroads may offer new avenues for understanding the simultaneously global and local nature of these cultures. The fundamental point I have argued is that conceptualising cultural multiplicities as rhizomes, lateral interconnections of social and political elements may have important implications for a contemporary understanding of 'identity' and cultural politics.

As Kobena Mercer has rightly observed 'identity' only becomes an issue when it is in crisis, when something assumed to be fixed, coherent and stable is displaced by the experience of doubt and uncertainty (Mercer 1990: 43). He suggests the preoccupation with talking about identity is symptomatic of the postmodern predicament of contemporary politics. What is alarming about the almost insatiable appetite for 'identity talk' is the degree to which these sentences — in both the grammatical and ontological sense — return to the same subject.

The debate on politics and identity in postcolonial and poststructural thinking has become preoccupied with the strategic justification for prime identities (Spivak 1990). The central issue has been how to reckon with fragmentation and rupture while keeping open the possibility of identity politics and agency. This is demonstrated in Stuart Hall's attempt to navigate between essentialist notions of identity based on a primordial self and the 'anything goes' pluralism of postmodern ideology (Hall 1987, 1989). His resolution is that arbitrary or strategic forms of closure are required in order to make politics possible. What I want to foreground is that there are other options for cultural politics. In short, a politics of the multiple that refuses the confines of the Subject while avoiding any banal form of assimilationism.[10]

The culture that I have tried to describe in this paper refuses to be located within the either/or ism of 'identity'. This music manifests itself in a connective supplementarity raga *plus* bhangra *plus* England *plus* Indian *plus* Kingston *plus* Birmingham. The culture which is produced relies not on entities of selfhood but on the process of becoming more than one.

Here I want to return to the metaphor of the crossroads. At the beginning of this paper I suggested that the utility of this notion was the way it captured a sense of convergence, particularly in the wider context of the global passage of cultural flows. The crossroads, however, is not just a place where routes converge, it is also the point where choices have to be made and directions plotted. I want to focus on this issue and examine the political bearings that are being established in Birmingham.

Michel Foucault, in *Discipline and Punish*, comments that around the plague a carnival of transgression occurred. He writes:

> A whole literary fiction of the festival grew up around the plague: suspended laws, lifted prohibitions, the frenzy of passing time, *bodies mingling together without respect*, individuals unmasked, abandoning their statutory identity and the figure under which they had all been recognized, *allowing a quite different truth to appear*.
>
> (Foucault 1977: 197 [my emphases])

It strikes me that there are a number of similarities between what I have described in relation to musical cultures in Birmingham and Foucault's telling description. The liminality of the dance-hall allows a similar process of cultural transgression and change. The infectious rhythms of the music suspend the social divisions which exist outside the dance and enable new forms of expression. Apache Indian's music demonstrates a quite different truth from the one commentators like Roy Kerridge invoked in the aftermath of the summer of 1985 and what came to be known as the 'Handsworth riots'. Kerridge and members of the media were quick to name the tragic deaths of two Asian shopkeepers as the result of a 'race riot', offering spuriously to 'explain' *Why Blacks hate Asians!* [sic].

A sensitivity to the politics of inter-diasporic connections may well provide the potential for developing new *historical blocs* (Gramsci 1971) of political commonality.[11] At an analytical level such an approach promises to remain sensitive to the particularities of local cultures while being alert to the global matrices of diaspora cultures. I have argued that sacrificing certitude for fragmentation may bring about new political possibilities. Rhizomes of anti-racist agency are being formed in the cultural intermezzo which reject both ethnocentrism and the psychic shackles of the 'either/or' model of identity. [. . .]

Something exhilarating is happening in the musical cultures that I have described, which point to new forms of cultural politics and begs a reconsideration of the way in which black music is analysed. Equally, the work of musicians like Apache Indian expand to new limits the utility of concepts like *antiphony* and *diaspora*. [. . .]

Notes

1 The emergence of Bengali sound systems is reported in *Artage* Summer 1991.

2 In Turner's later work he deployed a concept of liminoid social contexts (Turner 1985). Liminoid resemble liminal states, they are marginal, fragmentary, outside the central economic and political process. However, I have not deployed this notion here because I feel it implies a degree of stability and fixity which does not adequately reflect the intermezzo nature of the cultural processes I am describing. Equally, I do not want to characterise these social forms as in anyway 'deviant' or part of some cultural pathology. There is a danger that Turner's notion of 'liminoid social forms' may lend itself to such a reading.

3 I met Steven in 1990 and felt that his music signified an important development within Birmingham's cultural politics. Subsequently I conducted regular interviews with him about his music and its significance. This relationship is an ongoing one and to date we have conducted eight interviews.

4 There are similarities here with the experience of Johnny Otis and his place within the Chicano rock'n'roll (Lipsitz 1990). Otis was a Greek immigrant grocer and ship yard worker from Northern California and developed an interest in black music while growing up in a mostly black neighbourhood in Berkeley. Johnny Otis was a key figure in the early development of rock'n'roll. He worked extensively with black musicians and thought of himself as 'black by persuasion'. (*Editors:* Compare also Cutler, this volume.)

5 Quoted in *Independent* 19th September 1991. See also *Caribbean Times* 10 September 1991.

6 *The Voice* 28 May 1991.

7 This album entitled *Essential Ragga* sold 50,000 copies.

8 This is reinforced by the way in which Apache Indian's music has featured on Jamaican sound system, *Chok There* in particular was a big hit in Jamaica.

9 The *No Reservations* album sold rapidly in India during the summer of 1993 and went double platinum in a matter of three months. Apache Indian is the first artist to receive platinum records on Indian soil. Next year it is estimated that he will sell more records in India than Michael Jackson.

10 The notion of *hybridity* (Hall 1989, Bhabha 1990) might also be challenged as a way of framing cultural multiplicities. Hybridity as a concept may presuppose, as Mathia Diawara has pointed out, *that there are such things as pure Black culture and pure White culture that are transformed by mixing them* (Diawara 1991: 82). Curiously, then, the notion of hybridity, the very attempt to transcend the essential subject is prefigured on a spurious notion of cultural purity.

11 Another example where such an approach might prove useful is *vrakamuffin*. This music incorporates Cypriot, Greek and raga musical forms (vraka being the name of a male Cypriot costume). Musicians like Haji Mike — aka Michael Hajimichael — have developed an inter-diasporic *rebel culture* which has a similar political valency (Hajimichael 1993).

Discography

Apache Indian *Movie Over India* City to City SUNREC 001A
Apache Indian *Movie Over India hip hop remix* White label
Apache Indian *Come Follow Me* City to City CTC 1001A

Apache Indian *Chok There* Sure Delight SDT 41
Apache Indian *Don Raja* Jet Star SDCD 46
Maxi Priest/Apache Indian *Fe Real* White Label TENRDJ416
Apache Indian *No Reservations* Island CID 8001/514/112–2
Apache Indian *Chok Therel Movin On* Island CID 555
Apache Indian *Arranged Marriage* Island CID 544
Apache Indian *Nuff Vibes EP* Island CID 560
Apache Indian *Movin' On* Special CID 580
Bally Sagoo *Essential Ragga* Oriental Star SC 5141
Bally Sagoo/Nusrat Fateh Ali Khan *Magic Touch* Oriental Star SC 5130

Bibliography

Back, Les. 1988. '"Coughing Up Fire": Sound systems and Cultural Politics in South East London'. *New Formations* 5 Summer: 141–52.

Back, Les. 1991. 'Youth, Racism and Ethnicity in South London: An Ethnographic Study of Adolescent Inter-Ethnic Relations'. PhD thesis in Social Anthropology. Goldsmith's College, University of London.

Baumann, Gerald. 1990. 'The Re-Invention of Bhangra, Social Change and Aesthetic Shifts in a Punjabi Music in Britain'. *Journal of the International Institute for Comparative Music Studies and Documentation (Berlin)* 32.2: 81–95.

Benjamin, Walter. 1968a. 'The Work of Art in an Age of Mechanical Reproduction'. In H. Arendt ed. *Illuminations*. New York: Harcourt, Brace and World.

Benjamin, Walter. 1968b. 'The Storyteller: Reflections on the Work of Nikolai Leskov'. In H. Arendt ed. *op. cit.* 83–108.

Bhabha, Homi. 1990. 'The Third Space'. In J. Rutherford ed. *Identity*. London: Lawrence and Wishart. 203–22.

Chambers, Ian. 1990. *Border Dialogues*. New York: Routledge.

Finnegan, Ruth. 1970. *Oral Literatures in Africa*. Oxford: Oxford University Press.

Deleuze, Gilles and Felix Guattari. 1986. *A Thousand Plateaus: Capitalism and Schizophrenia*. London: Athlone.

Diawara, Mathia. 1991. 'The Nature of Mother Dreaming Rivers'. *Third Text* 13 Winter: 73–84.

Foucault, M. 1977. *Discipline and Punish*. London: Tavistock.

Frankenberg, R. and Mani, L. 1993. Crosscurrents, crosstalk: Race, 'postcoloniality' and the politics of location. *Cultural Studies* 7(2), 292–323.

Gilroy, Paul. 1985. 'Hip Hop Technology'. In P. Ayrton, T. Engelhardt and V. Ware *World View*. London: Pluto Press. 130–32.

Gilroy, P. 1987. *There Ain't No Black in the Union Jack: The Cultural Politics of Race and Nation*. London: Hutchinson.

Gilroy, Paul. 1991. 'Sounds Authentic: Black Music, Ethnicity and the Challenge of the Changing Same'. *Black Music Research Journal* 11.2: 111–36.

Gilroy, Paul. 1992. 'It's a Family Affair'. In G. Dent *Black Popular Culture*. Seattle: Bay Press. 303–16.

Gramsci, Anton. 1971. *Selections from the Prison Notebooks*. London: Lawrence and Wishart.

Gutzmore, Cecil. 1978. 'Carnival, the State and the Black Masses in the United Kingdom'. *The Black Liberator* 1 December: 8–27.

Hajimichael, Michael. 1993. 'The Representation of Cypriots in Britain'. Unpublished PhD thesis. Department of Cultural Studies, University of Birmingham, Birmingham.

Hall, Stuart. 1987. 'Minimal Selves, ICA Documents Number 6'. *Identity: This Real Me*. London: ICA/BFI.

Hall, Stuart. 1989. 'Cultural Identity and Cinematic Representation'. *Framework* 36: 68–81.

Hannerz, Ulf. 1989a. 'Culture Between Centre and Periphery: Towards a Macro-anthropology'. *Ethnos* 54.3–4: 200–16.

Hannerz, Ulf. 1989b. 'Five Nigerians and the Global Ecumene'. Paper given to the SSRC Symposium on Public Culture in India and Its Global Problematics, Carmel, California, April 26–30th 1989.

Hewitt, Roger. 1986. *White Talk, Black Talk: Inter-racial Friendship and Communication amongst Adolescents*. London: Cambridge University Press.

Hinds, David. 1980. 'The "Island" of Brixton'. *Oral History* 8.1: 49–51.

Hiro, Dilip. 1971. *Black British White British*. London: Eyre and Spottiswoode.

Jones, Simon. 1988. *Black Culture, White Youth: The Reggae Traditions from JA to UK*. Basingstoke: Macmillan.

Lipsitz, George. 1990. *Time Passages: Collective Memory and American Popular Culture*. Minneapolis: University of Minneapolis Press.

Mercer, Kobena. 1990. 'Welcome to the Jungle: Identity and Diversity in Postmodern Politics'. In J. Rutherford ed. *Identity: Community, Culture, Difference*. London: Lawrence & Wishart.

Mercer, Kobena. 1992. 'Back to My Routes: A Postscript on the 80s'. *Ten 8* 2 3: 32–39.

Oliver, Paul. *Savannah Syncopators*. 1970. London: Studio Vista.

Sivanandan, A. 1981/82. 'From Resistance to Rebellion: Asian and Afro-Caribbean Struggles in Britain'. *Race and Class* 23. 2–3: 111–51.

Spivak, Guyatri. 1990. *The Post-Colonial Critic: Interviews, Strategies, Dialogues*. London: Routledge.

Turner, Victor. 1969. *The Ritual Process*. London: Routledge & Kegan Paul.

Turner, Victor. 1984. 'Liminality and the Performative Genres'. In J. J. MacAloon Rite, *Drama, Festival, Spectacle: Rehearsals towards a Theory of Cultural Performance*. Philadelphia: Institute for the Study of Human Issues.

Turner, Victor. 1985. *On the Edge of the Bush: Anthropology as Experience*. Arizona: University of Arizona Press.

Les Back is Reader in Sociology at Goldsmith's College, University of London. He is the author of *New Ethnicities and Urban Culture: Racisms and Multiculture in Young Lives* (London: UCL Press, 1996), and co-author, with Vron Ware, of *Out of Whiteness: Color, Politics, and Culture* (Chicago: Chicago University Press, 2002).

Author Index

Subject Index